MW00575679

Roll!
Shooting TV News

You can take all the tea in China
Put it in a big brown bag for me
Sail right around the seven oceans
Drop it straight into the deep blue sea.

You can't stop us on the road to freedom
You can't keep us 'cause our eyes can see
Men with insight, men in granite
Knights in armor bent on chivalry

—*Van Morrison "Tupelo Honey"*

Roll!
Shooting TV News
Views From Behind the Lens

Rich Underwood

AMSTERDAM • BOSTON • HEIDELBERG • LONDON
NEW YORK • OXFORD • PARIS • SAN DIEGO
SAN FRANCISCO • SINGAPORE • SYDNEY • TOKYO

Focal Press is an imprint of Elsevier

Publisher: Elinor Actipis
Associate Acquisitions Editor: Cara Anderson
Assistant Editor: Robin Weston
Publishing Services Manager: George Morrison
Project Manager: Marilyn E. Rash
Copyeditor: Renee Le Verrier
Proofreader: Dianne Wood
Indexer: Ted Laux
Marketing Manager: Becky Pease
Cover Illustration: Matt Stallings
Typesetting: SNP Best-set Typesetter Ltd., Hong Kong
Text Printing: Sheridan Books
Cover Printing: Phoenix Color Corp.

Focal Press is an imprint of Elsevier
30 Corporate Drive, Suite 400, Burlington, MA 01803, USA
Linacre House, Jordan Hill, Oxford OX2 8DP, UK

Copyright © 2007 by Rich Underwood. Published by Elsevier Inc. All rights reserved.

No part of this publication may be reproduced, stored in a retrieval system, or transmitted in any form or
by any means, electronic, mechanical, photocopying, recording, or otherwise, without the prior written
permission of the publisher.

Permissions may be sought directly from Elsevier's Science & Technology Rights Department in Oxford,
UK: phone: (+44) 1865 843830, fax: (+44) 1865 853333, E-mail: permissions@elsevier.com. You may
also complete your request on-line via the Elsevier homepage (*http://elsevier.com*), by selecting "Support
& Contact" then "Copyright and Permission" and then "Obtaining Permissions."

 Recognizing the importance of preserving what has been written, Elsevier prints its books on acid-free
paper whenever possible.

Library of Congress Cataloging-in-Publication Data
Underwood, Rich.
   Roll! shooting TV news : views from behind the lens / Rich Underwood.
      p.   cm.
   Includes bibliographical references and index.
   ISBN-13: 978-0-240-80848-2 (alk. paper)
   ISBN-10: 0-240-80848-7 (alk. paper)
   1. Television cameras.   2. Television camera operators.   3. Television broadcasting of news.
I. Title.
   TR882.5.U53 2007
   778.59—dc22   2007010895

British Library Cataloguing-in-Publication Data
A catalogue record for this book is available from the British Library.

For information on all Focal Press publications visit our website at
www.books.elsevier.com.

07   08   09   10   11   10 9 8 7 6 5 4 3 2 1

Printed in the United States of America

Working together to grow
libraries in developing countries

www.elsevier.com | www.bookaid.org | www.sabre.org

ELSEVIER   BOOK AID
             International   Sabre Foundation

Contents

Credits

Frontispiece—"Tupelo Honey" words and music by Van Morrison. ©1971 (Renewed) by WB Music Corp. & Caledonia Soul Music. All rights reserved and administered by WB Music Corp. Used by permission of Alfred Publishing Co., Inc.

Chapter 1—Opener image: Illustration of a Lumière Cinématographs camera, c. 1896, courtesy of "Who's Who of Victorian Cinema"—*www.victorian-cinema.net*; rest of images courtesy Raymond Fielding

Chapter 2—John DeTarsio photographed by Dustin Eddo; images courtesy CBS News

Chapter 3—Images courtesy KAKE-TV

Chapter 4—Images courtesy KUSA-TV; Take 2: The Language of Lenses—illustrations by Paul Cohen

Chapter 5—Stephen Hooker photographed by Maggie Alexander; images courtesy WDSU-TV; Take 2: The Shot and Motion—illustrations by Paul Cohen

Chapter 6—Christian Parkinson photographed by Rob Pittam; images courtesy the BBC

Chapter 7—Ray Farkas photographed by Bob Burgess; images courtesy Off Center Productions; Take 2: Composition—photographs by Ángel Granados

Excerpt from "Hole in the Head" copyright © 2005 by Lerman Productions. All rights reserved. Lyrics reprinted by permission.

Chapter 8—Corky Scholl photographed by Kent Meireis; images courtesy KUSA-TV, Denver; illustrations by Paul Cohen

Chapter 9—Lisa Berglund photographed by Robert Coronado; images courtesy World Vision

Chapter 11—Images courtesy *Dateline NBC*, International Justice Mission and Investigative Mechanics

Excerpts copyright © NBC Universal, Inc. All rights reserved. Used with permission.

Chapter 12—Heidi McGuire photographed by Chris Weaver; images courtesy WFMY-TV

Note: All images in this book are copyright © 2006 by those who have so graciously given Rich Underwood and Elsevier, Inc., permission to publish them.

Chapter 13—Images courtesy KNSD–TV

Chapter 14—Sam Allen photographed by Frank Matson; images courtesy NFL Films, Digital Ranch Productions LLC, and Colorado Production Group

Chapter 15—Brian Weister photographed by Andrew McDonald; images courtesy KMGH Denver; illustrations by Paul Cohen; photographs by Ángel Granados

Chapter 16—Mike Elwell photographed by Mike Cerre; images courtesy GlobeTV

Chapter 17—Bart Noonan photographed by Steve Ager; images courtesy Reuters

Chapter 18—David Hands in Kenya photographed by Marin Dawes; images courtesy David Hands

Chapter 19—Images courtesy White Noise Productions

Chapter 20—Kevin Sites photographed by Bella Tochieva (first image), Dinesh Wagle/United We Blog (second and third images); other images courtesy Yahoo! News and Kevin Sites
Lyrics to "Truckin'" by Robert Hunter. Copyright © Ice Nine Publishing Company. Used with permission.

Appendix B—Images courtesy of Peter Hodges

Appendix C—Images courtesy of Bill Holshevnikoff

Appendix D—Images courtesy of Nigel Fox

Preface

When we think about our recent world history and talk of events such as 9/11, the wars in Afghanistan and Iraq, and countless other tragic, heroic, and life-changing events, our minds play back the images we've seen on television.

The images that we conjure up were first recorded by television photojournalists. These cameramen and women stand on the front lines, engulfed in the moment, their skill and visual sensitivities working to capture history on the fly.

How we see our world was first viewed by them.

The images tell the story, and they are crafted through lighting, lens selection, camera angles, and many of the same skills all camera operators use. However, these "operators" have honed an instant, instinctual feel for how they will shoot the world they've been paid to capture. They watch the world's top stories unfold through small black-and-white television monitors mounted inside their viewfinders.

At thirty frames per second, they choose how we will see ourselves, our joys and successes, our grief and terror, our births and last death rattles. The moments that shape our lives roll through their cameras. Unblinking, exposed, a moving record—our history.

From some far, remote corner of the world to a teeming metropolis or small hometown, they shift effortlessly their abilities to tell their stories with clarity, compassion, and honesty.

This text contains portraits of some of the best television photojournalists in the .world. All have received the highest awards and accolades from their industry. They are the noted leaders in their field and share an almost religious dedication to communicate what is true. Their images are arresting and memorable and stick in the subconscious of our mass media culture.

Foremost, they are storytellers, journalists with a lens. Their stories, the equipment they use, and the techniques that serve them every day are outlined in the following chapters.

Their stories have been divided to take the reader through a progression of skills that cover the world of television photojournalism. Each chapter takes the reader into a different skill or knowledge required of today's news cameramen and women. For the working professional, it is my hope that the insights provided by the stories in this book will serve to reinvigorate and offer a lasting homage to the profession of television photojournalism.

Notes on Text Format

The text in *Roll*! is set in two primary typefaces to denote the separation of voices between each chapter's interviewee and the author. This technique helps to create a fluid "train of thought" through the subject matter being discussed. By eliminating the timeworn format of "author said," "subject said," the halts in dialogue are replaced by relevant content that connects, advances, and clarifies the narrative theme.

The author's voice is set in *Times New Roman italic*. The typeface was chosen for its history in journalism. In 1932, under Stanley Morrison's direction, Victor Lardent drew the original Times New Roman typeface for *The Times of London* newspaper. Since its creation, it has become one of the most widely used typefaces for publications.

The interviewee's voice appears in Optima. The designer's "in-the-field" improvisation brought one of the world's most enduring fonts to life. While visiting the Santa Croce church in Florence, Italy, in 1950, designer Herman Zapf made his first sketches of the Optima typeface on the only paper he had available: an Italian 1,000-lire banknote found in his pocket. Zapf's sketches were designed in the proportions of the Golden Ratio and inspired by the Renaissance lettering carved into grave plates on the church floor, circa 1530. Today, Optima continues its memorial legacy as the typeface etched into the Vietnam Veterans Memorial Wall in Washington, D.C.

In addition to the two primary typefaces is a third. The chapter titles, and the running heads and folios, are set in DIN Light and **DIN Black**. *DIN* stands for *Deutsche Industrienorm* (German Industrial Standard). In 1936, the German Standard Committee selected DIN 1451 as the standard font for the areas of technology, traffic, administration, and business. The Committee chose a DIN font because of its legibility and ease of recognition.

Authors' professional titles and affiliations, equipment lists, and captions are set in a fourth typeface, ITC American Typewriter. Patented in 1868 by Christopher Latham Sholes, the typewriter became the tool of the storyteller. Its monospaced typefaces carried dispatches from around the world to newspapers, radio stations, and television news organizations. After being universally replaced by word processing software and computers, the typeface still evokes memories of intrepid journalists tapping out the latest scoop.

Acknowledgments

A special thanks to my wife, Kevin, whose love—and machete-like efficiency in clearing away the debris of daily life—made it possible to complete this project. To my parents, Al and Shirley, for their continued inspiration in my life. To my daughter, Hayley: Not a word was written without imagining it through your eyes.

I am extremely grateful for the support and enthusiasm of my original acquisitions editor for Focal Press, Amy Eden Jollymore, and to Cara Anderson, the associate acquisitions editor assigned to this book.

Thanks to Marissa Rocke for her research and transcriptions, and all the hours she put in from the beginning. Ángel Granados served both as my graduate assistant at San Diego State University and as photographer for many of the technical images in the book. Likewise, I have to thank the artistic talents of Paul Cohen for the illustrations he penned detailing the technical concepts of television news photography. The cover design was created by the very talented illustrator Matt Stallings. I'd also like to thank Amanda Rozier, who jumped in during the last phase to help wrangle photo clearances and final details.

Many of the images seen in this book required conversions from one format to the other. These images would not have been possible without the technical expertise of Greg Penetrante and the support of San Diego State University.

Travel played an important part in bringing this project to life. Leslie Overstreet and STA Travel did a wonderful job of getting me there with everything I needed.

I would like to thank Sharon Levy Freed, who runs the NPPA TV News Video Workshop in Oklahoma, for her assistance in locating the best in the business. Thanks also to Bob Fisher for his time and historical perspective.

And, finally, to all the TV news photographers who helped in this endeavor, thank you for your time, stories, and commitment to educating the next generation.

Introduction

Introduction

The History of Television Photojournalism from the Beginning

Bang !

Genesis 1.3—And God said, Let there be light: and there was light.
Genesis 1.4—And God saw the light, that it was good: and God divided
the light from the darkness.

*. . . and at close to 700 million miles per hour, light shoots throughout
the universe, illuminating our world for all the days to come.*

*How magnificent, the first living eyes—capturing the reflections of earth's
early environs, absorbing the hues and shapes that made prehistoric earth.
At the first blink, light enters the eye and is refracted by the cornea, travels
through the opening in the iris (called the pupil), then through the lens and
onto the retina. The retina contains two cell types called rods and cones. The rods handle
low light vision, while the cones handle detail and color. When light contacts these cells,
complex chemical reactions occur, changing light into electric impulses that are carried
via the optic nerve to the brain. The result is the experience of sight.*

*As the sun sets, light carries its qualities of hue, luminance, and saturation. Measured
in waves per second, or Hertz (Hz), the eye sees between 430 trillion Hz (red) and 750
trillion Hz (violet). These frequencies represent all the colors we can see in our universe.
But, there are more—unseen frequencies whose mysteries will be discovered far into the
future and affect the lives of everyone on earth. The mysterious (radio) waves exist in less
than a billion Hz, and gamma rays top the spectrum above sight, ultraviolet, and x-rays.
But for now, there is the awe of a perfect sunset. As the sun slips below the horizon, yellows
give way to blues and darker . . . reds disappear. The end of a day. With it comes a desire
to remember, to tell a story that will keep the experience alive for all time*

. . . to share our world.

A Timeline of Light and Shadow

Before 1000 A.D.

In 30,000 B.C., in a cave in what's now southern France, early Paleolithic man and woman captured their world in hundreds of paintings made from red ochre and charcoal. It's easy to imagine the effect flickering torches must have had on the mural of a running bison, its extra legs painted to help depict movement. Now referred to as Chauvet Cave, it is the oldest known art gallery. Cataloging and illustrating through art, the Aurignacian painters crafted one animal made of nothing but red dots. Pointillism eons before Seurat.

Around 2200 B.C., papyrus is used in creating documents. Seven hundred years later, in 1500 B.C., the Phoenician alphabet is formed. An exact understanding of written words could be shared then.

Aristotle describes a light after-effect—a persistent image—that slowly fades away after looking at the sun. In 300 to 330 B.C., Aristotle also questions how the sun can make a circular image when it shines through a square hole. This is the first reference to the camera obscura, *the forerunner to the camera. In Latin, "camera obscura" means "dark chamber." The Romans found that if bright daylight entered a dark room through a tiny hole in a curtain or window shutter, an inverted clear (although very dim) image of the outside world appeared on a white wall opposite the hole.*

Roman poet and philosopher Titus Lucretius Carus, in 65 B.C., describes the principle of "persistence of vision," the optical effect of experiencing continuous motion when sequential still images are momentarily displayed. This principle was proved one-hundred and thirty years later by Greek astronomer and geographer Ptolemy of Alexandria in 130 A.D.

In the fifth century A.D., highly polished bronze discs called "magic mirrors" appeared in Japan and China. When a small, bright light source reflects off the mirror and onto a screen, it projects an image, although no image is visible on the mirror itself. Therefore—the magic. The magic image is most often of the Buddha.

From 1000 to 1800

About 1000 A.D., Alhazen (Ibn Al-Haytham), a Middle Ages authority on optics, creates the pinhole camera and explains why the image is upside down.

A blurry devil dances across a wall, frightening everyone in the room. It is a "nocturnal appearance for terrifying viewers" as illustrated in Liber Instrumentorum *by Giovanni de Fontana in about 1420 A.D. It shows a man holding a lamp or lantern, and on the wall is a large projected picture of the devil. This is arguably the first evidence of a magic lantern.*

As Christopher Columbus sails the ocean blue in 1492, then arrives in the New World, Leonardo da Vinci combines art and science in creating the Vitruvian Man. *Six years later, in 1498, he paints "The Last Supper," which depicts the most important event in the Christian doctrine of salvation—the institution of the Eucharist. It has become one of the most widely appreciated masterpieces in the world. In 1519, da Vinci sketches a camera obscura. During the same time, the camera obscura's use as a drawing aid is being touted. The transition between medieval and modern times is defined by discovery, the arts and sciences, and is called the Renaissance.*

In 1589, the book Magiae Naturalis Libri Viginti, *by Giovanni Baptista della Porta, described the ancient art of projecting mirror writing. In 1658, it's published in English as* Natural Magick. *Della Porta was also the first European to publish information on the pinhole camera (which he did not invent) around 1600 A.D.*

During the early seventeenth century, Angelo Sala notices that powdered nitrate of silver is blackened by the sun.

In Rome, violent criminal Caravaggio paints "The Calling of Saint Matthew" in 1599–1600. It is a beautiful example of chiaroscuro *(Italian for "light-dark"), defined as bold contrast between light and dark, creating a three-dimensional experience through highlights and shadows.*

A German Jesuit priest, Athanasius Kircher, publishes Ars Magna Lucis et Umbrae *in 1646, in which he describes using a convex lens to focus images projected by sunlight or candle light.*

Dutch scientist Christiaan Huygens's father pesters him to send a lantern so he can "frighten his friends" with it. In the mid-1600s, Huygens, who is famous for his wave theory of light, does many experiments with lenses and develops a lantern as early as November 1659. Besides Huygans, elsewhere in Europe, the Danish mathematician Thomas Rasmussen Walgensten also develops a working model of a lantern projector. He is the first person to coin the term Laterna Magica. *Walgensten, realizing the technical, artistic, and economic possibilities, travels throughout Europe demonstrating and selling magic lanterns.*

In the seventeenth century, the camera obscura is used by artists and made portable in the form of sedan chairs. Dutch painter Johannes Vermeer, regarded as one of the greatest artists that ever lived, painted "The Music Lesson" and "Girl with a Pearl Earring." There is widespread speculation that Vermeer used a camera obscura to create some of the thirty or so paintings he did during his life.

In 1727, Professor J. Schulze accidentally creates the first photo-sensitive compound by mixing chalk, nitric acid, and silver in a container. Schulze notices a darkening on the side of the container exposed to sunlight. Schulze also discovers that certain liquids change color when exposed to light. In 1800, "sun pictures" are made by Thomas Wedgwood by placing objects on leather treated with silver nitrate. The silhouettes did not last long because there was no method of making the image permanent.

"Giphantie" by de la Roche is an imaginary tale where captured images from nature appear mirrored on a canvas that was coated with a sticky substance. The image would be permanent after it was dried in the dark. The author appeared to be a photographic prophet because he described an art and process that would occur a few decades after his death.

Ratified in December 1791, The first ten amendments to the U.S. Constitution are known as the Bill of Rights. The First Amendment states: "Congress shall make no law respecting an establishment of religion, or prohibiting the free exercise thereof; or abridging the freedom of speech, or of the press; or the right of the people peaceably to assemble, and to petition the Government for a redress of grievances."

From 1800 to 1900

On the third of May in 1808, following a riot the previous night, Murat ordered his Egyptian cavalry to set up a firing squad to shoot anyone who happened to be available. It was the first in a series of brutalities that engraved themselves on Francisco Goya's mind. In 1814, six years later, Goya asked the provisional government for an opportunity to "perpetuate by the means of his brush the most notable and heroic actions of our glorious insurrection against the Tyrant of Europe." His oil on convas painting of this event, "The Shootings of May 3, 1808," has been called the most horrifying record of war ever made in any medium.

Nicéphore Niépce combines photosensitive paper with a camera obscura in 1816. Brilliant! In 1826, he creates a permanent image. Peter Mark Roget rediscovers the persistence of vision principle in the 1820s. He's also famed as the author of Roget's Thesaurus.

Johannes Purkinje describes the change in relative brightness of the long wavelengths (reds) and short wavelengths (blues) as the ambient illumination decreases. His 1823 published report found that at high illumination reds appear brighter than blues, but at low illumination these same blues appear brighter than reds. The effect is referred to as the "Purkinje Shift." It explains the attributes necessary for "day for night" photography and is instrumental in the measurement of stars.

In 1827, taking almost eight hours of exposure, Niepce's the "View from a Window at Le Gras" is the first photograph. In 1829, Niépce agrees to go into partnership with Louis Daguerre.

The illusion toy, the Phenakistoscope, is introduced in 1832 by Joseph Plateau and sons. Pictures on one disc are viewed through slots in the other; when spun and viewed through a mirror, the pictures appear to move. In 1834, William George Horner introduces the Zoetrope based on the same principles except this time the pictures and slots are on the same rotating drum instead of two discs. Also in 1834, permanent negative images using paper soaked in silver chloride and fixed with a salt solution are created by Henry Fox Talbot. Positive images are made by contact printing onto another sheet of paper.

Louis Daguerre calls his discovery the Daguerreotype. A process which he founds in 1837 creates images on silver-plated copper coated with silver iodide and "developed" with warmed mercury. The French government awards Daguerre a state pension in exchange for publication of his methods and the right for other French citizens to use the process. The details of the process are made public August 19, 1839, proclaiming that the Daguerreotype "requires no knowledge of drawing . . ." and that "anyone may succeed . . . and perform as well as the author of the invention." "Daguerreomania" becomes an overnight craze.

A newspaper report in the Leipzig City Advertiser states: "The wish to capture evanescent reflections is not only impossible . . . but the mere desire alone, the will to do so, is blasphemy. God created man in His own image, and no man-made machine may fix the image of God. Is it possible that God should have abandoned His eternal principles, and allowed a Frenchman . . . to give to the world an invention of the Devil?"

In the year the photographic process becomes public, Sir John Herschel is the first to use the term "photography," derived from Greek words for light and writing. During that time, photographic images on glass slides were projected using magic lanterns.

In 1841, Henry Fox Talbot patents his process of negatives on paper under the name "calotype." Samuel Morse publicly demonstrates the telegraph for the first time in 1844. The invention of the sewing machine and other intermittent mechanisms in 1846 lays the essential groundwork for motion pictures. William Thomson (Lord Kelvin) develops his absolute temperature scale in 1848. Degrees Kelvin is the measurement often used to describe a lamp's color temperature: 3200K is the color temperature of tungsten lamps; daylight color film is balanced to 5600K.

In 1851, London sculptor Frederick Scott Archer improves photographic resolution by spreading a mixture of collodion (nitrated cotton dissolved in ether and alcohol) and chemicals on sheets of glass. Wet-plate collodion photography is much cheaper than daguerreotypes. In Paris in 1853, Nada (Felix Toumachon) opens a portrait studio.

In England, photographer Roger Fenton instigates the formation of a Photographic Society that is now called the Royal Photographic Society. In 1855, The Illustrated London News hires Fenton to photograph the Crimean War. On the front lines, Fenton processes his images in a flea-infested converted wine wagon that became an oven during the day and a target at any time. The summer heat often forces him to take his pictures before 7:00 A.M. In all, he shoots more than 350 pictures of the conflict.

Ambrotypes (direct positive images on glass) and tintypes (images on metal) become popular in the United States between 1855 and 1857.

"From the first, I regarded myself as under obligation to my country to preserve the faces of its historic men and mothers," said Mathew Brady in 1856. Brady opens a studio in Washington, D.C., to photograph the nation's leaders and foreign dignitaries. He's known as one of the first to use photography to chronicle national history.

Between 1861 and 1865, 7,000 negatives of the American Civil War are exposed by Mathew Brady and his staff. Although Brady shoots some of the images, he is more of a project manager, supervising photographers and buying photographs to ensure his collection will be as comprehensive as possible. Although the images in the collection are actually the work of many people, when they are published, either as prints or engravings, they are all credited "Photograph by Brady."

A sign, "The Dead of Antietam," is posted on the door of Brady's New York gallery. The exhibit displays photographs of battlefield corpses. In 1862, The New York Times said that Brady "brought home to us the terrible reality and earnestness of war."

Using a system he calls the "Pantelegraph," Italian physicist Abbe Giovanni Caselli is the first to send fixed images over a long distance. The "dry plate" process is proposed by English doctor Richard Leach Maddox in 1871. The process uses an emulsion of gelatin and silver bromide on a glass plate. In 1873, English telegraph engineers May and Smith experiment with selenium and light. The results give inventors a way of transforming images into electrical signals.

"Mr. Watson, come here, I want you!" Alexander Graham Bell invents the telephone on March 10, 1876, in Boston, Massachusetts. The word telephone comes from the Greek word tele- (meanings "from afar") and phone (meaning "voice" or "voiced sound").

"Do a horse's four hooves ever leave the ground at once?" That is the 1873 bet Eadweard Muybridge is asked to settle by Leland Stanford, the ex-governor of California. Five years later in 1878, Muybridge sets up a bank of twelve cameras with trip wires connected to their shutters. Time-sequenced photography is created as each camera takes a picture when the horse trips its wire. Muybridge develops a projector to present his finding. The answer to the bet is "Yes." He adapts Horner's Zoetrope to produce his Zoopraxinoscope and screens "The Horse in Motion."

On the kitchen table of his mother's boardinghouse in Rochester, New York, a twenty-three-year-old George Eastman invents a machine to manufacture dry plates. Eastman travels to London in 1879 to patent his invention. London at that time is the center of the photographic world. A year later, Eastman, and an associate named Henry Strong, set up Eastman Dry Plate Company in Rochester, New York. That same year, a daily newspaper, the New York Graphic, uses the first halftone photograph in its publication.

To transform images into electrical signals, George Carey builds a rudimentary system in 1880 that uses dozens of tiny light-sensitive selenium cells.

Heinrich Hertz's 1887 experiments confirm that electrical energy travels at the speed of light and describe the medium through which the energy travels as the "ether." He also proves that electricity can be transmitted in electromagnetic waves and that the waves possess many of the properties of light. His experiments with electromagnetic waves lead to the development of the wireless telegraph and the radio. The term hertz (Hz) used to describe radio and electrical frequencies is named after him.

George Eastman produces a still camera in 1888 that takes photographs on sensitized paper and sells it under the name Kodak. Also that year, French inventor Louis Augustin Le Prince creates a single-lens camera that he uses to make the very first moving picture sequences. The sequences are made by moving film through the camera's sprocket wheels that grab the film's perforations. Etienne Marey builds a moving picture camera that uses an intermittent mechanism and paper film strips.

The inventor of the electric light bulb and the phonograph, Thomas A. Edison, and his assistant W. K. L. Dickson, begin experiments for making and showing moving pictures. In November 1888, John Carbutt announces his successful production of photographic-quality celluloid, available in 20 x 50 inch sheets. Edison's laboratory decides to order a dozen Carbutt film sheets in June 1889, and the lab starts experimentation on its device called the Kinetoscope. Later in 1889, Edison travels to Paris to see Marey's camera, which uses flexible film.

Reverend Hannibal Goodwin likes to use fragile slides in his Sunday school. In 1889, he comes up with the idea of flexible, celluloid-based transparent film that is unbreakable. With a license from the Newark Celluloid Varnish Co., he proves that celluloid can be flattened, thinned, and used as an image base. George Eastman promotes the product for wide-scale commercial use. Dickson orders a Kodak camera to examine the film inside.

In London, William Friese-Greene makes motion pictures of people on their way to church. The simple scenes of everyday life are called "actualities." They are the very beginning of what become newsreels.

In October of 1890, Monkeyshines starring one of the Edison laboratory workers fooling around for the camera is W. K. L. Dickson's first motion picture. By 1891, Edison and Dickson are ready to patent and demonstrate their Kinetoscope viewing box and the Kinetograph camera, which uses Eastman film cut into inch-wide strips, punched with four holes on either side of each frame, allowing toothed gears to pull the film through the camera.

Sir William Crookes suggests that people could communicate using electric waves of specific wavelength on tuned equipment, or "telegraphy across space," in "Some Possibilities of Electricity," published in Fortnightly Review in 1892.

Léon-Guillaume Bouly manufactures the Bouly Cinématographe camera in Paris, in 1892.

At the 1893 World's Columbian Exhibition in Chicago, Thomas Edison displays the Kinetoscope. Also that year, the first public exhibition of films shot using the Kinetograph is held at the Brooklyn Institute. To produce films for their Kinetoscope, Edison and Dickson build a studio on the grounds of Edison's West Orange, New Jersey, laboratories. The studio has a removable roof and sits on circular tracks to rotate with the sun. Made of wood and tar paper, the studio is known as the "Black Maria" for the supposed similarities to police wagons of the day. The studio's first film is Fred Ott's Sneeze. It is also noted for the first close-up and becomes the first officially copyrighted film on January 7.

At 1155 Broadway in New York City, The Holland Brothers' Kinetoscope Parlor opens on April 14, 1894, with two rows of coin-operated Kinetoscopes. The film "business" begins. Celebrities Buffalo Bill and Annie Oakley are invited to Edison's New Jersey studio to be recorded on film with his Kinetograph.

Shot in the "Black Maria" studio and organized for the cameras by Thomas Edison, Gray and Otway Latham, Enoch Rector, and Samuel Tilden Jr., "The Michael Leonard and Jack Cushing Prize Fight" is decided in six rounds. Leonard wins the match.

Herman Casler files a patent application for an alternative to the Kinetoscope called the Mutoscope, which was developed with the help of Dickson and the Lathams. The Mutoscope uses a flick-book technique instead of using film. A sequence of photographs are mounted on a drum that is spun inside a cabinet. The flipping of photographs gives the impression of movement.

The name "peepshow" becomes the description of single-person viewers like the Kinetoscope and the Mutoscope, because of peeping into an eye hole to view the show.

In 1894 Europe, the Lumière family is the biggest manufacturer of photographic plates. Brothers Louis and Auguste Lumière design a camera that's both a recording device and a projecting device to compete with Edison's films. They call the camera the Cinématographe. It uses an intermittent mechanism modeled on the sewing machine and exposes flexible film cut into 35mm wide strips at 16 frames per second. Edison's camera operates at 46 frames per second. Lumière's 16 frames per second becomes the standard rate for 25 years.

Herman Casler demonstrates a camera called the Biograph to take "views" for the company's Mutoscope in March 1895. Later, a Mutoscope is adapted with a mirror device to project motion pictures. The partners—Casler, Henry N. Marvin, W. K. L. Dickson, and Elias Koopman—soon perfect a through-the-film projector, which they call the Biograph. They establish the American Mutoscope company on December 27, 1895. Dickson goes on to manage the company's London office.

In a Paris café named Salon Indien, the Lumière brothers hold their first commercial exhibition of their camera, projector, and films. The December 28, 1895, screening includes The Arrival of a Train, which is said to have caused a stampede. Early films are mostly documentaries or "actualités" (films of everyday life) like the Lumière's Lunch Hour at the Lumière Factory.

In London, Charles Morand Pathé buys pirated Kinetoscopes manufactured by Robert Paul and resells them at fairgrounds in France. His clients, tired of seeing the same films, encourage Charles to find more. In order to renew Pathé's stock of films, he meets engineer and inventor Marie Henry Joseph Joly and advances the necessary funds to make a camera.

In England, news films begin with cameraman Birt Acres photographing the opening of the Kiel Canal by Kaiser Wilhelm II. The Lumière brothers shoot the first news film in France. The topic is a holiday excursion of the Congress of the National Union of French Photographic Societies. The Lumière company later sends Francis Doublier and assistant Charles Moisson to Madrid to photograph a bullfight.

The Lathams succeed in creating a camera and a projector. The unfortunately dim projector uses a system that loops the film, making it less susceptible to breaks and tears. The "Latham Loop" as it is called, is still in use in modern motion picture projectors.

Thomas Armat improves the Phantoscope projector and renames it the Vitascope, then sells it to Edison in 1896.

In Paris in 1896, Charles Pathé and brothers Émile, Théophile, and Jacques found Société Pathé Frères. The first goal is to build cameras and projectors. A year later, the company becomes the Compagnie Générale de Cinématographes, Phonographes et Pellicules (Anciens Établissements Pathé Frères). Émile directs the phonographic aspects of the business while Charles handles the cinematographic.

Russian Alexander Popov begins transmitting wireless electrical signals more than 500 meters through the air. Italian Guglielmo Marconi accomplishes the same transmission three months later. Marconi can send signals more than a mile by the end of the year.

At the Grand Café in Paris, on December 28, 1895, one of the most famous film screenings in history takes place. Customers pay one franc for a 25-minute program of ten Lumière films including Feeding the Baby, The Waterer Watered, and A View of the Sea.

On January 14, 1896, Birt Acres presents a selection of his films to the Royal Photographic Society, including the now famous Rough Sea at Dover. Cameramen Francis Doublier and Felix Mesguich are the first roving motion picture correspondents, sent around the world by the Lumière Brothers.

After building on inventions and insights by Hertz, Nicola Tesla, and others, Marconi applies for the first patent specifically for wireless telegraphy technology and begins the process for starting a communications company in Great Britain.

Kodak begins manufacturing the first print film designed for projection, opening the way for the introduction of movie theaters.

On April 23, 1896, at Koster and Bial's Music Hall, six films are shown in the first public premiere of the Vitascope. Five of the films were originally shot for Kinetoscope, the sixth is Birt Acres's Rough Sea at Dover.

Before the 1896 election, William McKinley is photographed by Billy Bitzer for the Biograph Company. The 1897 inauguration of President McKinley, the oath, and the parade are photographed by Edison, making him the first president to be filmed in office.

In 1897, German scientist Karl Ferdinand Braun constructs the first cathode ray tube scanning device.

The Spanish-American War in 1898 is the first war to be covered by American cameramen and producers.

The Prestwich Model 4 cine camera is designed by John Alfred Prestwich and manufactured by the Prestwich Manufacturing Company in London in 1898. The camera's reliability is the main reason Australian photographer and cinematographer Frank Hurley chooses a Prestwich as his cine camera for the 1914 Shackleton Antarctic Expedition. Later, Hurley has to abandon his camera when the ice crushes the wooden ship Endurance on November 21, 1915.

In 1899, The American Mutoscope Company changes its name to the American Mutoscope and Biograph Company to include its projection and peepshow devices. Dickson sails to South Africa to document the Boer War for the British Mutoscope and Biograph Company. The war is filmed by cameramen from many countries. Dickson spends more than a year with British troops.

The Early 1900s

The word television, first used in 1900, comes from the joining of the Greek word tele (meaning "from afar") and the word vision.

The Pathé company merges with the Manufacture Française d'Appareils de Précision to

W. K. L. Dickson films the Boer War with a Biograph camera.

form the Compagnie Générale de Phonographes, Cinématographes et Appareils de Précision. From that point on, Charles Pathé develops the manufacture of both negative and positive film, the creation of factories and studios, and the making of cameras and projectors.

Ernest Francis Moy and Percy Henry Bastie's camera, also popularly known as a "Moy," is first made in England by the Moy & Bastie company in 1900. It's rumored that the first Hollywood picture was shot with a Moy camera.

Taking a single-frame exposure every four minutes, eight hours a day, a Biograph cameraman condenses the 1901 dismantling of the old Star Theater in New York. Projected, this spectacular time-lapse scene takes only seconds to watch.

The 1903 Pathé camera is often called a cracker box because of its light wooden construction. Hollywood is incorporated as a municipality in 1903.

For 12 magical seconds above the Kill Devil sand dunes, two bicycle mechanics from Ohio defy gravity and fly their craft into history on December 17, 1903, marking the first manned, sustained, powered flight. Before the day ends, Orville and Wilbur Wright's Wright Flyer will stay aloft for 59 seconds in Kitty Hawk, North Carolina.

Founded in 1904, the New York Daily Mirror *is the first daily newspaper in the world to be illustrated exclusively with photographs. Photonewspapers establish the basic categories used later by the newsreels: catastrophe, celebrities, pageantry and ceremony, sports, political and military, technology, spectacle, novelty.*

The first Nickelodeon opens in Pittsburgh in 1905. R. K. Bonine covers the 1906 San Francisco earthquake and fires for the Edison Company.

George Eastman first meets Thomas Edison in person during a 1907 visit to Edison's New Jersey lab. Eastman asks Edison how wide he wants the film to be for his new cameras. Edison holds his thumb and forefinger about 1–3/8 inches (35mm) apart and says "about so wide." The standard set that day has endured for 90 years.

Theater projectionist Donald Bell and camera repairman Albert Howell establish The Bell & Howell Company on Larchmont Avenue in Chicago, Illinois, in 1907. Their first camera is made of wood; the second is the 35mm "#2709 Standard" studio camera for professional cinematography. Its features include a body machined from cast aluminum, a four-lens turret, and a rack-over system, giving precise through-the-lens viewing and focusing.

In the basement of Boris Rosing's private lab at the School of Artillery in St. Petersburg, Vladimir Zworykin helps Rosing with his experimental work on television. Featuring a very early cathode ray tube as a receiver and a mechanical device as a transmitter, Rosing files his first patent on a television system in 1907. In December, Zworykin, having developed the prototype of the receiver, meets David Sarnoff, who eventually puts him in charge of television development for RCA. Later, Vladimir Zworykin says of his feelings about watching television, "I hate what they've done to my child . . . I would never let my own children watch it."

The voluntary Motion Picture Patents Agreement of 1907 sets specifications defined as standard for motion picture film: 35mm in width, 4 perforations along both sides of each frame, 4:3 or 1.33:1 aspect ratio, and a film speed of 16 frames per second.

In 1908, the American Mutoscope and Biograph Company hires one of the most important silent film directors ever: D. W. Griffith.

In 1908, André Debrie builds the wooden Debrie Parvo camera in Paris. The hand-cranked Parvo (meaning "compact" and of small dimension) at one time was the most popular European-made camera. By the 1920s, the Parvo is the most used camera in the world.

The French firm Pathé Frères is shooting approximately 30,000 meters of film a day in 1909. Their trademark is a golden rooster. In 1910, Charles Pathé introduces the Pathé Journal newsreel at 6 Boulevard Saint Denis in Paris. The theater is devoted exclusively to showing newsreel material.

The "Fight of the Century" on July 4, 1910, between Jack Johnson and James Jeffries is one of the most popular news films of the year. The first makeup formulated especially for film is created by Max Factor the same year.

The first produced, assembled, and released newsreel in the United States is Pathé's Weekly on August 8, 1911.

A 1912 cameraman's salary is about $35 a week, plus an expense account of around $65 a week. A cameraman shoots about 200 feet on an average assignment.

Pancho Villa signs a contract with Harry Aitkin of the Mutual Film Corp. in 1914 for exclusive movie rights to his battles during the Mexican Revolution in exchange for $25,000 and 50 percent of the royalties.

Pathé has 60 offices in Europe and 37 cameramen in North America, with the New Jersey plant processing 15,000 feet of film per week. Pathé offers a daily newsreel service starting on June 8, 1914. The Pathé Daily News uses nonflammable safety film stock that can be safely sent through the mail.

"Writing history with lightning," is how President Woodrow Wilson describes the highly controversial and technically brilliant Civil War epic, The Birth of a Nation by director D. W. Griffith. The film uses techniques of expressive close-ups, flashbacks, and cross-cutting that are still in use today. It is the first film to play in the White House.

Frank Hurley, the Australian photographer and cinematographer of the Shackleton Antarctic Expedition, chooses a Prestwich as his cine camera. On November 8, after Shackleton orders "abandon ship" of the sinking Endurance, Hurley dives into the freezing arctic water of the flooded ship to recover the precious photographic glass plates. Later, with Sir Ernest Shackleton, he chooses to keep 120, smashing the approximately 400 remaining plates. The Endurance sinks on November 21, 1915, at 68°38.5' S, 52°28' W. Hurley's photography is a lasting testament to their journey.

When the United States enters World War I, the Committee for Public Information, or CPI, produces its own newsreel, the Official War Review. William Randolph Hearst sends Joe Hubbell (his favorite cameraman) to Europe in 1917 to help make films for the Review. In Great Britain, The War Office takes over the Topical Budget newsreel and runs it as an outlet for official war film, changing its name to the War Office Official Topical Budget, then later the Pictorial News.

Founded in 1917, the Lincoln Motion Picture Company is the first African-American owned studio. Also that year, the University of Wisconsin at Madison begins radio transmission on station 9XM-WHA.

The Akeley camera, designed by explorer Carl Ethan Akeley for the Akeley Camera Company in New York in 1917, is nicknamed the "Pancake" Akeley due to its unique shape. The quick-change internal magazines let an operator reload in fifteen seconds. Director Robert Flaherty takes two Pancakes to Hudson Bay to shoot Nanook of the North. Aerial cameraman Elmer Dyer uses an Akeley on Howard Hughes's

Hell's Angels, *and Harry Perry uses the camera for most of the airplane work on* Wings. *The Pancake was still being made in the 1940s.*

In 1920, Philo Taylor Farnsworth, the fourteen-year-old son of an Idaho sharecropper, chalks his concept for the vacuum tube television display on a blackboard in his high school chemistry class.

KDKA Pittsburgh goes on the air in 1920 with the world's first "scheduled" radio broadcast. In 1921, a cine magazine for women, called Eve's Film Review, *is released by Pathé. The Mitchell Standard camera is introduced in 1921 too.*

The first feature film documentary, Robert Flaherty's 1922 Nanook of the North, *explores Inuit Eskimo life. Made one year later, the German film* Life in a Village *is the first "sound" documentary.*

Intended for amateur filmmaking, Kodak introduces 16mm reversal film and the Cine-Kodak 16mm motion picture camera in 1923. From the 1930s on, 16mm is considered a professional medium.

In magazine advertisements, Bell & Howell markets their new Filmo 70A for the "making of personal motion pictures." The ads run in The Saturday Evening Post, National Geographic, Harper's, *and* Country Life. *The camera sells for the exorbitant (for 1923) sum of $180. However, it does come with a lifetime warranty. The camera can shoot for 35 to 40 seconds, at 24 frames per second (fps), before being rewound.*

Based in Geneva, Ukrainian designer Jacques Bogopolsky—"Bolsky"—patents a 35mm cine camera (the 1924 BOL-Cinégraphe) designed for the growing amateur market. Bogopolsky later produced a 16mm camera, the Auto Cine.

The Odessa Steps sequence of the 1925 Battleship Potemkin *by Russian filmmaker Sergei Eisenstein establishes the montage technique.*

In Selfridges department store on Oxford Street, a crowd of Londoners watch the image of a ventriloquist's dummy's head on John Logie Baird's "televisor." Baird's demonstration of the first transmitted moving image takes place on October 30, 1925.

The top newsreel companies in 1926 are Fox Movietone, Paramount, Universal, Warner-Pathé, Hearst Metrotone, and the March of Time *monthly film "magazine."*

Wound by hand and almost indestructible, the Bell & Howell 1926 "Eyemo" is used by newsreel companies around the world.

David Sarnoff of RCA creates the National Broadcasting Network (soon to be known as NBC) in 1926 for national radio broadcasting.

In 1927, Fox's Movietone is the first sound newsreel and 24 fps becomes the motion picture standard as does the Academy aperture of 1.33:1, established by the Academy of Motion Picture Arts and Sciences.

Over 438 miles of telephone line between London and Glasgow, John Logie Baird transmits a television signal. Philo T. Farnsworth's Image Dissector camera tube transmits the first electronic television picture. Philo applies for a patent on electronic television.

Sound comes to the newsreel.

John Logie Baird's Baird Television Development Company, Ltd., makes the first transatlantic television transmission from London to Hartsdale, New York, in 1928.

General Electric begins regular television broadcasting with a 24-line system from a station in Schenectady, New York. The U.S. government issues the first name, "W2XB," to what becomes known as WGY's Television. By the end of the year, more than fifteen stations are licensed for television broadcasting.

William S. Paley takes over the United Independent Broadcasters network and reorganizes it as CBS (the Columbia Broadcasting System) for radio broadcasting.

Felix the Cat is broadcast in 1928, 1936, and 1937. A paper maché Felix is the first "stand-in" for television. The thirteen-inch figure is placed on a turntable for RCA's initial experimental television transmissions of 60-line pictures.

Buster Keaton stars in MGM's 1928 film The Cameraman. The Prévost Camera, manufactured by the Établissements Lucien Prévost in Paris, plays an important part.

Man with a Movie Camera, Soviet director Dziga Vertov's 1928 experimental, avant-garde film, is an excellent example of a "city symphony" documentary. Regarded as "pure" visual cinema, it shows Soviet workers and machines from Moscow, Kiev, and Odessa. The film exhibits radical editing techniques, special visual effects, juxtaposition of images, and double exposures.

A woman's eyeball is slashed with a razor blade in the opening scene of artists Salvador Dali and Luis Buñuel's surrealist masterpiece, Un Chien Andalou in 1928.

The BBC begins test television broadcasting for thirty minutes per day in 1929 using John Baird's 30-line mechanical system.

The all-newsreel Embassy Theater at Broadway and 46th in New York City opens with 544 seats on November. 2, 1929.

The 1930s and 1940s

"Television would soon serve as a theater in every household," writes David Sarnoff for the science page of the New York Times in 1930. The motion picture studios don't like this idea and begin to develop plans on how to deal with the new medium of television. A large television screen is set up at an RKO theater in Schenectady, New York, as an experiment for Theater Television.

The Baird Television Development Company made the first television program and the first live transmission of the Epsom Derby for the BBC in 1931.

Berndt-Bach, Inc., begins manufacturing the Auricon professional 16mm sound-on-film camera in Hollywood. The camera is primarily used for newsgathering and virtually all network news departments are using it by 1960. Later, Andy Warhol and Albert Maysles also use Auricons.

The NC (that is, newsreel camera) Mitchell is equipped with single-system sound. The sound is recorded directly on the film.

Technicolor is introduced in 1932 using three black-and-white negatives exposed in the same camera behind different filters.

Dedicated to "straight photographic thought and production," Ansel Adams, Imogen Cunningham, Willard Van Dyke, and Edward Weston form Group f/64.

Henri Cartier-Bresson buys a Leica, then begins his sixty-year career photographing people.

"My work is done. Why wait?" These are the last words written on a suicide note by 77-year-old George Eastman. He shoots himself in the heart with a pistol.

In 1933, Swiss company Paillard introduces the Bolex H16 16mm camera, a design loosely based on Jacques Bogopolsky's Auto Cine camera. The Bolex brand becomes a favorite of independent filmmakers and specialist cinematographers.

Motion picture camera manufacturer Mitchell introduces the "Blimped Newsreel Camera" shown on the previous page in 1934.

The 1935 Newman Sinclair 35mm spring-wound newsreel camera has dual springs that drive 200 feet of film through the camera without stopping. Of the top newsreels in 1935, Paramount is considered the most fair, balanced, and respected of the day. Hearst is the most controversial.

The notorious Czechoslovakian film Extase *(*Ecstasy*) is prohibited from entering the United States in 1935 because it contains nudity and sexual situations—the first time customs laws are used for this purpose.*

Experimental electronic television begins broadcasting in Germany, England, Italy, France, the United States, and Holland.

In Munich, Germany, in 1937, August Arnold and Robert Richter's company introduces the Arriflex 35 professional camera with a groundbreaking continuous through-the-lens viewfinding system.

"Oh, the Humanity!" WLS radio reporter Herb Morrison cries as the German airship Hindenberg *explodes 200 feet above Lakehurst, New Jersey, on May 6, 1937. All the newsreels have cameras rolling for the 34 seconds it takes the doomed ship to fall to earth and become one of the most famous newsreel stories of all time.*

Hearst's newsreel cameraman Wong Hai-Sheng films a scene of a crying baby in the rubble left by the Japanese bombing of South Station in Canton in September 1937. More than 136 million people are said to have seen the image, and it becomes one of the most celebrated symbols of the Far East conflict. The Japanese government is reported to have placed a 50,000-dollar price on Wong's head for filming the scene.

MGM releases Too Hot to Handle, *starring Clark Gable, as a newsreel cameraman, and Myrna Loy in 1938.*

Developed in 1938 by Edward R. Murrow, the 15-minute World Today *program on CBS is the first regular broadcast of daily news on radio.*

Broadcast on W2XB from the 1939 World's Fair in New York, RCA cameras shoot the first president of the United States to appear on television, Franklin D. Roosevelt. The World's Fair introduces the first TV sets (made by RCA) for sale to the American public. The mirror-in-the-lid TRK-12 sells for $600.

Telenews Theater in San Francisco opens September 1 featuring the invasion of Poland. Telenews soon opens thirteen theaters and sets up its own newsreel production company to supply other independent theaters and, later, TV stations. By the 1950s, Telenews provides 90 percent of the television news film in the country.

RCA-NBC goes on the air with "commercial" electronic television on April 30, 1939. The action is not endorsed or blessed by the government, nor will it be until July 1, 1941.

A college baseball game between Columbia and Princeton is the first sports telecast, on May 17, 1939. Princeton wins in the tenth inning, 2 to 1. Also in 1939, the first major league baseball game is televised between the Dodgers and the Reds, at Ebbets Field. That year also sees the first pro football game televised from Ebbets Field.

The first National Television Standards Committee (NTSC) of 168 members issues its standards on March 8, 1941. The television standards are approved by the FCC on April 30, and have remained in effect to the present day. Television would scan at 525 lines and 30 frames per second, composed of 60 fields per second interlaced 2 to 1, in a bandwidth of 6MHz. Electronic (commercial) black-and-white television begins broadcasting in the United States on July 1, 1941.

Starting at 7:56 A.M., on December 7, 1941, in less than three hours, Japanese planes cripple the U.S. Pacific fleet at Pearl Harbor. World War II begins for the United States. During the war, film comes from military cameramen and two pool cameramen from each newsreel company assigned to military theaters. Military censors have to approve all foreign newsreel footage, but there is no direct censorship of the big five U.S. newsreels during the war.

The Office of War Information (OWI) screens newsreel content through a covert organization called the Library of Congress Film Project, which is funded by the Rockefeller Foundation. "Will this picture help to win the war?" The OWI states that Hollywood filmmakers should consider this and several other questions before producing a movie. The War Production Board imposes a $5,000 limit on set construction, and Klieg-lighting for Hollywood premieres is prohibited so that possible enemy planes can't see a target.

Photographers Margaret Bourke-White, Robert Capa, Carl Mydans, and W. Eugene Smith cover the war for Life *magazine.* Churchill's Island *wins Best Documentary—Short Subject at the 1942 Academy Awards.*

Joe Rosenthal shoots the iconic still image, "Raising the Flag on Iwo Jima" in February 1945. The Pulitzer Prize winning photo captures six Marines raising the American flag after the battle for Mount Suriba-chi. The image is later used as the inspiration for the Marine Corps War Memorial in Washington, D.C.

The day World War II ends, Life *photographer Alfred Eisenstaedt captures a sailor's victory kiss and embrace in Times Square, August 14, 1945. It's one of the most reprinted images in* Life's *history.*

"With this issue is born a voice, one that has been mute much too long," proclaims an editorial on the front page of the first issue of the National Press Photographer *magazine. The National Press Photographers Association (NPPA) is founded in 1946.*

In 1947, Elia Kazan, Robert Lewis, and Cheryl Crawford establish The Actors Studio in New York City as a rehearsal group for professional actors. Later, under Lee Strasberg's leadership, the studio's clients include Marlon Brando, Marilyn Monroe, and James Dean. It's known for advancing the "Method" technique of acting.

The BBC produces its own newsreel in 1948. The television newsreel greatly increases the popularity of television with stories like the live coverage of the coronation in 1953.

Warner Bros.'s coverage of the 1948 Tournament of Roses Parade (Pasadena) and the Rose Bowl is the first to show a color newsreel. Eastman Kodak introduces 35mm tri-acetate safety base film to replace the flammable cellulose nitrate base used in the motion picture industry.

Don Hewitt begins producing the "CBS TV News" with Douglas Edwards in 1948.

The 1950s, 1960s, and 1970s

In 1950, James Dean's first acting job pays thirty dollars for the Pepsi-Cola commercial that launches his career.

"Gort, Klaatu barada niktu" is to become the most famous phrase in science fiction history. The alien words come from Robert E. Wise's 1951 film The Day the Earth Stood Still.

The first television magazine show, See It Now, *directed by Don Hewitt and produced by Fred Friendly, is broadcast coast to coast on November 18, 1951, using newly completed coaxial cable.*

The first practical VTR (video tape recorder) is developed by the AMPEX Corporation in 1951. In 1956, the first commercially feasible VTRs with two-inch tape reels are sold for $50,000.

In 1952, Eastman color film is introduced.

Cinerama (an anagram of the letters in "American"), the wide-screen aspect ratio 2.06:1, is created by three 35mm prints interlocked and projected from three separate projection booths onto a curved screen. How the West Was Won *is the last Cinerama film, in 1962.*

Fifty movie houses in thirty cities are wired together for the Joe Walcott versus Rocky Marciano heavyweight championship fight in September 1952.

Hollywood develops more wide-screen processes like Fox's anamorphic CinemaScope.

The NPPA awards Pathé cameraman Murray Alvey its first "Newsfilm Cameraman of the Year" in 1954. The award later becomes known as the "Ernie Crisp Television News Photographer of the Year."

Edward R. Murrow produces the See It Now *program on Joseph McCarthy on March 9, 1954, and on April 22 the Army-McCarthy hearings are televised live for thirty-six days to an audience of twenty million.*

The BBC introduces live, daily news with newsreaders in 1955.

Driving his new 550 Porsche Spyder, twenty-six-year-old James Dean collides with a 1950 Ford near Cholame, California, and dies. His Best Actor Oscar nominations for East of Eden *and* Giant *are given posthumously in 1955.*

In the late 1950s and early 1960s, the naturalistic, documentary-like cinéma verité (literally meaning "film truth") technique begins to flourish. The technique uses handheld cameras, nonactors, location shoots, and nonintrusive filming. It is also called "direct cinema" in the United States and "free cinema" in the United Kingdom.

"This instrument can teach, it can illuminate; yes, and it can even inspire. But it can do so only to the extent that humans are determined to use it to those ends. Otherwise it is merely wires and lights in a box. There is a great and perhaps decisive battle to be fought against ignorance, intolerance and indifference. This weapon of television could be useful," says Edward R. Murrow at the Chicago RTNDA Convention on October 15, 1958.

In 1961, John F. Kennedy holds the first televised presidential news conference.

Sony debuts the five-inch micro TV-5–303, the world's smallest and lightest television, in 1962. Sony also sells two-inch, open-reel videotape for the PV-100 (the world's first transistor videotape recorder).

AT&T launches Telstar (the first communications satellite) into orbit on July 9, 1962. That year, sex symbol Marilyn Monroe dies of an apparent drug overdose in a Brentwood, California, bungalow.

In 1963, the Ampex consumer VTR can be ordered from the Neiman-Marcus Christmas catalogue for $30,000. Merry Christmas.

Éclair introduces the NPR camera in 1963. The lightweight 16mm camera with quick-changing magazines helps further independent filmmaking and plays a part in the evolution of the cinéma vérité movement.

"The medium is the message," says Marshall McLuhan in his 1964 book Understanding Media: The Extensions of Man. *McLuhan theorizes that a medium affects the society in which it plays a role, not by the content delivered over the medium but by the characteristics of the medium itself.*

In 1964, California theater owners launch a campaign to ban pay cable TV. The measure (Proposition 15) passes but is later declared unconstitutional.

NBC is the first to produce all of its prime-time programming on color film in 1965. CBS follows the next year and ABC the following season.

Early Bird, the world's first commercial communications satellite, built by Hughes for COMSAT (Communications Satellite Corporation), is launched on April 6, 1965.

Sony introduces the CV-2000 videotape recorder for home use, as well as the first transistor condenser microphone, the C-38, in 1965.

During the mid-1960s, news becomes more important to local stations. Camera crews carry bulky sound cameras and usually an additional small, handheld, silent camera, both loaded with reversal film.

In 1966, WFBM-TV Indianapolis chief photographer Ernie Crisp wins NPPA's coveted "Newsfilm Cameraman of the Year" award. He will become vice president and president of NPPA from 1968 to 1970. Later, NPPA will change the name Newsfilm Cameraman of the Year to "Ernie Crisp Television News Photographer of the Year."

Sony demonstrates the first color home VTR in 1966. In 1967, it introduces the DV-2400, the world's first portable VTR.

On December 26, 1967, Universal Newsreel is the last newsreel, with a running time of six minutes. The 1967 Sony Portapak (out-of-studio video camera and recording system) ushers in the modern era of video.

Charles Kuralt begins his "On the Road" series for the CBS Evening News. *CBS develops "On-Time" the first time code editing system for video.*

Filmed at the Monterey International Pop Festival in California, Monterey Pop *(1968) features Jimi Hendrix, The Who, Janis Joplin, and many others. The concert documentary is a precursor to Michael Wadleigh's* Woodstock *in 1970.*

60 Minutes, *a weekly news magazine/documentary show for CBS, is created and produced by Don Hewitt, a former* Life *magazine reporter.*

General Nguyen Ngoc Loan, South Vietnam's national police chief, executes a Viet Cong officer on February 1, 1968. Eddie Adams' photograph for the Associated Press wins a 1969 Pulitzer Prize. NBC News cameraman Vo Suu shoots the same scene for television.

Jean-Pierre Beauviala establishes Aaton s.a. in 1970 to build an intelligent camera that would be lightweight, rational, and ergonomic. One goal is to give a single reference point to both film and audio takes, recorded on the film stock and on the magnetic audiotape. Beauviala's "cat-on-the-shoulder," 16mm camera project starts winning over camera operators, technicians, and buyers at the BBC, Swedish Television, and then Société Française de Production and French Channel One. In 1971, the first mock-up is shown. The delivery of the first Aaton 7A 16mm camera comes in 1973.

"Houston, Tranquillity Base here. The Eagle has landed," Commander Neil Armstrong reports to mission control on July 20, 1969. Tranquility Base *is on the surface of the moon, The Eagle is the* Apollo 11 *lunar module, and 600 million earthlings watch live television transmissions from the moon 238,857*

miles away. We watch and listen as Armstrong takes man's first step on the moon. "One small step for man—one giant leap for mankind."

The Maysles brothers, Albert and David, shoot the 1969 Rolling Stones tour and the free concert at Altamont Speedway. Their 1970 documentary, Gimme Shelter, chronicles the tour, the Altamont concert, and the tragic stabbing of an audience member by Hells Angels security guards. Sony introduces the VCR (video cassette recorder).

A small group of Canadian filmmakers and entrepreneurs design a new system for very large screen productions. Using 70mm film projected onto 80' x 100' screens, their IMAX (Image Maximization) motion picture projection system will revolutionize giant-screen cinema. The IMAX film Tiger Child premiers at the Fuji Group Pavilion, EXPO '70, in Osaka, Japan.

Cinema Products introduces the CP-16 camera in 1971. Designed by company founder Ed DiGiulio, (former vice president of engineering at Mitchell Camera), the small, lightweight camera is an instant hit and becomes a mainstay for television news and documentaries. DiGiulio earns Academy citations for technical achievement by developing crystal-control motors for film cameras. His motors eliminate the need for a sync cable between the camera and the sound recorder.

Home Box Office (HBO) sends its first cable television programming to 365 subscribers in Wilkes-Barre, Pensylvania, in 1972 and is the first pay-TV service for cable.

Sony is the first Japanese company to open a U.S. plant to manufacture Trinitron televisions in San Diego. The new U-Matic line of video cassette recorders is introduced.

In 1974, CBS vice president Joseph Flaherty asks Sony to develop a U-Matic model specifically for commercial broadcasting with the same image quality as 16mm film.

The RCA TK-76 19-pound portable camera is introduced at NAB 1976. It requires a separate recorder to record the images. By 1980, more than 2,000 cameras are sold worldwide to news organizations and production companies.

Sony brings its broadcast quality U-Matic system, the Broadcasting Video (BV) series, online. The system incorporates shooting, recording, and editing functions and heralds a new method of news reporting dubbed ENG (electronic news gathering) by Sony's Masahiko Morizono and Joseph Flaherty.

The half-inch Video Home System (VHS) is developed by JVC to compete with Sony's Betamax system. In 1977, RCA begins selling the first VHS video cassette recorders in the United States.

The 1980s and 1990s

Weighing only 2.8 pounds, the first commercial color video camera utilizing a completely solid state image sensor, called a charge-coupled device (CCD), is marketed by Sony in 1980. It is the smallest camera on the market. With only a 3.7-inch diagonal picture, the KV-4000 is the smallest Trinitron color TV available.

The first prototype of a single-unit compact color video camera–cassette recorder system is announced by Sony.

At NAB 1981, the first all-in-one camera/recorder ENG systems are exhibited. By 1986, Ampex, Thomson, and Bosch sign manufacturing and marketing agreements with Sony to produce Betacam products.

In 1987, the SMPTE working group on HDTV approves the 1125/60 standards document. The Japanese demonstrate an analog, high-definition television system called MUSE.

In 1989, the American National Standards Institute (ANSI) gives its final approval to the 1125/60 HDTV production standard.

The drama of Tiananmen Square, China, in 1989 is captured by the media in the scene of a young man standing in front of a line of tanks, unwilling to move.

General Instrument's Video Cipher division announces a digital high-definition system in 1990.

Televisions around the world show green night-scope images sent live from Baghdad as U.S. warplanes bomb the city and Iraqi antiaircraft guns fire into the night sky. On January 16, 1991, Operation Desert Storm's coalition forces, under the command of U.S. General Norman Schwarzkopf, attack Iraq in response to that country's invasion of Kuwait. After four days of fighting, the United States and allied troops halt their attack.

Televisions with built-in closed-caption display capabilities are introduced in the United States in 1991. In 1993, "wide-screen" 16:9 aspect ratio television sets are introduced in the United States.

Replacing the old 1934 laws, Congress passes the Telecommunications Act of 1995. The "Computer Chronicles" is the first television program delivered via the Internet in 1995.

In 1996, there are more than 100,000 World Wide Web sites, and that number is growing fast. There are 45 million Internet users, including 30 million in the United States. Search Web site Yahoo goes public; in three years, its market value will be seventy billion dollars. Mainichi Shinbum, a Japanese newspaper, delivers its editions online.

The Federal Communications Commission (FCC) approves a digital HDTV standard in 1996. The first Web logs, or "blogs," appear on the Internet in 1997. Streaming audio and video content is also starting to show up on the Web.

In 1998, 1,280 TV stations and 3,250 newspapers have online Web sites. The first desktop computer feature film is The Last Broadcast. CBS broadcasts the first HDTV-format NFL game.

KOMO 4 News Seattle is the first to broadcast HDTV daily local news in 1999.

The Twenty-first Century Begins

In 2000, Sony's HDW-F900 Camcorder with digital 24-frame progressive high definition is used to shoot Star Wars: Episode II.

September. 11, 2001. 9/11. On that morning, America and the world watch their televisions as terrorists hijack domestic airliners and fly two of them into the World Trade Center, one into the Pentagon, and crash a fourth—United 93—into a Pennsylvania field. Evan Fairbanks's camera is rolling on a shot for a documentary about Trinity Church when the planes crash into the towers. His video is shown that day by Peter Jennings, later by Connie Chung, and the next morning on Good Morning America. Two months later, the 25-minute video is shown as part of an exhibition at the New York Historical Society, where a critic calls it "a Zapruder film for our time."

The controversial Fahrenheit 9/11 wins the top prize, the Palme D'Or, at the Cannes 2004 Film Festival. Michael Moore's political film breaks the record for the highest opening weekend earnings for a documentary.

The March of the Penguins (2005) costs $8 million to make and earns almost $78 million. It's the second-highest grossing for a non-IMAX documentary.

In 2005, KUSA-TV in Denver, wins NPPA Station of the Year for the tenth time. The photography staff at KUSA has brought home this award in 1977, 1984, 1986, 1987, 1990, 1992, 1997, 1998, and 2000.

This book gets approval from Focal Press, and the advance check arrives December 17, 2005.

Behind the Scenes

On January 1, 2006, production on this book begins. The idea was always to interview the best television photojournalists from around the world. Timing is everything, and the latest NPPA Station of the Year and Photographer of the Year are both from the last television station I worked at: KUSA-TV in Denver. I spent many years there and still have friends throughout the station and in that area.

The beginning of this book will be easy; some of the best guys in the world are old friends, and one trip lets me get through four or five interviews. My first interview, at which I am able to work out my interviewing methods, is with a very patient John DeTarsio in San Diego, where I live now. Later, I interview Greg Stickney as well as Mitch Wagenberg on assignment in San Diego.

Aside from a snow storm during my Denver trip, the interviews get done without a hitch. I use a small digital Sony voice recorder and then immediately back everything up to a laptop, then burn a CD, and send the file off for transcription. If I can't get promotion stills, I shoot head shots with a tiny Canon digital camera.

My next journey is to London for interviews with photographers from the BBC and Reuters. It's a wonderful experience, and the guys I've only known through e-mails and an occasional phone call turn out to be great.

The feel of the book is starting to develop nicely just as travel funds evaporate. The book advance is gone, and I still have a few more interviews to do. After a few weeks of feeling like I might not get to interview the rest of the photographers face to face, a slightly brilliant idea hits me. Web cams. I buy two Web cams, made by Logitech, and send one to Heidi McGuire in Greensboro, North Carolina. With a few technical glitches, we get through our interview, and, with a little more experimentation, this method keeps improving. I do Web cam interviews from Kansas City, Washington, D.C., Seattle, and Cyprus. In the end, a large portion of the content in the book is gathered face to face. The rest requires many phone calls and e-mails to flesh out the stories.

Now, after more than a year of work, countless interviews, phone calls, cups of coffee, sleepless nights, CD-ROMs, DVDs, reference books, and an eternity on the Internet: Please enjoy the stories, ideas, and work created by the best television photojournalists in the world.

CHAPTER 2

John DeTarsio

A Storyteller's Story

John DeTarsio
Freelance Photographer

**CBS News *48 Hours* and *60 Minutes*, *Dateline NBC*, ABC News *20/20*
and *Primetime Live***
NPPA Ernie Crisp Television News Photographer of the Year, 1994

*I*t is almost sunset as muddy tires under a grey-green transport van pull to a stop just a few minutes outside Beslan Airport, North Ossetia, Russia, where freelance television photographer John DeTarsio and crew have spent more than an hour gathering up their gear. Beslan is at the foot of the Caucus mountain range, and Hell and gone from anywhere—the flight in was grueling.

The well-worn van has seen many miles; so has the driver. They're etched on his face like the scratches on the hood. Setting the brake, he lights a cigarette; burnt sulfur fills the cabin, and at the end of a long exhale, "Mi zdes." Even with the windows cracked, the blue smoke stings. Through dirty windows the day's withering light illuminates what seems to be fields of flowers. It's beautiful, but it doesn't look like the hotel. DeTarsio's Russian translator relays the driver's words, "We're here." His eyes in the rearview mirror tell all before the translator finishes the driver's next phrase, "Mi u mogyili." A pause. The translation ends: "We're at the gravesite."

Slowly, and under closer inspection, the flowers' setting is revealed. Vivid colors, alive in the day's last glow, placed on gravestones, hundreds of gravestones, where just a few weeks before had been a field where children played. The driver stops the engine; DeTarsio and the crew get out. People are at the gravesite, laying flowers, walking from marker to marker. Silence, complete silence.

The transport van waits as DeTarsio surveys the site, making mental notes, getting a sense or feel for the place. Not about to invade the scene with crew and large news camera, he snaps a few images

EQUIPMENT

Sony BVW-D600 Betacam

Fujinon A15X8 BEVM-28

Fujinon 4.8 wide-angle lens

Fish-eye lens

Chrosziel matte box

Arri 100-, 200-, and 400-W lights

ETC 750 Source four-stage lights with 50-degree
   lenses

200-, 400-, 800-W HMIs

DIVA 200 and 400 Kino Flo lights

Chimera soft bags with diffusion

16 wireless microphones

Shotgun, Schepps, and stick microphones

Mini jib with 6-foot extension

MicroDolly

A. Gravesite in Beslan.

B. Remains of Beslan School Number One.

on a small personal camera. Like a writer takes notes, DeTarsio uses the lens as a digital scratch pad. Thoughts to keep for future reference.

On September 3, 2004, Russian military forces stormed Beslan School Number One. Chechen terrorists had held children, teachers, and parents hostage since their siege began three days before, early on September 1.

September 1 is the first day of school in this small town of 30,000. It's called "The Day of Knowledge" and is a big holiday, a day of celebration for the children. They bring colorful balloons and flowers as gifts for the teachers. Children and parents come to class together on this hot, late-summer day. Then, suddenly, the cheerful laughs evaporate in an instant as thirty-two terrorists attack the school at around 9:30 A.M., firing automatic weapons and herding 1,200 parents, teachers, and children into the gymnasium. "For three days, time is frozen," says Dariya Fadeeva, a sixteen-year-old girl from Beslan.

In the sweltering heat of the siege, hostages were not allowed water. The children shared flower petals as food. Small hands offering a token of nourishment when there was nothing else. Humanity is simple this way. The terrorists, wired on drugs to keep them awake, paced the school like caged animals.

On the third day, the terrorists began firing on hostages who were attempting to flee. Russian Spetznats teams stormed the school. Explosions echoed through the compound as the terrorists detonated bombs wired to the gymnasium and themselves, taking with them the children of Beslan and laying waste the hearts of the Beslan community.

Of the 1,200 hostages, 331 died: 186 of those were children. More than 700 were wounded, and the event left 26 children orphans.

This Is John DeTarsio's Story, and This Is Where He Begins . . .

There are three things I want to accomplish at the start of every story. One, I want to get a sense of place. Two, I want to give an idea of who the characters are, and, three, give an idea of what the journey is going to be. Those things make for a strong story beginning and, if told well, will engage the curiosity of the viewer.

The cemetery seemed as big as two football fields, grave after grave after grave. It was a lesson for us. Some people had built little school desks right next to the graves with photos of the children placed nearby. Most of the people had brought bottles of water and soda, because the children were so dehydrated in their last hours. So, symbolically, they brought them water. Row after row of kids who had died in this terrorist act. It was a great way to start to understand the story. I wanted to walk through the scene and find the little things, the kind of shots that express emotion. I'll look for someone bowing his or her head quietly. I know the story is going to be very still because what we'll be shooting is only what's left in this town. The main event is over. There is a gutted-out building and a graveyard and some people to interview. When we arrived, we realized it's not a rich community; it's a very hardworking community. They're people just like us, and these people feel the pain just like us and they're living through this. . . . I started to think about my own kids' schools and something just like this happening. Even the ones that lived now have to live with the fact that half of their friends are gone, are dead. When I walked into this cemetery and, seeing the small town they're in, the enormity of it just hit like a ton of bricks.

So, when I went to Russia for a three-week shoot—visually, I already knew some of the building blocks that would tug the heartstrings. But, when I'm working for the major networks, much of the agenda is already set up. There's a field producer who's already been in place for weeks. He knows who the English speakers are, he has pre-interviewed characters, and he has lined up many of the locations to shoot. When I'm working on a program with an approximate budget of $250,000, I am only one part of a huge project, just one piece of the pie. However, it is a joy to recognize other kindred spirits on your quest for story and good TV. Visionaries like *48 Hours'* executive producer Susan Zirinsky and producer Joe Halderman keep this business exciting—to say the least!

But there are a couple of decisions I made that first day in Russia: The interviews were going to be very dark and basic. I wasn't going to do a lot of fancy lighting. I was going to make it very hard and cold visually. I knew how that would work next to the incredible behind-the-scenes footage *48 Hours* had acquired.

A good story is much more than just information, assembled in order, packaged around commercial slots and show bumpers. To give it life, it needs a pulse, it needs elements the audience can relate to if they're going to follow you on your journey. We needed to bring the story to life. To show that life goes on, and give a sense of place to this horrific story. To do this, I'm looking for shots of someone getting a hair cut, a local soccer match, two people holding hands. I'm looking for shots to show these people are just like anyone else. These are the building blocks that will inject emotion into the story. *Empathy is the bond that keeps the viewer connected to the soul of the story.*

Visual storytelling means taking a lot of pictures that are not necessarily specific to the story but give detail and put flesh on the bones. The little doll on the windowsill had nothing to do with the story *(see next page)*, but it was something we saw as we went by. It was a visual reminder of the children left behind—alone. The little kids playing soccer in the courtyard had nothing to do with the school, but it was important for us to get the sense of life.

To give a personal sense of what happened in the school house, to bring it alive and give a feeling of being

Fadeeva's interview is dark, with basic lighting.

The doll in the window is used as a visual reminder.

there, a handheld POV (point-of-view) shot is an effective technique. I'm using wide angles inside the building, running through it, walking through it, spinning around to show havoc and try and bring some life to the images. Shots of just the outside of the building are not really going to do anything. I'm looking for a shot of the wall with the clouds going by and rolling for five minutes to time-lapse the shot to show the passage of time and the building connected together. I'm looking for anything to bring some movement into what was now very still.

The big challenge when you are shooting a story that's already over is bringing it back to life. I tried to use variety in my shots, so when they got back to the editing room they would have a lot to work with. I shot the school building every way I could. For example, I got compression shots of bullet holes in the walls of the building, then stuck the camera on the ground next to a bullet hole on a wide-angle lens so you could feel how deep the bullet hole was. I shot time-lapse shots in the day, morning, and night. *A compression shot is created with a tele-photo lens—where elements in the scene are stacked, usually with a shallow depth of field. A wide lens extenuates depth. Time-lapse shots add motion to still buildings as clouds and sun rays move against the solid structure. Time-lapse conveys a passage of time and the lasting qualities of a structure against the elements.*

I tried to bring movement and intensity to the bland picture of a gutted-out building. I do have this rule of variety. I try and switch angles and focal lengths as much as possible. I switch lenses all the time when I shoot B-roll. *B-roll is an old film term. The A-roll is the primary content roll; it carries the reporter's stand-ups, narration track, and interviews. The B-roll has all the shots that illustrate that content. The term* B-roll *will appear and be discussed throughout the book.*

When I'm shooting and moving, it's always with a wide-angle lens. We did a walking interview with reporter Peter Van Sant and Fadecva Dariya, our main character, walking down the street as she was showing us the town. Again, adding more movement to what could have been a very

"still" shot. I shoot with a wide-angle lens, and all the camera movement happens with my feet and body. We were interviewing her, but for a while she was just walking us through what was going on and not really aware of the camera. As she pointed out where people gather, I was whipping my camera around to show some urgency, to bring us back into that movement.

Fadeeva and reporter Van Sant in a walking interview.

One of my favorite techniques that I would use in local news works very well at *48 Hours*, who always wants real-life moments. The goal is to capture footage that feels genuine and real … not affected by the TV camera. But gathering those real-life moments is tough when the entire crew is watching every move of the character. By putting a wireless microphone on the character and then interacting one on one (photographer and character), it helps the characters let their guard down and relate to the photographer behind the camera rather than performing for the camera. It's a great way to capture people being human beings and not actors. *When a scene's power and truth are strong enough, the scene remains etched in the viewer's mind. It becomes a memory that connects the story to the emotions of the viewer. The lasting effect is knowledge.*

The most graphic shot was actually an interview with the vice principal of the school. The whole interview was in Russian, and in two whole hours no one moved; we were all so still. It was so quiet you could hear the tape turning in the camera. She was telling us her story, and we were all intrigued. I was watching her face as she spoke, watching her emotions; then a moment later the translator would speak in English. She got to a part about how they couldn't get up for the restroom, and they weren't allowed a drop of water, and people were passing out and falling down. She described how it got so bad; she told us the story about day two when they were totally dehydrated.

This woman said she started to drink her own urine and her son said, "Mommy, save some for me." It took every ounce of strength to not sob aloud like a slobbering idiot. We all started crying, she started crying, even Producer Joe Halderman was quietly crying. That was the low point; it was the saddest thing. The interview ended, and everyone in the room went over and hugged her. She was our hero.

The CBS 48 Hours *program "Hostage" was assembled with the images and story content gathered by John DeTarsio and the crew of producers who went to Beslan, Russia. Film techniques of flashbacks, time lapse, and a haunting a capella musical score enhance the storyline. The show combines DeTarsio's work with Russian video of the siege when it happened, still images from a Russian photojournalist, actual video shot by the terrorists, and interviews from people who survived. The show is punctuated with the information, data, and hard news content that surround the event (see more photos on next page). Of all the techniques used to bring this story to life, the most powerful is silence.*

During the interviews, when the people of Beslan would pause and gather their thoughts or reflect on what they had just said, the interviewer did not jump in with the next question to fill the void; DeTarsio did not cut the camera. They just let the time hang there, quietly waiting for the right time to resume—rolling. The producers and editors bravely let these pauses play out on screen, silence—dead airspace, perfect. We know the hearts of these people more by the silence than by the recounting of events. Throughout the hour we don't know who of their friends and family has survived as they tell their stories about three days in September. The interviews are the string that holds the whole show together and takes viewers on their journey as we wait with them to discover who has survived.

I expected to go into the story as a journalist, and I was an emotional wreck the whole time I was there, and all I wanted to do was go home. But once I got home it didn't end and one night as I was crying on my couch I realized the story was what had me so depressed. I thought it was the bad accommodations, the bad food, or the fact that I might possibly have to miss Thanksgiving at home. But it was the story and the fact that these people lost their loved ones. It got to me. I was depressed by this story, that all these people had lost their loved ones, and kids had lost all of their friends.

A. DeTarsio and Van Sant interview a Russian still photographer who captured the events as they unfolded.

B. Some *48 Hours* "Hostage" footage came from Russian sources. This shot shows a hostage being raced to the hospital.

C. The terrorists themselves shot some of the footage used in the *48 Hours* "Hostage" program with a camera taken from a hostage. The footage was found in a ruined camera in the school's remains.

The Storyteller's Backstory

How do you end up here, back home, crying on your couch—remembering a journey to some far-off land? What does it take to work at this level? Who are the best television news photographers? There were lessons in the Beslan story. The ones who go farthest in their careers are the ones who have a heart—have a lot of passion, who understand human nature and emotions—because that's going give you the instinct to understand where the energy of the story is.

If I come into an office to do an interview with someone I don't know, I look around the room before the interview and maybe I see a picture on the shelf and I say, "Hey, it looks like you have a nice family. How old are your kids?" Just from genuine curiosity. That's the kind of thing that's going to make the person I'm shooting with be more real with me. I would say a photographer that connects with other people and can make other people feel comfortable is probably going to be the most successful in an overall sense. Of course, that photographer is not going to go very far if he doesn't understand the basic building blocks. To be technically the best, you have to study composition, have a natural eye for composition, and understand sequencing.

There are many names that are applied to the men and women who shoot television news: photographer, photog, videographer, photojournalist, television news photographer, shooter, cameraman, camerawoman, cameraperson, camera-op. Not all are considered kind terms or even accurately describe the job. I'm a freelance television photographer. I think the intonation of "cameraperson" feels like an operator. "Shooter" seems like a brainless kind of a thing. I don't mean to be pretentious about it; I'm not a television visual artist or video interpreter, but I'm a photographer. To me a photographer is a photographer, not a camera operator. *A photographer is someone who "writes with light." It's the writing part that speaks to the idea of storytelling, and it's the storytelling part that separates the best from the rest. The term "photojournalist" more specifically refers to writing news with light.*

Why work as a TV news photographer? It's one really rewarding life. That's plain and simple. Whatever town you are in, you are right there. You are watching news and life go by; you get to witness history as it happens. I used to think of myself as a historian. Maybe something ends up in a time capsule a thousand years from now and they pull it up and they are going to see that right now our world has real living, breathing, loving people, and not a whole bunch of suits going to press conferences.

My reason for going into television was because I like people. I like being around people. I like different challenges every day, different jobs every day, different things to do every day, meeting different people every day. Getting to know a little about something different every day. If you like new experiences, meeting new people, and the responsibility that comes along with all that, then that's why you become a television news photographer. Oh, and you should also like taking pictures.

There are many avenues into shooting television news. Everyone has that split in the road when they know it's the turn they're supposed to make. I was at a rugby match in college, and some local news guy came up and took some pictures of the rugby match. I just thought, wow, he gets to go and stand on the side lines, take a few highlights, shoot some pictures, move on to the next thing—what an exciting life! He's always on the go; he's a cowboy. I want to be a cowboy. It was the moment when I realized that's what I wanted to do.

Of course, you don't just step into the top slot the day you decide this is your calling. There's lots of hard work ahead. My first job out of college was at KOLD-TV, Channel 13, in Tucson, Arizona, making $11,000 a year working as a studio camera operator. *A studio camera operator works and stays in the studio and shoots what the director from a control booth tells him or her to shoot. More often than not it's a head shot of an anchor reading the teleprompter. A teleprompter displays the words the news anchor is reading right over the lens, so it looks like he's actually talking to the audience. Many of these studio camera jobs have been outsourced to robots—not cowboys.*

When I had some free time, I used to take pieces from the news, raw footage from stories the night before and the script, and I taught myself how to edit. I was able to exploit that and get a job as an editor; that was my way into becoming a news photographer. It is really hard to get any real hands-on experience in television news, yet everybody wants you to have hands-on experience.

A Really Bad Day

So your time has come; you get to step into the saddle; everyone will be able to watch your creation, scrutinize it for the rest of your career. Pressure, there's no pressure. Slap the reins, kick in your spurs, what could go wrong? The most disastrous day of my life. It was in the early 1980s, and I was an editor for less than a week when two photographers came up to me and said, "Here's your chance. We need a photographer, follow me." They took me to a locker, gave me a camera, showed me a car, and sent me on my way.

My assignment that day was with an RCA TK76 camera that didn't even have a shoulder brace, and I was carrying a thirty-pound recording deck tied to the camera. The TK76 was powered by a big belt I wore around my waist. My assignment was to cover a grand opening of a historical museum. I got to the shoot, and I couldn't even get the camera turned on. I had to get someone from another station to come over and look at it. Basically, the contrast and brightness in the viewfinder were off. He went back, and I could see them all kind of giggling at me, the new guy. Same thing with the deck. I couldn't get it turned on and had to call them over. They came over and discovered I didn't have a battery in the deck. It was really embarrassing.

Then the shoot started. There were stagecoaches bringing dignitaries to do a press conference. I'm trying to shoot as the stagecoaches come in, and all the other guys pop their cameras off their tripods, go follow the people, running into the building, and I couldn't even get the camera off the tripod. I go inside, and all the media is on one side of the wall and I'm wondering why they are all crowded up next to each other. At that time I didn't realize that you don't shoot people in front of a window. So all I got out of the mayor's speech was a black silhouette against the window. That day went on, and at the end all they got out of my entire experience there was a freeze frame that appeared over the shoulder of the reporter. And it was green because I didn't hit the proper switch to set the white balance. I went home and I cried. My humble beginnings.

Life Goes On . . .

So you dust yourself off, and you hop right back on the horse. I remember a defining moment. There was this organization, the NPPA [*National Press Photographers Association*] that had quarterly video clip contests. I wasn't involved at that time, but someone at the station had gotten some regional quarterly winners. There was a story from San Francisco that was about messengers who rode bicycles through the town. The photography and the story were so amazing. I'd never seen anything like it. I watched the story maybe 500 times, frame by frame. It just intrigued me and inspired me, and that's where the road started to turn. That's where it sparked, and slowly through the next decade or so I built towards that kind of work and found my potential and who I was.

'Til this day, I'm still discovering who I am and what I can do. I'm always thinking, "God, I hope I don't screw this up." When I won National Press Photographer of the Year, I remember I didn't want anyone to see my reel because I was afraid anyone who watched would discover I was a fraud and know that I didn't deserve the award. There's a little insight into my sick mind.

Once I felt like I had reached my peak in Tucson, I sent out a lot of résumés, but really kept hitting the San Diego market hard. I wanted to be there so badly I actually accepted a camera assistant job from KFMB Channel 8, the CBS affiliate in San Diego, where my job was carrying the deck and microphone. But I knew I'd move my way up. I borrowed a camera on my days off. I'd open up the phone book and find something like a horse shoer and I'd go out and shoot the guy putting shoes on this horse. Then I'd take the images and use music to make a photo essay—I used to call these photo essays my "Maker" series. I would give them to the executive producer; he would air them, and next thing I knew I was promoted to news photographer.

A year or two later, I was courted by KNSD, the NBC affiliate in town. There I headed up the photography department, and my little photo essays turned into real stories told with natural sound. Eventually, I realized using my voice to fill in the blanks wasn't so hard. The real hard work was gathering the right pictures and piecing them together in story form. From there, it seemed a natural leap to become a reporter as well as a photographer. I kept moving up until they made me an executive producer.

Moving Up the Ladder

An executive producer in television news is not a field position; you are not an executive storyteller. You are the person in charge of the nuts and bolts operation of whatever show you've been assigned. You have more responsibility and get more pay. But budget and management supersede being there. The front lines, the wild frontier of current events, are a distant memory. You're now a wealthy rancher staring into the sunset as all the other cowboys ride off into untold adventures. You'd love to go with them.

I was doing a lecture in Ireland about television news photography and I was with John Larson, a network correspondent for *Dateline NBC*, whom I knew through local news. He never tried to talk me into a life as a freelance photographer, but he did tell me if that time ever came he would do what he could to make sure I didn't starve, that I would at least get some work.

One night we were talking about how I had to have management meetings when I returned to my desk job back in San Diego, and it was like the whole house of cards came falling down. It clicked that I wasn't enjoying my job. It was that fast; that was that. I realized I had never been more comfortable than when I was behind a camera. I had normal worries during a shoot. Am I going to be able to deliver? Am I going to get this job done? Am I going to have anything on the air tonight? But once my eye was behind the camera, that was it. I was comfortable. I was back in the saddle.

On to Freelance Work

Network news is different from local news, and freelancing puts you out there without much of a comfort zone. Not only the stories change, but also the people you work with. The way they work might be very different from what you're used to. And now, in addition to being a photographer, you're also a businessman. The plus side: you're galloping full speed on the edge of history as it happens—anywhere in the world.

It was a huge jump. I had no idea going into it. The basic skills I brought from local news you can't trade. I think that is what makes me successful in this business. I can change directions really fast. I can maneuver my way through a story. I believe if you come from local news, you can do anything. However, it is a huge culture shock. Jumping from local to network, you're working with a lot of Ivy League graduates. Learning how to deal with these people on a day-to-day basis is still a real challenge. I had to learn quickly how to conduct myself as a business owner, as opposed to being in local news, where you could bitch about this and bitch about that and just be yourself.

When you go into the freelance business, you don't get to screw up anymore, you have to bat a thousand. Not only do you have to bat a thousand, you've got to be a bit of a salesperson, which I wasn't used to. I'm always a video journalist and storyteller, but now I'm also a salesman trying to sell the producer that I've got it under control—even when I'm scared as hell. With *60 Minutes*, you have to know what their product is and deliver exactly what they expect. Yeah, I want to put a little bit of me in everything, but I need to give them *60 Minutes* product. Same thing with *48 Hours*, I'd better know what they want and how to deliver what they need so they come back for more product. I have to think of myself as a businessperson/salesperson.

I am no longer in that wonderful world of local television news. When you're in local television news, it's all about you and how you want your work to look. That's what I miss about my time in local news. I could pursue my own visual fantasies about how I wanted to build the story. Now it's a different game. Another huge challenge was lighting. In local news you don't really learn a lot about lighting because you don't do a lot of lighting since you're moving at such a quick clip. That was the biggest learning curve for me, and I truly wasn't prepared for it. It was a huge, huge culture shock. It's not just gathering the lights; it's learning how to use them in the situations my new clients required.

When I made the jump to freelance, luckily I was stupid. If I really knew what I was getting into I probably wouldn't have had the guts to do it. I had a house, a wife, two kids and a dog, a big mortgage, and I quit my job. I needed about a hundred-thousand-dollar investment just to get started. And then, "Hey is anyone going to call me?" Had I understood the competition, I don't know if I would have gotten started. But now, here I am. My life can be strange.

My schedule says that I'm free for the next three days. I'll go to the gym, come home, pull out the paper, listen to the water fountain. All will be peaceful and quiet—until the phone rings. Five minutes later, I could be trying to pack up thirty-five cases of gear, getting airplane tickets, coordinating hotel rooms, rental vans, and crews, before jumping on a plane to fly across the country for a week. Luckily this life works with my personality. Most freelance crews are a two-part team. I am most fortunate to have an incredible partner on my photographic journeys, my soundman for nearly the last ten years, Dustin Eddo.

Always a Storyteller

The best television news photographers are considered storytellers first. Though that is never an official title, it usually shows up in the first phrase that describes their work. Their ability to visually tell a story elevates the work they do as journalists to a level above that of a camera operator. They all have had the experience of telling a complete story with just their pictures and the sound they capture on location.

I once heard a quote that I love: "Visual storytelling means telling and presenting stories in a way that takes full advantage of the curiosity of the viewer." If you don't take advantage of the curiosity of the viewer, then what's the point? To me, any good story is about a journey and that's where the curiosity factor comes in—in that you take the viewer through the journey. So once you find the journey in the story, once you find some place to take the viewer, then the viewer is going to be curious and will want to know what happens and how it resolves. Early on in the "Hostage" story, we all knew that the journey of the story would be the three days of the "hostages." We would slowly bring the audience along in the same way that the three days unfolded, and then in the end we would find out who of our character's loved ones made it through, and who didn't.

I like to think how Steven Spielberg would put this together. He'd have a wide master shot, he'd have a cutaway, he'd have a reaction shot, he'd have an over-the-shoulder shot, wide, medium, tight. He'd do all these things. While Mr. Spielberg has the luxury of time, big budgets, real actors, huge lighting crews, and set directors, in news you have to attempt to do these things at the speed of life. In other words, you have to anticipate, you've got to be one step ahead of the action. Example: Someone is at the ATM. You have to get that master shot of someone walking up. Then you've got to move to where the card is going to go into the slot while he's pulling out his wallet, so you have that next shot. You can't stage it if you want to keep your character comfortable and real. That is really the goal. In order to get good stories, keep it real (not staged or faked—real-life people can't act!).

The Tools of Photographic Storytelling

Heart

It's clear from John DeTarsio's story, and almost everyone else interviewed for this book, that having heart is at the top of the list. The best television news photographers all share a passion for life and a love of people. They are students of the human condition, and are compassionate and sympathetic to the world on the other side of their lenses.

The Imaging Device

The camera: I refer to it as an imaging device because of all the shapes and sizes that can be considered a television camera. It is the storytelling machine. How the cameras work may change; the optical laws of lenses and light do not. The camera will control the shutter speed, or how fast each image is frozen in time, the white balance, the quality of your images in terms of color, contrast, graininess or noise, sensitivity to light, and the aspect ratio. In connection to this tool is the recording device, usually mounted together in a camcorder. A recording device simply stores your shots on some kind of medium, tape, film, or hard drive for later viewing.

The Lens

The manipulation of the optical characteristics of the lens is a prime element in photographic storytelling. A wide lens portrays a scene differently than a telephoto lens, and depth of field can direct the viewer to the most important part of the story. This is your most active, tactile tool. If you understand the storytelling properties of lenses, you can tell your stories with any camera or device.

Sound

Not strictly considered a tool of photographic storytelling, this one will often fall on the photographer to record. Knowing what microphone to use and making sure you get clean, usable audio is essential to telling your story. You record the interviews and the reporter stand-ups. These will most often be the building blocks of your story.

Natural Sound—NATSND

Nothing conveys a sense of place better than the natural sound of being there. Record natural sound all the time!

Support and Motion

Support refers to anything you put the camera on. A tripod, baby legs, and high-hat are all tools for supporting the fluid head. The fluid head allows the operator to smoothly pan (move left and right) and tilt (move up and down). The tripod is essential for rock-solid images. Some techniques require shoulder mounting the camera; this should be done for a reason, not just because it's less fuss than a tripod. Every method of support and camera height conveys a different feel for the scene.

Light

This is the tool that let's us see our world. The quality of light can paint a mood and create an impression that can influence the experience of a story. Whether it's natural light from the sun or man-made, the photographer's manipulation of this tool is the basis for photography. It's important to note that the absence of light or the placing of shadows is considered the same tool.

Editing

All of the field work is done. Now to tell the story, your work needs to be edited. Editing will determine how your story is told, where the beginning will be, where the story will end. It will establish pace or the tempo of your story and will reveal details at just the right moment. Your story lives or dies with this tool, so make sure you shoot with editing in mind.

Words, Voice Track

This is about television news, so there's going to be words, lots of them, hopefully not wall to wall (meaning nonstop talking from the first frame to the last). You'd like some room to bring up natural sound or let an event play out. Share your thoughts on what you've shot with the writer and/or reporter; it will affect how they construct the final script.

Music

Music can have a place in television news. Most often, it's used in longer-format work like feature stories, sports, and mini-docs. Music is a very powerful communication tool in that it generally sparks an emotional response based on the performer's intent of the music and the viewer's past experiences. A sad song, is a sad song. Instantly, it cues the audience that the story is going to be emotional.

Now, what to do with these tools? (The tools will be covered extensively in the upcoming chapters.) Go make great stories that will enlighten your community and make the world a better place by capturing your history as it happens. I say "your history" because it is yours, you are paid to go out and experience the world and bring it back in a truthful, visual accounting. Your stories will be about the people and events in your world—that means the stories are exclusively about them—not you. But the truth of the moment is in your hands. So own it!

Back in Beslan

On the statistical side, Russian scholar and former CBS News Moscow correspondent Jonathan Sanders offers this information regarding the events at Beslan School Number One:

Numbers, especially in a chaotic place such as Russia, are slippery things. One thing is very clear numerically: the siege and bungled attempts to

A. Inside Beslan School Number One, a memorial honors the lost students.

B. A closer view of the photographs used in the memorial.

Loved ones bring water in memory of the thirst of the hostages who were denied food and water.

relieve it exacted a greater toll of human life than all but one act of modern (1881 to the present) terrorism, the destruction of the World Trade Center. However, few of the direct victims in the World Trade Center were children, let alone primary school boys and girls.

The coverage of Beslan, and the ethical issues raised in live broadcast of such events, caused the BBC to alter its guideline for television coverage of terrorist situations.

Under the BBC's editorial guidelines for hijacking, kidnapping, hostage taking, and sieges they now install a delay. The guidelines point out the importance of this, particularly when the outcome is unpredictable and the recorded material may not be suitable for broadcast.

Note, too, most of what the world saw of the crisis and its aftermath drew on the courage and fine eyes of Russian cameramen. Whatever the many limitations imposed on journalists of the increasingly heavy-handed Putin regime, Russian broadcasters continue to have the grace to always provide on-screen credit to the men (there are very few Russian camerawomen) who actually capture the images used to tell stories.

The CBS 48 Hours *program was reworked into a film narrated by Julia Roberts for Showtime. "Three Days in September" received critical praise from* Variety, New York *magazine, the* New York Times, *and the* Daily News. CBS sent the finished *48 Hours* "Hostage" program back to someone in Beslan. They had to take it to the next town over, where there was a big enough theater. They held a couple of showings that received standing ovations. All these people wanted was their story to be told. They were grateful.

Where does the story end? With a closing shot, and so often its negative action. It's almost cliché to see John Wayne fading into the sunset with his horse, but it works! Why do you think so many people use it? It clues in the audience that the story has come to an end. Closing content is what we have learned from this journey and the journey ends.

A good story, a good yarn. Nothing can beat that!

Take 2: Storytelling

Picture a campfire out in the forest somewhere. There's a full moon and the wolves are howling as you settle into the night. It's your turn to tell a story; all eyes are on you as the firelight flickers on your face. You are the television for the evening. This is a lesson in storytelling in its basic form. It's the way stories have been shared for ages. So what is a story? And what makes one good? And when you know that, how can you apply that to the art and craft of camerawork?

"There is a full moon over the forest and the wolves are howling" is not a story, it's just information. It's one component of a story, in that it describes the environment or setting. So, let's mark "environment" as one of our components. News can be just information and not a narrative story. "It will rain tonight" doesn't qualify as a story, either. You'll need an event or set of events. They can be problems, conflicts, or a realization. The start of a thunderstorm can be an event. So now we have the second component, "an event." You'll need characters, people, an animal, or anything that can be affected by the event. So there's a family from Chicago huddled around a fire just like this one. A dad and three kids. We have a third component and the beginning of a story.

"There was a full moon over the woods and the wolves were howling. A family from Chicago had just setup their tents and made a fire when lightning cracked. The rain started pouring and the woods rustled with the paws of unknown creatures." You've got them hooked; now take them somewhere. The journey begins. The journey is the fourth component and the middle of the story.

"The family had just zipped up the tent when the worst of the storm hit. The howling of the wind and the wolves was deafening. All of a sudden the floor of the tent started to move, it felt slippery. The dad poked his head out of the tent just as a roaring torrent of water sent him, the tent, and the kids racing down a ravine. Picking up speed as they went, the children started crying for their dad as he held on to the tent for dear life. Just when it couldn't get any worse, menacing teeth sank into his jeans, just missing the skin." You reach over and grab the ankle of the person next to you for effect. They jump with an uneasy giggle.

You howl like a wolf. This is the climax, the height of action in your story. This is what makes the journey worth taking. This is the fifth element. " 'Hold on to 'em, boy,' a voice screamed from the shadows. A dark cowboy descended the hill with his flashlight. The dad's pants started to rip as the teeth held him in place. With both hands, the dad was just able to keep the soaking tent from slipping over the edge and into the racing river. Looking over his shoulder, the dad noticed it was not a wolf or a cowboy. It was the ranger and his trusty companion, King, a large but friendly Alaskan Malamute. King released his grip as the ranger helped the family up. 'We heard there were some campers in these parts, and knew it would flood out as soon as it rained. King here caught your scent the moment we got out of the cab,' the ranger said.

As they walked back to the ranger's jeep, the dad from Chicago shook the ranger's hand and King licked the face of one of the boys." And that's the end.

So there's the story. With a few elements we were able to construct a basic campfire story. We'll call it "Terror in the Woods." Let's look at the components again.

- *Beginning: environment, event, character—full moon, forest, wolves, a campsite, a family from Chicago.*

- *Middle: journey, climax—the rain starts pouring, the tent slips down the hill, and at the worst moment a wolf bites the dad's leg.*

- *End: resolution—the wolf is really the ranger's dog and the family is saved.*

Often in news we hear that story is constructed of "who, where, what, why and when." The five Ws. Because the word "how" does not start with a "W," it is often just left out. But, we'll apply "how" to this story just the same. We can easily answer these questions in "Terror in the Woods."

- *Who? The family from Chicago, the wolf/dog, and the ranger.*
- *Where? At a campsite in the woods during a storm.*
- *What? A camping trip turns bad when a flood and a wild wolf attack a Chicago family.*
- *Why? The storm started and the family was in a flood plain.*
- *When? At night.*
- *How? How was the story brought to a conclusion? By King digging his teeth into the dad's jeans, the dog was able to slow the slide down the hill and save the family.*

Notice two things. I gave the story a name. It has its own personality; it's unique. Also note the "what?" "A camping trip turns bad when a flood and a wolf attack a Chicago family." In moviemaking, this would be a logline, a very brief description of a story. One or two lines, tops. When describing your story, the title and logline or "what?" should roll off your tongue. These simple thoughts should guide your story. Make a commitment to "what" the story is. Use the rest of your narrative skills to embellish this central core. If your "what" or "logline" turns into multiple run-on sentences, you don't have a very focused story. Do story first.

Take a few moments and create your own campfire story, developing yours like we did in "Terror in the Woods."

Now, Let's Take "Terror in the Woods" and Shoot the Story

You've got to get their attention right off the bat, so let's start with a silhouette shot of a wolf against the moon—the most graphic, visually arresting image first. The first shot does not have to be a wide establishing shot, but you'll need to establish the setting soon. We've set the tone; it's going to be scary.

Where are we? A wide shot establishing the campsite in a clearing of the woods will show the viewers where we are. We hear the dad say something about it not sounding like any animal in the Chicago zoo. Now we know where they're from. The lightning flashes and we see a close-up of dad's face as he tells the kids to get into the tent. The flashlights project the family's shadows against the tent as they settle in. There's a close-up of raindrops falling into a pool. There's another howl. It's good to keep the pace up and remind the viewers that this family is not alone.

The floor of the tent starts to wiggle around; a low, wide-angle shot would show this well. Then three quick close-ups of the kids getting scared by the moving floor. These are essential; they are the reaction to the action. This is the human element that connects the viewer emotionally to the story. We see the dad's face pop out from the zipper in the tent, then a look of horror. From his point of view, we see a river of water hit him right in the face. Of course we use protective housings for the camera. The dad and the tent start washing down the hill. We pan with them as they slide. We want to see inside as the kids get tumbled about. Dad's hands clenched onto the tent and then another howl. A close-up of the snout of a wolf/dog biting down on dad's leg. Through the rain we see an indefinable figure that looks a little like a cowboy running down the hill and screaming; this could be a medium shot.

The tent comes to a stop at the edge of the river, the camera perched on the edge of the river to show how close they came. In the same medium shot as earlier, the indefinable figure is now recognizable as the ranger. A close-up shows the dog release his bite and seem to smile. The kids are coming out of the tent as the dad gets up in a wide shot. In a close-up, the ranger says, "We heard there were some campers in these parts, and knew it would flood out as soon as it rained. King here caught your scent the moment he got out of the cab." And in the final shot, they are walking away from camera, back to the ranger's jeep in a wide scenic shot that shows the forest, the crumpled tent, and all the characters. Our story is done, roll credits!

Try to visualize your story this way. It is important that you learn to tell and appreciate good stories. Of course, in news you are not telling campfire stories, you are telling real life—but there are basic similarities to all stories. In news, you will probably know the where *before you shoot a frame. You'll also know the* when, *since you'll be there as it's happening; or if it's an accounting of a past event, it will be the reason you pulled out your camera in the first place. You'll probably know the* who *or learn that quickly.* Why will *often require research. It's the* why *that often dictates the journey, or the reason to keep watching the story. That leaves what. Again,* what *the story is about should be able to be summarized in a sentence or two. "What" the story is about is what your job is about.*

Throughout this book, we'll be covering the tools and techniques of visual storytelling and the world of television news photography.

CHAPTER 3

Larry Hatteberg
The Chain of Command

Larry Hatteberg

Anchor/Broadcast Journalist

**Former television photographer, photojournalist, reporter, chief photographer,
assistant news director, news director, executive news director
KAKE-TV, Wichita, Kansas
NPPA Ernie Crisp Television News Photographer of the Year, 1975 and 1978**

*I*t is a bright Saturday morning in Wichita, Kansas. The town is waking up to the beginning of a long holiday weekend—the Fourth of July. Independence Day is just two days away. Parades, picnics, and fireworks mark our nation's birth, and the official starting point of summer. Children are outside playing—laughter and giggles fade in and out with the songs of morning birds. The sun's rays, carved by trees, brightened by humidity and tiny particles floating through the air, open flowers and warm the gentle perfume of neighborhood gardens. This feels like a safe place to live, again . . .

Larry Hatteberg is up too, puttering around, chasing chores with a pleasant disposition familiar to all of Wichita. His thoughts bounce between holiday plans, family, work, and just plain nothing. The phone in his home office chirps to life. Maybe he'll let the machine get it. The second ring, it's a bit early, could be important. By the third ring, Hatteberg is making an honest attempt to pick up before the machine beats him to it. Without a moment to spare, the headset is snatched from its base, "Hello."

"Will you accept a collect call from the Sedgwick County Detention Center?" Hatteberg's day takes a dark turn; the next thirty minutes will change his life and plunge him into a first-person accounting of unimaginable torture and death. "Yes." Hatteberg's heart rate climbs close to that of a marathoner; the day's trivia evaporates, replaced by a singular focus. Record this, get the recorder, hit record, am I recording? Yes.

The operator clicks over the call. "Mr. Hatteberg, this is Dennis Rader. So, you getting ready to do the Fourth of July fireworks thing?" the voice on the phone

EQUIPMENT

Canon XL-2 Mini-DV camera with lens
Wide-angle lens
2 Lectrosonic wireless microphones
Sennheiser shotgun microphone
Miller fluid head tripod and "high-hat" for low shots
HMI 400W lights
2 Lowel "Rifa" 500W soft lights
4 Lowel Pro 250W lights
2 Lowel Broad 500W lights
3 Arri 250W lights
Assorted light stands
Portable florescent lights and camera crane

asks in a charming manner. Hatteberg can feel the hair on his neck start to rise, his skin crawls, the room seems colder. None of these sensations are commonplace to this seasoned journalist. But this morning, he's just accepted a personal call from Dennis Radar, the BTK killer. BTK for bind, torture, kill.

Wichita was not always as safe as it is today. Dennis Lynn Radar stalked this city and brutally murdered at least ten people between 1974 and 1991. Coincidentally, 1974 might have been the first year Rader saw Larry Hatteberg on the air with Larry's introduction of "Hatteberg's People," a series that still runs today. The people of Wichita knew they had a serial killer in their midst. With fear and fascination, they absorbed every detail the news organizations put out. Taunting the police and press, BTK would send notes and poems detailing his "projects," as he called them. In 1982, he dropped out of sight only to resurface with a flurry of eleven letters between 2004 and 2005.

Rader is the only serial killer known to disappear for so many years and then reappear. He is also the longest-running serial killer. In the end, Radar's desire for attention, a computer disc, and DNA samples led to his arrest. It isn't every day that you have a serial killer talk to you at home and want to talk about killing people. You don't want to make light small talk with a serial killer, but I answered his question, one of which was, Will I have the Fourth of July off work. "I'm not going be able to do that." *Hatteberg knows this phone call will put him into overtime for the next couple of weeks, maybe longer.* "Well that's too bad," he said. "You should get some time off and spend it with your family and shoot fireworks."

I had to really muster all my professionalism to make it happen because he caught me a little

bit off guard. I really didn't expect him to call me on a Saturday morning or really any time. So I asked him every question that I could think of to ask in a thirty-minute period. "How can you kill a child?" "What makes you kill?" He had told me that he had planned to kill again. That he had another female victim picked out; he was ready to do one more. He told me that the children he killed were simply collateral. He did not expect them to be home. He talks about the killing of people the same way the rest of us talk about picking up the laundry or buying a dozen donuts.

Rader had been to KAKE-TV as a child and an adult. He came to watch a cowboy show that we

A. Many of the BTK letters went to KAKE-TV prior to Rader's capture. Once captured and jailed, Rader exchanged letters with Hatteberg, which led to a major KAKE-TV exclusive.

B. Hatteberg communicated with BTK over the air in an attempt to stop him from killing and to keep him talking in hopes that he might make a mistake.

used to have on when he was a child. He was at the station when we brought in Rin Tin Tin, and he had taken a number of tours through the station. He knew a lot about me. He knew the names of my coworkers. He told me that the reason he communicated with us was that he liked our station and he liked the people on it and he specifically liked my work. He liked the "Hatteberg's People" segment.

In an unbelievable portion of the conversation, he told me that he wanted to be on "Hatteberg's People" because he felt that in his work as a code enforcement officer in Park City, Kansas, he had done some good work and he wanted to be recognized for it. I told him, "You know, killing ten people tends to negate the good cop angle. It pretty much shoots it down."

I asked if he had an accomplice, and he said no but he always had his little friend with him. I said, "Well, who's your little friend?" He told me it was a demon and he even drew the demon for me, so we had a drawing of the demon. He first knew that he was far different from anyone else back in elementary school. Having sexual fantasies in elementary school that he knew no other child was having. By the time he was in the eighth grade, or a freshman in high school, his future was cemented. His serial killer was there. What caused it, we still don't know. We know that it occurred, but to this day we still do not know why . . . and we may never know.

The call ends cordially. Hatteberg asks Rader if he would talk with him in person at the Sedgwick County Detention Center. Rader agrees and the following Monday, Rader, Hatteberg, and Anchor Jeff Herdon meet with Rader for thirty minutes. Hatteberg hangs up the phone assessing his new situation. Other than in court, this is the only time that BTK, Dennis Rader, has talked publicly about the killings.

Hatteberg's first order of business: Alert the station. Within minutes, the well-oiled gears of KAKE's news organization are spinning. Now I had to call the news director because he's my immediate boss. This was going to be the top story whenever it ran and it was going to run in a ratings period. The news director then notified the general manager. The story would also need extra resources and we'd be interacting with our dual affiliates, ABC and CNN.

The news director let me pretty much do this story how I wanted to do it. It will be a two-part story run over two nights. The decision is made to delay the broadcast to get things ready and make the best of it. The networks don't know about the story yet.

The news director lays out his vision of the coverage to the executive producer, the assignment editor, the anchors, and the assistant news director. He tells the show producers what show it's going to run on. The 5:00 and 6:00 producers will have little preview pieces in their shows. My story will be the lead story at 10:00. He tells the assignment editor his vision for the other stories that will support the "BTK Exclusive." There will be follow-up stories from the police department point of view, from the citizen point of view when they hear this—how they feel about it. We will be working with the promotion department, and the promotion department will be running ads all day long saying, "Coming up tonight . . . an interview with BTK exclusive to KAKE-TV."

The executive producer works with the show producers to make sure all of the elements fall into place and that the newscasts flow smoothly. The assignment editor knows the content that the show producers need and assigns field crews to get the stories. These can be either photographers alone or reporter/photographer teams depending on what is needed.

The reporters assigned to the BTK collateral stories are doing research and setting up interviews and shooting times. The reporters collaborate with the assignment desk for scheduling.

The photographers go by themselves or with a reporter and shoot the stories. When the crews come back, the reporters write their stories, share information with the writers for lead-ins, cut their audio tracks, and hand the material to the editor. When the photographer comes back, he gives the tape to the editor or waits for the script and edits it himself. The writers write lead-ins and story content not covered by the reporters.

The stories get edited, the copy gets loaded on the teleprompter, the anchors put on their microphones, and . . . in three, two, one, the red tally light on top of camera #1 glows. "Good evening . . ."

The story is introduced by Larry Hatteberg on camera; then the interview is played while graphics spell out the conversation on screen. The ratings, as you might imagine, in our area were off the charts; everybody was concerned about BTK. You have to understand the mindset of the people in Wichita: They could not get enough of the BTK news story. Everybody wanted to know every nuance of this story because the community had lived with it for thirty years.

The networks went nuts. They could not believe that a local guy had an interview with BTK. All the networks had flown in lawyers and their top reporters, producers, and anchors. They were all in Wichita and they were all trying to get the interview. When we went on the air with it, they just came unglued.

So I became, for a short time, a "media darling," appearing on all of the network shows—the morning shows, the evening shows, the cable shows. It was quite a rush. It was fascinating being on the other side of the media hoard for that particular experience. I learned a lot about how I wanted to be treated as a subject, something that most photojournalists don't get a chance to experience.

It's easy to see how things work in a newsroom by following the chain of command on the BTK story. As a thirty-year veteran of the television news business, Larry Hatteberg has worn many hats, often all at the same time. Having served as a photojournalist, reporter, and anchor, he is well qualified to examine the intricacies of the newsroom chain of command. Following the "Chain of Command" diagram on the next page, you can get an idea of the amount of communication that must happen in a newsroom. A few obvious observations: The most arrows come from the news director and the most arrows hit the editors. True in this diagram and allegorically true in real life.

Newsroom Chain of Command

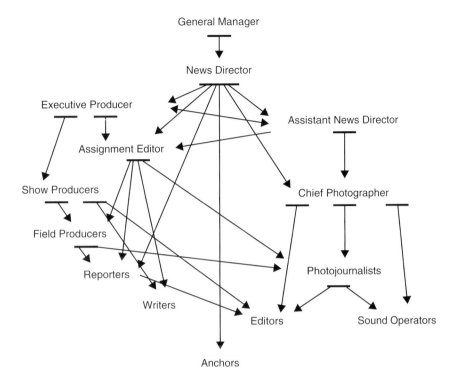

Newsroom Chain of Command

General Manager

We'll start at the top and work down, beginning with the general manager. The general manager is in charge of the entire station operation. That's news, sales, programming. Everything that has to do with the television station, he is in charge of it. The general manager, then, is also in charge of the department heads who are under him. That would be the news director and the heads of the programming department, the traffic department, and the sales department—whatever departments a particular station has. Those are the four main ones, and all of those people would answer to the general manager.

The general manager should set the vision and the tone for the station. The vision, for example, might be that we are going to be a community television station—that we are going to be a television station that sets the tone for community involvement. We want to be involved in everything the community does. We want to be there when the community does bad things and let them know that they've done bad things, and we also want to be there to pat them on the head and tell them they've done some really good things; so the general manager will set the overall vision for the station.

Interaction with photographer: Might fire you if you dent his car.

News Director

The news director works at the behest of the general manager. The news director is usually hired by the general manager, and reports directly to the general manager. The news director sets the tone for the news department based on the general manager's vision.

Now, many news directors today have a vision of their own and, if the general manager is sales oriented and has a sales background, he may let the news director set the vision and tone for the news department. We're seeing that a lot now in local television stations where the news director actually sets the tone for the coverage and actually has the vision.

He may also tell the reporters and the photojournalists the style of reporting and photography that he wants. He may say, "This television station is going to be all spot news. It's going to do nothing but spot news. I mean, if something is going on in the community—the plane crash, the murder, the knifing, the grass fire—we're gonna be on top of it and we're gonna be there. And we're gonna be known as the station that brings you the news first." So that is what I mean by a news director setting the tone.

He may tell the chief photographer, who works under the news director, how he wants to see the video—whether he wants to see the video as a package or as a voiceover, and the style of the video. He may say, "You know, I don't really care much about editing; all we want you to do is go out to the scene and do the video and we'll just put it on the air live as a reporter is talking over it." You will see another news director who will say, "I care very much about editing and everything we put on is going to be edited and it's going to look very good." So it's going to depend on the personality of the news director, and it's different for each and every shop.

Interaction with photographer: Probably hired you based on the recommendation of the chief photographer. Also might fire you if you dent his car.

Executive Producer and Assistant News Director

The executive producer works primarily with the show producers, not the field crews. It is the assignment desk and the assistants on the assignment desk who work primarily with the reporters and photographers. The executive producer may have three or four show producers under him. He may have the morning show, the 12:00 show, the 6:00 show, the 10:00 show, the 5:00 show; all those other producers will work under him.

The executive producer is really in charge of the overall look of all shows and working with them to make sure that stories aren't repeated. If there are new angles to stories, those stories are going to be run again in a second newscast during that day. The EP is checking the writing and the quality and the accuracy of every newscast.

Many times, the executive producer is also the assistant news director; it depends on how large their television station is. If it's a large one like in Denver or Chicago, there would probably be separate people in those positions. As you get down into the smaller television markets, that position tends to be morphed into one person.

Interaction with photographer: Can't fire you if you dent his car. Likes good photography because he needs a good-looking demo tape, too. You'll ruin his day if you miss your slot.

Assignment Editors

There is usually a morning meeting. It's a different time at every television station across the country. At our television station, it takes place at nine in the morning. The assignment editor meets with the news director and the executive producer and any other staff members that are available, and that includes reporters and photographers. In the meeting, they will discuss what's going on that day. Usually everybody gives his or her opinion. Everybody gives their thoughts as to what's important, and then the news director, along with the executive producer and the assignment editor, will lay out what stories they're going to cover for that day. At our station, the photographers are welcome to attend. What I find most of the time is that many photographers are already out the door covering stories at that particular time, so it's really rare that photographers get to attend that.

Stories come in every way you could imagine. For example, in our computer system the assignment desk is listed. For every day of the week, a reporter can go in and say, "Hey Jay, I'm working on this story; I think it would be great for tomorrow." And they will put that in the computer for the next day. Meanwhile, the assignment desk is assembling stories that they think might be good story ideas for the next day. They're getting them by phone, they're getting them by e-mail, they're getting them on the wire, they're getting them through news releases in the mail. Every way possible. Then these are all put into an electronic file, and that file is looked at the next morning to see what story possibilities they have. Then, after the morning meeting, crews are assigned to cover those stories. That's the function of the assignment desk.

A similar meeting occurs about 1:30 in the afternoon for the 2:00 P.M. to 11:00 P.M. crew as to what stories are going to be covered. Again, same deal applies. If a photographer can be there, if a reporter can be there, great. The reality is, usually they're running and gunning and not able to attend the meeting. Television has become a very "right-now" business. There is not a lot of planning for the next day done the day before. And, as a result, everybody has to hit the road running. It is really the unfortunate nature of the way television is today, and that's too bad. But, it's a reality.

So the photographer and reporter will be in touch with the assignment desk via cell phone all day long. The assignment desk will be talking to them and changing their assignment if need be, telling them of a new location, coordinating meetings and interviews. It's just a constant communication all day long, and that's very, very important. As the afternoon progresses and the deadlines get much tighter and the shows are looming, then the communications process is just absolutely vital between the reporter, the photographer, and the assignment desk. In the television news business, the assignment that is given at nine in the morning isn't always the assignment that ends up being shot. Sometimes the assignment isn't there. Sometimes the facts have changed; it isn't the story that everybody thought it was. In many cases, the assignments are changed while the reporters and the photographers are in the field. That's why communications are important.

The assignment editor is the person responsible for telling everybody what's available. Then the executive producer gets involved when they're building up what each show is going to have in it, what each specific producer is going to have in each show.

The assignment editor will then assign the hardware that's needed for that story. Are they going to need a portable laptop? Are they going to have to edit in the field? Are they going to need a microwave truck? Do they need a satellite truck? Are they going out of town? Do we need to hook them up with airline tickets and a motel room? He's kind of the transportation guy, too. Sometimes if it's a larger assignment desk, that falls off to an assistant assignment editor who might be in charge of crew transportation and crew housing, and then setting up and making sure that the crew has a live truck to operate out of once they get there. Getting them back, getting the crew's story back to the television station. It starts to get pretty complicated.

Interaction with photographer: Again, no car issues; you could probably borrow it and go four-wheeling without getting fired. But this person can make your life heaven or a living hell. Move him or her to the top of your Christmas list.

Chief Photographer

The chief photographer answers to the news director, and will set the tone according to how the news director wants his video to look. The chief photographer will then pass that down to the other photographers and editors. The chief photographer's role is being the guy who makes sure that all the equipment works and everybody has their assigned cameras. That everybody's car is in good condition. That the live trucks are ready to role at a moment's notice, and everybody has videotape, or whatever they're recording on, available to them. The chief photographer will locate and recommend photographers to be hired by the station. The final hiring is usually done by the news director.

Interaction with photographer: He will fire you if you dent his car. Had everything to do with you getting hired, all those raises, and good work schedule. You owe him big.

Show Producers

The show producers are in charge of getting each newscast on the air. Once they see what the menu is for the day, they will go in and say, "Gee, I'd like to have this murder that occurred last night at 5:00; I'd like to give that a full package at 6:00." The 6:00 producer will say, "Well, we ran a package at five, so I'm going to do a VO. VO is the acronym for voiceover—the news anchor reads the story as the video rolls on it at six. And the 10:00 producer may want to do a reader on it by the time it gets to be 10:00. So they're all bidding for different treatments of the same story.

Interaction with photographer: If you dent his car, it's the same as the executive producer except he may lack the life experience to let it roll off his back so easily.

Reporters

Reporters "report" the story. They are researchers, writers, field producers, and on-air talent all rolled into one. They often enterprise or uncover a story. The assignment desk assigns their daily tasks. In many markets, they are given "beats" (specific areas of specialization) like health beat, city beat, economic beat. A reporter in television news is a field position.

The relationship between photographer and reporter should be a fifty/fifty one. No person in that crew of two is more important than the other. They both have a job to do. They both need to put their egos aside to do their jobs. Now, we've all worked with reporters who will say when you're being introduced to somebody, "This is my cameraman." Well, it's not really the case. Reporters don't own photographers the same as photographers don't own reporters. They are both equally responsible for the *story*. They should be able to work together. The photographer should be able to tell the reporter, "Hey, you don't need to write these words because I have this piece of video and natural sound that says the exact same thing you've written, so we should be able to cut out the words." The reporter, on the other hand, should be able to tell the photographer, "Gee, we really need some natural sound in this area, or we really need to use a little bit of different video here."

It's really hard to set your egos aside sometimes, but you must remember that the story is the most important thing. It isn't the reporter and it isn't the photographer. It's the story. So you work as a crew, live and die and fail as a crew, not as individuals. If the story goes bad, both are called into the news director's office the next day, not the reporter and not the photographer, but both people are there. So it's incumbent that they have a good working relationship. They have to respect each other, and understand that both of them have difficult jobs to do under incredible time pressures; it's incumbent on them to work together.

The photographer usually drives the car because it's usually the car he's assigned to. If the reporter is smart at all, the reporter will help carry equipment. You have to be responsible for each other.

The really good reporters in the television news business help carry things. They help set up the lights. They pack the stuff away in the car. They know a lot about the photography aspect of it, which is wonderful. The reporters who don't can find themselves out of a job after a while because photographers would much rather work with those who not only are good at reporting but also know a lot about photography. So I think the good reporters are also good photographers.

Good photographers should be looking out for how reporters look, how they're coming across, and helping them with their work. The good photographer is going to say, "You know, we really need to set up lights here to make you look better." And, if the reporter is smart at all, he'll say, "You know, that's a really good idea because I need all the help looking good that I can get." Unfortunately, in this generation of photojournalists and the way television news is covered today, lighting is becoming a lost art, and that's really unfortunate because it makes the reporter look bad, it makes the station look amateurish.

Many reporters will tell a photographer, "We don't have time to set up lights." I've heard this a thousand times and my feeling is, and a lot of other professionals' feeling is, that we don't have time not to set up lights. Because it makes the subject look better, it makes the reporter look better; it's professional. It's what professionals do out on a story. The reporters who understand that, you can tell their work because they look very good. Every reporter who works with a quality photographer always remembers that photographer because he made her look good in the field. When you're sending out those resume tapes, you want to look as good as you possibly can—a good photographer can make you look great; a bad photographer can make you look terrible.

Interaction with photographer: No car issues; they probably drive the same thing you do. Reporters have a constant, daily, close relationship with photographers. It's definitely a team. You share each other's successes and failures. You probably have been married and divorced with less drama than you experience with reporters.

Writers

The writers take the vast amount of written material that comes into a newsroom from the Internet, news wires, and press releases and rewrite it for the anchors to read. They usually write the VO or VO/SOT (voiceover/

sound on tape—pronounced "vee oh" and "vee oh es oh tee," respectively—video over the anchor's voice followed by a sound bite or interview) portions of the show. Sometimes writers will write all of the on-air talent copy. Sometimes the on-air talent will write their own introductions, story lead-ins, and exits.

Interaction with photographer: If you're the only one sent out on a story, you've got to make notes and give the information to the writers. Dent his car? How could you tell?

Editors

The editor has to take what everybody gives him and then he has to make miracles happen in some cases. So he is at the mercy of the photographer; he is at the mercy of the reporter. He can only use what they give him and his own creativity. If it's a larger station, there will be separate editors; there will be people who are full-time editors. A photographer will usually end up cutting his own story 99 percent of the time. At the network level, obviously, they have separate editors for everything. But at the local stations, most of the time, you cut your own story unless you're in the larger stations in Minneapolis, New York, L.A., and then it would be given to an editor.

The responsibility of editors is to take everything that you've given to them and turn it around into a meaningful story—using the best video, the best audio—and they have to do it quickly. I admire them very much because they work under the deadline. The *real* deadline. If the field crew has procrastinated in getting the information to them, then the editors have less time to do their job, and that's unfortunate, but it happens daily in television.

The editor answers to the show producer, the reporter, the photographer—and the chief photographer is often their boss. In some newsrooms, there is a chief editor position. This person assigns the editors and keeps the workflow through the editing bays running smoothly. The editor interacts with the show producer much more than the photographers would. In many stations, the photographer never comes back to the station after the assignment is given out. That's due to the fact that sometimes you work in big markets and you can't get back to the station—the traffic is too big.

You have to serve many masters, and you have to satisfy them all. And you don't always do that, sometimes you have to slam the stuff together because you've received it too late. If an editor is doing a package for five and the stuff is given to him at a quarter to five, that package is not going to look as good as it would look if he got the stuff at three. I mean, it's just a physical act that you have entered and it takes time to do it.

Interaction with photographer: Make sure you shoot tight sequences and that your raw tape isn't a disorganized mess of shaky shots that runs too long and goes nowhere. Sure, you may have ten outstanding scenes, but if the editor can't find them quickly, he can make you look like an amateur. You should be more worried about the editor denting your car.

Anchors—On-air Talent

The anchors present the work that you've done all day. They are the front men and women who deliver the news and, as such, they have a responsibility for the success of the station, and the success of the station means that everyone else can keep their jobs, maybe get a raise, buy a house. The ratings a station receives are often related to the on-air talent. Focus groups and ratings decide their fate. They are often involved in the community as representatives of the station and have a certain "star" status.

While not just pretty faces who read teleprompters (devices that project words in front of the camera lens so it looks like the talent is talking to the audience instead of just reading—an occasional head nod and a vocal cadence emphasizing the odd word helps this effect), many news anchors are seasoned journalists at the top of their trade. Some hold executive positions in the newsroom and exert a large influence over the news content.

Interaction with photographer: Will spend every waking hour trying to get you fired if you dent his or her car. You can make it up to them by taking the extra time to light them nicely on those rare occasions when they venture out into the field.

Sound Operators

Networks and large stations also have sound operators. Anyone working in news will tell you that sound is at least as important as pictures, and sometimes more. The sound is the content that can make a story.

Interaction with photographer: What car? You're driving. Sound is one of the most important elements you have for telling a story. This guy's been through it all with you, and as a team you deliver flawless video and sound.

Field Producers

The field producer is a portable assignment desk with added responsibilities for the story. The field producer is in charge of the story. In local news, field producers are assigned only on very large stories. The difference between a field producer and the reporter is the ability to go on air. At the network level, the field producer many times will line up the interviews for the reporter. They will pre-interview people so when the reporter sits down, he pretty well knows what this person is going to say. The field producer is also in charge of the transportation, getting the crew from A to B, making sure that they have their meals, making sure that they have housing.

Interaction with photographer: Won't let you stay in the nice hotel if you dent their car. The quality of your life on the road is firmly in their hands. Where you stay, what you eat, and when the interview is scheduled are all determined by them.

Photojournalists/Photographers

Photojournalists or photographers use their cameras and lights to visually portray the story. More often than not, recording sound falls to them as well. They either work with reporters or are assigned by themselves depending on story content and staff availability. They are sometimes called on to collect information or do interviews, and usually they are the editors of their stories.

Interaction with photographer: The other photographers, they're family; you can't let them down. Hell, take my sedan, go four-wheeling, no problem.

The History of Hatteberg

Larry Hatteberg's first experience in a newsroom came in 1963, but his passion for photography started years before that. My father bought me a movie camera back when I was in the seventh grade.

I loved that movie camera, but I also loved still photography. I had decided in junior high and senior high that I wanted to be a still photographer, newspaper photographer, or magazine photographer. Then I suddenly discovered that everybody was a newspaper photographer and everybody was a magazine photographer.

So I had this little movie camera, I was fascinated with it, and I thought, well, television might be it. But I thought I had no talent for television. That'll never happen. I'll have to end up being a still photographer.

I went to a college in Kansas specifically to work under probably one of the greatest still photographers in the 1960s, Gary Mason, and I went only to work under him. I was a pretty good technical photographer. I could get you a very good technical picture. But Mason took me aside when I first started working for him, and he said, "Larry, your stuff is technically perfect. But you know what? Your pictures have no soul, soul of the person in the story line." And then he showed me how to do that. He showed me how he worked. He showed me how to listen to people. How to acquire that soul of the subject and to put that in my photography, and that's been the secret all these years. He had a great gift, and it was the gift of his intelligence and his sensitivity. So I owe this man my career. He changed my life. He taught me how to work with people, how to listen to people, and how to capture that soul that gives you an intimate portrait of an individual. And that's been my life.

During that year at Emporia, I met some people who were involved in the television station that I'm working at now. It now appeared to me that television might have a good future, because not many people were involved in it yet. I thought I might be able to make a larger mark in television than I would in the newspaper world. So I came to Wichita for my freshman and sophomore year in college. I applied for a job at KAKE-TV. After several rejections, they gave me a

A. Hatteberg with a Bell & Howell DR-70 filming President Johnson. The DR-70 was the main working camera of the television photojournalist in the 1960s and early 1970s.

B. Hatteberg with KAKE's sound film camera. Portable cameras in the 1960s and 1970s weren't that portable. The camera he's holding is an Auricon Pro-600, which held 400 feet of 16mm movie film (about 11 minutes worth).

summer job developing still pictures in the still lab. I started out as a part-time helper in the still lab during the summer, and at this point in time, almost forty-three years later, I am still on that summer job.

During the years, I left the lab and I became a photographer, a television photographer, photojournalist. I was doing both the reporting and the photography at the same time. Then I became chief photographer, assistant news director, news director, executive news director, and absolutely hated it. At the end of the day, I couldn't see anything creative that I had done. The only thing I was doing was solving other people's problems. I just really hated my life at that point.

I told the management I wasn't happy and they said, "Well, we don't want you to leave. We want you to stay here. We think you'd make a pretty good anchor." So I started anchoring, and that was in 1986. From 1986 to the present, I have been anchoring the newscasts and also shooting the "Hatteberg's People" segment.

VHS cover of *Kansas People*.

Hatteberg's People

I shoot the "Hatteberg's People" series every week. I love photography. But I also anchor a television show; I also write; I also report. It is those skills that have permitted me to travel the world and to take my show on the road to thirteen countries and all over creation. I think it's important for photojournalists to understand that they, some times, many times, have to be a chameleon in order to survive. They have to change their colors. They have to change their spots. You have to have many skills to survive in a television newsroom. Life changes, the requirements change, and I think that photojournalists, photographers, should be open to their other talents. That's how I survived in television for forty-three years—making myself open to other talents.

Much of Hatteberg's current life is surrounded by the art and craft of photojournalism. Having won the top award twice, his point of view is respected throughout the industry. My objective has been to focus on people, to tell a story through people, and to let people tell the story as much as possible. I believe that viewers will listen to real people talk more than they will listen to what a reporter has to say. I do a two-and-a-half- to three-minute feature on this individual; I may have three, four, or five lines of copy in it, but really probably no more than that, because I want the person to tell their own story. Nothing is more powerful than when people talk from the heart, because when they talk from the heart, the viewer knows that. The viewer listens.

I never talk to the subject about the story, about the equipment, how expensive it is, or how many people are going to be watching them on television tonight. Those subjects never come up.

When I first meet the individuals, I talk to them about what they are interested in, what motivates them, what moves them. Then, when we get into the story concept, I never say, "Excuse me, I'm going to white-balance the camera," or "Could you move over here?" We just start within a very relaxed mode and they're doing what they want to do.

What my role is, is simply to be a good listener. What I found out over the course of time is that if you listen and keep your mouth shut, people understand that you are interested in them as a person, not a story, and if you're interested in people they will open their hearts to you. Once they open up their hearts, then it's like white lightning.

So you tell your story through the subject. If I just act as the subject's producer, then they sell their own story. It becomes more important to the viewer because that person sounds like them. It's not a reporter telling them a story, it's the subject opening his heart to the viewer. That's the key.

Photojournalism is an art form that people like me and a lot of other people across the country really have to fight for on a daily basis. Anything that we can do to keep the art form alive, we want to do.

Television's great power is to transfer experience, not fact but experience, and you do that through the art of storytelling. Storytelling is so important. We all learn it from the time we grow up. We learn by telling and by listening to stories. That process never ends. Those of us in television, who have the power and who have the cameras and who have the access to the television stations, must keep this art form alive and, hopefully, we can interest a whole new generation of photojournalists in the power of television itself.

Hatteberg continues his long-running "Hatteberg's People" series and, with some relief, announced on August 18, 2005, that Dennis Lynn Rader had been sentenced to serve ten consecutive life sentences, without the possibility of parole for 175 years.

Wichita, Kansas, a safe place again, safe from the likes of Dennis Rader—BTK and his demon.

CHAPTER 4

Eric Kehe

The Photographic
Department—People
and Equipment

Eric Kehe
Director of Photography

KUSA-TV (9News), Denver
NPPA Ernie Crisp Television News Photographer of the Year, 1997

A dark, gray sky hangs over ribbons of red and white—car lights that carve the freeway on this chilly January morning. Rising exhaust fumes, illuminated by the headlights behind each car, act as a visual clue to the outside temperature. It's winter in Denver, a light sprinkling of snow is falling on Speer Boulevard as Eric Kehe pulls his SUV news truck into the parking lot at KUSA-TV. His morning has started like half the rush hour commuters in this city—get up, work out, pack the kids off to school, stop for a coffee on the way in—inch your way to work. As his eyes adjust to the light in the underground lot, he takes a mental note of whose news car is in their parking slot and whose is not. The missing are either out on a story or stuck in the same traffic he just survived.

Kehe is one of the top photojournalists in the world. He is director of photography at the only TV station to win the NPPA Television News Photography Station of the Year ten times and to have been home to five NPPA Ernie Crisp Television News Photographers of the Year. He himself won the award in 1997. His title, director of photography, is unique in this business—the station retired the title "chief photographer" in honor of Brian Hostetler, chief photographer when a helicopter accident tragically claimed his life. Although Kehe's title is different, he continues a tradition of fostering an outstanding team of photojournalists.

And today, like many days, he's going to shoot the worst story on the assignment board. The one no one else wants to do. He'll take one for the team.

EQUIPMENT

Sony DVCAM DSR500WS camera
Canon 22 × 8 lens
Anton Bauer Ultralight camera light
Carbon fiber Gitzo tripod with Sachtler 18p
    fluid head
Anton Bauer Dionic lithium batteries
Wide-Eye-Century zoom-through and/or
    converter (cap)
Lectrosonic wireless UHF UCR 201/adjustable
    frequency
Sennheiser shotgun microphone with windsock
Stick Mic-Shure VP64
Sony ECM-77B lavalier
Camera rain cover
Light kit: Omni, Tota, and Lowel Pro lights; soft
    box, gels, scrims, dimmers, umbrellas, stands,
    clamps, Westcott reflector (sunlight/silver)

Kehe's office is lined with plaques commemorating the photographic history of this station. Engraved with the names of past and present photographers, it's easy to see the sheer volume of outstanding work that's come out of this department. But, after that initial impression, there is a deeper realization. These awards not only represent photographic skills, they represent stories. Stories from this community; stories that mattered; stories that enlightened, entertained, and effected change. These are the stories of the commuters stuck in rush-hour traffic, and the awards represent them, their lives, triumphs, and sorrows. These walls recount the history of Denver as told through eyes that care about every image they see, every life they witness, every story they pursue.

Kehe dumps the last of his coffee, bitter and cold, in the trash. A few photographers wander in and say, Hello, as he checks his e-mail, the daily grind of someone in this position. Messages from management, equipment vendors, people looking for jobs. "Dear Mr. Kehe, I would like to come work at KUSA. Do I need any special training to do what you do?" There should be a form letter for this one. From the big picture to the most minute details, running this department, acquiring the best equipment and hiring the best people are what Eric Kehe's job is all about. Lots of desk work keeping the department together and running smoothly is the order of the day. And he'll still need to shoot a few things before the 5:00 News.

This is Eric's life. He has earned it and he has the respect of the staff and the station. It's just a few minutes until the morning editorial meeting; his photographic fate for the day will be sealed during the next half hour.

The morning editorial meeting is where the day's stories will be decided. Kehe enters the room; there's already a flurry of unorganized chatter. It's here where he'll make suggestions on which stories have the most visual potential and who might be the best photographer to shoot them. It's the most dysfunctional meeting you'll ever attend in your life. Somebody tries heading it up, but it never works out that way because everybody's got an opinion and wants to express it. It's an environment filled with "type-A" people and they're all going to express themselves. It's just kind of a Battle Royale in the morning as to what stories we're going to cover and who's going to cover them and what the assignments are, what the treatments are for those stories.

Kehe is battle hardened and has earned his way into these meetings. He's also ensured that the eight or so daytime photographers are here as well. It's mandatory. Everybody throws out their story ideas, and there are some good visual stories. You kind of see the photographer's eyes perk up, and they're eyeing the reporters and saying, "You and me on this one" and "That would be a good one." Sometimes those stories never get selected and sometimes they do.

The news managers realize that you have to have a healthy balance of stories, and so they're kind of intermediaries in helping us get some occasional visual stories built into the newscast. Photographers, we want to shoot every visual story that comes along. Obviously that would be our preference. And the assignment desk, they're just trying to make everybody happy. So there's a little bit of conflict there. You can see where it might create some angst, but for the most part we realize we need to have a healthy balance of news that day. The goal is to work towards that; we just sometimes disagree on how to get there. A lot of the time, I do step in and say, "No, this

ADDITIONAL EQUIPMENT FOR EACH PHOTOGRAPHER	
Car	Employee handbook
Maps	Gate remote
Emergency kit	Cell phone/camera and
Gas card	charger
Press plate	Pager
Scanners	9News badge and door
Nomex	card
Jackets	

ERIC KEHE: THE PHOTOGRAPHIC DEPARTMENT

is a great story. This is a visual story. If you don't have a reporter for it, let's get a photographer out there and do an 'f/stop' on that."

F/stops are photo essays, and they have become a brand name in 9News's content. Established in the mid-1970s, these essays have been an essential part of the photographic tradition at 9News. Their evolution has grown from beautiful images put to music to what now resembles complete short-subject films. Always highly visual, these are the assignments that show off the photographers' storytelling abilities. Laced with natural sound, wireless interviews, music where appropriate, these stories not only depict an actual sense of "being there"; they've evolved into legitimate news content.

So I do kind of play cop in deploying resources. If I disagree with the direction that something is going, or if there's a great visual story that they're going to pass over, then I'm the intermediary. I step in and say, "That's all great, but we'd still like to figure out a way to get this story done."

The producers are looking for leads for the four, five, and six o'clock newscasts to get the ball rolling. Of the stories they've decided on today, these are the packages: The Bronco Fanatic, Spelling Bee, Forensic Lab Opening, and Denver Public School Plan. *"Packages" are complete stories on tape with a reporter generally voicing the track and showing up in a stand-up or bridge.* So now, all the photographers are thinking, Spelling Bee would be a fun story. That'd be visual. The Forensic Lab Opening, that would be pretty cool because you're going to get all the new gadgets and whistles.

Because we are a visual medium, we have to play to our strength, and our strength is that we have great people with great vision on our photo staff. So some of the stories we're going to do just because it's a great visual opportunity. When some other story might be more important, we're going to find a visual way to treat that story, and we'll still try to plug a photographer into the more visual story. So we try to balance out the hard, nonvisual stories with some visual feature stories.

Lots of times in the morning meeting, I'll figure out what stories we're going to have to do that none of the other photographers want to do, and that's the story I'll take. *Today's assignment for Kehe, a VO/SOT (voiceover followed by sound on tape—an interview) on school board redistricting, downgraded from a package.*

I figure, if our photographers are out on the streets all the time and they need good stories and good opportunities and I'm only out there part of the time, I can bite the bullet on this one. I'll get through the day so they can have a chance to do something else. That's better. But, consequently, you should see my résumé tape of the last five years.

The current staff at KUSA consists of twenty-three photojournalists and eight editors. "Photojournalist" is their title on show credits and whenever someone is speaking specifically about their storytelling contributions. We're more than photographers nowadays because we get the story side of it, but over the years we've had all kinds of names, so we'll answer to anything— shooter, photog. *Between each other and in this interview, you'll often hear them referred to as photographers.*

The images on the next three pages are from KUSA's NPPA reel. Eric Kehe and some of the photographers offer advice about what makes each of these images special and give some insight on the thinking that goes on behind the lens.

A. Kehe shot this image, one of the first taken at an industrial park fire. He always tries to knock off a couple of wide, establishing shots without missing any crucial moments, so later he can concentrate on close-ups and detail.

B. Virtually the same shot as the first, but without any foreground or depth. It's important not only to get the smoke and flames but also to get the people who are affected by the fire. Flames are just flames. It's the people who make each story different.

c. Byron Reed shot this story about a controversial art mural being displayed at South High School in Denver. It caused quite a stir among students passing it. Byron used his wireless microphone and moved it around as much as possible to get a variety of opinions. Many students had good and bad comments about the mural, which showed images of drugs and alcohol, teen pregnancy, and racism. Some students were so upset they left school early, which caused school officials to remove the work within 12 hours of its installation.

D. Not only did students have an opinion on the mural; some teachers took notice.

A. Corky Scholl shot a story about bees that took over a house. He got as close as possible in order to get compelling close-ups of them and to get good natural sound of the bees buzzing. When shooting nature video, try to zoom in as close as possible to capture the fine details a viewer doesn't get to see under normal circumstances. Corky was wearing a bee suit, so he didn't have to worry about getting stung.

D. This shot is of the church through the front doors. Shane used the music from the service to open and close the vaccine story, which provided an interesting angle.

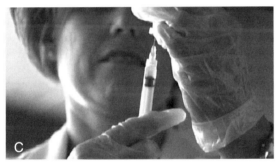

B. Shane McEachern shot this story about shortages of flu vaccine. When the vaccinations were given at a local church, many senior citizens' prayers were answered. This woman helped organize the clinic. Shane shot this interview in her element. He backed away, shot her through a door, and became a fly on the wall, so to speak.

C. Shane shot the process of vaccinating patients without ever showing a needle going into their arms, which is hard for most viewers to watch.

E. Photographer Brett Alles shot a "cheerleader" at a former all-boys high school as he rallies the crowd. The school is now coed, but still supports the all-male cheerleading group called "The Rowdies." Costumes, makeup, and dancing are standard fare at Friday night football games.

A. There's a lot of hootin' and hollerin' when the Rowdies are on the sideline at Regis High in Aurora, Colorado, so there's a lot of natural sound in this piece. This group of all-male cheerleaders makes sure the crowd gets the full high school football experience.

B. Lou Davis shot this story about baseball in a rural community. This is an interview with one of the administrators at Brighton High School. The shot is in his office much like he might be talking to one of his students—very natural with him, comfortable in his element.

C. Television is a two-dimensional medium, and Lou looked for ways of adding layers and a third dimension to his shots. By focusing on the foreground, he softened the background, which adds nice depth to his shots.

D. Most photographers think they need two shots in a sequence to capture action and reaction, but some of the best images are when both are handled in the same frame. Lou widened out to include another player watching hitting practice.

E. The surprise in this story was that the school is so overcrowded that the kids can't practice in the gymnasium, so they resort to practicing in a barn. This was the reveal shot and the story's turning point.

A. This is an interview with the coach in his natural element with foreground.

B. This is the closing shot of the barn with a slow zoom-out and the natural sound of baseballs under the reporter's voice track. It gave the story closure and a sense of finality, like the last page of a book.

C. This is a shot by Dan Robbins, who traveled to Yellowstone, Montana, to shoot a story about bear-proof dumpsters. It was driven by moments as the grizzlies sniffed, licked, tipped, and destroyed various dumpsters. He used lots of natural sound to bring the story to life. He worked at the mercy of sunlight, but looked for good lighting to separate the bears from the dark background.

D. This story, shot by Dave Delozier's, is called "A Ton of Cookies." The small town of Olathe made an effort to send cookies and cards to troops in Iraq in time for Christmas. Here a little girl decorates cookies. Delozier is very good at identifying and capturing emotion. He composes his pictures and anticipates action to build steady, match-action sequences. He held this shot until the girl grabbed the can in the foreground so that he could sequence it with her decorating the cookie.

When we won the 2005 NPPA Television Station of the Year, I looked around the room and said, "This is a newsroom accomplishment. You can't just have a team of great photographers and go out and do this. There are so many demands and pressures on any given day. You really have to have the support of the entire newsroom." So I went down the list; I thanked

- The assignment editors, who came out with a lot of the story ideas and assignments, who gave us the time to go out on the street and do the story justice.

A. Residents at a nursing home joined in the cookie-decorating effort. Young and old worked for weeks to contribute to the project. The woman here had a special connection—her son is a helicopter pilot stationed in Baghdad, so she knew how much cookies would mean to him at Christmas. Shooting news is more than capturing the process. For Dave, the story was more than about making cookies. It was a story about the people who made the cookies.

B. Finally, kids from a school in town added messages to the cookie boxes. They created hundreds of hand-written Christmas cards to be sent along with the decorated cookies.

C. This shot is from a story by Corky Scholl about King James a homeless blues player. Corky saw the moon in the sky as James was playing music on a downtown side-walk. He positioned his camera underneath James so that his head and the moon could be composed in the same shot. He then zoomed in to compress the shot a little.

- The producers, who found the time in their newscasts, who took an interest in those types of stories. Because, you know, there's a lot of blood and guts that you can fill a newscast with, and it is really easy to fill a newscast with that type of material. So it's a special commitment on the part of the producers to say, "No, we're going to leave that guy alone. We're going to free him up so he can go down and concentrate on this other story that we feel is newsworthy."

- The writers and the reporters, who are just exceptional storytellers. They take the time to write properly and they study the art and craft well enough that they know how to get the most out of the images.

- The news managers, who value this type of product in the newsroom.

- The live truck operators, who pull cable and set up live shots in the freezing cold.
- The maintenance workers, who keep our cameras up and running and keep our equipment fixed so we can do our jobs and not have to worry about our equipment.
- The chief engineer, Don Perez, who makes sure that we have the newest equipment and the best technology inside the newsroom.

So there is a big superstructure that supports what we do here. It takes everyone's effort to win Station of the Year.

All photojournalists at 9News are encouraged to try new things, experiment and stretch their photographic and storytelling abilities. The staff enjoys a legendary esprit de corps *established more than thirty years ago, and it's as vibrant today as at any time in the past.*

The success of the photographic department at KUSA can be traced back to the mid-1970s, when the station was known as KBTV. It was then that news director Roger Ogden (now senior vice president of Design, innovation and strategy for Gannett and president and chief executive officer of Gannett Broadcast) and chief photographer Tom Baer made a commitment to the photographic quality of their newscasts. It's clear that their early influences created a legacy of photographic quality that has spanned decades.

In 1977, the station won its first NPPA Television News Photography Station of the Year award and staff photographer Sam Allen won NPPA Ernie Crisp Television News Photographer of the Year. That year, the work of the photographic staff set the level of quality and attitude for every other photographer who would work at the station in the years to come.

To sustain a department takes more than the individual efforts of the photographers. Many people contribute to what, in the end, is the photographic signature of the work at 9News. It all started at the top with Roger Ogden. That commitment to top-level photojournalism guided his decisions and priorities on equipment purchases and hiring the right personnel and the photographic and artistic needs of the staff—completely supported by management.

The photographer's work was critiqued nightly, not only by the news director and chief photographer but also by the rest of the photo staff as well as anyone within viewing distance of the newsroom monitors. The entire station was vested in making great images and visual stories. A slight error could get you jeers; a good job would get a shrug; and, with something special, the newsroom would light up. That moment—the entire staff lived for it.

Although not as famous as "SKY 9," the news helicopter that had its own toy version available in stores, the photographers at 9News would often got on-screen credit for their work and became known in the community for their visual contributions.

To illustrate the commitment KUSA has to its photojournalists, the station offered scholarships to the prestigious American Film Institute in Los Angeles. Photographers Dan Wood and Sonny Hutchinson both spent a year in the program before coming back to KUSA, where they shared what they had learned. It was a calculated investment in the photographic quality of the station that paid off.

That early commitment to the visual identity of 9News has remained through countless management changes at all levels. It's part of the brand; it's part of what the station stands for in the community. It's reliable, predictable quality and honest, interesting stories told by the best in the business. No matter how the news sets change or the on-air talent's hairdos recede, the visual continuity in the station remains with the photographic department.

They come from all over the United States, from small markets and large, to work at this station. It takes a special set of qualifications to get in the door. Eric Kehe has a screening process—he knows who will work, who will be the right fit, who will add to the department and keep it growing. There's a lot at stake; he doesn't want things to fall apart on his watch. When I look at a résumé tape, I can really tell how creative a person is. I can typically look at twenty seconds of a person's résumé tape and tell you if that person has potential or not. And a lot of that has to do with effort.

How much effort did you put into each and every individual shot? And if there are four shots in a twenty-second sequence, I can break down each one of the shots and say, Yeah, he tried; yeah, he moved; yeah, he tweaked; yeah, he got that shot so I can forgive that; yeah, he sequenced it all together. Yeah, this guy hustles, and he doesn't miss a shot.

I have this sheet that I call the "Pyramid of Success" (shown on the next page). And it has the basic building blocks of what a good photographer is. First of all, you, need a good base or the rest of the structure crumbles. On that base are things like good attitude, the ability to demonstrate basic skills, and being good ambassadors for the station. I've designed it in such a way that once you master these skills and perform at these levels, you're ready to climb up the pyramid.

It's kind of designed after Maslow's Hierarchy of Needs. Just as basic human needs are water, nutrition, and shelter—and from there you move up the hierarchy to achieve the top, which is self-realization and a complete understanding of yourself—I challenge all the photographers to perform the basic functions, so they can move up to things like storytelling and creativity and get outside the box.

Pyramid of Success

Self-Actualization or Realizing Potential

Excels at
– Journalism
– Storytelling
– Writing
– Producing
– Lighting
– Editing
– Audio
– Photography

Opportunities
– Effort
– Fairness
– Goal setting

Creativity
– Thinking different, unique
– Using new tools to potential
– Taking risks

Safe
– Defensive driving
– Operating and working around live trucks
– Good choices and habits
– Back safe

Responsible
– Maintain car and equipment
– Learn from and be accountable for mistakes
– Organized and clean

Healthy
– Physically, mentally, and spiritually capable of performing all aspects of the job

Demonstrates Basic Skills
– Shoot, light, and edit

Timely
– On time and ready at beginning of every shift
– Turn in timesheets, gas receipts, expense reports, and so on, when due
– Responsive to e-mails, schedule changes, and requests for help

Communicative
– Check in with desk, editing, producers, and managers
– Report when coming and going
– Use cell phones, 2-way, and pagers

Involved
– Attend editorial meetings
– Recommend story ideas and ideas for execution
– Sense of team/camaraderie

Positive Attitude
– Can-do spirit
– Solid work ethic
– Strong ambassador
– Consistent, reliable, dependable, tolerant

To become a member of the photography staff at 9News, there are some things you must be able to do. You must have a good eye. You must be a solid editor. You must be motivated. You must have a great attitude, and for me that especially means being a team player. Because we are a team. I can't have an "A Team" or a single guy that gets all the good assignments and a "B Team" that gets all the crap assignments. It's just not going to work because there's going to be jealousy and animosity amongst the staff.

Everybody does everything here. Everybody shoots good stories. Everybody shoots sports, weather, and closes for the end of our newscasts. Everybody does everything here, and because of that we are a team. If Dan gets a great assignment today and he's going to be out all day, I know that I have to step up my performance and cover all the things that Dan isn't free to do. I have to shoot two packages so he can have this opportunity to do a great story because he hasn't had a chance in a while, and I know that Dan will do the same for me next time. So being a good team player and having a good attitude is critical for building a good team and a good sense of camaraderie.

Then, as the photographer develops, we move into things like creativity and storytelling. There aren't a whole lot of great storytellers out there in this country. Typically, you see it in the reporting and writing but not so much in the photography. But that's typically a skill that we develop here and hone in on. Once the photographer demonstrates good lighting techniques, and good editing techniques, and can gather clean audio, then we can move on to the next level of things.

The guys at the top of the pyramid, they just have the complete package. They have an understanding of the newsroom at all levels. It's about getting information to the producers and the reporters. It's having a complete understanding of the story when they're out in the field, so they can get all the elements that are necessary to tell the complete story.

They already know they have to get the information back to the art department so they can do the graphics. They know they need to let the newscast producer know that, "Yeah, I've got a great sound bite for a tease to lead the newscast with." They're going to tell editing, "I'm going to help out; I can get the five o'clock package. I'm going to need your help with the four o'clock VO/SOT." So it's the guys who have this great awareness of what it means to be a part of a team in the entire newsroom—those guys, they click and they get it and they're not so wrapped up in getting "their" story or a single shot that they forget the big picture of the newscast.

When you get the guys who have mastered their skill sets, they don't have to think about it anymore, about shooting wide, medium, and tight, shooting a sequence and moving and getting it from another angle. And they don't have to think about turning on their microphones or what filter to use or what the color balance is or what color temperature is the light here. When they don't think about it anymore and they get totally involved in the story, those are the guys who have elevated their game up into the storytelling level. And they just get caught up in the moment and they get caught up in the character.

I think Corky's piece on King James is a perfect example of that. He just kind of became one with this guy, and he was so wrapped up in telling all these elements about King James that it was beyond the technical. Even though, technically, it's beautiful and it's perfect, you really get a good feeling for this guy and he really got inside that guy's head. And that's what the next level of photography is all about. *Corkey Scholl's story is in Chapter 8.*

It's knowing how to personalize a story. You know how to capture emotion. And you know how to get all these moments of surprise that come into a story. And then you don't think about it anymore. It just happens. They know exactly how to bring it all together. Because you can meet a King James, but if you're shooting blue video and it's shaky and it's distracting, or your audio's not clean, the story is going to stink. So you have to demonstrate the basic skills of photojournalism before you can move up to the next level of the pyramid.

I hear a complaint from a lot of other photographers in small stations or small markets that are not very good television stations. They say all the time, "Well, we never have the opportunity to do that type of story." I'll say to them, "That's a bunch of bunk." Everybody has an opportunity. Every time you put that camera on your shoulder and you walk out the door, you have an opportunity to do that. It's just whether you exercise it or not. Whether you take advantage of the assignment or not and how much effort you're going to put in to it.

Because I can get a story about homeless people out on the street, and I can go out and I can shoot a bum on this corner, and I can shoot a guy holding a sign on that corner, and I can shoot traffic rolling by and somebody giving him a nickel, and I've completed my assignment and I'm done. But the next level is really personalizing the story—getting to know that guy, making a commitment that I'm going to go out and meet this guy on weekends and nights and do whatever I have to do so that I can really tell this assignment well. As long as you have a camera, you can do that.

The 9News Camera—A Setup for Storytellers

All ENG (electronic news gathering) cameras are camcorders—the camera and recorder are in the same unit. They make images by converting light into digital signals; then those signals are recorded to tape or digital media located in the recorder part of the device. All ENG camcorders use a zoom lens. The zoom is a variable focal length lens that goes smoothly from one focal length to the next without a shift in focus. A zoom lens uses convex lenses that always invert their images, so the image at this point is upside down.

The amount of light that enters the camera is controlled by the aperture, a variable opening that allows light through the lens. The f/stop ring on the outside of the lens controls the diameter of the aperture. An f/2 would let much more light in than an f/22. The lens directs light and focuses the image onto a charged coupled device (CCD) or chip. A charged coupled device is a microchip covered with light-sensitive "photosites." When light strikes the CCD, the photosites produce electrical current.

In a single-chip camera, the light hits the surface of the chip. In a three-chip camera, the light is divided into three primary "additive" colors (red, green, blue) by a prism, and those light waves hit three separate chips, generating three separate red, green, and blue "signals." The signals these chips generate are then recombined into one signal by a "coder." Either after the single chip or after the coder (depending on the camera), the signal is processed and inverted to right side up.

The images these signals carry have either a 4 × 3 or a 16 × 9 aspect ratio and move at 30 frames per second NTSC in the United States or 25 frames per second PAL in Europe. The frames comprised two interlacing fields that replace the image at 60 and 50 cycles, respectively. The video signal and any sound coming into the recorder part of the camcorder are then recorded onto tape in a cassette or some other digital medium.

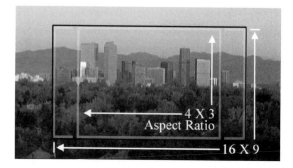

The signal is also sent to the viewfinder. The viewfinder has a diopter on it so that you can focus your eye on the tiny video monitor inside. Often the image in the viewfinder is black and white. There will be lights that tell you when you are rolling, are out of tape, or have a dead battery. Many cameras give you the option to put even more information in the viewfinder such as audio levels, f/stops, and time code.

Analog camcorders store their images and sound as a continuous recording of magnetic patterns. Digital camcorders record signals made out of binary code, 1's and 0's. As long as the playback can read the data, flawless duplicates can be made and dubs will retain the same quality as the original. (For further information, see Appendix A, Video Formats.)

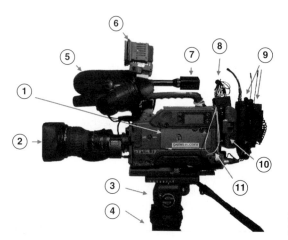

1. Sony DVCAM DSR500WS camera
2. Canon 22 × 8 lens
3. Sachtler 18p fluid head
4. Carbon Fiber Gitzo tripod
5. Sennheiser shotgun microphone with windsock
6. Anton Bauer Ultralight camera light
7. Lectrosonic UH190 plug-on cube transmitter
8. Lectrosonic wireless transmitter
9. Lectrosonic wireless receiver UHF UCR 201/adjustable frequency
10. Anton Bauer dionic lithium batteries
11. Ear piece

Eric Kehe Walks Us Through the Typical 9News Camera

Sony DVCAM DSR500WS Camera

The camera weighs between fifteen and twenty pounds the way we have them set up. It records the image in a 16 × 9 aspect ratio. It's fantastic; it's cinematic. It's what you're used to shooting in film and this is the way pictures are meant to be seen. So, it's very aesthetically pleasing to your eye as opposed to a box, which is the 4 × 3 format. And you can exercise the true, true rule of thirds (see Chapter 7) in 16 × 9, and you can't in 4 × 3. So, it's better composition that way. It's DV, so it's compatible with our Avid Unity Editing system. We can dump video and audio into our system very quickly, at four times speed. So if I have a twenty-minute tape, I can get it all into the computer in five minutes.

And with the Unity system, everybody has access to the footage around the newsroom, all at the same time. I also like it because it's a manually run camera, not like some of the industrial or home cameras that go into an auto mode that controls the focus and controls the color temperature. I can control this. This is my tool; I tell it what to do. Most other cameras tell you what they're going to do. I paint a picture with this camera with a simple brush and paint. I am not putting any layers, any effects, nothing on it. I am thinking about as pure an image as I possibly can.

In the black-and-white viewfinder, the only information I see other than the image is the battery indicator light. The tally light is a red light that let's you know the camera is rolling. We all turn this function off. The worst thing that someone wants to hear is "Okay, they are recording now," and then they freeze. It has a filter wheel that goes from one to four. Filter #1 allows the most light into the camera and is clear—balanced to a tungsten color temperature of 3200 Kelvin. You would use this filter under low light and in interior settings where there is artificial light. Filter #3 is the second most transparent with an orange #85 color filter to compensate for a daylight color temperature of 5600 Kelvin. Filter #2 matches the daylight #85 filter with one-eighth neutral density to reduce the amount of daylight entering the camera. And, filter #4 doubles the neutral density to allow even less light into the camera. As you go from #3 to #2 to #4, you have to adjust the *f*/stop to a wider opening. As you open the iris and alter your *f*/stop to a wider opening, you lose the amount of depth of field in the shot. The filter wheel will allow you to set the correct color temperature and control depth of field to roll the background out of focus. A very helpful tool.

Further back on the operator's side of the camera is the on/off switch, a switch for color bars or camera, and a gain switch. The gain switch can be toggled between 0: no gain; 9, 18, and then hyper gain at 36. Hyper gain makes the image very noisy, but can sensitize the camera to see in very low light. There is a selector switch for white balance, either a factory preset or A and B options with memory to store white-balance settings.

Around the front of the camera is the white-and-black balance switch. Shoot something white under the same lighting conditions you'll continue to shoot under and lift the switch up. The camera will automatically set the correct color temperature. Push the switch down to set black balance. Black balance tells your camera what "black" is. You do not shoot a black card. I take white balance twenty to thirty times a day, but I only have to black-balance once a day.

Also at the front of the camera is the shutter switch. The shutter is variable. You use it to sync up monitors so you don't see a scan line roll through the image, and to freeze action with the higher speeds. I use it mostly for sports or when I want to slow things down or really see in detail what is happening in slow motion. The monitor switch—I always have that turned off because it will flash when it doesn't have any more tape or battery.

The viewfinder displays a zebra pattern. I have mine set at 80 percent. I always shoot with the zebra on; it just helps me know where I am at with my exposure.

I use running time code, or I use record time code. Whenever you push the button, it picks up time code from the last place you stopped. A lot of guys will use real record time code; it just constantly runs. So if you sync up your time code with a reporter at the other end of the room, whether you stop the camera or not, you will be on the same page with that reporter. I can set it to time of day, which helps the sports guys if they are recording a game or if someone is logging it from a press box.

Canon 22 × 8 Zoom Lens

The lens has a 2x extender on it to double the focal length and a macro so you can focus on things very close to the lens. Some of the wide-angle adapters need this feature to work. For me, it's a great lens. It's an all-purpose lens; it's great for shooting football and telephoto stuff. We are shooting 16 × 9, so it goes wide enough, and we also have the wide converters that are helpful on it, so you can even go a little wider. We have a Century converter that allows you to zoom through the focus. Century also makes a converter cap. You can't zoom through them; you just stay wide and operate your macro to set focus.

Sachtler 18p Fluid Head

Most of the photographers use a Caddy Sachtler head. The difference between the 18p and the Caddy is that the 18p has four settings for your springs; the Caddy has two settings for your springs, which control the balance and resistance to a neutral setting. Both have good adjustments for tilt and pan drag, which smoothes out those moves.

Carbon Fiber Gitzo Tripod

This tripod is light and quick and does not require a spreader. I can work pretty quickly with it. I can get down on the ground like a high hat and I can also get about eight feet up in the air. It's got independent legs so I can alter the length of the legs. I can put it up on steps; I can put it on a rock; I can make it work inside a car. I can put one leg on the back seat, one on the armrest, and one on the floor. I can just twist it and maneuver it to whatever is going to work.

Sennheiser Shotgun Microphone with Windsock

The shotgun is connected to a Lectrosonic UH190 plug-on cube wireless transmitter and mounted on a Dan Wood-designed quick-release shotgun mount. The microphone is great for sharp directional sound recording.

Anton Bauer Ultralight Camera Light

This lightweight Ultralight runs off camera power, so there's no extra battery to carry. You can flip in and out a dichroic filter for daylight and/or diffusion to soften the light. It's mounted on an articulated "light arm" that gets the light up off of the camera so it won't burn the shotgun windsock. It also lets us throw shadows so it doesn't look like the lamp is right on top of the lens. You get a little contrast, you get a little drop shadow off it—anything for a little bit of depth. The "light arm" is designed by Dan Wood, one of our photographers, and is available at *cameravaults.com*. The Ultralight is great in spot news situations.

Lectrosonic UH190 Plug-on Cube Wireless Transmitter

Attached to the shotgun microphone, I can send the reporter or an intern off and they can get good sound from quite a distance away. So they just move the shotgun around getting natural sound, which is one of the hallmarks of the work here. Natural sound tells the story.

Lectrosonic Wireless Transmitter

I keep my lavalier connected to one of the wireless transmitters so it's always ready to go. It is what I use for my primary interviews. It's always right there, ready to go, so I can just pop it off and hook it on somebody. Typically, I will get to a story, figure out who my main character is, and the first thing I will do is pin it on that person. I'll just follow them around and let them tell the story through their eyes.

Lectrosonic Wireless UHF UCR 201/Adjustable Frequency

Many cameras are rigged with two wirelesses. One for the shotgun and one ready on a lavalier microphone.

Anton Bauer Dionic Lithium Batteries

They have as much juice as a big brick and they are a lot lighter.

Ear Piece

I always have my ear piece in whenever I shoot because you want to make sure what is going in is clean.

Lighting is an essential part of the photojournalist's equipment. This is a typical kit issued to the photographers at 9News. I have an Omni Lamp, which is a 250-watt lamp, a Tota Lamp that goes from 750 to 1000 watts—I have mine on 750 because I put a Chimera softbox on it. When I light an interview, I always have my Chimera on. It gives me a nice soft light that I can really control, especially once I put the egg crate in. Everyone uses Chimeras. Some people have Dido lights, which are lights that you can put little scrims in and throw patterns on walls. Also, a Pepper light, either an Arri or a Pro-light. It's a small instrument used to backlight people so they pop from the background.

Typical lighting for me is three-point lighting. My key light is the Chimera, my fill light is the Omni, and my back light is my Pro-light.

We all look for external light source opportunities too. If I have a light in the background like under-cabinet lamps, I'll pop those on, just to give it some depth.

There's also a collection of photographic equipment used for those special stories. We have a Sony PD150 camera, which is a very miniature camera and it shoots DV, so it is compatible with our systems. It doesn't have the resolution of the big broadcast camera; it has smaller chips. But it is real small, real compact. Lots of guys, when they go mountain climbing, that's the camera they generally go with. But that's changing.

We are experimenting right now with next-generation high-definition cameras that are miniaturized and compatible with our system. I also have a TRV7, which is a small Sony camera that looks like a small home video camera, that we do investigative stuff with. I know that some places are off limits to us and if you look like a tourist you can still get the shot. We have undercover vans with drapes and tinted windows you can shoot out of. We have a lipstick camera we mount onto fixed-wing airplanes so you can get that exterior shot looking into the cockpit. You can mount it anywhere on a car and just tape it down or Velcro it down. We have different mounts and rigs to mount the PD150 and the midgi-cam, so you can get in these really interesting angles and it will be rock solid.

We have a Tamron 1500mm lens that we use for undercover or wilderness shoots. When you shoot nature pieces, you are not going to get real close to the hawk or the grizzly bear, or want to.

We have an Ewa bag that the PD150 sits in and one guy in particular, Tom Cole. He'll do kayak pieces; he is always underwater shooting with that thing. The Ewa bag is a sealable pouch. You put the camera in and add some weight so you can swim down and around and get interesting and different angles to tell the story.

Now that all the equipment is accounted for, one of the most important aspects of photography is making sure your equipment works. There's no point in going out on a great story and pointing your lens at the best shot anyone has ever seen, only to come back with bad or unusable images or, worse, nothing. Check all your equipment thoroughly. Plug everything in and record a tape. Now play back the tape. Make sure everything is working flawlessly. In order to know exactly how your camera "looks," you'll need to view the output of the camera on a monitor. The monitor has many settings; it is imperative to set up the monitor to the color bars generated by your camera. That way you'll have a true idea of the picture quality of your camera. (Refer to Appendix B for how to set up a video monitor.)

For Eric Kehe, setting up and testing cameras is part of his job. He'll make sure the existing cameras are operating properly, and he'll evaluate many new cameras and photographic products as they become available. Always looking for the right tool to do the job better. We are one of the Gannett flagship stations; that puts us in an enviable position as a beta test station. We get to play with the newest toys, gadgets, and systems that are out there. If we can make a case for a piece of equipment or tool that's going to help us do our job better, tell stories better, or give us an edge over the competition, Gannett will typically support the purchase.

We're looking forward to the next generation of cameras. We're looking at memory cards, hard drives, blue laser, and disc technology. We'll figure it out, and when we do we'll set the agenda for the rest of the Gannett stations. If they want the help, we'll train them and get them up to speed.

With the right equipment, the right people, and the right atmosphere, KUSA is a learning environment. The station supports training and education, and shares its resources with the industry. There was no special moment that I said, "Okay, I'm there; I've arrived." But once I put that string of stories together in 1997 and had a successful year in contests, then NPPA sends you out on the road. You do Flying Short Courses and workshops. And then you figure out the vocabulary and the nomenclature to explain what you do to other people.

It was the next year where I realized who I was and what I was about, because you have to do a lot of introspection and ask yourself, Why did I do it this way? Why do I like shooting from a corner? Am I good at capturing emotions? Emotion is a basic building block to telling a good story. I've always identified the emotion of the story and shot for images that move people, that make them care. So it was the year afterwards when I really had to do an analysis of myself and figure out who I was as a photographer. Then it all kind of clicked and came together. I grew more the year after I became "Photographer of the Year" than anytime before.

The station has a training budget for the photo staff. They are given time off every year to instruct and train at seminars and workshops. There's a lot of value in having our name out there because the best photographers want to come here and work in this environment. You've got to keep your name out there to keep the reputation, so you can continue on with the tradition.

The photographers are constantly trying new things and pushing and challenging each other. It's fun when you can do that, and it's great to be in an atmosphere where it's competitive. It's a friendly competition, and not only are you working hard for yourself, but you wish well for the guy you're competing against. We're proud and pleased when someone wins an individual award, but as a group it's a big honor to share Station of the Year. I don't think we could have won that if everyone was just looking out for themselves and didn't care about the product that everyone else was putting out. That's what I'm talking about. The big picture stuff.

You may have a great story, but if your overall product stinks, nobody's going to watch it. You have to be in a position where you put great newscasts together. The only way you can do that is if everybody's working together. We believe that to be a good television station, you must have a strong foundation, and that foundation is good stories and good pictures.

Because without good pictures, we're just radio.

Take 2: The Language of Lenses

Lenses "select" the image that is to be captured from our camera position. The controls on the lens determine much of the visual attributes of that image.

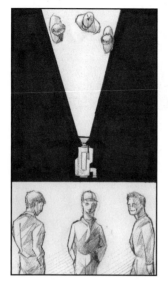

Normal lens

A modern video zoom lens has a focus ring, a motorized zoom control, an aperture ring (which selects the f/stop), a macro adjustment (which allows objects to be focused closer to the lens), a focal length 2x extender, and a back focus adjustment screw.

All of these tools control the communication of the image. Will the shot compress the elements in the frame? Will the background be in or out of focus? These are just a few of the questions you'll answer by manipulating the lens.

All video cameras use a zoom lens, which is of variable focal-length. Focal length is the distance between the film plane, or CCD, and the optical center of the lens when the lens is focused on infinity. The focal length is designated in millimeters; the lower the number, the wider the angle of view; the higher the number, the narrower the angle of view. A zoom lens lets you smoothly "zoom" through all the focal lengths of the lens while keeping the image in constant focus.

All cameras have what is considered a "normal lens" (see image at the left). Such a lens reproduces objects with the same natural perspective as the human eye. What is considered normal is determined by the size of the gate or CCD chip. For 35 mm film, a normal lens is 50 mm. For 16 mm film, it's 25 mm, and for a 2/3 chip video camera, it's also 25 mm. That's because the size of the 2/3 chip is very close to the size of 16 mm film.

For cameras with smaller chip sizes, the focal length of what is considered normal will also go down. Lenses with shorter focal lengths than "normal" are referred to as wide angle, and lenses with longer focal lengths are called telephoto.

Although a normal lens reproduces images with roughly the same optical characteristics as the eye, it does not make the camera record the event as the human mind perceives it. The sense of vision requires both eyes and the mind to capture an event. Having, two eyes allows us to perceive depth in relation to other objects, with a camera and single lens, depth is defined by focus and the optical characteristics of the focal length of the lens. A wide-angle lens expands the perception of depth, while a telephoto lens compresses the perception of depth and the distances between subjects.

While the eye does not zoom (note: Zoom moves are thought to be unnatural since the human eye cannot zoom), the mind can focus or concentrate on the most minute detail, excluding everything else in the periphery, then, an instant later, expand to comprehend a grand vista without changing position. Having a variety of focal lengths at our control allows us to approximate an effect of concentration. Through the lens, we control the amount of visual information we select to communicate with each shot and sequence. Is it an isolated, minute detail, or is it a grand vista showing the immense scope of our shooting environment? These are the elements controlled by the lens.

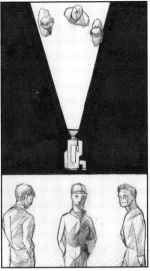
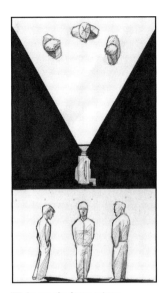

Telephoto lens view. Normal lens view. Wide-angle lens view.

Focal lengths do not equal shot sizes. A wide-angle lens does not immediately make the shot a wide shot. A telephoto lens does not always need to make a close-up. Keep these concepts separate in your mind. A wide-angle lens will naturally make the shot wider, but what if you move closer to your subject? What if you move very close? You can make a close-up shot with a wide-angle lens, and you can make an establishing shot with a telephoto lens.

In the figures on the next page, you can see how a close-up changes by changing the focal length while keeping the subject the same size in the frame. The middle figure is the normal lens. By moving away from the subject and zooming in to a telephoto shot, the image compresses. The background seems much closer to the subject, and there is very little detail to his environment. The figure to the left of the normal shot shows a wide-angle lens. Note that the facial features expand due to geometric distortion. Also note that we see much more of the background. So, in the telephoto shot, we see a bald man with glasses against a small section of wall, and in the wide-angle shot, we see a bald man with a large brain engulfed in his room of planet pictures. We learn more about the man from his environment in the wide-angle shot than we do in the telephoto.

But what if it is an intensely personal story about the man's triumph over his impaired vision? Wouldn't you prefer the frame to be filled with just him—isolated, telling his story as we focus on his glasses and nothing else? This is what storytelling through the lens is all about. The example illustrates—with the same location, subject, and equipment—how a story's emotional impact can be vastly different from one photojournalist's impression to the next. It's not only artistic interpretation, it's the effective communication that the photographer intended.

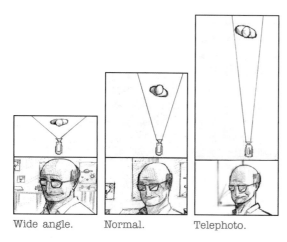

Wide angle.   Normal.   Telephoto.

Focal Length Characteristics

Wide Angle

A wide-angle lens views a larger area than a normal lens. Pull out from a "normal" lens size to wide angle, and the subject will shrink in size. A wide angle can allow the photographer to work closer to the subject while retaining the same subject size in the frame. It exaggerates depth beyond what would be considered normal. Movement toward and away from the camera seems to be faster than normal. The apparent speed increases the closer the subject is to the camera. Wide-angle shots tend to be more graphic in nature and often contain strong visual lines. But, because of geometric distortion, these lines can bend on extreme angles. They also tend to communicate more about an environment than a normal or telephoto shot.

The characteristics of a wide-angle lens also lend themselves to hand-held work. Images appear to be more stable than with a normal or telephoto lens. But be aware—strong vertical or horizontal lines in your frame can accentuate the movement in a handheld shot. A wide-angle lens has a very large depth of field; almost everything is in focus.

Normal

Normal lens views are similar to the perspective of the human eye. This is everyday life. Viewing subjects from fifteen feet to infinity will appear normal in terms of depth. A normal lens shot can easily become an "average" shot. Nothing special, just a tool to fill out a sequence. Work harder to make these shots carry the same dynamic communication and visual interest as the wide-angle and telephoto shots that you create.

Telephoto

Telephoto lenses view a smaller area than a normal lens. By going telephoto, the subject appears larger in the frame. On a zoom lens, you're zooming in. A telephoto lens makes distant objects appear closer. It compresses depth, which makes elements in the frame appear closer together. The greater the distance from the lens, the more this effect is noticeable. A telephoto lens has a shallow depth of field. At closer distances, foreground and background elements will go out of focus more easily.

"Selective focus" is a very effective storytelling tool. It can isolate the viewer's attention or shift it to separate elements in the frame. "Rack focus" refers to this shifting of focus from one element to the next, and it is done most often on a telephoto lens. A soft focus foreground and background can add to the illusion of depth taken away by the compression characteristic of the lens. Because of the compression characteristic, subjects moving toward and away from the lens appear to be moving slower than real life. Note: This is the exact opposite of a wide-angle lens.

We've discussed three variables of focal length. A zoom lens contains all the focal lengths between the widest and most telephoto settings. Get to know the characteristics of wide and telephoto in their extremes so that, in more subtle changes in focal length, you'll know what characteristics you're changing. In practicality, you'll see changes in the communication of your images from the smallest adjustments in focal length. To limit depth, while you isolate and enlarge your subject in the frame, zoom in a little. If you need a more exaggerated effect or a closer subject, add an extender to the lens. If you want to tell more about the environment and make the shot look a bit more graphic, widen out.

Using the Lens

Before making sure your lens is operating properly, adjust the diopter in your viewfinder. This ring (located by the eyepiece) will allow you to adjust the focus of the viewfinder to your eye.

Next, make sure the lens's back focus is set. Shoot a subject that has a lot of detail; there are charts that help this process but, in the field, anything with details will do. Zoom in and set focus. Zoom out to the widest setting and adjust the back focus ring. There usually is a locking screw that must be loosened before rotating the ring. Rotate the ring until all the details in your shot are sharp. Tighten the locking screw and zoom in and out several times to make sure that the focus is holding throughout the range of the lens.

Set focus by zooming in all the way on your subject, and adjust the focus ring until the image is sharp; then zoom back out to your shot. You do this because of the characteristics we outlined earlier. The more telephoto, the less depth of field or the more critical the focus. By zooming in, we are looking at the most critical focus for our distance from the subject. Zoom back out and we add more depth of field, so we are safely in focus.

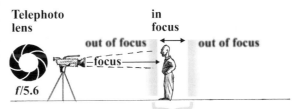

Depth of Field

Depth of field is the area in front of your lens where everything is in focus. Depth of field increases with wide-angle focal lengths and decreases with telephoto focal lengths.

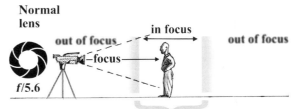

The aperture controls the amount of light that hits the chip or image sensor. It also affects the depth of field. The aperture is variable through the positioning of leaves that shrink or expand the opening. The size of the opening is calibrated in f/stops.

F/stops generally range from f/1.4 to f/22. Light meters register measurements greater and less than this, but this is the normal range of current lenses. The openings progress from f/1.4 to f/2 to f/2.8 and through f/4, f/5.6, f/8, f/11, f/16, and f/22. Each f/stop up allows half as much light to get through; each f/stop down

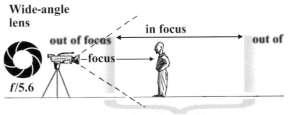

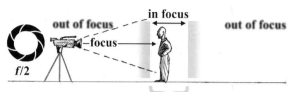

Depth of field

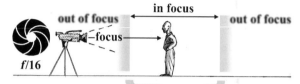

Depth of field

allows twice as much light in. So f/2.8 allows twice as much light in as f/4, and f/5.6 allows half as much light in as f/4.

In the illustrations about lenses on the previous page, you see that the f/stop remains constant; only the focal length changes, expanding the area that will be in focus. If we change the aperture, the lower the number (wider aperture, allowing more light in), the less depth of field we have; the higher the number (smaller aperture, allowing less light in), the more depth of field.

So if you need more exposure because your shot is too dark and you can't add more light, as you open the aperture you'll decrease depth of field (see images below). If you want the effect of a decreased depth of field (to be more selective with your focus), reduce the amount of light coming through the lens either by lowering your lighting or adding neutral (uncolored) density in front of the sensor. Most cameras have a filter wheel that allows you to add neutral density, thus lowering the amount of light entering the camera.

Depth of field decreases the closer your subject is to the camera. On telephoto lenses, although the focus is always critical on distant objects, the selective focus becomes more noticeable the closer you are. The farther away your subject is, the more depth of field you have. (See top two images on next page.)

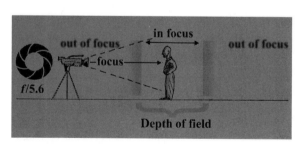

Depth of field

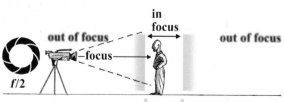

Depth of field

You'll notice there is less depth of field in front of the focal point than behind it, and as subjects get closer to the lens the effect is more pronounced. With this in mind, you could roughly guess that by moving the focal point forward from your main subject, you may be able to keep important foreground and background elements in focus. (See bottom two images on the next page.)

Nothing has more depth of field than a wide-angle lens shooting a distant subject at a very high f/stop. Nothing has less depth of field than a telephoto lens shooting a close subject with a low f/stop. By thinking in these extremes, you'll quickly learn how to communicate with your lens by using all the variables in unison.

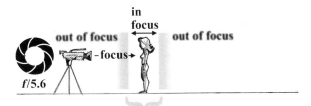

Depth of field

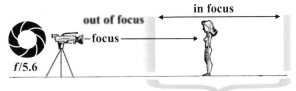

Depth of field

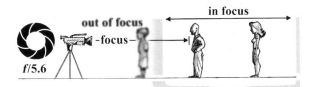

Depth of field

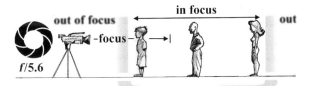

Depth of field

Once, while discussing all the terms used for describing television news photographers, Jim Berger, photojournalist and friend, jokingly referred to himself as a "lensman." Decades, and thousands of assignments later, I think he had the idea right. In news and in most photographic ventures, it's the lens that does the most work. The photographers' ability to understand, manipulate, and work this tool to their visual will is what separates the great photographers from ordinary shooters.

CHAPTER 5

Stephen Hooker

Camera Techniques
for Spot News

Stephen Hooker
Chief Photojournalist

WIS-TV, Columbia, South Carolina
WDSU-TV, New Orleans, Louisiana
WYFF-TV, Greenville, South Carolina
South Carolina Associated Press Television Photojournalist of the Year
Louisiana Associated Press Television Photojournalist of the Year
RTNDA Photojournalist of the Year, South Carolina

A strange and ominous moaning calls Stephen Hooker from a troubled sleep. He has never slept here before. Through blurred and blinking eyes, consciousness takes hold as he looks up at yellow goal posts and crowds in the stands. Decades of victories and defeats have been decided right under Hooker's sleeping bag. Camping in the Superdome is not a lottery prize; no one paid to be here; it is not a dream vacation. They are here because she's coming; they hope she'll be gentle or pass by without harm. This morning, huddled inside the protective egg, the crowd isn't watching the field, their faces lifted as if hoping for salvation. She sings from the rafters. The moaning turns to shrieks, and the sky is torn open. Katrina announces her arrival by tearing a hole in the top of the Superdome. The worst is yet to come.

Born as "Tropical Depression Twelve" over the Bahamas on August 23, 2005—within a day her strength grew to a tropical storm—she was named Katrina. Her size and power continued to expand in the Gulf of Mexico until she became a Category 5 on the Saffir-Simpson Hurricane Scale. Category 5 is the top rating

EQUIPMENT

Panasonic DVC-PRO camcorder (WDSU-TV)

Ikegami HL 45L docked to a DVC-PRO tape deck (WIS-TV)

Panasonic AJ-SPC700P camera shooting on P2 memory cards (WIS-TV)

Canon with a 19x zoom lens

Frezzolini Micro-fill 35-watt camera light

Miller carbon fiber Sprinter II with a DS-25 head

2 Lowel 250-watt Pro-Lites with barn doors on Avenger stands

Lowel Rifa 44 250-watt bag light

3 25-foot extension cords (two retail)

2 Lowe's battery-powered fluorescent work lights

2 300W dimmers, power strip, assortment of gels for color correction or effects

Not part of the fast kit: 1 Berkey Colortran 600-watt light and stand for exterior background light; Lectrosonic wireless system, Sony ECM-44 lavalier mic, and Electro Voice RE-50 handheld mic *determined by sustained winds above 156 miles per hour. Katrina's winds were now topping out at 175 miles per hour.*

Stephen Hooker and the staff at WDSU start to make preparations for Katrina's visit. The rule is, if you work in television news, in a major emergency your family is on its own because you can't leave. The junior weatherman prophesied that the storm would come directly at New Orleans. I cursed him because I knew that would trigger my wife to leave early. She left town in light traffic carrying all our important papers and our dog.

Under a sunny sky, Hooker's goodbyes leave him to close up his house. The heat and humidity, common to New Orleans, makes it feel like just another day. By mid-afternoon, he locks the front door and takes a final look at his house, wondering what the next few days will bring. Preoccupied with thoughts of his wife and home, he drives to the station, knowing work will soon narrow his focus and replace the what–ifs.

On August 28, Mayor Ray Nagin orders a mandatory evacuation of New Orleans. All inbound lanes on the freeways are reversed; the only traffic moving is out of the city. This change in traffic is called "contraflow."

As soon as I walked through the door, I could feel the electricity in the station. I was immediately sent to meet a live truck at the beginning of the contraflow on Interstate 10.

Traffic was already backed up waiting for the extra lanes to open. There was no time to lose.

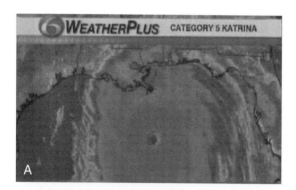

Having abandoned our normally scheduled newscasts, our news was now on the air nonstop and the contraflow was to open in a few minutes, at 4:00 p.m. On location, I ran over to a highway patrol trooper to find out the sequence of events to open the flow. That became my shooting map for the next hour. The sun was low in the sky, and I wanted it behind me so the reporter and the contraflow opening would be sunlit and look good. Ideas bounced back and forth until the

A. Storm clouds and rain begin hitting the Gulf Coast while hurricane-force winds are just a few hours away.

B. I-10 is about to open its inbound lanes to make six lanes flowing out of the city.

C. A double crawl provided both general information on disaster services and damage and personal messages of viewers trying to contact or alert family members and friends. Businesses also used it to inform employees.

STEPHEN HOOKER: CAMERA TECHNIQUES FOR SPOT NEWS

People unable to evacuate go through security checks before entering the Superdome for the evening. They expect to return to their homes by the following afternoon.

reporter and I had our plan. We choreographed and practiced until the producer gave us a thirty-second warning. *The contraflow opens as Hooker's camera goes live on the mass exodus of an American city. Many of the motorists will never return to call New Orleans their home.*

Back at the station, news director Anzio Williams gathered everyone and laid out our assignments and schedules for the next two days, taking us through the storm. Our station's hurricane plan staggered our field crews and station staff so we weren't burned out before the storm hit. We all expected Katrina to veer off at the last minute and hammer Mississippi as in the past. My assignment was to go to the Mississippi coast Sunday afternoon or, if the storm continued as predicted, I was to go to the Superdome. *By late Sunday, Stephen Hooker and the staff of WDSU's news operation knew Katrina was heading straight for them. There would be no escaping her temper.*

I was disappointed that my assignment was now the dome. It was going to be boring, just a few thousand people sleeping over in the grandstands. The National Guard had prepositioned tons of food and drinks. The dome was self-supporting with huge generators and plenty of fuel for several days. We did a number of live shots outside the dome as people lined up and were admitted inside. Later, I drove our live truck up to the second level and positioned it on the safe side from the approaching storm. Once inside, the media was allowed to set up on the field. We got a few shots of the crowd in the stands and settled down to sleep out the evening.

Established as a "refuge of last resort," the Superdome opens for those who cannot leave the city. Ten thousand people including Stephen Hooker, spend the night. Katrina hits New Orleans the morning of August 29. Now a Category 3, her 125-mph winds pound every building, window, and roof, while the water from the storm surge threatens the levee system.

Completely awake, the nightmare unfolds as Hooker powers up his Panasonic camera and presses record. This is his job and the moment everyone feared is on them. A lot of preparation and experience preceded the color bars that mark the first recordings that day.

Katrina passes through New Orleans in the early morning hours with 145-mph winds.

A. The special protective cover has been ripped off the Superdome roof along with many underlying steel panels.

B. Early-morning light, water, and fierce winds stream into gaping holes in the Superdome's roof.

C. A reaction shot: Evacuees look up as Katrina comes in.

The red light in his viewfinder glows as Hooker points his camera toward the ceiling. More than 270 feet in the air, a white glow grows in size. The hole is getting bigger. Built to withstand 200-mph winds, this can't be happening. But it is.

The glowing shape is the story that moment, but if anyone were to see only this image, they'd be hard pressed to say the white blob moving on the screen is the top of the Superdome coming off. Yet Hooker stays with the shot, steadying himself to see what will happen next. It is the "action shot." Nothing else matters while this image has the potential to change. What happens on the roof could have dramatic effects for the thousands of people watching in disbelief. After a few moments, the tear stabilizes. Hooker knows how to make sense out of this situation for anyone who will watch it. He tilts down to the crowd. Faces looking skyward, pointing; families moving out of the rain that's streaming in—this is the "reaction shot."

Action/reaction is the basis for all news coverage. It's not just the catastrophic event unfolding in front of the camera; it's the reaction of the people who witness it. Their faces and actions tell the story. Hooker does not stop rolling. The situation is still fluid; the ceiling could let go any moment. He's panning the crowd looking for moments that compel him to stay longer. (Panning is horizontal camera movement. Tilting is vertical camera movement.) His right eye focused in the viewfinder, the left one occasionally opens to survey his surroundings, searching for any clue that will tell him the ceiling will give way. His camera still rolls, the pans and tilts not intended to be used; he's just reframing for the next reaction shot when Katrina rips the hole open even more. Hooker stays on the reaction. This refugee's look says more than the growing white shape on the ceiling. Intuition tells him what five seconds feels like and, when he's sure there won't

WDSU reporter Ed Reams and his photographer document the Superdome damage
in the wake of Katrina.

*be another expression, he tilts up to capture the
new damage.*

*The importance of Hooker's methods should
be etched in the mind of anyone shooting news.
As bullet points they are:*

- *When you arrive on scene, shoot the
  object that may change or vanish first. Stay with it until the situation has stabilized or until you
  feel free to make a different shot. This could be minutes or hours.*

- *As you become comfortable, work to make the shot better, stabilize the camera, get tighter if
  you can.*

- *Always try to predict where the action will go and be prepared to get the shot.*

- *Do not turn off your camera in a fluid situation; look for the red light and look for it often. It
  is not unheard of for photographers to accidentally stop recording when they think they are
  recording.*

- *Keep aware of your surroundings. Look and listen for clues that the situation is changing. When
  you feel that you can shoot something else without missing the "big shot," find reaction shots.
  Look for images that convey how people are reacting to the event.*

- *Stay on each shot at least five seconds. Seven to ten seconds is better. Count out the time until it
  becomes intuition. A rookie mistake is coming back with footage that doesn't settle down into any
  one shot for more than a second.*

- *Action/reaction is a two-shot sequence. Try to expand that sequence with shots that convey the
  environment in which the event is taking place.*

Note: *Roll fifteen to twenty seconds of color bars—some people prefer a minute—then a few seconds of
black before you start rolling. If you are recycling tapes, watch this beginning area for tape damage, and
when it starts to occur, retire the tape.*

By 1:00 P.M. Monday, the wind had died down enough for us to get out and shoot the damage
around the dome. Many high-rise buildings had most of their windows blown out. The Hyatt was
a mess. I got the live truck going, and we went back to the station to regroup for the storm aftermath
assignments. But first, everyone wanted to go home to check on their damage.

We weaved our way around downed trees and power lines as I took a carload of fellow
employees to their homes. I couldn't get to mine due to high water. We began to return to the
station and the nearby hotel we would use until power was restored at our homes, when we met
up with Jefferson Parish sheriff, Harry Lee. I couldn't believe what I saw and grabbed my camera.
He and his deputies had several people in handcuffs after a spree of looting. We considered it an
isolated incident and thanked our luck for being in the right place at the right time. As we continued

back to the station, though, we began to see more looting. I was shocked at the breakdown in the social fabric. Suddenly, hundreds of years of cultural and social mores had dissolved into anarchy in only a few hours. Forget law or order; this was a free for all without bounds. We began to feel in danger and hurried back to the station.

As we all met up, we swapped stories of our overnight experiences until bedtime. The next day, refreshed, we gathered at the morning assignment meeting ready to go out to shoot post-storm stories when a policewoman came running in. Because there was no phone service, she said, she wanted us to know that the Seventeenth Street Canal levee wall was breached and houses were being flooded. We said we'd send a crew there immediately and she interrupted saying the water was already too far down this way. We were about to change where the crew should go when she said, "You don't understand. I've just come from city hall four blocks away, where the water is four feet deep and rising!" We looked down and saw that her pants were wet to her waist. The news director ordered us to load up all the news cars and evacuate over the Mississippi River Bridge.

Fifteen minutes later, we convoyed out our gate and onto the expressway ramp. As we rolled out, people came up begging to be taken away. We just looked at them, unable to stop, knowing that we had no more room in our vehicles. We rolled by and up the ramp.

The worst of Katrina is happening. The wind damage proves to be nothing compared to the water damage from the storm surge and levee failures. The Big Easy, as New Orleans is called, is devastated to an extent that is almost unimaginable. A large U.S. city is laid waste by nature, and man's inability to predict and tame her elements will cost 1,836 people their lives.

Two days later, with my wife further evacuated to relatives in Columbia, South Carolina, I returned to our rendezvous point, our sister station in Jackson, Mississippi. Two hours later, I was one of two photographers along with two reporters and our satellite truck operator headed back to our station in New Orleans. The station's transmitter was destroyed during the storm. Our stories would be sent back to Jackson by satellite and put on the air from there. A security force accompanied us—seven deputies from the Tulsa, Oklahoma, SWAT. Their job was to protect us and to go into our station to clear and secure it for us to enter. Since there was no fuel, food, or water, we were loaded down with as much as we could carry in and on each vehicle.

My news car reeked of gasoline fumes, and we joked about being a 70-mph Molotov cocktail. When we arrived in the dark early morning hours, we were struck by how empty and bleak everything was. At the first I-10 overpass before entering the city, there was an eerie blue-white glare of portable work lights illuminating hundreds of people huddled along the highway as Blackhawk helicopters kept landing and taking off in the cloverleaf areas. Several buses arrived, and the people wearily boarded them. There were fires everywhere you looked across the horizon from the top of the bridge, because the city is so flat you can see for ten, fifteen miles. There must have been half a dozen fires across the city and nobody to respond to them, so they just burnt on and on. It was just incredible. Tom Fitzgerald, my fellow photographer, shot that story while I concentrated on the helicopters ferrying out evacuees. At daybreak, we entered the city from the West Bank, since the flooding had covered the interstate in town. Our station was secure and dry because it had been built near the river and was on higher ground.

A. The levees now breached, people make their way to safety.

B. Uncontrolled fires spring up across the city, with no equipment available to put them out.

For the next three months, Stephen Hooker and the small band of journalists and SWAT members live at the television station while braving post-Katrina New Orleans. Because of the anarchy and danger, we never went anywhere without our own security force. Each crew had two members of Tulsa SWAT go out with them. They were first armed with pistols; then, after seeing the situation, they had their AR-15s with laser aiming devices brought in. After a few days, we stopped trying to keep our bodyguards out of our shots. They were part of this bizarre environment, and they became part of some stories. People were desperate. They wanted our water, food, and vehicle with cans of fuel hanging on the back and sides. It was like *Mad Max.*

Simply put, what Katrina did to New Orleans is a catastrophe of epic proportions. Everyone who once lived in her path experiences tragedy and loss, including the news crews who cover the story. We were part of the story, our lives were turned upside down, our families evacuated, and our homes damaged or destroyed—just as our story characters experienced. Many times, we just stopped taping and held each other and cried right along with our subjects, then picked up and continued. We lived like the military in the field—sleeping in the edit bays, eating MREs (Meals Ready to Eat), washing with bottled water, using portalets. We had only packed three days of clothes so, after two weeks sister stations sent us clothes (embroidered with station logos) by special courier.

I shot rescues, fires, and devastation. Everything was spot news.

What Is Spot News?

Hurricanes, fires, shootings, floods . . . spot news is an unplanned event, often dangerous, where life and death hang in the balance as the camera rolls. It has an immediacy, the outcome of which could affect the lives of many viewers. It generally runs at the top of the newscast, the "A" section, earning it the phrase "If it bleeds, it leads." Spot news is often criticized as sensationalism. But consider this: Nothing is more important or carries more weight than life and death. Whether it pertains to our world, country, city, neighborhood, or family, the spot news event has altered the lives of those involved. Even one life should earn our compassion and interest for a small amount of air time.

Mr. Viewer: "I don't need to see that." Think again. You might not like what you see, but you may need it. Spot news exists to show viewers what is affecting their lives and the lives of their neighbors. It's immediate information that may save viewer's lives or help them make decisions to stay away from an unsafe location. A tragedy happens a few blocks away. Could it happen to you? Could you prepare for or avoid the same danger? Not likely without some knowledge of the situation.

Life and death are dramatic. The images can be disturbing and arresting at the same time. It's hard to watch a train wreck; it's hard not to. What the viewers see at home is nothing like the real experience of being there. The image they see is a selected portrayal of the moment. Photojournalists are horrified by what they see, too, and sometimes their need to share the moment leads to capturing images that no longer tell the story in anything other than a scientific or biological way. Blood and guts is not the story; people are. A tragedy that can be seen on someone's face has more storytelling power than any physical wound.

The dead don't need a close-up; the living do.

Fighting for the A section slots, weather occasionally wins out due to the fact that it will affect the most people. Katrina was A section from the beginning. Viewers desperately wanted to know what was going on. Were their houses and businesses still standing, was anything left, anyone still alive? Two news crews can cover a few stories a day under normal conditions; the aftermath of Katrina required a different technique to cover the volume of stories developing in New Orleans.

The Whip Technique

We went out to start doing stories, and we were going to do them in a traditional manner. For a news package, you'd go out, interview people, get some B-roll shots. The reporter logs the tape and writes the story on the way back to the station; you edit it, and your story is done.

We were on the air twenty-four hours a day, every day of the week, with only two news crews. All anyone wanted to know was what was going on; viewers wanted to see their neighborhoods. They didn't care about the damned story. So the photographers stopped driving. The reporters drove the cars

A. WDSU reporter Heath Allen records a report as he evacuates from the St. Bernard Parish Emergency Preparedness Center following the storm.

B. Flooded neighborhoods become unrecognizable from the air.

to the stories, and the photographers just shot out the window. Sometimes, it was hard to recognize the neighborhoods anymore. The station would just air the shots of us rolling through the neighborhoods and talk about what they were seeing while using our locator information.

There were also helicopter shots of New Orleans. But you couldn't tell from a helicopter where you were, unless you shot downtown or the Superdome. Then you knew where you were. You couldn't recognize neighborhoods; it showed just a bunch of houses under water. For the evacuees at the evacuee centers scattered around the country, this wasn't enough. So that's why we shot this way. We just rolled and rolled and rolled. We drove for five or six minutes just rolling, and it would go on the air that way.

The news director said, "You can do it in a minute, you can do it in ten minutes. I don't care. We need video, video, and video, and somebody standing up there to tell us what's going on. If you can't find somebody to talk to, then you tell us what is happening, what you're feeling." So we'd wing it. The reporters would just talk off the top of their heads. As time went on, we got better and better. From that point on, packages were out; there was no time to shoot and cut stories in the traditional way.

We called it a "whip." Other places call it a "look-live" or "walk and talk" because there's walking and a lot of talking.

There's one whip where the reporter takes his mother back to her home that has been flooded, and they go through it for the first time. It looks like a package. It's basically four shots. For the last shot, I'm inside and they're outside. I'm shooting through a broken window and they're talking about what they saw and what it means, and she says, "Hey, well, we've got each other and that's all that matters." It was a powerful moment. We were in and out of there probably in ten to fifteen minutes. That's all it was, and it was a great story. It took us maybe a week and a half to get to that level of sophistication. But that's the only way we could turn out the

WDSU reporter Fletcher Mackel takes his mother through her flood-damaged home for the first time while his twin brother, Travers, and Helen Moreno watch and break down in tears back at WDSU's temporary news set in Orlando.

quantity of video and the number of stories we needed. So if a reporter has the gift of gab, like a QVC salesperson, where they can talk about anything, you can do a great whip.

When things started to get back to normal, they wanted to do traditional packages again. I didn't remember how and fought to keep doing whips. Once we got good at it, I just loved them.

Handheld Versus Tripod Use in Spot News

Because of the fluid nature of spot news, it is often necessary to go handheld. This will allow you to react quickly as the situation changes around you. Shakiness in a spot news story is not an appropriate storytelling tool. While going handheld allows mobility, the images still need to be steady and the steadier the better.

Don't only think of it as going handheld; think of it as shooting without a tripod. Look for things to place the camera on or brace it against to make the shot steady. If you can prop yourself against something solid, do it.

Do not hold your breath and lock your knees; you'll just keel over and ruin your shot. Balance the camera and balance your body, don't struggle to hold the camera steady, and readjust if it doesn't feel right.

A wide-angle lens will be steadier than a telephoto. The longer the lens, the more you will see your body's movements affect the camera. Going wide means you'll have to get physically closer to make a close shot. This will often put you "in the moment"—be careful.

Avoid strong vertical and horizontal lines in your composition. Strong lines give away movement.

A fluid situation does not always mean the best shots will be handheld. Consider using a tripod when the best shots will be telephoto. Back off to your best angle a safe distance away from the event. Go telephoto and use the lens's 2x extender to get you close to the story. A steady telephoto shot over a shaky handheld shot of the same subject will win every time.

After you place your tripod, stay at that position if the situation is still fluid and can change at any time. As the situation stabilizes, move the tripod and get another set of shots from a different location.

When I come out of the car, I've got my tripod in one hand and I've got my camera on my shoulder. I'm carrying them both. I'll be shooting off the tripod, and if I see something going on, I come right off the tripod and run over there in order to get the shot handheld, because otherwise I'm going to miss it. So you'll see both handheld and tripod in the same story.

When you're handheld and moving forward, you're walking from the waist down. You kind of walk like Groucho Marx when he's half crouched; that's the best way to get the steadiest shot. If you walk like you're dancing, like you're trying to do a really smooth waltz, you're going to get a great shot. This is a dance.

Handheld and moving backwards can be tricky and dangerous. When you're backing up across sidewalks, around fire hydrants, past telephone poles, over curbs, in the streets with traffic coming, all you're doing is looking into the viewfinder. If you've got a good reporter with you, he's got a hand on your belt behind you, saying things like "Curb down in three, two, one." He'll just whisper in your ear. It's a heck of a lot better than when you've got a rookie out there saying, "Oh Steve, look out." Look out for what?

When I don't have someone helping me back up, I'm shooting wide. I've got the viewfinder a few inches away from my eye and I'm glancing into it once in a while and I'm also looking where I'm going. I have pretty well mapped out where I'm going to go before I start rolling. I'm also considering how many other cameramen I'm going to be competing with, going shoulder to shoulder while we're walking backwards. I just hate it, it's a horrible shot, it's the worst shot you can do.

A camera, some tape, a charged-up battery, and the good fortune or experience to be in the right place at the right time are all it takes to shoot spot news. But each type of event has its own set of conditions that a photojournalist would be well advised to consider. For Katrina, Stephen Hooker had the experience to keep safe and get the great stories. Experience he'd gained from years of disaster coverage and his time as an army combat commander.

Stephen Hooker's Tips for Disaster Coverage

One of the most embarrassing things that can happen to a news crew is to become a news story. There is video of cameras being ripped out of the hands of photographers who got too close to waves, or live trucks being turned on their side by strong winds or soft sand. Those things amuse viewers who already wonder why we are out in a storm in the first place. It's tragic, however, when someone gets hurt, even a news crew. Make your personal safety paramount.

Storm-experienced managers have learned to prevent burning out their newsroom staff and field crews just when they need their crews alert and energized most, when the storm hits their area. As the storm approaches, a lot of effort goes into informing viewers about preparations and evacuation. Resist the temptation to throw everything and everyone at this phase of the storm. There are two more phases: the storm itself and the aftermath cleanup. Two days before the storm hits, crews should go to twelve-hours-on, twelve-hours-off shifts. That schedule will last for at least two weeks after the storm passes. For Katrina, we were on this schedule for two months.

Facing into the wind and rain may seem the place to be for the most dramatic video, but it has a lot of disadvantages. First, the camera lens is so wet, viewers cannot see much. It is also the most dangerous position for reporters to have their back to unseen flying debris, not to mention photographers locked down in a live shot position unable to move quickly from junk traveling eighty miles an hour toward them. The best place is on the downwind or protected side of a solid structure. The lens stays dry, the reporter is safe, and viewers can still see destruction happening in the background.

Park your news vehicle facing the wind. Over several years of covering storms, we lost two car doors and a trunk lid because this wasn't followed. The reporter opened the door, the wind caught it and jerked it out of his hand. The door hinge was bent so badly that it wouldn't close again, and they rode out the rest of their storm assignment in a perpetually wet car.

Trees are falling, and downed power lines are still live. Do not pursue a course that you cannot extract yourself from at any time. No one will be able to help you until days after the storm has passed. Always plan a way out.

No stores are open, no restaurants are serving, and gas stations are closed, too. So what need is there for money or credit cards? In fact, if you need something like a boat ride into flooded areas, most emergency people will help you. There is that one time, however, when cash is the key. Thirty bucks may get you that lift in a high-wheeler to just the right spot.

Most storm-hardened stations begin their storm plans with a line about taking care of your family and home first. Once they are safe, you can concentrate on your job better. As you say goodbye to them, remind them that phone lines and cell phones will be down for days and you will not be able to contact them directly. Make sure your station has arranged with a sister station located out of the zone to handle employee/family inquiries and relay messages to you and them.

As the storm approaches, employees of gas stations will be evacuating and fuel will no longer be available. Seize every opportunity to top up. Once the last station closes, they will not reopen for days. The only fuel will be fifty miles out of the zone, provided those stations still have power.

Everything eventually gets wet. Keep personal items in clear resealable plastic bags so that you can see what's inside.

Never wade into moving water. Even a slow current, waist deep, can knock you off your feet. In murky water, you cannot see what you are stepping on or into. Contaminated water in the streets of New Orleans was so feared that our station banned us from going in it except by boat. The smell was so bad we used masks in case we inhaled spray or other airborne germs. Even though we were banned from the water, we still wore boots because we invariably found ourselves in some water or mud. When we returned to the car, we removed our boots into bags. Then at the station, our boots went through a decontamination process of three bleach-and-rinse baths. Our cars were covered with contaminated mud that smelled so bad we parked them on the other side of the lot. We could not wash them because there was no running water, only bottled water. We carried large bottles of hand sanitizer and used them constantly.

Cuts and scrapes become particularly dangerous because there are no medical centers open. Your first-aid kit is your only line of defense. For serious problems, you will have to travel twenty or thirty miles away to the nearest evacuation center where there might be emergency personnel. They will also know where the nearest open medical facility is located.

Making it through a disaster with great footage and minimal injuries requires experience, intuition, and preparation.

Packing for Disaster Coverage

Normally, I carry an overnight bag with a change of clothes, three pairs of socks, toiletries, a sweater, and a complete set of rain gear, including boots. Flashlight, wipes, paper towels, plastic bags large and small.

For hurricanes, all of the preceding plus three days of clothes and six pairs of socks. The station has a hurricane kit for each news car that has utensils, food, bottled water, toilet paper, and a five-gallon gas can.

Stores won't be open so cash and credit cards are useless. Especially credit cards without power to run a charge. Fuel up at every open gas station no matter how full your tank is. Within a few hours they will all be closed for weeks.

Don't stock up on cookies, chips, or candy. After the first day, you'll want real food. MREs are great supplemented with fresh fruit like apples and oranges. Tuna is always a winner.

Stephen Hooker's preparation allowed him to stay on-station and continue providing important cover-age throughout the disaster. Weeks turned into months; the stories ranged from heartbreaking to uplifting glimpses of hope. The emotional roller coaster is part of the job. When you stop feeling, you can't tell stories anymore. So, you just let the pain hit and deal with it the best you can.

You go into a grocery store that's finally open. They only have one cashier because there are no employees, because there's no place for employees to live, because there's no power and their homes are flooded. But they're trying to open up the store, and the shelves are all empty because it's like the Soviet Union 'til you get delivery trucks in there. You go down row after row of empty shelves like in some third-world country. Then you see some products down at the end all stacked up; you ask what it is. It's moth balls. You can't eat moth balls.

But you're standing in the grocery checkout line, and lines go from the cash register all the way to the back wall of the meat counter. And everybody is standing there—forty-five minutes or an hour and a half to check out. Nobody is quiet. They push into the line, and the next thing someone says, "Hey, how did you do?" And then it starts. Everybody down the aisles is talking about the damage they had, the people they can't find, who got lost, who's still evacuated, things like that. Everybody sharing their stories. It's the most incredible thing I ever saw and experienced, so compassionate yet so heartbreaking, so incredibly heartbreaking.

EXTRA EQUIPMENT FOR DISASTER COVERAGE

300W to 500W power inverter for news car to charge batteries and run 250W light

Extra batteries for wireless transmitter/receiver

Baggies and rubber bands to cover and protect the wireless

A/C power supply

Battery charger

Audio—XLR turnarounds, impedance pad

Video—BNC cable and BNC turnaround barrel

Lens cloth

Sandbags to anchor lights

Light rope in short lengths to tie things down

Camera storm cover

Camera light rain cover

Black gaffer tape, not duct tape

Mag light

Black plastic garbage bags to protect exposed equipment

Clothing: 18" high rubber boots, rain suit, cap, sweater, three pairs of socks, change of outer and underwear, basic toiletries

Accessories: wipes, hand sanitizer, two face towels, paper towels, and plastic bags

For disasters, standard disaster kit with food, water, and a first-aid kit

It's six months later and Hooker is in a different state, at a different station, with a different job—chief photojournalist at WIS-TV Columbia, South Carolina. He's trying to sell his New Orleans home after paying a $20,000 repair bill. Katrina left Stephen Hooker better off than most. He salvaged his past and moved to a more temperate climate.

Spot news is an unplanned event with immediate interest, divided into current and aftermath categories. The screams of Katrina's brief and violent life now gone, the flooding and looting more or less at bay,

Stephen's stories live as memories for the millions who watched an American city wash away.

Take 2: The Shot and Camera Motion
The Shot

A shot *is one continuous take of a scene. Each shot contains story content and visual interest on its own. Combined and connected, the shot's communication starts to flow into a sequence, releasing the magic of television and bringing the story alive. These basic building blocks make up the visual foundation of a story.*

These shot descriptions describe the scene or the subject, not the angle of the lens. They refer to the size and relationship of elements within the frame and the intended communication of the shot. The focal length of the lens can vary on each of the shots described in the following sections.

Establishing Shot

An establishing shot *is usually the opening shot of a sequence and tells us where we are. It is most often also a wide shot, shot with a wide lens.*

Wide Shot

A wide shot *is any shot that encompasses the entire scene. A wide shot can be a sweeping vista or an all-encompassing view of a kitchen. A wide shot of a kitchen is inside an establishing shot of the house.*

Master Shot

Used in the master scene technique, a master shot *is generally a wide shot where all the action takes place. The shot lasts the duration of the repetitive action, either ongoing (as in the assembly of a widget on an assembly line) or staged (directing the action). The master scene is used as a blueprint for the rest of the closer shots that, in repetitive action, will match-cut with the master shot. These closer shots are called cut-in shots.*

Full Shot

A full shot *contains all of the subject you're shooting. A full shot of a person standing would be head to toe; a full shot of a jumbo jet would be nose to tail. Both examples fill the frame.*

Medium Shot

A medium shot *is closer than the full shot and shows more details about the main subject. On a person standing, it would be from the waist up; on the jumbo jet, it might be the front half of it the plane showing more of the airline's logo.*

Two Shot

A two shot *is any shot that has two characters only.*

Single Shot

A single shot *is any shot with just one character. A "clean" single is a shot without any hint of another character. A "dirty" single might include a bit of another character's shoulder and is any single shot in which you can tell another character is nearby.*

Close-up

Close-ups *show intimate details about the main subject. Television is often referred to as a close-up medium due to the relatively small screen size, where wider shots lose detail.*

Head and Shoulders

Just as the name says, it's a close-up showing only head and shoulders.

Extreme Close-up

The extreme close-up *is the closest the camera can get. Eyes and mouth, just eyes, or a gold tooth.*

Over-the-shoulder Shot

Just as the name says, it's over the shoulder *(OTS) of one character looking at the subject or other character(s).*

Reverse Shot

A reverse shot *is any shot that looks back across the scene opposite of the last shot. It's the reverse shot that gets most photographers in trouble for "crossing the line." Stay on the same side of "the line" established in the last shot. (See Screen Direction in Chapter 12.)*

Answering Shot

An answering shot *is either an OTS or a close-up reverse shot, used in shooting dialogue where one character "answers" the other. The focal length, lens height, distance, and horizontal angle should mirror the preceding shot.*

POV Shot

POV *stands for point of view. It is any shot that is supposed to represent the main subject's visual experience. It can be static, but often refers to a handheld shot that captures the experience as seen through the main subject's eyes.*

Action Shot

An action shot *is defined by its relationship to a reaction shot. It is the shot the subject is reacting to. While most shots in television news should have action in them, some may not. The only reason not to search for action in a shot is if the lack of action is central to the concept of the story. However, even then the smallest amount of action can be very powerful. In a desolate ghost town that's been abandoned for decades, a few static shots could communicate that quite well. If a tiny dust devil rolls up the street blowing an old newspaper in the process, that's good action that advances the story. Look for grand action; look for subtle action.*

Reaction Shot

A reaction shot *is any shot in which a subject reacts to the action of the preceding scene. It gives a human, emotional element to the action.*

Cutaway Shot

A cutaway shot *is any shot that is used to cut "away" from the action. Cutaways help the editor condense screen time and fix screen direction issues. It's important to keep cutaways relevant to their moment in the story. Think of cutaways as atmosphere shots and use them to convey details about the environment.*

Cut-in Shot

A cut-in shot *must match the action and appear connected to an adjacent shot. It implies a closer look. This shot term is often used in describing the closer shots used in the master scene technique.*

Opening Shot

An opening shot *is any shot that starts a story. It could be a wide shot or a close shot. It could be an Alaskan mountain range or the close-up of an eagle screeching. Use whatever shot sets the tone and grabs the attention of the viewer.*

Closing Shot

A closing shot *is the last shot in a story. It lets the viewer know the story is over and should convey any final emotions intended for the viewer. The endangered eagle flies into the sunset—perhaps one day we may never see eagles again.*

Camera Motion

Camera moves can help tell the story. Different moves communicate different messages. Take care to use camera moves only when the story dictates and not simply to add motion to the shot. It can be very jarring to cut in the middle of a camera move. All moves should have a static start and a static stop of at least five seconds.

Static wide shot.

Pan.

A rookie mistake is shooting every shot with zooms and pans that start and end on nothing, making it impossible to edit and painful to watch. If you're going to do a move—get there. Have a reason for going from point A to point B. Don't make twenty- or thirty-second slow moves; they probably will never be used in news. All camera moves alert the audience that someone is manipulating the camera.

Consider camera motion options for a story on a scenic Alaskan overlook where a crowd gathers to watch bald eagles fly at sunset.

Pan

A pan *is a horizontal pivot of the camera. A camera pans right and left. It would be natural to follow the person joining the crowd. It would also be the move you'd use to follow the eagles across the horizon. New visual content can also be revealed by a pan. A young man is hiking by himself at the start of the pan, but as it follows him we see the crowd. If there was no prior knowledge of the crowd on the overlook, the pan shot would reveal them and further the story.*

Tilt

A tilt *is the vertical version of a pan. A camera tilts up and down. A tilt shot can also reveal new* visual information. If we see only bald eagles flying against the mountains, a tilt down will reveal the crowd gathering on the cliff.

Zoom-in

A zoom-in *eliminates environmental details in the frame as it enlarges the main subject. You see the subject from the beginning of the move until the end. Once the zoom is started, you generally know where it will end up. The only changes are that the subject is growing in size and importance within the frame. A zoom-in "points" the viewer's attention. The crowd on the cliff is becoming the central point of interest in this shot.*

Zoom-out

A zoom-out *broadens the field of view, adding more environment to the shot. New visual content is revealed by a zoom-out. The eagles are peacefully gliding around the mountains, but as we zoom out, we see they are not alone. People are gathering on the cliff.*

Camera moves can be dictated by the type of camera support, or what that camera is mounted on. The figure on the next page illustrates four types of camera support that dictate what kinds of shots can be made.

Tripod

A tripod *shot will allow you to smoothly pan, tilt, and zoom. The solid support will keep the image steady on telephoto shots as you follow the eagles. Move the tripod often; raise and lower it to make better shots. Baby legs are short tripods; a high hat places the fluid head and camera almost on the ground.*

Tilt.

Zoom in.

Zoom out.

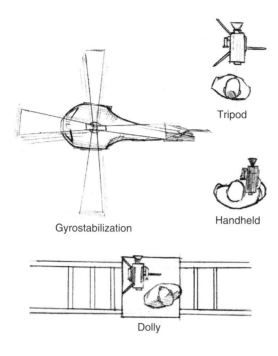

Tripod

Handheld

Gyrostabilization

Dolly

Handheld

Handheld *camera work draws the viewer's atten-tion to the camera operator and does not lend itself to good, strong graphic images. On the positive side, it may give the viewer a sense of being one of the participants watching the eagles. When handholding, try to balance the camera on your shoulder; there should be no struggle to keep it there. Set a slightly wide, comfortable stance with your feet approximately shoulder width apart. Keep your elbows close to your body. Stand straight, don't lock your knees, and take long shallow breaths to keep your shoulders from rising and falling. Stay on the wide end of the lens to avoid shakiness. Going handheld allows for quick responses to unplanned events.*

Dolly

A dolly *shot allows the camera to move smoothly along a horizontal plane. The camera can pan, tilt, move left and right and forward and back. A dolly-forward is called a* dolly-in; *backwards, away from the subject, it's a* dolly-out.

Some dollies allow the camera to be raised and lowered on a pedestal. The move is called ped-up or ped-down. Often, the dolly runs on tracks to further smooth out the move and keep repetitive takes exactly the same.

The dolly could follow the newcomer as he joins the group, creating a tracking shot. *Tracking shots attempt to keep the subject in frame.*

It could be placed along the cliff and move left to right, pointing out toward the mountains as we move by. This would be a trucking shot. *Trucking shots do not try to keep the subject in frame; they move past it. Tracking and trucking shots can be made on any camera support that rolls.*

Gyrostabilization

Helicopters are commonplace in gathering news. Aerial shots can pan, tilt, track, truck, zoom, ped-up, and ped-down with altitude. With gyrostabilization, *the camera can also zoom in quite close without noticeable shakiness. The bird's-eye view would be very helpful in illustrating our bald eagle story.*

A Final Note on Camera Support

Almost anything can be used for camera support. Figure out where you want the camera; then get inventive. I was in the habit of using my wallet to prop up the front of the camera when I put it on the ground for low shots. With a little fidgeting, I could wedge the lens up to the angle I wanted. Unfortunately, while in main-land China, I tried this trick and accidentally left my wallet by a small lake, never to be found again. Be innovative; just don't use important items to secure the camera.

More on Moves

Moves in, either by zooming or moving the camera, bring the main subject closer and begin to limit the amount of environment information. Moves out shrink the main subject, but also add environmental information. With a move out, there is always new information entering the frame.

Many camera moves will force the camera operator into uncomfortable positions, positions that will be impossible to maintain for very long. Always start in the most uncomfortable position and finish your move where you're naturally more comfortable. Ending in the uncomfortable position will often force you to ruin your shot.

In compound moves of panning, tilting, and zooming, don't try to start all motions on all axes at the same time. Start with one move; then a moment later add the others. Camera moves become more transparent when following a subject and more obvious when moving through a static scene.

Understanding how various camera shots and motion techniques can advance the story is an essential element in television photojournalism.

CHAPTER 6

Christian Parkinson
General News—From Kings to Commoners

Christian Parkinson

Broadcast Camera Journalist, BBC London

*T*he winter wind chills everyone standing on Cowley Street. Trying to stay warm in brightly colored jackets, they huddle and wait. Late in the afternoon, the temperature drops a few more degrees. Teams from everywhere gather on the walkway; there's an energy in the air—a sense of competition.

Christian Parkinson can see the crowd, steaming mouths talking trash and treasures. The latest gossip, love affairs, and inside tips. He knows most of the players, and he'd love to be part of the party. But, he can't. Yearning, like a puppy on a leash, Parkinson is tied by coax cable to a live truck half a block from everyone else. The truck's mast marks his presence like a team flag. It's almost 4:00 P.M.

All of a sudden, as if someone had smacked a bee's nest, the crowd takes on a singular buzz. Only one thing matters: Sir Menzies Campbell exits the hall. The newly voted leader of the Liberal Democratic Party will make his way to party headquarters near Parliament in Central London. He'll make the short walk engulfed by the media as they follow him down the road. The scrum starts.

Scrum is a term from rugby; it's when eight men join arms and then ram into another eight men. That's what we call it when we are at a big press event and we are all on top of each other trying to get the shot. I hate it, but I love it at the same time.

EQUIPMENT

Sony DVCAM DSR-500 camera
2 Sony ECM-77 lavalier microphones
Sony radio lapel microphone
Sony WRT847 radio stick microphone
Sennheiser MKH60 shotgun microphone
3 300 W Sachtler Reporter lights
Sachtler 150W Reporter light
650 W Strand Redhead
150 W Dedolight
Vinten Vision 10 tripod
Lastolite Gold reflector
Magic arm
Pag Powerarc top light

The scrum around Sir Menzies as he moves toward Parkinson's live position.

The pack moves toward Parkinson, thirty to forty heads backing up. Microphones, boom poles, cameras of all makes and formats record the walk. Everyone is walking backward, focused on Sir Menzies Campbell. There, in the center of the walk, stands Christian Parkinson, about to be mowed over by a human engine, powered by the collective need to "get the shot."

As this pack got closer, I heard the producer telling me to run over and join the mob. But, I made a snap decision to hold my ground.

Back at BBC Television Centre, Parkinson's video signal is being broadcast live. I held firm and made the other crews part around me rather than trying to force my way to the front. That's when the old left hand comes in useful. You just gently move them. That's where size can be important if maybe you are a little bit taller. Although it doesn't make you a better cameraman, it can be useful in these situations. Guiding more than pushing allows you to get the shot that you need most of the time. It's never a good thing if you get nasty, because it will get you another time. Be firm, be confident, and be polite.

Parkinson also has some help. A soundman offers to guide him should he decide to back up and join the scrum's march. Parkinson holds his ground; the event is coming to him. The scrum moves around as he eases his lens into a better position. A slight physical suggestion steers the less seasoned from running over him; the oldtimers can sense he's there and move like chess pieces to the next position of greater advantage.

I felt the cables being tugged a bit. People where getting them caught up in their shoes and that was a bit worrying. The BBC is very hot on health and safety, so we run our cables along the edge of the road and not across. Someone must have found a way to get tangled. Then it all came together.

The scrum parts. The visual excitement of the shot grows as the last journalist's head rolls through the viewfinder on his way down the street, revealing: Sir Menzies Campbell perfectly framed in Parkinson's camera. It was very satisfying when he popped up right in front of my lens and was waving to his supporters in the upper floors of the building.

Christian Parkinson not only captures Sir Menzies Campbell's face as he makes the walk; his decision helps tell the story of the event. The scrum itself illustrates the importance of the moment as it grows in the

frame until the isolated "subject of the hour" is revealed. It's a much better tactic for storytelling than a bouncing Sir Menzies Campbell head filling the frame for sixty seconds. You dread it and sometimes you feel like scum when you do it, but you do get an adrenaline buzz when you get the shot.

"GOT IT." Sir Menzies emerges from the pack right in front of Parkinson's camera.

About five minutes later, as soon as he'd gone inside, everyone sort of disappeared. Myself and another cameraman then had to rig up for a two-camera, live interview with the guy for the top story of the day. *The BBC has plenty of other resources on the event—radiocams, and mini steady cams—all going live.* Over the past year, the use of "radiocams" has transformed the way the news networks cover big stories. "Radiocam" is the generic name for the new generation of transmitters that can be attached to the back of the camera to send pictures and audio back to a receiver and, thus, negate the need for tricky cable runs. This means you can now go live to the middle of a "scrum" outside court, or even into a riot if need be.

But it is Parkinson's shot, captured the "old-fashioned way," that leads the newscast live and, later, replays to lead a packaged segment on the 6 o'clock news.

This type of story is just one of the many that BBC broadcast camera journalists are asked to cover. The position use to be called "location camera supervisor"; the title changed to reflect the content responsibilities of the job. Christian Parkinson shoots general news and thinks it's the greatest job in the world.

General news *refers to the day-to-day coverage of general interest stories. These are the stories that document our daily lives. They are about us. They are not often flashy or arty; they tend to be informative and dry. But Parkinson likes to "lift" the work a bit, make it something worth watching, and his efforts are plain to see in the style of his stories. General news is always very topical, its "time of interest" very short. So those who work in general news are always under extreme deadlines to go on air, making a "lift" even more difficult to achieve. Add to the tight timeline the need to fit into any circumstance, and you could think of BBC broadcast camera journalists as chameleons who have mastered space and time. They are where they need to be, comfortably chatting with anyone from any social background while creatively solving technical, visual, and content problems.*

Of Kings and Commoners

The more I do this job, the more I think that it isn't necessarily your camera skills but people who can get along with anyone. Someone who can walk into a prison and make the inmates feel comfortable and talk to you. And then the next day, go to Buckingham Palace and interview the Queen. You can make the best pictures in the world, but if you can't get people to relate to you, and you relate to the people, you're never going to get great shots anyway. That, to me, is the most important thing. You need patience and understanding, especially with the general public. Remember, you do this every day, but to a lot of people you interview, this might be the only time in their life they'll do this. You need to be able to go into an interview and make the person feel comfortable and relaxed. The ability to get on with people is a big deal.

The BBC's business model seems custom-made for general news. The BBC is actually very good in the fact that's it's a public service broadcaster and "Joe in the Street" is paying my wages—I like to think working for the BBC, you do have a certain respect for people. *The BBC is funded by license and has no commercials. People in the United Kingdom pay roughly 130 pounds a year for a color signal.* And, it's that money that pays for the BBC. I think the BBC can be more independent because we aren't worrying that we are upsetting advertisers. In that, I feel the BBC has a certain freedom in the way we tell our stories. It also means we are answerable to the public more so than a commercial station and, therefore, as representatives of the BBC, we have to have more respect for the people in the streets.

One thing I like to try and do is get people involved. If someone is polite with me in the street, I have no problem letting them look in the camera viewfinder, explaining to them what I'm doing. Recently, in the wake of the July 7 bombings, we spent a lot of our time around the Muslim areas of Yorkshire. I don't think a lot of people understood why we were there. So, I was deliberately engaging with the local kids to make them and the people feel involved and comfortable with our presence.

The subject matter of general news is as varied as life itself. However, the basic techniques used to capture these stories remain tried and true. The story itself will start with research and discovery to determine what the story is about. You'll find the information on the wire, or newspaper, or wherever the lead came from. More information can come from the interview. There are three basic elements that are shot in the field for a television news package.

Basic Field Elements

The Interview

This is used for personalizing a story as well as attributing information. As journalists, you may not be 100 percent sure of the facts, but when someone else tells the story, it's his or her interpretation and fair material to use. (Example: A farmer saying aliens landed in his wheat field is very different from a reporter saying aliens landed in that wheat field.) If you say it and it's wrong, it could be libelous. Sometimes an interview is used for discovery as well. In any case, it should be inspiring to both the reporter and the broadcast camera journalist to think of ways to further the personal aspect of the story and plan creative shots that are relevant to the package.

The Stand-up

Reporter stand-ups have been a mainstay in television news since its inception. A perfect stand-up would be essential to the advancement of the story. It would be the best way to impart critical information that could not be illustrated by a shot, not an excuse to build the reporter's face time on air. So, yes, this is a challenge. One: Are your shots stronger and more interesting than a reporter's head? If not, work harder. Two: There will always be stand-ups, so do your best to integrate them into the story and make them seem less like a pasted-on afterthought of ego. Bridges (the reporter connecting two segments within a package) rather than opens and closes would be a good suggestion.

The Shots That Tell the Story

Your images should bring the story to life and illustrate in a way that is memorable and engaging. Don't think of it as just B-roll—covering the interview and the reporter's voice track; think of your images as relevant to the

Making politics relevant—filming with party members during a Conservative leadership election campaign.

very nature of the story. This is TV, and as a reminder, it's an expensive box in someone's house. Your story is invited; make your stay worth the viewer's while. Give them something valuable.

The challenge in every general news story is to be creative, come away with pictures that will put together an interesting package. I always like to do the interviews first, so I can introduce myself and put them at ease. Maybe have a cup of tea with them. Then what I always look for is a place where there is a little depth to the shot where I can get something visually interesting. Anything is better than a shot straight against the wall, but at the same time I'm not upsetting their existence. They don't necessarily want me to be there. I sometimes explain to them not to look at the camera but to look at the reporter. I ask them if they have been on TV before and nine times out of ten they haven't, so I just to explain to them how it all works.

The value of general news coverage is community coverage; it's making a story specifically to inform and be understood by the local community. You can't necessarily sit at home and relate to someone starving in Africa. You can't necessarily relate to a millionaire politician whose wife has just left him. But, people can relate to someone like them, telling their own story in their front room. It needs to be something people can relate to. That sort of interview does give a human face to the story. If you see images of a kidnapping in Iraq, it might be hard to relate to, but, if you see an interview with the mother of one kidnapped who is crying in the living room, then there is that human aspect. Let's face it, yes, it's one world and many like to think of themselves as citizens of the world, but a lot of people only relate to people like them. Whether it be race or country, it's easier to relate to someone locally. That's why we do the stories we do.

Parkinson's methods are common among BBC broadcast camera journalists and the other camera positions further up in rank. Senior BBC broadcast camera journalists *and the top* picture correspondents *do the training and encourage experimentation—as long as the story is served. Parkinson has developed his own favorite techniques and shortcuts, but follows a standard path when exploring a story's potential.*

Parkinson's Interviews

First you look for where you want to do the interview, where the light isn't too bad and the scenery is interesting. Think: What is the purpose to the interview? Is the background important to the context? You have to think about what this is going to cut in with. Think about how wide the framing should be. Do you want it to be tight or a medium-long shot, down to the knees?

An interview with a comedian—the subject lent itself to a handheld moving style. Always try to reflect the mood of the piece in your framing.

"As the interviewee makes his point, I move into a mid-shot. You have to be careful when doing this and try to 'hit' the soundbite with your move."

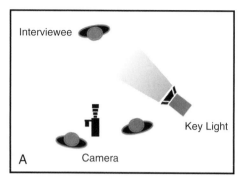

A. A lighting diagram.

B. A typical Parkinson interview—a hard key light with a colored lamp giving some interest to the back wall.

C. Parkinson reframes often during the interview.

You want the reporter right next to the camera so the eye line's right. Always use two microphones. Put microphones on the reporters and have them talk to the interviewees, and have interviewees spell their names, all while you get the audio levels set. Always monitor audio.

Put a key light on the other side of the reporter to carve pleasant shadows that define the face. So it's you and the camera, then the reporter, then the light (see top figure). That's the most basic rule and, if you stick to that and get the exposure right, nine times out of ten your picture will come out looking good. I carry two lights with me to every job: a 300W Sachtler with a stand and a 300W Sachtler with a magic arm. Always have at least one light with you.

Usually, I only have time for one light because I'm being rushed. One trick that I do to make a dull, rushed situation look like I took time and made it arty is to use one hard key light upstage from the other side of the reporter. Get a nice bit of shadowing on the side of the face and keep the shot tight. It will look lit and like you took some time.

If you have time, sometimes it's nice to use more lights. Your bog standard three-point lighting would be: upstage key, soft or hard depending on your preference; a soft fill on the camera side so you still have a little modeling; and a back light on a magic arm, giving a nice rim and a bit of separation between the shoulders, the back of the head, and the background. The back light just lifts them from whatever is behind them.

A fourth point of light would be putting light on the background to add a bit of depth to the shot and to specifically show something that's in the background. It could be books or something that might be relevant to what the interviewee is talking about. It may also be used just for contrast. It would look odd if you had a nicely lit guy being interviewed and a dark cabin behind him. What's back there? You know you want to see what's back there. Let's have a look. Let's put a bit of light on it and make the shot a bit more interesting.

When doing location lighting, it's important to know how many lamps you can plug in without blowing the circuit. Electricity is measured in terms of voltage, amperage, and wattage. Voltage measures the force or

A. A four-point lighting diagram.

B. An "unstaged" interview: This man started making an interesting point. Instead of asking him to change seats and lose the moment, Parkinson found an interesting angle and went with it: "Sometimes you have to be prepared to wing it."

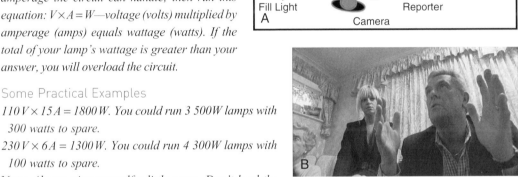

pressure of electricity. Amperage measures the amount of electricity used. Wattage measures the work that electricity does per second. Lamps are rated in watts. How many lamps can you plug into a home before the circuit blows? First, find out the voltage on the circuit you're using, then how much amperage the circuit can handle; then run this equation: $V \times A = W$—voltage (volts) multiplied by amperage (amps) equals wattage (watts). If the total of your lamp's wattage is greater than your answer, you will overload the circuit.

Some Practical Examples

*$110V \times 15A = 1800W$. You could run 3 500W lamps with
  300 watts to spare.*
*$230V \times 6A = 1300W$. You could run 4 300W lamps with
  100 watts to spare.*
Note: *Always give yourself a little room. Don't load the
circuit to the maximum. (For more on lighting, refer to Appendix C.)*

    While I'm setting up, I try to find something to talk about with the interviewees. Something we both can relate to. If they have some football trophies on the fireplace, I get them to talk about football to get them loosened up. It's the most important thing to get them talking about whatever and get them comfortable. I start recording, not being secretive about it, and have a chat with them to get them loosened up.

    It's the worst when the reporter just comes up with his papers and says, "All right, we're starting, go." Too many reporters don't understand that and will be too formal. They also will sit there with their guest and not say a word as the cameraman, me, gets set up. So, I often am the one who talks to them. When the lights are up and I'm back at the camera, it quiets down and the reporter starts. A first, simple question that will never get used eases us into the interview.

    I might zoom in during a question or, if it's an emotional answer, I might do a slow, creep-in zoom. But, a caution: Zooming can be hard for the editor because they might want to cut out right when you are zooming in, and that looks awkward. If you are a beginner, when in doubt, don't zoom in; stay still. If in doubt, reframe during the question.

    If we have time at the end, I will move frame and get a tight profile shot and ask the reporter to ask the two key questions again, just to get a couple of nice, different shots. No interview is

A. Movement is a great way to draw the viewer into a stand-up, as this example from Parkinson's work in Moscow demonstrates.

B. Here in Rome, Parkinson wanted to show a moving and developing story, so this stand-up was done with a slow walk through the gathering crowd at the Vatican.

C. This shot comes at the conclusion of a stand-up in a shopping mall. Parkinson started very wide and then walked through the shoppers to find this reporter.

complete without the standard set-up shots. I get a wide establishing shot favoring the interviewee to identify the interview's location. Another shot is an over-the-shoulder of the interviewee looking at the reporter, and then I push into a single close-up of the reporter to use as a cutaway if the editors need it.

Parkinson's Stand-ups

There is quite a bit of difference between doing a stand-up live and one for a package. On a stand-up for a package on tape, I will try and be more dynamic and more experimental or creative in terms of framing than I will be for a live stand-up. I'm much more likely to do a walkabout on a standup on tape than I would on a live because, with a live there are obviously so many more factors involved and so much more that can go wrong.

I don't like "Reporter stood next to sign." I just really hate it. I hate zooms, so I like to walk around and use the wide-angle lens. I like to put the reporter on a wireless microphone then walk through a crowd of people. At the back of the crowd I find him continuing the standup, then we walk together as he finishes his bit.

I love that sort of thing. I'll always be thinking, "How can I just lift this a little?" Even things like taking them twenty yards ahead of the sign, and have it slightly out of focus over their shoulder, instead of them being right next to it.

The reporters always want to look stunning, don't they? They will always thank you if they look good. So, just give them a little lick of light. Even if you're in the middle of a field, just get your battery light, put it off to one angle a little bit, give them a little sparkle in the eyes even if nothing else, and they'll always thank you for it. Even if it looks no different, in their eyes you made the effort. Often, more important than them actually looking better is that you made the effort.

Most reporters hate the idea of you filming looking up at them. So, most of the time, you shoot from at least head height. It's pretty rare to film from a low angle. If the reporter needs a little sprucing up, then that's just common courtesy to let them know if their tie isn't straight or their hair is sticking up.

So I'm always thinking: (1) How can I make this visually interesting? (2) How can I make the reporter look good? (3) How's it going to fit into the overall style of the piece?

So I'll often say, "What's it coming off the back of? What's gonna come next?" Always ask the reporter what they are going to say. Too many cameramen think of themselves as just cameramen, and they're just there to make it look pretty. And they forget that what the reporter says will affect how they shoot it and the style that they shoot it in. Too many think, "We'll that's a nice shot—not really bothered about what they're talking about." If you understand the story you're telling, then you'll come up with different ideas and ways of illustrating it.

Parkinson's Shots That Tell the Story

A lot depends on the style of the piece. If it is something I know is going to be free flowing and I don't really know what's going to happen and where it's going to go, then I'll be handheld unless I'm at a distance; then it would look terrible handheld. If in doubt, I shoot handheld. I just think it gives you more freedom and you think more. I think a problem too many people have is that they are obsessed with their tripod. It can sometimes limit your creativity by thinking, "This is my spot and all my shots happen from this spot." I'll shoot handheld and look for interesting things to set my camera on. If I rest my camera on the pavement with a couple of tapes just raising it up, I get a beautiful shot that's steady and interesting. Don't limit your creativity by being tied to a tripod.

I love what I call dirty shooting, where there might be bottles on the table and I'll shoot through the bottles with them in the foreground of the interview. It's a different way of lifting a dull shot. *Dirty shooting means trying to get objects in the foreground, shooting through things (see figure below).*

Basically, what we do is so cliché and so easy to parody, and often the camerawork is cliché. There are time constraints, and people fall back on clichés because there's no time to do it any different. I often look for quick ways to make it look like it's not been done in a hurry. So I use this dirty shooting technique to make it look like I've introduced a style when, really, it's just a way to try to lift it out of the average.

I'm a big fan of Big Close-Ups—they really give your shots more power and impact. If you are shooting a street sequence, look for that shot of the policeman's face or the beggar's hands—a pull focus between the two would be even better.

*(*Pull focus *or* rack focus *is the shifting of focus from one subject to the next in the same shot. A shallow depth of field accentuates the effect.)*

An example of "dirty shooting." Try to make the shot three-dimensional by using objects in the foreground.

Always look for the killer shot—the one that makes the editor stop spooling the tape. Two killer shots can make a whole piece. Always think "opening" and "closing"—you need a shot that can be scripted to—I often have potential script lines in my head when I see a shot and will often pass it on to the reporter, who may or may not use it. The other thing when shooting B-roll is sound. Always look for that sound of the gates closing or the rifle being cocked. These sounds give you so much more to play with when you are editing. An up sound like that can allow the editor to full-stop a sentence.

The Sun Never Sets on the British Broadcast Signal

Parkinson never forgets his audience—the regular people—living regular lives. Londoners and expats, people all over the world, tune in to the BBC to see news that's familiar to them. The BBC has put Parkinson on the road more these days. His footage is starting to show up from all over the globe. The BBC shoots on two formats. Domestically we use DVCAM, while abroad we use Beta SX in order to be compatible with most local broadcasters, who are still on SP. My camera is a DVCAM DSR-500. It belongs to the BBC, but is permanently allocated to me. I know its eccentricities and don't get caught out by changed menu settings, and so on.

The BBC way of doing things is unique. For Christian Parkinson and the other broadcast camera journalists, the working schedules and travel opportunities create a very rewarding life. Most people here do four days on and four days off. But then they ask you for these days and other days and to go abroad. They are quite flexible in the system. We get five weeks paid leave a year. The days average twelve hours, but at the same time the assignments desk is very good and can be flexible if you need to change some days. The time it gets more difficult is when there's a breaking story and they call you. Or, if you are off somewhere shooting and something happens and you are the only one and have to stay there until it's done. They're a good employer; they treat us well. If you want the extra hours, they're there. If you want to spend more time with your family, then you can do that, too.

The most rewarding thing is knowing you were there. Recently, I was on a date in the corner of a café, and there were highlights of the year on *Sky News*. I must have looked a bit cocky after it because I was saying, "Oh, I was there," after each clip. To me, that's the most rewarding thing to the job, to be able to look back and know you were there. I can say to my family, when they see certain old footage, that I was there and that was my shot.

I was there in St. Peter's Square, minutes after the new Pope was announced. History had just been made; the Pope was crowned.

I was there in Thailand covering the one-year anniversary of the tsunami to show how much the people had recovered and brought their lives back. I welled up at one point during a ceremony on the beach—they released 5,000 burning lanterns into the sky, representing the souls of the people who had died. It was an indescribable experience.

And I was there, too, outside countless courtrooms. Waiting for the scrum. Standing in the rain for ten hours at a time. Knowing, even if you get the shot, and it's a great shot, no one's ever going to thank you for it because you're expected to get it. That is what I get paid for, that's essentially why the BBC employs me.

So we stand and wait. There's nothing else to do but talk to your colleagues. Sometimes cameramen will agree if one goes to get coffee, if they miss the shot, they can dub someone else's shot. Camera crews help each other out. There's that kind of relationship within the brotherhood of cameramen.

Standing outside of court . . . the best place for making friends.

A door swings open. Fifteen top lights turn on; Styrofoam coffee cups fall, crushed under dirty boots, worn tennis shoes, and wicked heels. Cameras mount up, eye pieces glow blue with the image of the accused. Strobes flash like lightning, blowing out faces in their brief pulse, leaving instant shadows to disappear on the wall. Microphones fly on taught cables as the inquisition ensues. Everything gets very tight, very loud. More questions than answers mix with jostling journalists and equipment. It's sensory overload as the pack moves backward, teetering for balance. Equilibrium—something for science, some other time. Swirling around in this tribal dance could signal a new ruler or human sacrifice.

A black limousine door with smoked windows opens as the center of the whirlpool disappears inside. Slam! The surrounding flurry evaporates as the story drives out of view. But it's there, burned on tape, one man's digital legacy ready to air on the night's news.

The brilliant moment of adrenaline intoxication is over in a few moments. The scent of perfume and cologne from forty close colleagues is all that's left.

No need to go back for the coffee. A caffeine buzz just can't compete with a scrum.

CHAPTER 7

Ray Farkas

Interviews—Talking Heads
and Voyeurism

Ray Farkas

Independent Producer
and Director
Founder, Off Center
Productions, Inc.

ABC News, PBS, CBS News, HBO, National Geographic, Fox, NBC News
Emmy Award for Best Documentary, "Catch-22" (Special Classification—
  Outstanding News and Documentary Program Achievement), NATAS, 1996

"You don't need to shake my hand, it shakes just fine on it's own."

– Lyric by Phillip Lerman

Two operating lights hang like flying saucers above the table. Their glare shines off a shaved head. It smells like a hospital, clean—scary. Under a light blue gown, the patient twitches with tremors—an uncontrollable symptom of Parkinson's disease. There's no cure, just a hope that the DBS procedure will work where medications have failed.

DBS stands for deep brain stimulation and the procedure involves a surgically implanted, battery-operated device called a neurostimulator. It delivers electrical stimulation to the brain via implants that block the abnormal nerve signals that cause tremors.

Four cameras roll in the small, white operating room. Different angles of the same procedure fill the corners of the screen. The elements in each shot, meticulously composed. This is a Ray Farkas story; the documentary will have all the hallmarks of his work.

Dr. Chris Kalhorn of Georgetown University Hospital is about to go to work. This shift will last seven hours. He'll have plenty of company to keep the conversation going. Operating nurses and a neurologist dressed in hospital blues and face masks circle the table. But no one is as conversational as the patient—Ray Farkas. Ray Farkas: producer, director, patient with Parkinson's disease.

An oxygen tube is wrapped around his ears and under his nose. The operating light swings closer—Ray doesn't like lighting, but in this case he'll make an exception. With an IV taped to his shaking hand, he tells them he's ready. The doctors go to work: a titanium

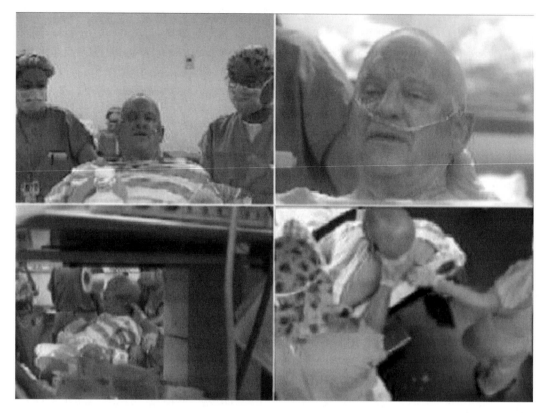

Farkas on the operating table after setting up the shots for his operation. Virtually all of the scenes are seen in a four-way split screen—partly because you can see more, partly so you don't concentrate on the very few scenes that might make you queasy.

crown is pulled over his head, fixed in place by latexed fingers. "Try to be stylish about it." Farkas's wife and daughter worry in the waiting room as he cracks jokes.

The overhead camera is static and unmanned. Good friend and cameraman Bob Petersen oversees the camera setup. Two cameras are operated by Farkas's sons, another by a friend (also a professional cameraman), and a portable camera by Darrell Barton, who's flown in from Oklahoma. Their surgical masks hide their concern as surgery begins.

The drill whirrs to life; the rising pitch suggests RPMs in the thousands. Farkas will remain conscious throughout the operation. The drill fits into a slot in the crown. "There'll be some pressure," Dr. Kalhorn says. Metal finds bone. The bit enters his skull as the cameras roll. Farkas smiles.

Something's smoking . . . it's the drill in Farkas's head. Wisps of vapor materialize from his crown. Unfazed by the high-tech procedure taking place above his eyesight, Farkas chats away. The beeps of industrial green operating equipment are constant. That's a good thing. So's the chatter. The surgeons need Farkas awake to test the implants. They drill two holes and feed one electrode into the hole above his right eye.

Throw the switch. Tiny electrical pulses race through wires buried deep in Farkas's brain. His left foot stops shaking; the neurostimulator works. It's a thrilling moment for Farkas, a dream come true.

"The surgeon explains about the electrodes he put in my brain. Great opportunity for a silhouette."

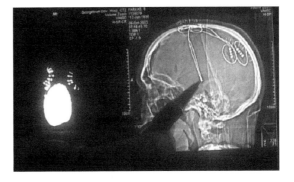

The other implant is set, the wounds closed, the first operation complete. A week later, there will be another operation to implant the battery portion, which is similar to a heart pacemaker and approximately the size of a stopwatch. Both operations will be resounding successes.

Six months after the operations, Ray Farkas's autobiographical documentary, It Ain't Television—It's Brain Surgery *(a musical comedy), is complete. Running an hour and a half, the film features two original songs written for Farkas, "Hole in the Head" and "DBS Tango." "If I Only Had a Brain," from* The Wizard of Oz, *plays for an additional comedic edge.*

The documentary starts in the OR with a quad split (the screen is divided into four squares) of the procedure. The procedure, an interview with Farkas before the operation, another interview after, interviews with family members, and interviews with doctors are all woven together for a lighthearted but impactful story of hope.

Interviews—that's what Ray Farkas does best. His unique style, techniques, and process challenge many of the standard interview methods. Yet, almost without exception, anyone who sees his work admires it. His interviews ring true, their content honest. Although he is not a television news photographer, he's included in this book because he asserts direct control over what the camera shoots: focal length, composition, and lighting. With a handheld monitor, Farkas directs the scene, sometimes to the dismay of photographers not yet familiar with what the outcome will be. They may feel their area of expertise is being encroached on. However, the end result is so profound, literally every photographer bows to his methods, confessing the best interview possible.

Ray Farkas's methods are not the be all and end all of interviews. In fact, he'd encourage experimentation, trying new methods as new equipment comes online. Some of his techniques are controversial—more on that as the chapter progresses. Farkas is hired to create his style of work; not all news stories that you'll be hired to do will work with this type of interview. Some news managers might insist on the "standard" way of doing interviews outlined in Chapter 6. As photojournalists, it is important to be skilled in as many techniques as possible, tailoring your work to the advancement of the story.

Who is Ray Farkas? From his Web site: I am the "foreground guy" and the "compression man" . . . but what I really do is sound. I am the tripod man, the long lens man, the wireless man—hardly very

"There's a line in the song: 'I thought I would marry my surgeon . . .' So I kissed him, knowing it would fit."

revolutionary. I steal everything from movies. In movies, you willingly believe you are eavesdropping. The illusion holds our interest. I try to hold your interest with photography that does the same. As a journalist, I am twenty-five feet more honest than you are, my subjects are twenty-five feet more relaxed, they are one or two or three lights more honest. I believe in art, in my craft, in eavesdropping, in honesty. I believe in symbolism and detail in picture and sound. I believe in my audience, in stretching their imagination, in treating them as I would you. I am Off Center because I believe in a sense of discovery, I believe in my craft, I believe in my audience.

The birth of Ray Farkas's style can be traced back to the Civil Rights Movement of the 1960s. I spent a lot of time for NBC down in Mississippi, and we were accused, not without some justification, of being part of the story. The white people in Mississippi were upset with us because they figured that the minorities were coming down just because we were there, because the cameras were there. That was part of the genesis of learning how to stay away from subjects, to stay out of the story as much as we could. To record it rather than be a part of it. That criticism is justified; a lot of times we unknowingly become participants in a story, rather than observers, which is what we should be.

From then on it was just gradual, little by little. I always like to stand back and look at things rather than get right on top of them. I mean, that's my whole theory of shooting.

Characteristics of a Farkas Project

Distance

The first hallmark of a Farkas interview is distance. Photographically, that means the use of a long lens and all the attributes that come with it: a shallow depth of field and a compressed image. It also means the machinery of recording the interview is kept at a distance as well, keeping the environment as real as possible. For this reason, the second hallmark is natural light.

Natural Light

One of the more controversial aspects of Farkas's work is that he avoids the use of lights, using them only when exposure absolutely mandates.

Another benefit of the long lens, foreground approach: You're not likely to need lights because the soft focus foreground (remember, you're pretty tight on the subject) gives your picture depth. So, you've lost another piece of intimidation.

I use natural light. I seldom, if ever, use light in an interview. My problem with lights is if you put up one light, that begets a second light, a third light—pretty soon

"A good friend, Phillip Lerman, wrote and sang two songs for my movie/video about the surgery. He performed them for me after the operation, and for the neurosurgeon, neurologist, and supervising nurse. One of the few times I used lights."

everybody seems to be wearing a beret, figuratively. Sometimes, I'll use a desk lamp as part of the picture—in front of the subject, but not obliterating them. In front of them, using it as a light and also using it to tell you something about the person. The person works at a desk, if you will. That sounds terribly simplistic, but in the context of a story, it makes sense.

I think lights are intimidating. I think you get further away from the truth when you put lights up because it's just like a shotgun mic thrust in somebody's face. Lights, shotgun mics, cameras five feet from your face: They all serve to make the scene more about the production rather than keeping us away from the scene and keeping it as normal as you can make it. So I don't use lights. Besides which, lights take time—you've got to get to your next shoot.

Composition and Foreground

Composition and foreground elements, the third hallmark, appear in every Farkas interview. I've never met an interview I didn't like, that I couldn't frame well. The subject matter is to the left or the right; it's seldom dead center. It's seldom the Mona Lisa. When I walk into a room, I look for not a background but a foreground. A background doesn't give you any depth, but a foreground does. It gives the picture a couple of layers. If the foreground's out of focus, it gives dimension to the picture; it gives depth to the picture, so I don't need lighting for depth. (See top figure.)

That's a major difference between me and a lot of people in this business. For instance, if I'm shooting a congressman, I'll look for the American flag and set the shot up so it's in front of him and he is to one side of it. It's a neat trick because it gives your correspondent or your producer a place to hide.

If I'm shooting an officer of a company or mayor or councilman, and the interview is in his or her office, I will do two things. I'll try to set the camera far away from him to reduce his intimidation factor. I'll put the camera out in the hallway and use the door jamb, the door knob in the foreground.

It makes perfect sense because that person is the official; he's the office guy in your piece. If you're doing a minute and a half, that's fine. If you're doing five minutes, that's fine, because every time you come back to that shot, you know he's the

A. "There's always something that gives you a feel for where you are. In the hospital, being examined before surgery—a scale, of course."

B. Gordon Liddy tells Ira Silverman all about Watergate. Ira is hidden behind the dark left edge of the frame. The conversation feels private.

Through the doorway, off center, Farkas and the surgeon.

official person. Whether you know that he's the mayor or not may escape you, but you know he's the official person because you see the door jamb. I also have the beauty of the camera being twenty-five, thirty, fifty feet away from him. I'll compress the shot so that the door knob falls out of focus, but you still know what it is. I want to know that you're the guy in the office. I want to know that the door knob is in front of you. I want to know that the flag is in front of you. I want to know that the jail bars are in front of you. Not behind you. If you put in a foreground, your subject might say, "What the hell are you doing?" Or your correspondent might say, "What the hell are you doing?" And they'll smile and they'll laugh a little bit. But, you've gained something—the camera is out of the room; they're that much more at ease.

Positioning for Conversation

Positioning for conversation is the fourth hallmark. Interviews are meant to be conversations. How many times have we said, "We just want to have a conversation," and as soon as the camera turns on, the person becomes a politician? I want a conversation. I want to know that somebody is talking to somebody—that it's not just a sound bite. So, that's one of the things I set up.

Now, take body positioning. Think of how you talk to each other in a bar or at a lunch counter. That's right—sideways, body facing forward, head turned to your friend or anybody else you shouldn't be with.

That's conversational and confidential. Try the same thing with your interviewees. Put your camera ninety degrees away from the desk. Ask them to turn their face toward the camera but not their body. Their natural inclination will be to swivel their chair to you (that's because they've seen too much TV). Be adamant; don't let them do it.

If you don't believe me, try it yourself. Sit at a bar; talk to the person on the stool next to you (you can even try this in your kitchen). Then sit at a desk and talk straight forward. You'll see: different body language, different conversation; less tense, more relaxed. It works with politicians and commoners.

"With my wife and our teenage son. This shot is stacked the way I like it, so there's no dead space between us."

Speaking Quietly

Whisper. Although not as recognizable as the other hallmarks Farkas always employs; he regularly asks his interviewees to hold it down. Hints you can pass on to your reporter: Ask the subject to talk lower, almost whisper if you must. Again, try it yourself. It's relaxing; you're not trying to project. The quieter you speak, the closer to the truth you get. Ask the subject to explain the answer as if he were talking to a bunch of first graders. Your subjects are used to seeing interviews on the six o'clock news where people make statements, mini speeches for the camera. You want to get them out of that. You want a conversation. Don't let them get away with words like "consequently." Interrupt, start them over. I'm in first grade; speak to me, simplify for me.

Don't just say we're going to have a conversation. We're going to have a quiet conversation. Everybody is looking for their fifteen seconds and will project when the camera is on. Stop them, quiet them down. It's not too far-fetched to suggest they almost whisper. That forces everybody to lean closer. Something happens. It gives the person who's talking to you the sense that they're confiding in you rather than talking to you.

Be the devil's advocate in an interview, both the hard-nosed ones and the supporting witness ones. Even warn your subjects, when the circumstances warrant, what you're doing. For example, tell the government prosecutor you think the triple ax murderer is a nice guy, a softy at heart. You will be paid back with passion in their answers.

While recording the whisper, be careful to make sure your sound levels are correct. The use of sound is hardly unique to Ray Farkas's work, but he emphasizes the creative use of environmental sound. Good sound will carry a bad picture, but a good picture won't carry bad sound. Every story we ever tell, every room, every building, every field, has its own signature sound—a ticking clock, the click of a keyboard, running water—if only we'd listen. That tells you something; it gives you a sense of where you are. It also punctuates the story.

Mixed together, these hallmarks create an environment open and conducive to capturing magic moments of conversation—moments that carry the heart of the story. Farkas's interviews are as much about the environment in which the interviewees exist as the interviewees themselves. Farkas's lack of intrusion allows the interviewees to remain comfortable in their environment by not altering the feel of the space. It is an office, not a small television studio.

We've always had the ability to get the inside story without actually being on the inside. Long lenses and wireless microphones have been with us for a long time. I think a lot of people in the television business are lazy. It's the easiest thing in the world to take the camera and run it up in somebody's face and jam the microphone in there. It's easy that way. But it's just as easy to approach him with the right mindset. Just stand back fifty feet across the street and send your correspondent or producer to the other side of the street with the microphone, which is ten times less intrusive. So you get closer to the truth. In my formulation: If I'm fifty feet away and you're five feet away doing an interview, my shot is forty-five feet more honest than yours because the person's not reacting to the camera as much.

The result is magic. It's all a matter of your approach. If I put the camera fifty feet away, there's probably going to be something that's going to intervene between me and them. And that's great—it's simple magic.

Ira with Bert Gordon in jail. Bert, a pilot, was a major drug smuggler—until he got caught. From *Ira's People*, a mix of crime and humor, that was originally broadcast on Court TV in 1999.

The rewards of shooting interviews with this method are evident in the moments that make a Ray Farkas project memorable. The value of a Farkas interview is in the content. What makes the content unique is the little things.

Television is a medium that can convey small truths and small moments much better than any other medium. Television can do something that newspapers, magazines, and print media can never do, which is capture the small moments. It's the moment when a person reveals himself in a small way.

It happens when most of us turn our cameras off. "All right, we got what we came for, let's get out of here." And the person that we're interviewing turns to his assistant or somebody else and says something remarkably honest and unexpected. Even if we were recording that by accident, more often than not we throw it away because we were looking for the big moment.

We're worried about tomorrow's headlines. Will we have the big story too? Yet that lost moment is more valuable than the hard facts pulled from the interview. It's something revealing about the person's character. The anchorman can always do the headlines and the lead-in.

We are still afraid of open space, of quiet, of rustling papers and room tone. We are afraid of pictures that make you look, make you squint, and say: "Did I see what I thought I saw, hear what I thought I heard?" We live in fear we've missed what the mayor or senator or O.J. said. So, we miss what television—and only television—can convey: a sense, a feel, and, ultimately, an understanding to go where the written word cannot take us.

There are three types of interviews Ray Farkas produces. All attempt to capture conversation rather than data. The thing that I like better than interviews is conversation. In other words, again, eighty-five percent of what we do in interviews is information. Only maybe ten percent is conversational. *His opinions are backed by decades of award-winning work, and he's quick to share his point of view with anyone who asks.*

Interview Types

Make a Talking-head Interview with a Reporter/Producer a Conversation

No matter which way you cut it, news (and documentary) photojournalism is, probably, eighty to ninety percent "talking heads." The stuff you rush through so you can get to the "good stuff"— marching bands, Blue Angel flyovers, sunsets. Which we then, mysteriously, call "B-roll."

In interviews, don't plop the camera down seven feet away—try thirty-seven or seventy-seven feet. Put the camera outside the door or across the room. What you'll get is that wonderfully compressed look—approaching heat waves on a summer road—not the standard six o'clock news, two-dimensional shot.

And, you've lost much of the intimidation factor, that camera-in-the-face that turns regular people into politicians and politicians into monsters . . . all projecting their fifteen seconds of fame (I know, it used to be fifteen minutes).

And, while you're at it, use that door knob or door jamb or trophy or whatever is germane to the subject in the foreground to compose and balance your picture and, incidentally, to give your reporter a part of the frame in which to hide. Try to include a little reporter shoulder in the shot—after all, this is supposed to be a conversation, not a sound bite.

All this gives you the feel that you're eavesdropping—a fly on the wall—which jazzes up the most mundane sound bites. Now you're beginning to make movies, folks. At the movies, people spend $8.50 to suspend their disbelief, to think they're hearing something intimate, hearing something they shouldn't.

Somebody told me after many years, "I know what you do, Farkas. You're a voyeur." And that's really the sense I'm trying to convey. You know you're hearing something that maybe you shouldn't be hearing.

Turn an Interview into a Conversation with Friends

Ninety percent of the talk we get is informational, not attack, not confrontational. So, try setting your subject up with somebody they normally talk to, and let them talk about your subject matter. People will talk to people they know a lot easier than they'll talk to you. We're strangers, and as I like to say, "There ain't nobody stranger than us." We're strangers. We're the evening anchor or the cameraman; we're an intruder in their lives. People will talk to friends and family members much more easily and differently than they talk to us. So, whenever possible, in situations big and little, if I see two people who are talking with each other, I use them to conduct the interview between themselves.

I may have to steer the conversation because people won't normally be talking at that moment about what you want them to talk about. We'll manufacture that conversation, so to speak. I'll ask, "Do you know about whatever subject . . . ? Would you talk about it again for our camera?" If they say yes, and they usually do, I tell them I'm going to put microphones on one or both of them and I'm going to step back across the street. Subtracting yourself for the moment will some- times yield surprising results, nuances, and information you might not get in a standard interview format. This doesn't necessarily replace your interview, but try it first if possible. There will inevi- tably be a few moments of ". . . what do you want us to do?" or just plain uneasiness (this isn't

A. Alex Chadwick of NPR at his listening post on the boardwalk for *Interviews 50 Cents*, a whimsical series originally broadcast on ABC's *Day One* and later sold as a half-hour, 13-part series, to CBS's *Eye on People*.

B. Alex in conversation on the Cape May-Lewes ferry.

C. Chadwick meets his match in Cape May, where *Interviews 50 Cents* originated—sometimes the simplest ideas are the best.

the way they've been trained to think television works). Trust me, it's worth the investment. After the first thirty seconds of embarrassed "We're on TV," they've got nothing else to do but be themselves.

Make a "Man-on-the-Street" on the Street

The purpose of a "man on the street" assignment is to "poll" the general public about a given subject. You go to a downtown street or a mall, anywhere where you think you can get a good variety of people willing to talk and offer opposing opinions on the topic. The most important stuff that we do is the talking heads, and that's the stuff we dismiss most easily. We say, "Let's go get the talking heads done, so we can get some of the good stuff," which we then call B-roll, which should be A-roll. It's all A-roll.

What is the man on the street, other than on the street? Why shouldn't you shoot that through traffic? Why shouldn't you show the environment that you're in? Why shouldn't you shoot from across the street with two people at the bus stop, conversing, and one person saying, "I love it," and the other person saying, "I think you're full of crap, I hated it." It's just another layer. We all do these.

Shoot from far away—say, across the street—through traffic, people, and cars between you. Again, the sense of eavesdropping. You want people to cross through your picture.

A. "My dog Lucky in the window. Again, outside looking in—a feeling of eavesdropping. A simple shot that says, 'I'm not there, someone's waiting for me.'"

B–D. "Three cameras—front, side, behind me—talking to the camera in front, lit by my desk lamp. I was just rambling on about my thoughts."

Ray Farkas's techniques also apply to other staples of the news-gathering business.

The News Conference about the News Conference

Try to resist the urge to yell "Down in front!" to the still man. Try putting your camera behind the row of other cameras, shooting (medium tight) through them so you clearly see the subject but also see those bobbing heads and camera lights, see reporters and photographers. After all, it's a news conference—shoot it like one.

"B-roll." The name B-roll will probably be with us forever, but the letter B *should not convey a second tier or lower-level work.* It's all A-roll, folks. Every picture has a sound and life of its own. If it doesn't, that's why your station loses channel surfers—it all looks generic. No such thing as wallpaper. Every frame counts; every frame has a life and look and sound of its own. Nothing is secondary.

What Is Television to Outspoken Ray Farkas?

Television is . . .

- It is losing audiences.
- It is the last unexplored frontier.
- It should be creative, imaginative, not a haven for the safe and the dull.
- It needs passion, not focus groups and surveys. Trust your own judgment, even if it is bad. Time will sort it out. I'm more interested in the passionate stamp collector than the consummate generalist.
- It is guilty as charged: of being intruders, not recorders.
- It needs conversations, not statements. We must come to listen, to watch. Instead, we come for what we came to hear.

- It is the "medium of impressions"; it is TV journalism, not just journalism.
- It is irresponsible if it tries to be a newspaper; we already have those.
- It must do what other mediums can never do; a sense of time and place.
- It is sloppy thinking in the field and "saving it in editing."
- It is B-roll when it should all be A-roll.
- It is in your face when it should be eavesdropping.
- It is believing you're important, taking yourself seriously, when there should be humor. We are not the story. We are not bringing down tablets.
- Yes, it is talking heads—and they are a great adventure. They should be shot with a sense of proportion (wide/medium/tight) to their importance.
- It is saying, "Don't look into the camera," when that it usually the most interesting and certainly the honest shot.
- It is understand that every picture has a life of its own; there are no neutral shots. Even symbolism should be interestingly shot.
- It is tripods and wireless mics. If it isn't, it will look like the world of camcorders. How do you differentiate your 11 o'clock news from *America's Funniest Home Videos?*
- It is framing with a sense of adventure.
- It is framing with a sense of proportion.
- It is framing always with a sense of place.
- It is composition

Trust Serendipity: On Location with Ray Farkas

Shooting with Ray Farkas is making fortunate discoveries by accident. Yet, for Farkas, his years of experience tell him these discoveries will happen more often than not if he shoots using his techniques. So there, fifty feet away, on the long end of a locked-off lens, looking over a door knob, is the camera, cabled to a monitor in Ray Farkas's lap.

I tell photographers, once we get the shot set, they can go out and have a cup of coffee. Just turn the camera on and go have a cup of coffee, because I'm never going to change that shot because that's the shot I want when they say or do whatever it is that I want on that shot. Cameramen have it easy working for me once they get over the idea that I've taken over half their life and their soul.

I've never held a camera in my life except when they've been thrown at me by angry cameramen. I once had a camera thrown at me; he said, "Here, you shoot it," and pitched a heavy film camera at me because I was telling him how I wanted it shot. Luckily, it had a soft landing in the field we were in. Cameras have always been a mystery to me. I don't know cameras; I don't know anything about equipment. All I know is, I know what I like on my monitor. I'll look at the monitor and I'll say, "Ooh." I mean, I make sounds that are better than sex when I see a shot that I love. I don't know how many camerapeople I've said that to, into their ear.

When I work with a cameraman for the first time, he'll say, "We need to get cutaways and then we need a reverse." And I'll say, "No, you don't need a sequence. One shot does everything." One shot pretty much covers all. It's easy.

So, you're on assignment, you've got a story to deliver, and there's a deadline. The shot is set up and the camera rolls . . . and rolls . . . and rolls. Many people would think this an irresponsible waste of videotape with no hope of any useful story content. And the camera rolls. . . . Your intuition, built on years of journalistic study, is screaming, "This is crazy, we'll never get anything." Farkas knows better.

It's wonderful, and then you just let them go and you don't know where it's going to go. It's a roll of the dice when you know you've got something. I said, "This is really great!" a number of times that I've come to regret. It's hard to say that I know that I've got it. But I get a general sense that I know. I've set up an interview with a picture and a frame that pleases me. So, when a person says something even halfway interesting, I say, "I've got it," because everything is right. I love the surprise of finding out that I've got it.

Farkas lets his stories breathe. He allows his stories to be themselves so that the stories evolve on their own. It might have taken a few more moments, more patience, more faith in the story, but the end result is a story that has its own pace, its own truth, and a value that's timeless.

Now, with his surgery behind him, Ray Farkas is back out conducting interviews and producing projects with his unique vision and passion for the industry.

Television news is often good journalism, but seldom good television. It generally fails to do what it alone can do—convey touch and feel and context. It has become a formula: wide, medium, tight, helicopter aerial of the flood, zoom in to mother crying. Stick figures and illustrations rather than pictures with a life of their own.

Reporters and producers and editors and crews have to be open to the possibilities of symbolism—attentive to small sounds, aware of the human face and voice.

Visually, your pictures should match the mystery you're unraveling for your audience and yourself. Don't ever lose the wonder of what you're doing. Try not to condescend to your audience. They're smarter than you think, and, besides, we all love a puzzle, as long as you show us the solution.

That staple of our business, the "talking head," comes in endless varieties and is endlessly fascinating. Treat it with the awe and glee of a beautiful sunset.

"... 'Cause they poked and they probed and they pushed and they pinched every inch of my old sorry carcass.*

And they sent me home mate, and I'm feeling just great, like a state-of-the-art is Ray Farkas."

– Lyric by Phillip Lerman

Take 2: Composition

No matter what the medium—canvas, celluloid, video—and no matter what the format—4 × 3 or 16 × 9—there is composition. Great composition engulfs the viewer in the photographer's selection of space from the real world. Composition is about space within a frame.

Composing a shot is the arrangement of visual elements within the aspect ratio of the frame.

Composition should enhance the intended communication by arranging elements within the frame to advance the story and tell more about the scene. Whether you fill the frame with details, lead the viewer to look at a certain portion by leading lines, or leave plenty of empty space (negative space), it all communicates something. It's the photographer's job to decide and select what is communicated. In addition to telling the story, shots should be composed so that they are interesting and pleasing to watch.

While pleasing composition varies greatly with individual taste, there are some basic guidelines that can provide a starting point. The most frequently discussed rule of composition is "The Rule of Thirds."

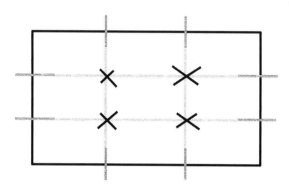

The Rule of Thirds.

The sun centered in the frame.

The sun positioned with The Rule of Thirds.

The Rule of Thirds

In The Rule of Thirds (illustrated on this and the next page), the frame is divided vertically and horizontally into imaginary thirds. You simply place elements in the frame along either of the lines and/or the intersections of the lines.

Apply The Rule of Thirds to your favorite images in this book. Many will naturally fall into this formula. The Rule of Thirds should be a starting point for composition but, like all rules, it is meant to be broken when you fully understand the craft.

Head Room and Lead Room

These terms refer to the space around your subject. Framing someone dead center in the picture is rarely good composition. Reducing head room—the space above the subject's head—fills the frame nicely and tends to force the image

The left vertical and lower horizontal lines dissect the train tunnel, and the glass ceiling starts just above the top horizontal line using The Rule of Thirds.

The woman's eye falls at the intersection of the left vertical and top horizontal line in The Rule of Thirds.

into The Rule of Thirds. Likewise, allowing for lead room—the space in front of the subject—also tends to force the frame into The Rule of Thirds, making a better composition. (See figures A through C on next page.)

Angles in Composition

Angles add the perception of depth to a shot. A television screen has only two dimensions, width and height. By shooting on an angle, we get to see the depth of the subject. Only by shooting the building on an angle do we get to see its true shape. (See figures D and E on next page.)

By shooting the man on an angle, we can get a better sense of the shape and character of his face (see figures A and B on page 129). The vertical position of the camera can have a subtle influence over how the viewer will perceive the subject. When the camera is at the same eye line as the subject, it appears to viewers that they are on par or equal to the subject. By raising the camera and pointing down, the man's stature diminishes, he seems less important. By lowering the camera and shooting up, the man appears larger and more important (see figures C through H on page 129).

Frame Within a Frame

By using foreground elements to frame your subject, the shot becomes more interesting, shows more information in relationship to the subject, and directs the viewer's eye (see figures A through D on page 130).

Having a person framed in the center of the image (A) is not so good. Tilt down to lose head room (B) then pan left for more lead room (C).

D. Flat.

E. Angled.

Leading Lines

Another way to direct the viewer's eye through composition is to use leading lines. The train station is a classic example. The lines naturally lead to where the train will enter or exit. Many other subjects will have natural leading lines that will help in composition; just make sure the lines lead where you want the viewer to look (see figures E and F on page 130).

A. Flat.

B. Angled.

C. Eye height.

D. High angle.

E. Low angle.

F. Eye height.

G. High angle.

H. Low angle.

A.–D. Four examples of a frame within a frame.

E., F. Leading lines.

A photographer's sense of composition is unique to the individual. You are creating, composing, and capturing your interpretation of the world. You are the sole author and artist of your images, so make them worth watching. Strive, in every shot, to show a dimension to your subject that is unique and speaks clearly and beautifully to you. Make your images memorable, arresting, and powerful in their communication as well as their beauty. Great photographers can elevate the most common object to a work of art by showing us (composing) their vision in a way we might never have imagined.

CHAPTER 8

Corky Scholl

Feature Stories—B-Roll,
Sequencing, and Great
Moments

Corky Scholl
Photojournalist

KUSA-TV, 9News, Denver
NPPA Ernie Crisp Television News Photographer of the Year, 2005

T*he old bed frame and dresser parked in the yard start to make a strange sound. It's either electricity or a few bugs* [bzzzzz]. *Another hot summer day winds down as Paul Upsol investigates. Stalking the unknown in his backyard, the sound gets louder as he approaches. A few insects are going to perrish today and Upsol is the executioner. Armed with a can of Raid, he peels back the green canvas covering the furniture to take a look. Forty thousand bees stare back.*

Backpeddling like Roy Scheider's character in Jaws*, he makes a quick retreat. If bees were sharks, "We're gonna need a bigger boat." Call in a professional, call the media.*

The professional is beekeeper Larry Brown who has a bee farm in Larkspur, Colorado. The media is reporter Andrew Resnik and photojournalist Corky Scholl. They're assigned to do a feature story about Paul's backyard bees and Larry's collection of the hive.

Now, in a full bee suit, Corky peers through a mesh hat as he sets up his camera. Everyone else stays back as Scholl and Brown approach the bees. Larry lights a smoker. Squeezing the accordion-like contraption, he moves closer. When a hive is threatened, guard bees release a phero-mone—it's an "alarm odor" that alerts the middle-aged bees in the hive (the ones with the most venom) to defend the hive and attack. Smoke dulls the guard bees' receptors, so they don't send out their alarm. It's worked for thousands of years; let's hope it still works today.

The smoke hangs in the calm air, stinging Scholl's eyes. Better the smoke than the bees landing on the net stretched

EQUIPMENT

Sony DVCAM DSR500WS camera

Canon 22×8 lens

Anton Bauer Ultralight camera light

Carbon fiber Gitzo tripod with Sachtler 18p fluid head

Anton Bauer Dionic lithium batteries

Wide-Eye-Century cap, zoom-through and/or converter

Lectrosonic wireless UHF UCR 201/adjustable frequency

Sennheiser shotgun microphone with windsock

Shure VP64 stick mic

Sony ECM-77B lavalier

Camera rain cover

Light kit: Omni, Tota, and Lowell Pro lights; soft box, gels, scrims, dimmers, umbrellas, stands, clamps, Westcott sunlight/silver reflector

A. Scholl puts on a bee suit to get close enough to shoot without getting stung.

B. An extreme close-up of bees and the honeycomb.

c. An extreme close-up of a bee on a bed frame.

in front of his face. With gloved hands, he brushes away the bees so they won't get caught between his eye and the viewfinder. Through the lens, it's just between the bees and Scholl. He sets a shot that establishes the environment: Bees are starting to fly outside the hive. He doesn't just zoom in; everything moves—tripod left, right, up, down—composing shots as he goes. Wide, medium, tight is a progression of story, not just a higher focal length. As Scholl gets closer, the buzzing gets louder. Sounding like a weed whacker, beekeeper Larry starts up a gas-powered vacuum cleaner. The easiest way to collect bees is through the suction hose. Bees by the score disappear through the black tube as they're sucked off the face of the honeycomb.

Rotating the focus ring to the closest setting, Scholl moves his camera another foot closer, then another until the image goes soft. An inch at a time, he backs up until the image is sharp again. This is minimum focus for his zoom. He's as close as he can get without going to macro. Macro allows the camera to focus closer, but you can't zoom through it and keep focus. So, while you may be close to the subject, you won't be able to make it larger in the frame. At Scholl's current setting, the full zoom works and he can get very, very close. Scholl's progression of shots has gone from wide, to medium, to close to extreme close-up (ECU). His camera is used as a tool for discovery. Scholl is making a "photographic study" of the bees and their journey.

Shooting out of the bee suit makes it harder to shoot, but it's worth it because you can get super close-up shots of the bees, where the bees fill the entire screen. Because bees are ominous; bees are scary. The closer you can get, the bigger you can make them, the more you can kind of feel their ominous presence. Getting so close to the bees that you can stick a microphone right up into them as they are swarming really helps. Audio of bees buzzing is a very compelling element of the story. The story wouldn't be as much fun to watch without the sound—just hearing those bees buzzing.

This is a perfect project for Corky Scholl; much of his influences come from nature photography. I read a lot of photography books, and I look at a lot of nature photography and study still photog-

A wide shot with all the elements—a bee walking on the lens, the beekeeper, and a woman watching from behind a screened window.

raphy. I'm very interested in that; that's kind of what got me into the profession. I think the more images that you look at, the more great photography that you get stuck in your brain, ingrained inside of your head, the more you'll be able to kind of imitate that when you're out shooting.

My shots have a lot of sunsets and a lot of golden light. Someone once said several of my shots look like they could be on a postcard. I guess that comes from just looking at postcards and studying: "Okay, what makes this picture great? What makes this such a great picture that it's plastered on a postcard and sold to hundreds—thousands—of people?"

I like to just get creative shots, and that's what I love to do. I got in to this profession because I loved composition and loved colorful shots.

The "B-Roll" of Bees

The interviews were recorded earlier—slices of life to punctuate the story. The rest of the story unfolds shot by shot. They are often referred to as B-roll shots, a term Scholl doesn't like—it has secondary, inferior connotations and doesn't describe the story relevance of the images he creates. "Relevant video" more aptly addresses the shots' story content. However, for now "B-roll"—steeped in film history—is internationally accepted.

The term "B-roll" is left over from the days of newsfilm. In editing, two film rolls were made and then married for projection. Separate rolls allowed for dissolves and effects between shots. The A-roll carried all of the narration track, the image, and sound of interviews and reporter stand-ups—all the sync sound and, to a large part, all the story content. The B-roll was made of all the pictures used to illustrate the story, cover the narration track, and any other A-roll portion that needed covering.

Today, depending on where you're working, "B-roll" can refer to any shot needed to cover a story (with a "Just go shoot it" attitude) to the best assignment going. Note: No one gets assigned A-roll. That term died out with videotape and nonlinear editing. Now everything should be "relevant" to story content. When we talk about B-roll here, we are talking about pictures and natural sound, used to illustrate and advance the story, that are not sync sound.

Every shot, every element, in a story should advance that story and take the viewer on a journey. The art of news photography is creating compelling, graphic compositions that communicate environment and emotion. Strung together, they take the viewer on a progression of discovery until the mystery is revealed.

Opening shots establish the context of the story in an arresting visual to captivate the viewers and keep them watching. Closing shots sum up the story's meaning and generally illustrate leaving the story to continue on with life. The cowboy rides into the sunset.

Before you actually go out and shoot, you kind of know generally what kind of shots you're going to need. But then, once you actually get into the environment, that's when the spontaneous

The closing shot: Kid running away—going back home.

creativity really kicks in and you start seeing things.

I decide to structure the story around the process of the guy removing the bees because that's a process that has a beginning, middle, and an end. It's a natural story.

Unfortunately, we weren't able to stay until the end of his collecting the bees because of our deadline. I still needed a closing shot. A kid came in and asked the beekeeper what he was doing. I had my wireless microphone on him, so when he told the kid to run away, I had the audio and the kid running. So, we just ended on the kid running away, which was a funny closing shot. I think it turned out to be much better than the guy loading up the beehive and driving away—more of an ending for the neighborhood.

Sequences "Tell" the Story

Scholl selects what the viewer will see. While each one of his shots is unique, he's also calculating how they'll cut together. He's planning how to advance the story in editing by shooting sequences. A sequence is more than one shot used to communicate an idea. The "telling" of the story happens through sequences. Spiced with emphasis and punctuation, sequences tell the story; they break down real life into a language that can be visually told. Think of them as visual sentences. Through a progression, they take the viewer on a journey from the story's beginning until the end.

The basic news sequence is "action/reaction"—illustrated in the figures below. In a story about bald eagles in Alaska, you might shoot an eagle flying from a nest—the action. How special that moment might be can be captured in the expression of a boy; his "reaction" gives the story a human element.

While action/reaction can be captured in one shot, in this case by panning from the eagle to the boy, it becomes a sequence when two or more shots are used to communicate the story. By creating a sequence, you can use only the best moment of the eagle and the best reaction from the boy to tell your story, leaving the pan and other, less interesting moments on the edit room floor.

The phrase Leave it on the edit room floor *means edit out and discard the footage. It is left over from film editing when the strip of film was literally thrown out.*

An action/reaction example.

Sequencing: Shooting a News Story

In our "Alaskan Bald Eagle" story, we know where a nest is located. It's a well-known viewing area and sightseers come from all over the world to watch the eagles soar above the trees. But, funding for the refuge has fallen off and the endangered birds could find themselves in trouble without the rangers and veterinary staff to oversee the park.

The following diagram shows how you might shoot this story from an eagle's eye view with camera positions and angles, as well as the corresponding storyboard illustrations of the shots.

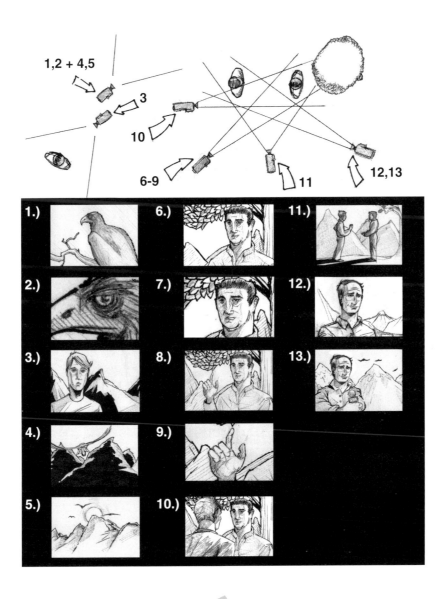

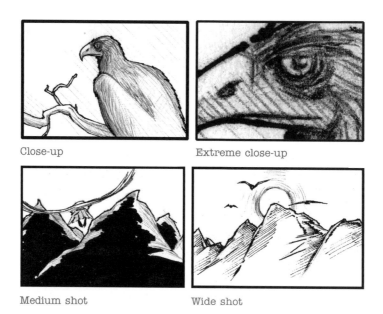

Close-up

Extreme close-up

Medium shot

Wide shot

Shot 1

When you first get to a location, shoot the thing that might change first. In this case, the eagle might fly away and you'd lose your story.

While shots 1,2 and 4,5 are shown from one position (see figure above), in reality you're changing positions and lens settings to get the best shots you can. You're also likely to shoot and use many more than four shots. Keep your shotgun mic on to capture natural sound of the eagles screeching.

Shot 2

Start getting closer as you work. Go all the way to extreme close-ups. Do a photographic study of your subject. With any luck, you'll get them flying from the branch and circling the area.

Shot 3

A boy reacts to the eagles as they fly away—"reaction" shot. This part requires instinct, a sense of the story, and some knowledge of human nature to know the right time to leave the "action" and get the "reaction" shot. If an eagle is doing amazing aerobatics, you stay on the eagle no matter how many "Oohs" and "Ahhs" the boy is making. There will be the right moment—when you've shot enough eagles and they're still flying around—when you can change your shot to get the reaction.

Shot 4

Look for opening shots, something that will establish the story. Eagles flying over the mountains would be a good establisher. Your strongest, most visual shot will likely lead the story. You want the viewers to stay on the couch and watch the rest of your story.

Shot 5

Look for a closing shot—maybe it's the eagle flying into the sunset. It should be something that finishes your visual story.

Shot 6

Set up for the interview. Consider the background: Will it change? Does it help tell the story? The interviewee may be on screen longer than any other image in your story, so make the setting great. Work to put elements in the frame that help to communicate the story, such as the eagle's nest in the tree behind the ranger.

Listen to the interview, not only to ensure good audio quality but also to get clues for additional shots that will make your story even better.

Shot 7

As the interview develops, you may want to zoom in for a closer shot, either for emotional impact to isolate the interviewee or to give the editor another option. Again, instinct, a sense of the story, and some knowledge of human nature will guide your decisions on when to zoom in.

Shot 8

Watch for repetitive action in anything you shoot. The ranger pointing to the eagle every few sentences is part of his personality. Keep this motion in mind for the end of the interview.

Shot 9

When the interview is over and you've got what you need, the reporter should continue discussing the story. Use this time to get a close-up of the repetition—in this case, the ranger pointing.

Shot 10

Move the camera to an OTS (over-the-shoulder) shot to show the relationship of the reporter to the interviewee and provide a medium shot of the interview setting. This shot might be used to introduce your subject.

Shot 11

Move the camera and frame a wide shot of the interview setting. This is the shot that graphically establishes the location of the interview.

Shot 12

Move to a shot of the reporter, the "reverse." If he is going to ask a question on camera, this is the shot to use. As they talk, just get general reactions from the reporter. Wait for those natural moments as he checks his notes and looks back up. Try to avoid a nodding head, although sometimes that's all you'll get.

Talk to the reporter about the interview. Was anything new said that should be shot? If so, continue shooting with the new information garnered from the interview.

Shot 13

If there is a reporter stand-up to do, discuss what will be said and look for a backdrop that supports the reporter's commentary.

Now you're done shooting this story. In Chapter 15, we'll cover the editing that needs to be done for the Alaskan eagle story.

Scholl's First Shots

From the beginning, Scholl's passion for photography led him to a career in television news. It was the central focus of his life and remains so today. When I was in high school, I liked photography. I liked the artistic aspect of it. I liked taking pictures and experimenting with The Rule of Thirds and color and all of that.

I decided that going the route of broadcast news would be a way to do photography every day and get paid for it. So, after high school, I went to North Central University, a small, private college in Minneapolis that had a broadcast journalism department.

After college, I started my career at a small cable station in the Minneapolis area. They did news for thirteen suburbs, and so it's kind of a small-market type of deal, even though it was in Minneapolis. I enjoyed the job a lot, but it wasn't where I wanted to end in my career. After about a year, I decided that I wanted to move on and start looking at the next step.

I'd heard of this guy named Mark Anderson who had won NPPA Television News Photographer of the Year in 1993. He was the chief photographer at KSTP, which was the ABC affiliate in Minneapolis. I e-mailed him and told him about myself and he replied saying I should feel free to send a tape and he would critique it and tell me what kind of stories to have on the résumé tape. And maybe give me some advice on where to go next in my career.

I sent my reel and he watched it and he decided to hire me. I got a call out of the blue one day and he said, "Hey, this is Mark Anderson," and I kind of got excite. He said, "How would you like a job?" That totally blew me away; I wasn't expecting it. I hadn't even applied for the job and got it.

As a young photographer, to be there with all those talented photographers and so many great people to learn from—you can't really ask for anything more than to be around these great legends in the television photography business. So, I learned a lot and that was a great break.

Hold for Future Release: Time to Do a Story Right

Corky Scholl later joined the staff at KUSA, where he won NPPA's Television News Photographer of the Year in 2005. On his reel is a feature story called "King James." Feature stories offer a more in-depth look at a person or issue in the news. By their nature, feature stories encourage photographers to explore and experiment more. It's a chance to flex their photographic muscles.

At KUSA, there is an aggressive HFR (Hold for Future Release) program. They encourage feature stories with high production value. When there is a story that requires multiple days to capture, the assignment editor schedules the story as a HFR. The photographer and/or reporter who are working on it are set free—without the demands of the assignment desk or the nightly newscast.

This happens only when daily news gathering allows, although every effort is made to facilitate HFR stories. They're the ones you can build a reputation on. These are coveted assignments and shooting days, and are not handed out without careful scrutiny. If they are going to allocate news resources, the final product had better be great, and the "King James" story is.

"King James" *is the story of a musician living in subsidized housing. After living on the streets, he decided he wanted to make a CD to raise money for the homeless—not too far from homeless himself. Scholl found King James and followed his life and music. From the alleys he once lived in to the recording studio,*

A. In the alley where he once lived, wide-angle composition and leading lines point to King James—a summary of his environment.

B. King James on his harmonica; he knows the blues.

C. King James realizing his dream through music.

D. King James in a shot that's a good example of frame-within-a-frame composition.

Scholl spent twelve nights shooting this feature story. Several of those nights were scheduled as HFR, but the rest were shot on personal time—hours well spent on a story Scholl was committed to.

Make Stories Happen: What the Best TV News Photographers Do

They don't wait for great stories to come to them; they go out and make great stories happen. They're looking for great stories, and they take initiative on the stories that they shoot. The best photographers are the ones with great attitudes, who think, "Every story is a challenge; every story has a potential to be a great story." They're always thinking of ways to bring the story to the next level.

It's being willing to make the calls and set up stories yourself. If you're out in the field and there are things happening and you see somebody that you got to get on tape, don't hesitate to just do the interview yourself. If you don't see a reporter around to do the interview for you, you need to be able to just do that yourself. Ask the questions yourself and get compelling sound and great moments without anybody kind of leading you around and showing you what to do. Just take the initiative and do it. More and more, the jobs of photographer and reporter are going to overlap, and you're going to have one-man bands even in large markets.

For me, it's important to take ownership of my stories, and that's what's going to advance the story to the next level. If you're just relying on the reporter to do a good job, relying on them to do all the work setting up stories, then you're not taking ownership.

The best stories that I've done are stories that I've just gone out myself and done. The interviews: Set up the interviews, got on the phone myself, made the calls, talked to these people, and really got to know them. I really invested all the time and knew what the story was about, rather than just getting into my car with the reporter, listen to some music on the way there, and then get there and ask, "What's the story about?"

It's important to really be involved in the process even when you're working with a reporter. Talk to them when you're driving to your story about what the story's going to be about. Talk about how you're going to visualize the story, what kind of shots you'll need to tell the story.

When you've done enough stories yourself—or you set them up and structured the story yourself and told the story yourself—when you've done enough of those, then you kind of know how to find the juice of the story, how to structure a story. Then you can talk with the reporter about that. Then you can start talking more intelligently in a more informed way with the reporter about how he could structure the story and make the story really compelling.

It's Not Just Shots: It's Moments

I shoot wide, medium, tight, super tight with everything. I just make sure that, every time, I switch the camera angle. I like to get a couple of really wide shots that kind of draw your eye into the picture somewhere. Then a lot of tight shots, close-ups. Tight shots are more personal; there seems to be more emotion in a tight shot. I'll always be looking for the "moments" because that's the most important thing in photojournalism. It's not your sequencing skills, it's not your beauty shots; it's the moments that you capture. The Berlin Wall coming down is going to be more compelling than the greatest sunset that you've ever shot.

Whatever the shot, it's important to anticipate that something might happen. Be aware of the environment as you wait for that moment to happen in front of the lens. You're trying to "be there" with the lens, sitting in front of the moment that's about to happen.

You always try to anticipate when a great moment's going to happen, and you really never know. But, there are clues that something is going to happen. We've done a lot of stories lately, where we're at an army base and soldiers are coming home to meet their wives and families. You know there'll be a great moment at some point where the soldiers run up and hug their wives. That's where the juice of story's going to be, in those moments of the reunion.

You do want to get all of the establishing shots and the nice tight shots of the flag waving and people waving. You want to work hard to have all of that, but you have to realize that that's not what's going to make your story most compelling. The most compelling part of the story is their emotional reunion. So, you're always waiting for that moment. Just use your senses and know something's about to happen and be prepared. A lot of time is spent just waiting.

In television news, it's hard because you have the daily grind and the expectations to feed the beast on a daily basis. So, you're always going, going, going, and, really, to get great moments,

Beekeeper Larry Brown in his bee suit.

you have to just stop and look around and be aware of your surroundings and just be prepared. Maybe roll for five minutes on a shot waiting for that moment to happen. You have to sit there for five minutes, but when that moment happens—that's the most important thing. It's going to make your story better and it will pay off.

A moment doesn't have to be just an emotional thing like a family reunion. It could be a space shuttle blasting off—that's a moment. Then the reaction of the people as they're watching—that's another moment. It doesn't even have to be human emotion. The *March of the Penguins* has great moments. It's penguins, not people, but still you can relate to it somehow. Still you come away feeling something because they've worked hard and captured great moments.

So, a moment can be defined in a lot of different ways. In nature photography, it might be an eagle swooping down into its nest to feed its chicks. Always try to capture the moment—try to capture something that will connect with the viewers, not just fancy edits and beautiful shots.

That makes the shot relevant, not just generic B-roll. The "moments" give life to your shots, punctuation to your sequences, and impact to your stories.

Behind the netting of his bee cap, Corky goes the extra mile to get those great moments, taking the time to place his camera where others wouldn't. The extra mile puts him closer to the bees, closer to the sound—closer to the story.

I try and get as close as possible. Especially with the bees or any animal, you want to get so close that it's closer than somebody could get in real life. That way, watching becomes an experience because they can't just go outside and see bees that close. So, you're delivering something special. Delivering a shot of a bee that fills the entire screen, and it's practically coming out into their living rooms.

That's the value of a good close-up shot—that's relevant.

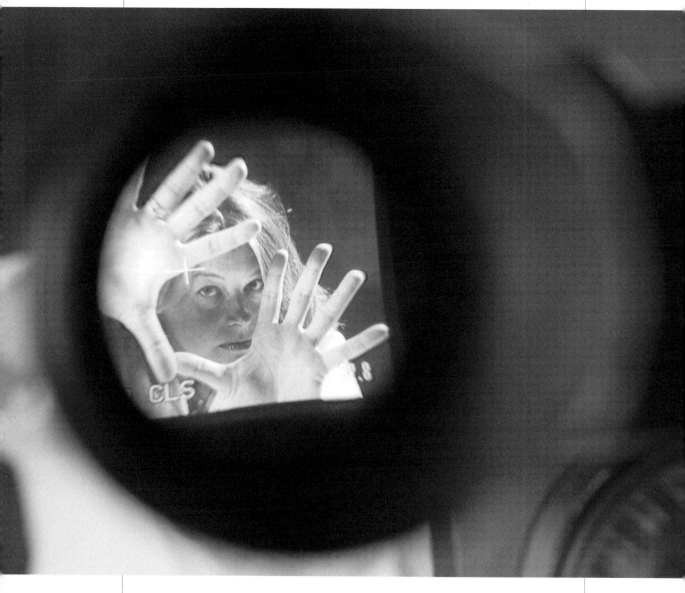

CHAPTER 9

Lisa Berglund

Truth and Filmmaking—
Objective and Subjective
Camerawork

Lisa Berglund

Freelance Photojournalist and Editor

NPPA Ernie Crisp Television News Photographer of the Year, 1995

"You must do the thing you think you cannot do." Eleanor Roosevelt's quote has become my professional motto. –LB

The old Toyota SUV bounces down a dirt road in Huambo Province, Angola. The chrome hood ornament centers the drive, far away from the edges of the road. Villagers stay to the center, too; the closer you venture to the edge, the closer you are to death.

The road, bordered by unusable cropland, is the only safe place to tread. Lisa Berglund knows this, too; it's why she's here—Not for the dangers but for a story of hope. This is a new assignment for Berglund, now a world away from her life as one of the top photojournalists in TV news. She's the only woman to have ever won the NPPA Ernie Crisp Television News Photographer of the Year award.

The Toyota pulls to a stop not far from what looks like a large cement match ready to be lit.

"Perigo Mina."

White letters against a red tip scare the farmers away. If they can't read, the skull and crossbones clearly tell the story. And for those who can read English, "Danger Mines" may be the last thing

EQUIPMENT

Sony BVW-D600 camera with Fujinon lens

Sachtler Speedlock tripod and head

Anton Bauer batteries, charger, and Gold Mount belt pack

Lectrosonic UCR 195 UHF wireless receiver and transmitter

Lectrosonic UM 195B and UM 400 wireless transmitters

Lectrosonic UH 195 and UH 400A wireless cube transmitters

Lectrosonic UCR 201 wireless receiver

Sennheiser ME-88 microphone

2- and 4-bank Kino Flo Diva lights

Lowel Omni, Rifa, and Pro-Lite lights

Anton Bauer Ultralight 2 with dichroic filter

Photoflex 42-inch Lite Disc reflecter

Sony ECM-77B condenser microphone, PVM 8020 color video monitor, VTR playback adaptor, and headphones

Angevine Optics wide-angle lens

Canon XL2 digital video camera

Century Optics wide-angle lens

Some families walked two-and-a-half days to reach a World Vision food distribution center in Lunge, Angola, often passing through fields of land mines—"Perigo Mina."

they'll read. It's estimated that more than eight million land mines have been left in the fields from thirty years of civil conflict.

Berglund looks down from her seat, her first step outside the vehicle could be her last or, worse, the beginning of a nightmare that would last a lifetime. The nightmare takes no imagination; its living testimony is scarred on a crippled boy hobbling on his homemade crutch. The missing leg and potholes blown in the road prove the devastation created by land mine explosions.

Lisa is here to look closer. The land mines have not only injured scores of men, women, and children; they've made the farmland unworkable. This is a famine. More people will die from starvation than from the mines. Berglund steps out on the dirt.

The skull smiles: if not her, someone else, if not now, sometime later. Not the odds or comfort level Berglund likes to operate under. But this is her story; she's chosen to tell it, and she'll do it her way.

Berglund left her comfortable Seattle office to come on a famine tour that will take her from Angola to Niger, West Africa. The video she's shooting is called From Locusts to Land Mines *and illustrates the battle her new employer, World Vision, is fighting, to ease hunger in these desperate villages.*

As I got out of the truck and began setting up my camera, I could see a family off in the distance. They were working in the field, trying to make enough money to feed their family. They were working in a field, in a field of land mines. Something took hold of me at that moment. I wasn't sure if my friends, my family, or the World Vision donors would ever really understand the desperation, how hunger can drive you to do unimaginable things, and how the people of Angola and Niger were risking their lives, to help save the next generation.

From the minefields to small villages, to the faces of children barely alive—Berglund captures the problem. Every image in her black-and-white viewfinder is a heartbreaker. For the harder images, she keeps her eye to the viewfinder, not wanting to spend too much time in full color; this will be hard enough to watch later. Even images of the relief effort are difficult; there's hope—but only so much.

In stark contrast to the pain and suffering are moments of happiness that transcend daily hardships, Moments that jump through the lens in bittersweet clarity. A child laughs, about what we can only imagine, but the laughter is as real and cleansing as that of any child back home. A mother beams an ecstatic smile as she receives food for her family. True joy caught on tape. Berglund's video will be used to raise funds for the relief effort. That's why it's so important and why she's traveled so far.

Berglund's style is based solidly in her photojournalist roots, even though this is not a news story. Since leaving local news, much of her work has had a journalistic feel to it. There is honesty in her method of visual storytelling. From Locusts to Land Mines *will be a story told by Berglund. There's no shy, passive observer shoot from the shoulder work here.*

This is active storytelling, taking accountability for the honesty of the story. This is Lisa Berglund's vision; she's sharing her understanding of the story through her eyes. Her take on this story will be communicated and visually portrayed differently than anyone else's. In the end, the information will be the same—the dead, the maimed, the starving, the relief effort. Numbers, dates, places—all facts, all the same. But the experience of being there, the moments that move Berglund to press "record" and move closer—all are unique to her and her story alone.

Pride and determination carry Berglund through this story, from place to place, shot to shot, building sequences as she goes. Through intuition, skill, and luck, her decisions on camera placement will a moment later capture the action and emotion that define her work. It's like she knows the future, where the best shot is likely to be and what action will happen there before it does. This is not black magic or some form of clairvoyance. Thinking ahead and planning her next camera position is what puts Lisa Berglund's camera where her heart is—deeply in touch with the flow of the story.

In another village of starving children with skin stretched painfully thin over tiny bones, Berglund shoots a woman stirring a meal meant only for animals. It's the husks of grain that would normally be thrown away. Tonight, it's dinner. Flies pester infants too weak to blink or move away. Their pain is exhausting.

Berglund again works "ahead of the moment." In a wide shot that conveys the desperate conditions, her composition leads to the stirring bowl. The motion is repetitious. This is the action that can be cut on. It's intuition that will tell her how long to hold the wide shot and if anything new is coming. Quickly, she moves to a close-up of the woman's hand stirring the grain. Three rotations should be enough. Back out to a shot of the woman's face and her interaction with her children. Which handful will go to her? Which one will help keep her child alive? Through Berglund's lens, we watch the gut-wrenching decisions, turned "matter of fact" with each drop of food.

Throughout the shoot, Berglund changes shooting methods to fit the circumstances, often moving close enough for the children to touch the lens. At this range, it is very personal. No long lens from across the room can capture this kind of intimacy. You've got to be in the mother's space—see what she sees. From this point of view, her images are very subjective. It's a first-person view of the subject.

Viewing Different Points of Truth

If you compare visual language to literary voice, a subjective camera represents first person and illustrates the vision of "I," a personal experience shown as the main

In Niger, West Africa, Zeinabou Sita makes a meager meal for her family.

147

A "first-person" close-up of parents and their children at Bailundo Central Hospital in Angola. Today the children will receive measles, polio, DPT, yellow fever, and BCG (for tuberculosis) vaccines.

subject sees it. As the camera moves away from a direct depiction of an individual's visual experience and swings away from that person's eye line, it illustrates less what "I" might experience and more what someone else, "You," might experience. In literary terms: second person. In television news, this view is often the point of view for standard interviews. The camera is close to the interviewee, but her attention is drawn off-camera toward the reporter.

As the camera continues to move further away from the subject and out of eye line, it becomes more "objective," moving from the visual second person to third person: "They." This third-person point of view is as objective as you can get. You are a distant observer. Camera angles, lens selection, composition, and lighting create the gray area between completely subjective and almost completely objective—almost. No image can be completely objective and removed from the experience of the photographer.

As photojournalists, we capture our subjects through our individual set of preferences that influence each frame we shoot. Preferences and variables in the filmmaking/newsgathering process make each shot, sequence, and story unique.

Lisa Berglund is well versed in film technique; it's the language that let's her tell her story. Mastering that language in the world of news is what makes great photojournalists. Like all languages, it is the presentation that carries as much meaning as the actual words or, in this case, images. There's a story to be told, but the inflection (the unique qualities of each shot) combined into a sequence color the final outcome.

If you send two photojournalists to the same parade, they will come back with two different sets of images. Although the event is the same, their perceptions about the story, the people they choose to interview, and the way they frame their shots will probably vary widely. It's not that one is necessarily more accurate than the other, or less truthful. The facts can look different to different people.

Now consider ten or a hundred photojournalists working anything from an important local story to one with international repercussions. With so many differences, which story "tells" the truth? They all should.

News Must Be Honest

It's our charter, it's the thing that must rise above all else. The viewer's trust should never be violated. An often stated goal of television news is to "remain objective." Objectivity in news means the content is unbiased and based on fact, without the influence of personal feelings, prejudice, or interpretations. But are all these definitions even possible in photojournalism? Or desirable? Certainly, without question, a news story should be based (anchored) in fact—unbiased and without prejudice, absolutely. But, what about influence by personal feelings and interpretations? These "subjective" aspects are impossible to ignore and make complete objectivity impossible.

What the Viewer Expects; What We Deliver

People watch the news to get honest information about their world, but information alone is boring. Imagine a half an hour of someone reading statistics in a monotone voice. If you're like most viewers, you tune out after a few seconds. We make information personal and interesting by telling stories. The more personal, the farther away from "objective" we get. Less objective does not mean the story is not well balanced, fair, and honest. In fact, "subjective" influences may give the story more clarity in depth.

Information and Story

Information is seen as truth. Story is open to interpretation. Information is just head knowledge, merely facts, figures, and data. Stories are things you care about, things you remember and tell other people. Stories make you feel something—sad, happy, angry. They have meaning for everyone and universal truths that people can identify with. Facts and figures don't stir emotion in the viewer, but stories do.

They are best told, and more authentically told, when we let people speak for themselves. When we allow stories to unfold before us, and slowly uncover things we didn't know (things we could never know), the results can be amazing. Sometimes, few words are necessary.

Information alone is not a story. Information is objective. Story can't be objective; it is subjective. What turns information into story?

Objective information becomes story with a journey. A beginning, middle, and end. The more a story evolves, the more subjective it becomes. The "telling" of the story makes it more subjective by influence of the teller.

As a camera tilts up to see an airliner crash into the World Trade Center, that shot falls into the most objective type of image, unpredictable reaction to an event. There wasn't much time for personal influence by the photographer. But, as the event unfolds, the photographer's images become more subjective, more connected to his or her vision of the event. The images get more personal. The photographer has gone from observing to conveying. Again, a transition from objective to subjective.

Subjective and Objective Photography

Subjective photography is photography that is influenced by the attitude of the photographer—photography that tries to convey a certain point of view. Objective photography is photography that attempts to remain neutral.

Subjective Photography Adds the Human Element

Subjective photography adds heart to the story and allows for visual interest. I want my stories to be interesting and visual and fun to watch, but I don't believe that's lying to the viewer. I think it's just giving them a different perspective on a story.

Although it should be the aim of every photojournalist to remain as neutral as possible, subjectivity is unavoidable. For better or worse, we are telling stories the way we see them, and we have a certain amount of control over the environment. In the end, we have a great responsibility to viewers not to mislead them in the choices we make.

Maintain Your Objectivity?

Objectivity in terms of passive observation does not lend itself to detailed content or storytelling. Standing on the corner of Fourth and B Streets, with a normal lens on a tripod four feet in the air, can certainly capture the activity of the intersection in an objective manner. But the viewer's knowledge and understanding of all the aspects of that street corner are very limited. As soon as the photojournalist moves the camera to convey an opinion of "what else" is important, the less objective the coverage becomes.

The objective and subjective points of view seem to be controversial in many circles. The challenge is that we are subjective beings trying to tell stories through an objective lens. I don't believe photojournalists can ever be 100 percent objective when shooting video and telling stories with their images. Past experiences, opinions, likes, dislikes, prejudices, impulses—they all affect what we see and, ultimately, dictate our perception and our storytelling. We're constantly defining the reality by what we put in that 4×3 or 16×9 frame. It's really easy to lose your objectivity.

We definitely run the risk of using our tools in a way that distorts or emphasizes certain elements of the natural environment.

If you were shooting a story on people with large noses, it would be quite easy to use harsh lighting and side profiles to accentuate that feature. I believe in sensitivity and compassion, not exploitation. Although it can be difficult at times, I always try to put myself in that person's shoes. Is this the way I would want to be portrayed? Would I feel comfortable with the way the video was shot if I were on the other side of the lens? Am I stealing someone's dignity by shooting it this way? *If the nose story is sensitive and about the hardships of freakishly big noses, harsh light would be cruel. If by accident the location you were shooting in had harsh light, would you try to soften it? Would you make the video look more pleasing?*

Some photojournalists would; some would not. Each would have to make that determination based on the actual details of the story. But what if the nose story was a lighthearted feature about a large nose convention in town? The participants would be there to show off their unique profiles. In that case, creativity rules; most photojournalists would push the limits of their storytelling abilities.

It is important in this process of discovery that the photojournalist looks to the people and situations in the shooting locations to discover the story, not solely to a newsroom manager. I have seen instances where the assignment editor or show producer has dictated what the story should entail and what images should be shot long before the reporter and photographer left the newsroom. If the team listens to those instructions without deviating—even if the events develop differently—their story has great potential to become a distortion of reality. Photojournalists must be empowered to tell a story as they see it unfolding. We have a lot of tools that we can use, and we need to use them wisely.

The wise use of the tools means the active use of the tools. While it may be easier not to be involved with the story and maintain a distant point of view, the truth of a story is manipulated by passive-objective photography as well. Not getting involved in placing preferences on your camerawork still has communication consequences. One of my pet peeves is something I see quite a bit on television. It drives me crazy when I see stories about children, and every shot is from the point of view of the photographer's shoulder, looking down. It makes the children look powerless and unimportant.

The farther away from the photographer's eye height, the more subjective the image is. I love to get down at their level and talk to them, eye to eye. It acknowledges their relevance and offers them dignity. We should treat the people we're interviewing, and our stories, with respect.

It's essential to care about all the elements that make up your stories. Each element, each decision, can and will affect the final communication. Some elements we control, others we can't; some we could but should not. Great photojournalists "capture" great moments; they do not re-create them. They do not alter reality for their lenses; they anticipate it.

Great Stories Come from Great Moments—Anticipate the Future

Lisa Berglund's intuition puts her in front of the moment that's about to happen, ready to roll. While some events would inspire anyone to shoot, others are made up of photojournalist's preferences. Anyone would shoot the flames of a house fire while trying to guess when the roof will fall in. The best photojournalists anticipate that shot, but also know there will be a moment when the building can't be saved and that resignation will be visible on someone's face. Who will that be? When will it happen? Intuition, experience, and luck converge to guide the lens.

While Berglund manipulates her camera for the story she wants to tell, she does not manipulate real events. She does not ask the crippled boy to walk through the village again just to get the shot. If she missed it, she missed it. Move on.

Great photojournalists are those who know how to capture moments. There is a fine line between being in the right place at the right time and learning to anticipate. In the business of television news, this can be very difficult. There are so many factors that go into capturing just the right moment. Sometimes patience and foresight are the keys; other times you just get lucky. Success mostly comes from having experience sensing how stories unfold.

Being in the right place at the right time has a lot to do with being aware of the world around you and learning to anticipate life's actions. Whether it is a car crossing in front of the lens to create a really cool wipe, or a woman shedding a single small tear over a baby who has died, some actions are easier to anticipate than others.

I used to be terrible at shooting police walks. (That's when they move the guy from the house he was holed up in to the waiting police car.) I would stress out so much on those shoots because you never know when they're going to come out of the house. There were always at least three other video cameras anxiously waiting, and just as many still photographers. Inevitably, I would end up in the back of the pack trying desperately to shoot over everyone's heads. The shot was always shaky and out of focus, underexposed, and far away. Truly a mess.

One day Brian Puchaty, my chief photographer at the time, gave me a great tip. He told me that no matter where the person was walking from, to always place myself in the nook behind the opening of the car door. Then, no matter what, I would always have a great shot of them going into the car. I tried it one day, and it worked like a charm! I was never again yelled at by the assignment desk for not getting the shot. That kind of thing comes with experience. The more times you shoot a particular event, scene, or action, the better you become at anticipating what's going to happen next.

I once shot a story on a father, Jim, who made the decision to stay home with his children while his wife went to work. He started a club called Dad to Dad, a support group for stay-at-home fathers. I talked quite a bit with the producer about how we wanted to shoot the story before ever picking up the camera. And, although we didn't block out every shot and cutaway, we did look at our story as a whole and try to decide how we might tell it. What might be our opening shot? Would we need to transition from inside the house to outside? What shots might help with those types of transitions? What surprises did we want to see unfold? Could they unfold on tape, rather than in narration? Having thoughts like those kicking around in your head while you're shooting is crucial to great video storytelling.

As your story unfolds in the field, and you begin to piece it together in your head, shots become less lucky and more intentional. One of the surprises we wanted to capture on tape was the fact that Jim was a stay-at-home dad. I wanted to capture the moment his children woke up and came downstairs looking for him. To capture this moment, we had to arrive early in the morning. We videotaped his wife leaving for work, Jim doing chores around the house, and so on. At one point, Jim was downstairs folding laundry. I knew I needed to capture as many sequences as I could of him doing laundry, but I also knew his girls would be waking up at any moment. I put myself in a prime position where I could capture Jim folding laundry in the foreground, but still maybe with a child appearing at the top of the stairs in the background.

I sat there for what seemed like forever. Then, finally, a little girl peered from the top of the stairs. Was that luck? No. It was an intentional attempt to capture a moment. Now, there have been just as many, if not more, times when I have missed the moment by being impatient, running out of time, second-guessing myself, or just simply misjudging the timing. Sometimes you can anticipate life's actions, and sometimes you can't.

In addition to anticipating the great moments, you have to anticipate the actions that will help build a sequence, shot by shot. Will you need a close-up? Does it have to match-cut, or is it a cutaway? Work ahead. Anticipate the motion and actions that will carry the sequence from shot to shot.

Photojournalists tell stories by shooting sequences. When you really think about it, your eyes see in sequences, too. If I am walking into a baseball stadium and a cute guy catches my attention, my eye doesn't slowly zoom in on him. Rather, it cuts directly to his cute, smiling face. Crucial to telling stories through sequences is learning to anticipate what's coming next. When I turn and see my boyfriend staring at me with disgust, my eye doesn't pan around to his angry face; it cuts to it. If I can anticipate his action well enough, I can have my camera rolling on the close-up of steam coming out of his ears. That's how sequences work in photojournalism.

Of course, this is much easier to do in a chocolate factory, where every push of a button, whirr of a cog, and wrap of a candy bar is repeated like clockwork. Shots involving repetition are easy to anticipate.

You have to study your surroundings, intentionally set up your shot, and wait patiently for the right moment.

Not wanting to wait for the right moment, tied to the desire to attempt dramatic filmmaking, can lead photojournalists to stage the action. Staging happens anytime you stop reality and take control of the scene in order to shoot something that did not happen naturally.

Staging Is a Manipulation of the Truth

Viewers tune in to newscasts with an expectation of objectivity and the representation of truthful events. Staging is the most controversial topic in photojournalism today. *The controversy comes from the gray area surrounding staging. While all agree you would never ask a grieving mother to cry again, many would have no problem asking a bicyclist to go around the block again for a story on bicycle safety, or, lift the bicycle off the ground and spin the wheel to show a close-up of the brakes grabbing.*

While the staged action in the bicycle safety story is a manipulation of the truth (or reality?), the final edited story is illustrated in a more informative way than either running alongside the bicycle hoping to catch the moment or eliminating the close-ups altogether.

As much as possible, I try to preplan my shoots, to position myself in a time and place where I can capture the story as it is unfolding. I will get up early in the morning if I need to shoot someone making coffee, starting their day, and heading off to work. I won't try to re-create those shots at four in the afternoon. If, while I'm shooting that sequence, I miss the tight shot of the coffee being poured into a mug, I won't re-create that either. Instead, I will find another way to edit the story.

I truly believe the viewer knows the difference. They know when actions are not authentic. Staging doesn't just alter the action; it also changes the environment around you. When you stop capturing what is naturally unfolding and start creating sequences of what you want the story to be, you lose all sense of authenticity. When I am shooting, my goal is to disappear into the background. The more I can make people forget I'm there, the better photojournalist I'll be.

I believe in shooting sequences, repetitive action, and as many angles as I can in the time allowed. I do not, however, believe in stopping life as it unfolds in order to capture those elements.

It's important for every photojournalist to be introspective and decide for himself or herself where to draw the line. At the end of the day, will they feel comfortable with the way they shot their news story? Is there anything they'll regret? I come from a pretty conservative background. From the beginning of my career in news photography, I learned that staging was not appropriate and that, as a journalist, it was my responsibility to allow the story to unfold naturally, not to create it as I went along. I can't say that I don't struggle with staging, because I do. I'm always questioning myself and the way I shoot and produce stories.

One of the biggest questions is, are you misleading anyone by the way you tell your story? Are you asking someone to re-create something that already happened or to do something they wouldn't normally do? If you're shooting a story on a golfing prodigy, and you're videotaping one of his practice rounds, it would be dishonest to stage him hitting a hole in one. That would be manipulating images in order to tell the story you want. It's simply untrue. Now, that's an extreme example. Every day we are faced with situations that aren't so cut and dried, and sometimes the line is not all that clear.

The line blurs when repetitive action allows for match cuts that illustrate one event in one timeline, where the outcome from each individual shot's action is different and random. The golfer swings 30 times while you're shooting. You shoot him swinging with a wide angle; you shoot a close-up of the ball being hit off the tee; you shoot another set of close-ups of the golfer's face. Later, you move to the hole and shoot another ten balls landing around the hole. None of those shots can be assembled to show the exact swing, facial expression, and ball position as one actual swing. If, in the edit, he swings and makes it close to the hole and shows an expression of happiness, we'd think that shot was good for him.

The same sequence could be assembled differently. By changing the reaction shot to a disappointed expression, the viewer's impression is changed. "He got close, but he thinks he should have done better."

The photojournalist captured the events just as they happened, making a photographic study of the golfer's practice and the motion of the club and ball, but because action and reaction change with each repetition, reassembling the shots into a duplicate of reality is impossible.

Editing applies more "subjective" pressure to the story, particularly where match cuts are involved. Match-cutting from single-camera photography is also a manipulation of the truth. It falls on the editor to create a truthful illustration of the story. Editing can solve the honesty issue of match cuts by making a "montage"—random combination of shots—to show "some of the action of the day" as opposed to "This string of shots actually happened in this order."

I am always thinking about how the story could be edited. I have no formula as to what I shoot first, or if I'm on or off the tripod. The story completely defines that for me. If I show up at the scene of a water rescue, I will most likely run out to the beach with my tripod, drop it in the sand, and then run handheld to the edge of the water to shoot them coming into shore. Once the scene has died down a bit, I will pick up the tripod and shoot more sequences from different vantage points. The story dictates the order in which I gather my footage, whether I'm on or off the tripod. Regardless of the order, I will always try to shoot as many sequences as possible, with as many focal lengths and angles as I can, as long as I'm not compromising the story.

When the Story Is a Re-creation

Staging and all the tools of filmmaking are fair to use in a re-creation. If you are re-creating a murder scene or doing a story on a house that is haunted, I think there is room for staging. If it's clear to the viewer that this is something that happened in the past, staging can be an effective way to help tell the story. The bottom line is you should be truthful. If you're not honest with your pictures, your words, and how they all come together, then you're not being fair to the viewer. In the end, everyone has to decide for themselves where they draw the line on staging.

A Special Effect Is a Major Deviation from Reality

Special effects should never be employed outside of special circumstances and re-creations. These filmmaking techniques are fun to watch, but their use may call into question the journalistic ethics of the news organization. It's a little trickier now that we've gone digital. The effects are endless, but are they really helping to tell your story, or are you just trying to do something different and cool for the sake of doing something different and cool? It's great to try out new styles and tricks, to figure out what works and what doesn't. But it's more important to ask yourself, "Is this technique helping to tell my story, or is it distracting from it?"

Truth in Filmmaking

Many filmmaking techniques are essential to telling truthful stories. Lighting is required for proper exposure in many instances. While the "reality" might be that artificial light does not exist at your location, you won't see a thing without it. So you put a light—a subjective influence—on your story. A light mounted on top of the camera makes for flat lighting, and the reporter squints, so you move the keylight. The reporter is much brighter than the background, so you lower the intensity of the reporter's light and add a light to the background. The harsh shadow on the reporter's face could be softened—add a fill.

All of these additions to reality make the image more subjective and alter the true environment. Some would argue, "Never change reality." In practice, you must, and while you're doing it and making subjective decisions, they might as well be good ones that advance the story. Better to see the background as well as the reporter.

As you apply the tools and techniques of filmmaking, you are influencing reality. While the debate over altering reality will continue for some time, the constraint of the medium will make it necessary.

The debate over altering reality exists in motion pictures as well. Director of photography Ron Garcia, ASC, wrote an article for TheASC.com *about an experience he had filming a night shot.*

During the filming of *Twin Peaks: Fire Walk with Me*, we had to shoot a night scene between Laura and Bobby while they were waiting to do a dope deal in the woods. David Lynch did not want to use any movie lights at all! He wanted the kids to use a flashlight (just one). I explained about photographic darkness, but this was David Lynch, King of Blackness in Spirit and Photography—he was adamant about the scene not looking as though it was lit. He asked, if I used motion picture lights, where the light would come from naturally in the middle of the forest? I said the light would come from the same place the music comes from—he didn't laugh!

Garcia's point is well made. We are communicating with a medium that has its own rules and parameters. We cannot carbon copy reality; we interpret it through the tools of the medium. We create "television reality."

Watch any newscast and count the elements that aren't reality. The news set, animated graphics, bumper music—all are added to enhance the basic news content and retain viewers.

Subjective Influences Retain Viewers

The bottom line is "Are we getting the ratings?" I know I'm shooting the same story as the photographers next to me, but how is my story going to look different from theirs when it hits the air? How is it going to stand out, and how will it keep the couple sitting on their sofa from changing the channel? Or, if they turn it to mine, why will they keep watching? The answer comes from finding those unique angles, unique shots, and unique people to profile. Hopefully, those techniques will play some part in retaining viewers. If not, at least I've exercised my photography skills that day, and stored away some great new idea for the future.

Even at press conferences, I like my video to look different. Sometimes, I'll take a chance and break away from the rest of the group. I'll try to get a shot with something else in the foreground, like other cameras or someone watching who is affected by the outcome of the event. I think it's good to take chances once in a while.

Creativity Is a Subjective Influence

Creativity is essential for any medium to survive. We can live through boring lives, careers, and relationships, but we won't spend two seconds with a program or article that's not creative and interesting. It's easy to be drawn into using filmmaking techniques just to improve the creativity in a story.

Lisa Berglund has found her own balance among journalism, filmmaking, staging, and creativity. I thrive on creativity. I would not be a photojournalist if I could not be creative with my camera, my eye, the angles, the lighting. I could never just point and shoot without caring deeply about how the finished story looks and how it affects those who are watching. Objectivity is very important to me, but so is creativity. So, I walk this line with respect and admiration for both.

It is extremely important to take creative risks. I really believe that's the only way to grow as a photojournalist. Unless you get yourself out there, and put your ideas into practice, you will never grow.

Sometimes the things that scare us the most are those that will help us grow the most as human beings and as photographers. I think everyone reaches moments in their career and in their personal life when they know they need to rise to another level. There is something scaring them (shooting a first photo essay, learning a new software program, pursuing a certain relationship), and they know deep down that they need to conquer that fear. If you can push yourself through that first layer of indecision—the first layer of being petrified—you'll become a much better photographer, editor, or person.

The most fulfilling stories for me are the ones that scare me the most. Maybe it's just me, I don't know, but I thrive when I am forced to push beyond what I think I can do. And, as a result, I grow into a much better storyteller. In fact, I'm at that stage in my career right now, knowing I want to work on a documentary, but being petrified to jump out into it.

Lisa Berglund's creativity as a photojournalist and storyteller has been acknowledged with the industry's top awards. At her first job, after graduating with a degree in religious communications from Whitworth College, Berglund ran a hand-cranked teleprompter for KXLY-TV in Spokane, Washington. From there, she worked her way from editor to photographer and photojournalist. It was hard work but worth every bit of the effort. Berglund is now recognized as one of the top photojournalists in the world.

Lisa Berglund's Guide to Success

Beg, borrow, or steal (well, maybe not steal) as many reels as you can from photographers you admire. Watch them, study them, memorize them, pick out the things you like, and learn something from those you don't. Watch movies, television shows, and commercials to gain a better understanding of sequencing, lighting, sound, and storytelling. Although it may seem much different than television news, all those techniques can be applied to your shooting. I love to study cinematographers and photojournalists, taking ideas I think work well and applying them to my own storytelling.

It doesn't always work. It's easy to take ideas out of context or try too hard on the technical aspects, forgetting the importance of the story. Sometimes we just need to relax and chill out and document what's going on around us honestly and with integrity.

I believe that storytelling is evolutionary. The videos I produced ten years ago are drastically different than those I produced last year, which are different from the ones I am producing today. As my knowledge grows, so does my level of self-critique.

The best photojournalists are those who are curious, love people, and are passionate about telling stories. You could have twenty cases of the best video equipment on the planet, but if you don't understand storytelling and aren't interested in dissecting the human condition, you will never become a great photojournalist. Great photojournalists will push themselves beyond their comfort zone. They take chances and learn from their mistakes. They don't complain about newsroom politics, but rather work within the system to produce great stories. Great photojournalists put the same amount of effort into a fifteen-second VO as they would a more complex, visually rich feature story. They learn to think on their feet, anticipate, tell stories, consistently meet deadlines, and interact with dramatically different types of people.

They are creators and innovators.

My World, My Story

I remember when I was younger and new to photojournalism. My dream was to show people things they might never see if it weren't for my camera lens. I wanted them to feel what I feel when I'm out in the field. I wanted to take them places they would probably never go and help them realize what life is like for a child struggling to survive in villages like those in Angola, Honduras, or Sri Lanka. I wanted to tell stories. Thankfully, and by the grace of God, that is what I have been able to do . . . to help people understand more about the world through my lens.

I can remember as a child, sitting at the kitchen table after dinner. I can still hear my mother's words, "Lisa, eat your asparagus! There are so many starving children in the world who would love to have that asparagus." My reply to that one was easy. "Great, send it to them!"

I'd seen images of starving children on the television screen. They seemed so far away and distant. I wondered if they were real. I had never seen a child that hungry in real life. Well, I found myself standing in the middle of a Doctors Without Borders clinic in Niger, and I was face to face with children who were truly on the edge of survival. There was a time when I was videotaping that I thought, "This child is going to die while I'm standing here shooting this video."

I really thought this experience would draw me closer. That seeing these children in person would be different than seeing them on television so many years ago. But you know what? They still felt far away. They still felt distant.

Why? Because I kept them there.

It wasn't until a month later, while sitting alone in an edit room, that those images finally became real. I remember watching that same child on a video monitor, in an edit room, thousands of miles away. This time, I broke down in tears.

You see, it's not about the asparagus. What my mom was saying all those years ago had nothing to do with asparagus. What she wanted was for me to take my eyes off myself, and lock them onto the world around me.

Sometimes the viewfinder provides a convenient barrier between the story and us. Sometimes it's our own fears and insecurities that keep us distant. The children I videotaped in Niger aren't statistics . . . they are real people, with mothers and fathers and dreams for the future. That was my story.

Lisa Berglund's video From Locusts to Land Mines *helped raise funds for the relief effort. Berglund's honest and emotional depiction of the famine increased the awareness of starvation in these impoverished countries. Her creative efforts helped bring hope to places where it had not been before.*

Creativity in photojournalism means being subjective in an industry that touts "objectivity" as its prime directive. Apply your influence to the story you're telling. That makes the responsibility to illustrate the truth all the more important.

Be the truthful arbiter of what's in front of you. Own up to your authorship of the moment. Create "well-balanced," "truthful" representations of news events and stories.

Be subjective, be accountable, be honest.

Embrace the "subjective" while holding "objective" ideals.

We are the eyes and ears of the world today. I love introducing the world to people; I can't think of a more satisfying profession.

CHAPTER 10

Ian Pearson

Legalities and Ethics—Do
the Right Thing

Ian Pearson
Media Consultant

Pearson Communications, Foundation for American Communications

*F*our lanes of speeding commuters sling-shot out of the Waldo Tunnel separated by less than the width of a handshake, except no one here is in a handshaking mood. Hands clench steering wheels as the drizzle-slick highway abruptly drops and slaloms right, left, right, then, for good measure, narrows to three lanes. It gets worse: Dead center, through their windshields, towers what may be the most seductive distraction in the Western world: the Golden Gate Bridge.

Ian Pearson steals a peek. His commute reads like a Gray Line tour: Bridge, Presidio, Market Street, maybe a little Pacific Coast Highway on the way home. Pearson sees it all through two sets of eyes: like everyone else, as world-class scenery but also as a longtime news executive viewing an ethical minefield. Complete with flashbacks.

Pearson first entered journalism as a radio-TV reporter in Duluth, Minnesota. From there, he went on to manage newsrooms in five cities, including Houston and, most recently, San Francisco.

The bridge's south tower looms, reminding Pearson of Ken, a young man who jumped. My station, like all others, had a policy not to cover suicide attempts (or bomb threats). Don't encourage them, went the thinking.

But Ken had survived! Pearson tracked him down years later for a documentary, only to hit an ethical wall: This would be an "exclusive," but didn't it violate station policy? The documentary covered the bridge's history, including its notoriety as a suicide magnet. "The minute I jumped, I knew I wanted to live," he told me, which strongly argues that attempting suicide is a mistake and, coming from him, had unique credibility. So we used it.

Just past the bridge comes the Presidio, the scene of a historic visit from Pope John Paul II. In the media frenzy before the Pope's visit, a priest source carelessly confided to me the Pope's ultra-secret parade route. I agonized: If I report it, am I compromising the Pope's security? Or, is it okay, since my source didn't tell me *not* to report it?

As Pearson exits the Presidio. To the west, in the distance, lies the Pacific Coast Highway, which each year becomes the finish line for the famous Bay-to-Breakers race that attracts 80,000 people. The year I first oversaw this station's coverage, race organizers threatened to deny my live crew finish line access because exclusive rights had been sold to a rival station. But wasn't this a public highway? Didn't 80,000 people make this a bona fide news story? Could I win a legal fight?

Pearson turns left toward downtown San Francisco. In the thicket of tall buildings ahead lies the "Jukebox Marriott," so nicknamed for its shape. Once, on the penthouse floor, I scored a one-on-one interview with Mikhail Gorbachev. No sooner had the station triumphantly aired the first clip than the union steward approached me. "You're not union," he warned. "Having your voice on the air is a violation." *This, just minutes before the next newscast planned to lead with Pearson's story. Now what do you do?*

Cable cars chatter down Hyde Street toward the wharf, a cultural icon in the company of Alcatraz, China Town, and local rock legends The Grateful Dead. Pearson recalls passing the desk of a reporter who had recently done a story on "The Dead." The reporter returned with a pile of freebie CDs. I knew the dollar threshold for reporting payola, and the freebies probably didn't exceed it by much, but I couldn't help wondering, "How many of this reporter's other story decisions have come with spiffs attached?"

Locals call San Francisco "The City," and like any "city," there's a dark side, the side that keeps newsrooms busy. One day while managing the news, Pearson's phone rang. The light signaled it was the news director: "That SWAT shooting we covered live this morning . . . the photographer panned over to show police on the roof. Now it turns out the killer was watching TV and the police just called. They're furious. Come to my office."

The light turns green at the intersection of Geary and Gough, and Pearson snaps back to the task at hand—driving to an interview about the legalities and ethics of photojournalism.

Ian Pearson now heads Pearson Communications, a media strategy and production service in Tiburon, California. As a consultant for many years to the Los Angeles-based Foundation for American Communications (FACS), he lectured on media relations at Harvard Business School, UCLA, and dozens of other universities and nonprofits. Pearson's experience in managing newsrooms has given him a host of examples to use when discussing the legal and ethical issues of television photojournalism.

Legal In Houston, our photographer is arrested for crossing police lines at a crime scene and his camera is confiscated. Thanks to the photographer's own alertness, we convince a jury he was wrongly accused.

Ethical At a tension-filled school board meeting in an aging auditorium, the lighting is so muddy that, lacking AC power, our photographer tries a sun gun, only to have the crowd demand that he stop.

It's important to note: laws and community standards, which in part establish ethical behavior, change from town to town, state to state, and country to country. What was unacceptable two years ago is now tolerated. The tolerance for infringements also changes from one news organization to the next. While there are codes of ethics established by the NPPA (National Press Photographers Association) and the RTNDA (Radio Television News Directors Association), no set of standards will cover every situation in every loca-

tion. It is imperative that all photojournalists be aware of the standards set by the community, the courts, and the news organization for which they are working.

With so many variables, it is easy to see the complexities that may arise in the field of photojournalism. This chapter attempts to give an overview of some of the legal and ethical questions that face photojournalists. It is not to be used as legal advice. When in doubt, get a professional opinion from management and/or a lawyer retained by the news organization.

This chapter is heavily slanted toward U.S. law and ethics, but much of the content can be adapted for other countries.

Legalities and Ethics Are Often Intertwined

Federal laws, or laws that pertain to the entire population of a country, may seem written in stone, but in practice, many are often left to local interpretation and punishment. Local laws often follow local customs and ethics. Many of the photojournalists Pearson has hired have come from cities outside his market. The quicker they acclimate to their new environment, the better photojournalists they'll become.

Photojournalism being what it is, a lot of the folks practicing it will move town to town, city to city, and country to country. They quickly learn how much conditions can differ from one place to the other. How comfortable are the local residents when cameras are thrust in their faces? If you work in a large city and one day find yourself covering a story in a small town, you may overwhelm the residents there. If you show up where people aren't used to seeing cameras, they might try to deny you reasonable access to a crime site or a scene of grieving. At times like these, you might have to be an educator and explain to people why you're allowed to do this. Not easy to do if you're not sure yourself.

The law may be on your side, but if you barge in and someone ignorant of the law blocks your path, you might be ejected, arrested, or have your camera confiscated or broken. You'd miss the story, which might not have happened if you'd used a little up-front sensitivity.

Getting the story is what you're paid for; jail time is not.

In other countries, this issue of shifting ethical boundaries works much the same. You might find yourself in trouble for photographing women's exposed faces if they are required to wear burqas at all times. In some cultures, you could offend a married couple by asking them to hold hands for your cutaway shot.

To condense the questions and issues surrounding both legal and ethical matters and place them in a more practical format, Pearson combines the issues under a "What You Should Know and When" checklist. He starts with "before employment," then "before the story," "during the story," "after the story," and the "future." These are by no means all of the legal and ethical questions you'll face, but they should serve as an opening to thinking in terms of these issues.

Pearson's "What You Should Know and When" Checklist

What You Need to Know **before** *You Accept Employment*

This information will vary with each employer. It's important to have these questions answered. Newsrooms should have a written policy manual as well as documentation for all copyright agreements. Be familiar with them.

___ Is your employer a bona fide news organization? Is it covered by fair use laws?

___ Who retains copyright to your images?

___ What ethics training or policies are there?

___ Who's the "go to" person in the newsroom for ethical questions and problem solving?

___ Does the news operation have access to a lawyer, and is it someone who knows media law?

What You Need to Know **before** *You Go to a Story*

Knowing what the story is about and anticipating legal and ethical entanglements can help keep you out of trouble, and may help to advance your access to the story.

___ Is there pool coverage and, if so, what are the special rules?

___ Do you need credentials? Are special ones needed? Was access preapproved? Is there a contact person?

___ What are the state laws? Hidden recording, quasi-public access, shield laws, and sunshine laws all will vary.

___ What are the newsroom policies regarding coverage of suicides, exposed bodies, funerals, SWAT live shots, and obscenities, and their subsequent use in stories?

___ What are the local media standards? An example might be: No microphone flags on podiums during press conferences.

___ What are the community standards? Will you cause an uproar by showing gays kissing? Nipples showing through T-shirts? Open caskets? What is acceptable in one location may be taboo the next town over. When in doubt, ask your news management.

What You Need to Know **at** *the Story*

Things move quickly in the field. Being familiar with your organization's policies and the local customs is essential to make snap decisions, decisions that could keep you out of trouble and free to continue doing your job.

___ What are acceptable versus unacceptable photo techniques (telescopic lenses into private homes)?

___ Editing in the camera: Do you shoot the exposed body, or the protest sign showing the aborted fetus, and trust your editor not to use it?

___ What are your rights to access, to use lights, make noise, deal with the photographer who blocks your shot?

___ Procedures if you encounter resistance: What if citizens block you or police arrest you or if someone objects to your videotaping?

___ Local diplomacy tips will improve access and defuse confrontation.

___ Getting involved in the story: Is it okay to follow a mob into stores it loots? Wrong to photograph the hit-run victim rather than rendering aid?

What You Need to Know **after** *the Story*

The issues don't end when you stop recording. In fact, in some cases, they've just begun. Make sure you and your employer have a complete understanding of your responsibilities regarding the footage you've just shot.

___ How may any super-sensitive material you shot be used?

___ What risks are there that your video will be misused in future stories?

___ Do you alert management if someone you photograph demands not to be shown?

___ What to do if a citizen or company or medium asks for a copy of your video?

___ How do you convey to management any problems you encountered?

What You Need to Know **about** *the Future*

Laws and local customs change all the time. Technology and its effect on business and communities help accelerate the change. We will continue to adapt as new issues shape our craft and responsibilities.

___ Shifting ethics brought on by one-man bands, Internet, quasi-news shows

___ Changing community standards

___ New technology for surreptitious recording and image manipulation

---

In 1841, Thomas Carlyle in "On Heroes and Hero Worship" attributes the term "Fourth Estate" to Edmund Burke. He writes, ". . . does not . . . the parliamentary debate go on . . . in a far more comprehensive way, out of Parliament altogether? Edmund Burke said that there were three Estates in Parliament, but in the Reporters' Gallery yonder, there sat a fourth Estate more important than they all." *This quote, referring to the news media at the time, established the term "Fourth Estate" to describe the press and their capacity for civil advocacy and ability to frame political issues. "Fourth Estate" points directly to the power the press has in society.*

It is reasonable to argue that the Fourth Estate, with its power as advocates for the people and authors of impartial news and information, should be governed to ensure its ideals and protect journalists and the subjects they cover. To a degree, the industry is both self-governed by organizational policies and codes of ethics, and externally governed by laws that empower or restrict its activities (not to mention the cutthroat nature of media who would gladly point out a competitor's misdeeds or failures).

In much of the Western world, the news media share the same rights and are afforded the same protections as private citizens in general. There are also policies that are written and interpreted to allow the news media to do their job but that are not extended to the general population (for example, access to a White House news conference).

At the top of any legal discussion regarding the media in the United States is the First Amendment to the Constitution. The First Amendment states:

Congress shall make no law respecting an establishment of religion, or prohibiting the free exercise thereof; or abridging the freedom of speech, or of the press; or the right of the people peaceably to assemble, and to petition the Government for a redress of grievances.

The Reporters Committee for Freedom of the Press publishes The First Amendment Handbook *in print and online. It should be essential reading for all journalists. The introduction to the* Handbook *tells the story of its inception:*

On a Sunday afternoon in March 1970, a group of journalists and media lawyers, concerned over FBI attempts to find the sources for journalists' reports on radical groups, gathered at Georgetown University to create an organization that would be available around the clock to provide legal assistance to any working reporter, anywhere in the United States, without charge. For more than 30 years, The Reporters Committee for Freedom of the Press has carried out that vision, giving legal advice to thousands of journalists and producing publications to help them do their jobs. *The First Amendment Handbook* is one of those publications.

The handbook covers libel, invasion of privacy, surreptitious recording, confidential sources and information, prior restraints, gag orders, access to courts, access to places, Freedom of Information Acts, Sunshine Laws, and copyright. (See the RCFP Web site at http://rcfp.org/handbook/ *for the complete Handbook.)*

When you examine many of the laws that govern photojournalism, you realize a couple things quickly. It is not statute law; it's case law. That means that a particular case was brought before a judge or jury whose ruling provides a precedent for future media conduct.

Photojournalism and the Law

Photojournalists really need to understand at least the basic legal fundamentals. Knowing the law tells you what your rights are, yes, but also how to explain them when challenged and where to draw the line on unethical conduct. You will be more confident in the field and less likely to find yourself in trouble.

In the following subsections, Pearson cites specific examples of how the laws that apply to all journalists may have unique implications for the photojournalist.

The Right to Privacy and the Media

There are stories that are obviously worthy of coverage, which photojournalists have an absolute right to cover when they occur in public, even though participants may object at the time or later. For example, a woman entering an abortion clinic, a dazed survivor of a horrific traffic accident, or even just a couple smooching in the park on the first day of spring (but beware: If your story implies the woman is having an abortion when in fact she is not, consider your career over).

People venturing out in public have to expect that in doing so they sacrifice a certain degree of privacy; there is a "reasonable expectation" that they could be seen, witnessed, or photographed. And that's a strong criterion that courts consider in a case. However, a competing ethical consideration arises if, for example, you photograph a couple in public performing a sex act. Let's say you put it on the air or in the newspaper. All of a sudden everyone in the community is looking at it in shock and, more than likely, there's a lawsuit.

What's at issue here is much more complicated than the photojournalist saying, "They are in a public place; I can photograph them," and the opposing side saying, "We were doing something intensely private; you can't photograph us." Rather, what comes into play is: How newsworthy was what they were doing? Was it necessary for you to show it or show as much as you did, or was your coverage gratuitous or reckless? It gets down basically to common sense: How much does it have to do with the story? The ethical hair-splitting here can get intense: If you photograph a public official engaged in sex with a prostitute, do you show the politician's face to prove who it was, but blur the prostitute's face because showing her would be gratuitous?

Or, take the seemingly simple assignment to photograph street crowds for a story about census figures. Every photojournalist would self-edit out the passerby picking his nose because using it is clearly tasteless and distracting. But, what if, unbeknownst to you, the crowd you photograph includes a man and woman having an affair, and they sue? Well, you had no way to know that, and the couple had to expect that they could be photographed while in public. But what if the couple saw themselves photographed and called your newsroom just before deadline, demanding that you not use the shot? In a jury's mind, the difference between right and wrong might literally depend on how many minutes you had to find an alternate shot.

So, everywhere you go, there are judgment calls. If someone does challenge your decision, you can be called into court, right or wrong, and then it's not just the law you're arguing with but community standards. Yes, it's a public place, but could you easily have used an alternate shot and avoided damaging someone's reputation? Did you use a shot to further the story, or was the shot unnecessary and over the line—whatever the line is?

Access

Sometimes you're granted access and it blows up in your face. The classic case is the renter who lets you in to shoot his rat-infested apartment, whereupon the landlord sues. In case law, it may depend on whether you showed just the tenant's quarters or the rest of the building's interior. Access is very tricky; you need to know if the person granting you access—or in some cases denying access—has the authority to do so.

When I was a news director in Houston, we sent a very talented rookie photographer to videotape a combination car crash and police action. The next thing we know, there's a phone call saying our photographer's been arrested for crossing the crime scene tape. So, I went to the police station, where they allowed me to reclaim the camera and talk to our man. The officers at the scene said he had crossed the police tape, but our man said that wasn't the case at all.

We fought the charge and it went to trial. After the officers testified that our photojournalist had crossed the line, we rolled the videotape and it showed that he had been photographing on the permissible side of the police tape the entire time. It showed the jury that the officers were wrong, and we won. One lesson here is that you can be squeaky clean and obeying the officers, and still be arrested and not get the story on the air. You should also have that camera rolling at all times. Finally, the photographer was well behaved during his arrest; if he had fought the officers, he could have faced "resisting" even though he hadn't crossed the line.

Our photojournalist did everything right, and it was an honor to stand up for him. Unfortunately, there are many times when photojournalists are pushed around or confronted with capricious limitations. It pays to know your rights and how to preserve them without inflaming a situation.

Copyright and Legal Protection

When photographers work for a news organization, the rights for footage they shoot typically belong to the organization. For freelance photojournalists, the situation is different. They may choose to retain full or partial rights to their work. They need to know how policies of conduct differ from client to client, and they need to know their liabilities as contractors.

What about legal protection? If a citizen you photograph feels his rights were violated, he'll go after the deep pockets—your news organization. Even so, both the photojournalist and the station will very likely be dragged into the legal matter together. And if, back to our earlier example, our photojournalist sneaks around police lines and it's provable, there's a good chance he will not be supported by management and will face internal discipline.

Fair Use

For news programs, "fair use" generally means the overriding intent is to educate or inform and not to profit. For example, if two photo crews are permitted to photograph a newly promoted CEO at work, the news crew is covered by fair use and need not have the CEO sign a release, but the crew shooting a corporate commercial should. For photojournalists, it's important to know whether your so-called "news organization" really is one, especially today, when it's hard to know if some of the television programs out there are news or entertainment or infomercials.

Errors in Judgment

Negligence in the newsroom may also have profound legal ramifications. You need to know what you are going out to shoot. I recall a case in which a news outlet dispatched a photographer to shoot a residence, without informing the photographer the home belonged to a suspected drug dealer. Not surprisingly, the photographer was attacked and beaten badly. A court found his news organization negligent for not warning him. A more commonplace mistake occurs when a photojournalist shoots generic "people shots," including faces, without being informed the story is about, say, increased drug use in society. Just that bit of information would have caused the photojournalist to defocus and avert a defamation lawsuit.

Knowledge of the legal system and local ethics will make you a better photojournalist and a better storyteller. Staying onsite and in tune to the community you're photographing will produce better results than if you're thrown in the back of a police or military vehicle, handcuffed and without your camera.

To help guide journalists in their ethical decision-making process, many organizations issue a "Code of Ethics." This code reflects the principles the organization holds as paramount for its members to follow. The Radio Television News Directors Association's Code of Ethics applies to all electronic journalists. (See the RTNDA Web site at www.rtnda.org/ethics/c.e.html *for more about this.) More specific to the field of photojournalism, the National Press Photographers Association has its own code of ethics. (See the NPPA Web site at* www.nppa.org/professional_development/business_practices/ethics.html. *for the code and other details.)*

The Culture of Photography

As a photojournalist, you have to know the basic laws to know what's wrong and what your basic rights are. If you are a photojournalist, you have to know your community and know the culture of photography. Sticking a lens in a person's face is going to cause a reaction. All of us know from the body language what those reactions are and how they determine if you get a good story, or a stiff story, or no story.

Each town's press corps may have differing customs for microphone flags, station logos, pool coverage, and group lighting set-ups. Know what the customs are for the town you're shooting in. You won't find a place in the world where it's acceptable to alter someone else's lighting, certainly not without discussing it first.

Common sense is important, as is diplomacy, as are good "antennae." All of these deserve a place in your ethical roadmap because, too often, the law alone is not an absolute guide.

I've said there is a whole lot of gray area that makes a photojournalist's job that much more difficult but, at the same time, that much more powerful. Many times, terrific photojournalists push themselves out of the "safe" zone to get wonderful results that their competitors can only envy. The gift is being able to navigate the gray areas to become successful while avoiding the pitfalls.

Many of the techniques available to filmmakers are used by TV news photojournalists. Using those techniques to distort reality violates the public's trust in the media. Just ignoring the technical variables of video photography can lead to distortions in reality—the jailkeeper was not heartless but, by not white balancing and recording his image in all blue tones, he appeared cold. Visual accidents can have visual consequences.

Photographers will frequently impart their personal views onto the subject they are shooting. Uncontrolled bad lighting is no different in the end from choosing to cast hard shadows to create a dramatic image. One photographer didn't care; the other had control and understood the message. Yet both influenced the emotional impact of their shots.

To me, what's interesting here is that even simple laziness that makes someone look bad is, if not unethical, unfair. And the same goes for over-stylizing. I once interviewed a woman from ground level because that was the fad, but the result was so unflattering I had to reshoot. It wasn't the only time I was reminded these are people I am portraying, not creative playthings.

VISUAL TECHNIQUES AND ETHICS

Reflect Reality The general rule is to reflect, not distort, reality. Framing a police officer's interview to show the crime scene behind him is common sense. Framing a remedial class to show only minority students is wrong.

Some Techniques Can Be Right, Some Wrong Laying your own music under a funeral is wrong, but using music from the actual funeral is desirable.

Choose Wisely Not all "manipulation" is wrong. Zooms have been historically acceptable to draw attention, but using a fisheye lens to make an overeater look fatter is not.

Know the Local Standards They can vary from decade to decade, state to state, medium to medium. In the seventies, my overnight photographer got bored shooting his umpteenth traffic accident and shot one using snap zooms and swivel dutching. I climbed all over him. Today on *Cops*, he'd be a hero. In Houston, we never showed uncovered bodies while, one television market over, it was standard operating procedure.

Ethics in Practice

Staying abreast of ethics in photojournalism can seem like trying to tell time with a running stop-watch: It just keeps evolving. It's not a single dimension. The history in a community might shape or suddenly alter local ethics in a unique way. Would it surprise you that many residents around San Quentin turned hostile after a solid week of pre-execution coverage and satellite truck generators? Frankly, far too little emphasis is placed on staying abreast of local culture, laws, newsroom standards, community standards, or precedent-setting cases around your state and the country.

Even if the law remains the same, newsroom standards can change because of new management. One newsroom I worked in habitually aired a twenty-second VO of every homicide scene our crews shot, until one news director objected, challenging us to do "just one in-depth story" about the life that was lost. Ethics can also change as cultural standards do (most news outlets flatly avoided reporting bomb threats until 9/11 altered our consciousness). Competition plays a role, too. How many times do we air stories simply because we have "exclusive video," or refuse to cover stories because the competition has video but we don't?

Some of my most perplexing ethical challenges had nothing to do with life or death. Once, we sent a photographer-producer to cover the "troubles" in Northern Ireland, and he returned with terrific interviews that, due to the thickly brogued accents, were hard to understand. A heated debate ensued. Do we subtitle the sound bites—without them, much of the story was unintelligible—or would subtitles insult the interviewees and their many local sympathizers? To my regret, we did without subtitles.

In fact, much of our ethical gatekeeping flies under the public's radar. Yet it speaks well of newsrooms that most have rules that say, with a few exceptions, you won't show suicide attempts, rape victims, exposed dead bodies, or underage criminal suspects. We could use a few more standards like these. It's also heartening how often news staffs heatedly debate the pros and cons of showing a piece of photography; photojournalists often bring a unique perspective to these exchanges as the only ones who observed the situation "on the ground."

Good newsrooms have mechanisms to support photojournalists in the decision-making process. For starters, they talk these things over. It was also my job at KRON-TV to make sure the staff was informed of changing standards and to make sure they abided by these rules and policies. It's important for photojournalists to know if gatekeepers like this exist in the organization somewhere. There should be someone to call immediately about questions you have from the scene.

Newsroom Ethics

The news organization has the ultimate decision-making authority, yet often a photojournalist's sensitive material gets on the air without the chain of command being aware of it. Photojournalists have more responsibility than they might realize, as do other newsroom staffers.

Once, we dispatched a crew to cover a nuclear plant protest. Before the story aired, no managers were red-flagged that it included protestors shouting obscenities. Airing the obscenities rather than bleeping them was questionable enough, but not calling in management made it worse. It was a complete disregard of the chain of command, to say nothing of community sensitivities. It blindsided everyone down to the receptionist who handled angry calls. If you are given a policy when you are hired at a station, you better know it. And, even if the decision is made to air something shocking, the responsible thing to do is precede it with an audience warning.

Sensitivity Toward Grief

Remember, put yourself in your subject's shoes. Traumatic events evoke unpredictable reactions from those involved. Emotional pain can override rational behavior. You may have become accustomed to witnessing violent death, but, for many of the people you photograph at a news story, this is their first time. If the casualties are personal friends or family, their reactions could be beyond their control. Balancing compassion with the need to do your job can be difficult, but that's the job. Without compassion, you'll miss the true heart of the story and focus only on the gruesome details, details that may never be used.

Photojournalists who cover emotionally charged stories get only so far by arguing their rights with upset bystanders. The best photojournalists I've worked with know how to explain, "Look, I respect your grief, but it's important that the public see and know what's happened if anything is to stop it from happening again." And, too, good photojournalists ask themselves before they record a single frame: Is this a case where I stand apart from the crowd or the media who are irritating them, or is this a case where traveling with the pack is the only safe thing to do?

The Ethics of Life and Death

On the worldwide stage, atrocities are photographed. Often, no attempt is made by media witnesses to stop the atrocities. The reasoning is twofold: One, their images capture and expose those events for the world to see, and, two, those images would not be captured if, by intervening, the photojournalists suffer the same fate as their subjects. The end result: The event goes undocumented.

By witnessing, a greater good has been served. This position of capturing versus intervening is by no means absolute. Let's look at a different story. A child is trapped in a burning car that will explode soon. What should you do? Save the kid! Always. A life will always have more value than a 30-second news story about another traffic accident. Between the two extremes lies a lot of gray area. Follow your conscience.

Laws and Ethics Present Boundaries

Learn where the boundaries are for yourself, for the company you're working for, and for the location. Photojournalists on the front lines are less likely to be injured by the nuclear bomb than the sniper fire. And that's kind of how it is on the front lines of legal and ethical issues as well. There are fewer situations where you'll be thrown in jail but more where you'll be caught going slightly over the bounds, getting you and your organization in trouble. A huge chunk of photojournalistic ethics is not black and white.

Everything Changes

Today, describing the ethics of photojournalism is like trying to shoot the Daytona 500 with an Instamatic. It's a blur. New-tech phenomena are flooding the marketplace—and flooding our profession—with new tools, new distribution routes, and new dilemmas.

Any citizen using a cell phone camera and YouTube now can instantly show the world a hospital patient, a movie premiere, or your exclusive video shot off a TV set. Never mind that these acts might violate HIPAA, copyright laws, or your right to make a living. With millions of citizens already using these tools, prevention is in danger of becoming impractical. Then what about punishment? Again, prosecuting millions of abusers seems impractical. Most don't have deep pockets, and existing laws can't keep up with every precedent du jour.

What to do? We saw the recording industry crack down on music downloaders (or at least try to), and an imposing consortium of Japanese corporations pressure YouTube to remove copyrighted videos. But in this globalized age of ubiquitous Paris Hilton tapes, Web site beheading videos, and pirated movies, is enforcement doomed to be porous? Is it inevitable that a sizable appetite and market will survive beyond the reach of law?

And consider this. In our legal system, your right to photograph a private citizen increases if the location is one where citizens should have the "reasonable expectation" of being photographed. Historically, those locations were sidewalks, ballparks, and the like. But as cell cams proliferate at every dorm kegger and every teen's bedroom computer comes with a camera, and every corporate hallway has a surveillance camera, how long will it be before someone claims we should have a "reasonable expectation" of being photographed . . . well, anywhere?

The implications are too numerous to cover here, and that's not my purpose. To me, these evolving times make it imperative that photojournalists dust off our code of fundamentals:

- The definition of privacy may change, but violating privacy is still wrong unless outweighed by some vastly compelling public right to know.
- Copyright theft is still wrong, even if "Everyone is downloading it, stupid."
- Using handout video without attribution still erodes the public's faith that we can be trusted.
- Staging is still not reality, especially if it conveys a false impression.

And, as always, there will be exceptions: a newsroom decision to show shocking images or private acts or re-creations. But each exception deserves a healthy newsroom discussion and perhaps, too, a "viewer advisory" (plus some promotional restraint). Having managed five newsrooms and watching three of them ascend to first place, I know newsroom conduct can leave our audiences feeling appreciative rather than insulted.

The biggest threat photojournalists face today is what I'd call the sellout by inches. The "everyone's-doing-it" syndrome, the "no one will know I cheated" rationale, the "blurred-lines-mean-no-lines" excuse. We know better. It catches up with you. Just ask the seventy-seven television stations facing FCC action for airing VNRs (video news releases) without informing their audiences. Or my ex-anchor facing a lawsuit for downloading copyrighted games at his sports bar. Or the photographers whose out-of-control celebrity stalking led to California's new antistalking laws.

We've been here before. In the 1930s, the photographic foodfight during the Lindbergh trial became a big reason American courtrooms banned cameras. I remember four decades later petitioning the Oklahoma Supreme Court to lift this ban, and it was not easy countering the resentment still directed at our past brethren. Let's not leave that legacy to those who follow us.

Photojournalists face a huge choice. The sheer size and reach of information sharing today threatens to create an "anything-goes" field of ethics. The old rules don't fit new technologies, the old enforcement is inadequate to control abuses, and the number of abusers and the size of their audiences are immense. For photojournalists, the temptation to bend the old rules will skyrocket. How they respond will help shape the ethics of the future.

Quite an opportunity.

At the heart of it, the laws and codes of ethics that govern photojournalists state that the responsibility is to truthfully document society and preserve its history.

CHAPTER 11

Mitchell Wagenberg
Covert Camera—The Fangs
of the Fourth Estate

Mitchell Wagenberg

Specialty Cameraman,
Engineer/Inventor

Investigative Mechanics, Inc., New York
StreeTVisions Remote, Inc., New York
George Polk Award for "Made in America," ABC *20/20*, 1998
Peabody Award for "9/11," CBS News, 2002
Columbia DuPont Award for "Hopkins 24/7," ABC News, 2002
Emmy for "Children for Sale," *Dateline NBC*, 2005

*S*even motorcycles weave through traffic on the outskirts of Phnom Penh, once known as the Pearl of Asia. The off-road bikes scream like chain saws as they race down the dirt road towards their destination. The city blurs to countryside, from wealth to poverty. The passengers lean in unison with their drivers, avoiding potholes and oxcarts.

Twenty minutes later, with their two-cycle engines spewing clouds of blue smoke, the team pulls to a stop just outside one of the most notorious villages in Cambodia. One by one, the passengers hop off the back and the motorcycles disappear into the distance. The breeze from the ride is gone, replaced by an oppressive humidity carrying scents of burning charcoal, burning animals, and urine. The sweat comes on fast as they survey their surroundings.

Like cowboys in an old-west movie, they slowly walk up a dirt road into the heart of Svay Pak. On the other side of town, hidden and waiting, Cambodian Special Forces armed with automatic weapons are waiting to strike. Svay Pak is a village of brothels. The trade here is not only women or men—it's children—some as young as eight years old. The team making its way through town is made up

EQUIPMENT

Sony DSR500 DV cam
UMHD-DR100 Micro drive recorder
MMV-1000/MicroMV micro video recorder
MicroCam camera
IM/Compaz Covert Pan and Zoom camera system
Button cam, pin cam, hat cam
MAV-LANC on/off control verification
Infrared lights

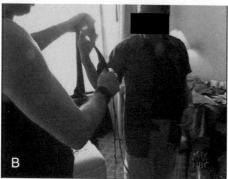

A. A shot taken in Svay Pak, Cambodia.

B, C. The team suits up with hidden cameras.

of Mitchell Wagenberg and a crew of six others from Dateline *and an NGO (nongovernmental organization), The International Justice Mission.*

As they walk down the narrow street, Wagenberg pushes the small button in his pocket. The button vibrates, alerting him that his undercover camera is operational and recording. The rest of the crew is wired as well, with cameras and recording devices placed in different locations around their bodies. I had a button camera on my shirt and a watch cam on my wrist; the investigator had a cell phone with a camera in it; another guy had sunglasses with a built-in camera. *Miniature recorders are shoved down their pants, positioned so they would be found only under the most explicit search or pat down.*

Wagenberg is the most sought-after undercover cameraman in the world. Through experience, custom video gadgetry, and tenacity, Wagenberg captures his style of high-quality, covert images in situations where a visible camera would be undesirable or dangerous. He's here because all of his "go to work" criteria have been met. This is a story Wagenberg wants to do, to be a part of, to effect a change.

Shortly, a fifteen-year-old hustler runs up and starts his sales pitch. They come over—they all smoke cigarettes—"Hey, Mister, how you doing? What's your name? Come see my girls!" They know the kids aren't going to get arrested; they've got the whole program down. *In this village, it's business as usual; his mother takes her cut.*

Wagenberg and team enter the small door to the brothel that was staked out weeks before. They're here to make a deal for a lot of young girls. The pimps think it's a payday for them. In reality, it's an attempt to rescue as many children as possible and send the pimps to prison.

Two Weeks Earlier

The Dateline *documentary starts in Phnom Penh, a tourist destination for those who come to see the Angkor Wat temple, the killing fields of Cheung Ek, and the cultural landscape of Cambodia. It's also a destination*

A. Mitchell's team suits up with hidden cameras.

B. Children for sale.

C. An American doctor confides to the hidden camera.

for a darker form of tourism. The name of their documentary says it all, "Children for Sale." Sexual predators—pedophiles—come from all over the world to this region for one reason: to rape children.

Within minutes of hitting the streets, a cab driver takes the crew to a whorehouse filled with children. Reeling with revulsion, the crew fights back the nausea as they pretend that they are sexual predators themselves.

The madam offers a member of the crew a child, a virgin, for $600. "You can take her to your hotel for three days." Six hundred dollars is double the annual income for an average Cambodian. Struggling Cambodian and Vietnamese families sell off their children for a few hundred bucks. The children work for years as prostitutes to pay off the debt. The undercover team covertly documents the negotiations for paid child abuse. They back away from the deal when they've recorded enough footage.

While roaming the city, the crew comes across an American doctor. They ask him, in a standard on-camera interview, why he comes to Phnom Penh so often. "The Cambodian people have been most welcome and most courteous at all times, and they've got some of the most remarkable architectural finds here." *Later, covertly, on hidden cameras, the doctor offers graphic details of his involvement with children.* "Usually I buy out three, three girls for 50 bucks. Take 'em for the whole night."

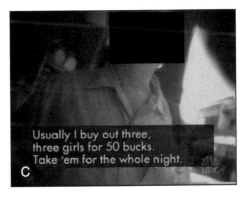

Usually I buy out three, three girls for 50 bucks. Take 'em for the whole night.

Child prostitution is part of the human trade in Phnom Penh, but nowhere is it more prevalent than in the small village of Svay Pak—a destination for pedophiles.

The International Justice Mission convinced the Cambodian Ministry of Justice to be part of a sting to document the sale of children in Svay Pak and arrest the pimps and madams who sell them. Wagenberg and NBC are along for the story of the operation. The Ministry of Justice offers Special Forces troops to back them up and make the arrests.

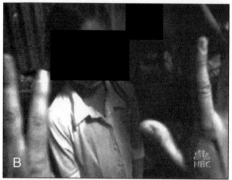

A. Children sitting in a brothel.

B. A Cambodian child discusses her fees with an undercover investigator. The camera is hidden in a button cam.

c. The bust begins.

In a Brothel of Children, Svay Pak

The sting is underway at the Svay Pak brothel, and the team is recording all of the setup. The plan is to buy the girls and take them out of the village for a sex party at a house they've rented a few miles away. The pimps are supposed to come to the house as well to watch after the girls. They'll be arrested by the Cambodian Special Forces as soon as they arrive.

The plan starts to fall apart early. On a previous visit, they recorded an off-duty policeman selling protection from arrest. They believe the same policeman has tipped off the pimps. They now insist that the "party" happen right here and right now. There is a rough back-up plan, but it will take some time.

There came a point where all of us were in separate rooms with at least three girls a piece, and we had to make the call. A member of the International Justice Mission used his cell phone to call in the Special Forces. Then we waited.

We brought some toys for the kids, some bottles of bubbles—pedophiles don't normally do that. The plan had unraveled and the pimps were getting nervous. You had to make some weird sounds in your room to make the people outside think that you're doing the dirty. These young girls, eight years old, they would just want to get down to business, and you would have to keep them occupied, teach them the ABCs, whatever you had to do.

Finally, the Special Forces and Police Arrive

When the troops started coming in, the girls started screaming. They didn't understand what was happening. They bolted for the door. I grabbed two girls by the hair so they wouldn't get away through holes in the wall. It was a very weird shot from the wrist camera I had on, but to me it was more important at that point to get the kids and not get that particular shot. The house had cages on it, barred doors. Some of the people in the neighborhood, when they saw the Special Forces

A. The military sweeps the town and makes arrests.

B. An investigator rescues a young girl.

coming down the hill, would lock the bars to make sure the girls wouldn't get out. One of the investigators lost his Mace; it rolled out under the barred door, and one of the locals took it and started spraying it through the door of the house, Macing all of us inside.

Although the sting doesn't go according to plan, it captures a dozen pimps and madams. The International Justice Mission's plan rescues thirty-seven children, thirty-seven little lives given a second chance and the freedom to be children again.

Mitchell Wagenberg, correspondent Chris Hansen, Dateline NBC, and the IJM show the world the hidden truth behind the brothel doors of Svay Pak and raise an awareness that could save thousands of children who are currently held for sale.

Who Is Mitchell Wagenberg?

Wagenberg is no less controversial than the subject of hidden cameras. A letter to the editor of the Columbia Journalism Review, *in response to an article on investigative journalism, refers to Wagenberg as a publicity averse mercenary who does the dirty work for the networks and doesn't ask questions. Wagenberg is no journalist, the letter states, and then asks, "Who is he? Why does he do it? How is he monitored? How many Americans have been secretly taped by him? What is his legal and moral rationale?"*

The next issue of CJR *publishes Wagenberg's response and leaves no doubt as to his job description or morality:*

As someone who designs, builds, and operates custom undercover gear for network investigative news organizations and also teaches undercover systems and techniques to dozens of state and federal law enforcement agencies, I am somewhat "publicity-averse." It goes with the territory and I take my job seriously. I do not "do dirty work" for the networks or anybody else. I do ask questions concerning the investigations that I am involved with. The reason I do this work is because I do it well and my systems and services are in demand by bona fide investigative units and agencies that I trust and believe in. These same organizations and agencies "monitor me" every single time I work with them. I need no "legal rationale" to do my work since it involves no illegal activity on my part, as opposed to many of the scam artists, abusers of power, and criminals that my undercover work and equipment have helped indict. My "moral rationale" is a belief in the traditions of journalism and muckraking as well as law enforcement and justice.

Reading (the letter) made me feel like some of those people who, after receiving their FBI file via the Freedom of Information Act, find out that they were on Nixon's enemy list.
I am honored.—M.W.

If you can find him, if he likes your idea, if he's available, maybe he and his team will shoot your project. For this interview, contact and setup took months. The interview itself took two hours and was likely taped by Wagenberg as I tape-recorded him. Several discussions and various versions of his blurred photograph were reviewed to ensure his identity was obscured to his liking. Wagenberg has energy and enthusiasm to burn, his 100-mph New York accent filled as many transcript pages as interviews twice as long. It's obvious that he loves the unique aspects of his work and is passionate about the stories he captures. To say Wagenberg is colorful is an understatement.

I'm not a spy. I'm not a plumber. I'm a cameraman who does specialty cameras. I'm a director of photography. I just do it differently. When I have the time to light somebody covertly, I use the same techniques as any photographer except my lights are infrared. I'll have a nice key, a nice fill, and some back lighting, but it will be infrared light at 950 nanometers wavelength, with different intensity instruments, diffusion, spots, and floods. Light that you can't see with the naked eye, but, when you put an infrared camera on it, that stuff looks really pretty for undercover footage. I learned all that by shooting commercials, fashion shows, network stuff when I was just working for production companies out there in the union, just doing jobs.

Earlier, I worked for a defense contractor. I did work with the USIA (United States Information Agency) teaching television engineering overseas in South Asia. I just took a lot of the tools that I learned back then and brought them into journalism. When you're in and out of the embassies, you meet people and one thing leads to another. That just warped into taking knowledge on that side of the fence and marrying it with the TV end of it. So, now, I'm trying to bring the best pictures possible to the undercover world.

If you see the FBI's footage of Abscam or Marion Barry smoking crack in Washington, that was some of the most miserable video. You can't even recognize who the hell's there, but for indictment purposes that's all the cops are going to need. Video is an automatic plea-out for the lawbreaker, for the suspect. Once there's video, the defense lawyers—they plead out. Where are they going to go? What are they going to say, that's not you? "That's not me." "Oh, that's not you?"

Some of the stuff that we're shooting now with high resolution makes it prettier. It is just something that we do. We do what the network wants with image quality, but the cops and the juries certainly don't mind it because it brings it all back home and they can really hear what's going on and it can make the case much more convincing.

There are some stories I just don't want to work on, and we don't. We just politely don't. You've got to know where to draw the line. I pick my poison, and, hopefully, I'm doing the right thing and on the right side. Occasionally, a motion picture wants us to do something, and they'll call and, if we feel that it's appropriate, we might get involved in some way.

Undercover Encounters Expose Crime and Corruption

Investigative journalism does just that—it investigates. The story is not laying on the surface for everyone to see; it takes some digging. These are the stories that are being covered up, kept private by people and organizations who, in many cases, cause harm to a person, community, country, or, in terms of industrial pollution, the world. Without a watchdog, who would call these people to account?

How would you find out what was happening in the world without hidden cameras? You just wouldn't. Hidden cameras are tools that are used constantly in every law enforcement arsenal, and these days they're in every arsenal of the top hundred television affiliates around the country. Take any big, major thing that's gone on. Who has exposed it? The Fourth Estate has exposed it. News people have exposed it. Intrepid investigative reporters are the ones that go out and do it.

Most of the stories that you see on primetime network news shows have come out of the *Washington Post* or *New York Times* or the *L.A. Times*. Walt Bogdonich is one hero in the business. He's a great news guy, comes from the *Cleveland Plain Dealer*, a great investigative reporter. When he worked for *60 Minutes*, I did some great stuff with him. Now he's back working for the *New York Times* and still digging away. Alan Maraynes is a great investigative guy I worked with at *CBS News, ABC News*, and now at *NBC News*. I am proud of the dozens of important investigative stories I have worked on with him and the many awards they have won.

Sometimes hidden cameras are used for no good reason at all, and other times they're used for great reason, exposing things that otherwise wouldn't be exposed—human rights abuse and animal rights abuse being two major things happening around the world.

Undercover Equipment

One of Wagenberg's companies is StreeTVisions Remote, and the other is Investigative Mechanics, which manufactures and sells advanced surveillance technologies. Wagenberg's company develops gadgets that would make James Bond's "Q" jealous. His company sells tools (undercover cameras and support) to law enforcement, government, and bona fide investigative news organizations only. In other words, if you're an idiotic reality show or entertainment magazine show, forget it; we're not interested.

We sell to intelligence agencies, too. *Wagenberg's client list reads like an alphabet soup of acronyms for clandestine super-secret organizations—all of which were deleted from the first draft of this chapter.* Basically, some of the same tools used by the intelligence agencies are used more and more by newspeople who can get access to them. There are agencies that order stuff from us to see how we did it, what we're doing. They take it apart, dissect it; they'll check it out. They just don't want to reinvent the wheel.

A lot of intelligence agencies have unlimited amount of budget. They have stuff that you'll never see. The stories are true. Years ago, they sutured recorders into trained pigeons who then landed in, let's say, the backyard of the Chinese Embassy and gathered information. You can't buy "pigeon cams" from us—yet. We don't injure animals in our business, and I'll bet it's difficult to teach them to make a steady shot.

There is certain gear that we can't send overseas—Title 3 stuff, which means it can be used on a consumer level or industrial level, but it can also be used in human rights abuse—so the U.S. government watches that quite closely.

I do a lot of undercover training with law enforcement and investigative news people. When you're going to go undercover, you consider your scenario before you pick what equipment you're going to use. What will your story be about? Will you be able to move freely? Will you be closely monitored? Is it dangerous?

Wagenberg's company divides the equipment into two basic categories: "Wired," which is his preferred method, with the recorder being placed on the operator; and "Wireless," which he leaves as a last resort due to potential transmission errors. After that the categories are broken down into "Above the Neck" and "Below the Neck." Anything above the neck, you've got the shot; anything below the neck, you've got to work it. You've got to really work a button or a necklace or a pin. I always put "Above the Neck" on a layman unless I have a second camera on them somehow. Sometimes you shoot with several cameras if you can get away with it; especially now that we have the small recorders, you're more likely to get the shot.

From Wagenberg's company's literature, the following table lists the advantages and disadvantages of various undercover cameras.

Advantages and Disadvantages of Undercover Cameras

Advantages	Disadvantages
Above the Neck—Examples: Hat Cam, Glasses Cam, and Others	
Easier to follow the action	Must face target
Can readily face target	Not always appropriate (hat, glasses)
More critical ID of individuals, actions, transactions, items, contraband	Hat: cable must extend to collar (long hair only)
Easier to "work" (not shooting blind)	Glasses—not for everyone
Below the Neck—Examples: Button Cam, Pin Cam, and Others	
Do not need to face target	Will not readily face target
Many more choices of outerwear/gear	Gender specific (tie, necklace)
Particular low-body applications (pager, belt)	Must "work it" to get shot (shooting blind)
Bag cam is self-contained (nothing on body)	More practice necessary

Wagenberg is constantly inventing and manufacturing new devices. Years of experience guide him from one solution to the next. His products have been developed in response to the unique demands of each story and undercover situation.

Glasses Cam

When you wear the glasses, it's a no-brainer. Glasses cam can't miss the shot; wherever you look, you're going to get it. The disadvantage is, I've got to stay on my target, and sometimes you don't want to be staring at your target. So, I will use a different method.

There are dealers who I know of that sell these to the entertainment shows. The problem that I have with that is it takes us two years to develop new glasses, and if an entertainment show gets hold of them, they zoom right in and show how it's wired. I've got guys doing investigative news and law enforcement agents who are in some hairy situations all over the world. It's dangerous. We don't want everyone to know what our gear looks like.

Button Cam

The button cams are great because the button cam you can put anywhere. We did a bust on a local bad dentist who was fondling patients who were under anesthesia, and one of my people went in with a button cam fastened on the top of a sneaker. You can imagine that shot sitting in a dentist chair when they went under. The dentist was caught red-handed. I can reframe a button cam to work as long as I'm thinking about what I'm doing. That's the problem—when somebody has to be thinking about pounds and ounces of drugs or caliber of weapons—working undercover and also thinking about getting the shot, that complicates the situation.

Lens

Buttom cam.

Screw Cam

The newest, hottest thing we've built is a Philips screw cam. The Philips screw goes right into a wall somewhere, anywhere. The camera's right inside, just like a button cam. These things aren't obvious, people aren't going to start looking at every Philips screw, every button you wear.

Cap Cam

The cameras we build in the baseball caps are lipstick-type cameras, really tiny ones that we build so it is exactly right. Then you use the brim to judge your headroom. I know that if I'm looking at you and my brim is cutting off right at your hairline, I've shot a composed, perfect picture.

Screw cam.

Mailbox Cam

The camera is mounted looking out the back of a mailbox pointing towards the house. The great thing about the mailbox cam is, when the guy is heading up the driveway he'll rarely look back and see the darkened backside of the mailbox. So you see the guy going into the house, then running out when he thinks it's over. By that time he has too many other problems than to focus on why the mailbox looks a little odd.

Sidewalk Cam

We've got a guy that we use in Pennsylvania who's great. He molds pieces of sidewalk with the rebar hanging out of it so I can pick it up. It's light as a feather and underneath is all hollow. You put in your transmitters, you put in the cameras, and you're ready to shoot.

Transformer Cam

We empty out the gray transformers you see on telephone poles and put cameras in them. It looks like a black band holding it on the pole, but it is actually a cutout where the dome camera is

Robotic cam.

Infrared light.

looking down at the facility, panning, tilting, and zooming.

Birdhouse and a Coconut Cams

I've got tons of birdhouses with cameras hidden inside. Got to have that; everyone should have one. The last great camera I built a while ago in Fort Myers, Florida, is "The Coconut Cam." We made a dome cam look like a coconut and put it up in the palm tree and now you're seeing both ways up and down the block.

Robotic Cameras

For *Dateline's* "To Catch a Predator," all the cameras in the "interview room" are high-end robotic. I'm getting 800 lines of resolution out of these cameras. They rarely even cut to the Beta cams when the reporter exposes the sting. They're using our cameras just to show the whole big picture because the robotics are that smooth and looking that good. The remote controller can move them on all axes: x, y, and z.

The cameras use optical zooms instead of digital ones for greater picture quality. We built the image quality up to such a degree that people can't believe it's a hidden camera. It's just images that people don't expect from hidden cameras.

Infrared

The infrared light you see on some camcorders is very spotty; it spots your face and kind of overexposes you. That light's wavelength is 880 nanometers. It lets you see in very dark places. If I have big 880-nanometer lights and we put them on trees to illuminate a whole yard, it's a very hot light to the touch and you'll see a red glow. I go a step above that.

I use infrared lights that are used more in the intelligence world and not the prosumer—those between professionals and consumers—or DP world. Their light wavelength is 950 nanometers, which is invisible to the human eye, but they put out just as much light. I have them as big as a 2K, and I have them as small as a button. The Russians are building some fabulous little, tiny infrareds the size of a quarter. They eat a lot of power, but they have lenses on them that can spread the light 120 degrees; it appears less spotty. We'll take them and use regular Rosco diffusion on them to diffuse that light just like you would any light. Light is light. I don't care if it's ultraviolet, infrared, or visible.

One-way Mirrors

My robotic cameras are in cabinets with two-piece, specially baked glass that act like mirrors. If you don't black out the back right, you can see through it, but if you black it out correctly, you can't see through it. The old one-way mirrored glass will knock you down three stops; it's very dark and you won't make good pictures unless the room is very well lit. The new glass that we have—you make incredible pictures with less light.

Remote Controls

We were one of the first ones that came up with remote controls that confirm recording status. That changed a lot of things for law enforcement and for investigative news teams in the under-cover world. Before that you were dead-rolling and you were walking around just hoping you were going to come back with that footage. When you push a button and it vibrates once and a little tiny light comes on, you know you're rolling. Three vibrates: off; constant vibrate: no video—your battery's dead or the cable came loose.

So, now, when I'm undercover, I think I'm getting great stuff and I feel this vibration: I've got to go to the car for my cigarettes, I've got to go to the bathroom. You've got to go because you know you're not getting video. Beforehand, you thought you were getting it, you came out and you had nothing. There is never a worse feeling in the world.

Wireless Transmitters

A lot of people go wireless, but wireless transmitters don't always work. I worked microwave for years, and I know the pros and cons. Wireless transmitters can spit and roll. If you're wearing a transmitter, and you're in a place like Manhattan and a bus goes by, microwave doesn't work. Microwave doesn't like metal or human flesh. Bad microwave looks like reception from bad rabbit ears—you're not going to make pictures. There are times, just for safety, you have to wear wireless because you need to see. Even if it's rolling and spitting, you need to see what's going on inside the place. It could be a dangerous situation, so you want a backup of some sort.

Miniature Recorders

We make some of the smallest digital video recorders available anywhere in the world. One version uses MPEG 2 compression and has full-screen DVD image quality at thirty frames per second, with up to eight hours of record time. We also make one so small it almost disappears in a closed fist. It records on an SD card for up to an hour of thirty-frames-per-second video.

Another recording device is our MMV-1000 micro video recorder that records DV-quality video onto Micro MV digital tape with a sixty-minute record time. It also has a built-in 2.5-inch screen for viewing the footage.

Several different minature recorders.

A miniature recorder.

High Definition

I have my first HD dome cams built already. I've got my infrared 1080I high-definition cameras—I put on my own hot heads. Now we're working on HD1080 and 720P button cams and little tiny hard-drive recorders that we're going to record HD right to drive. We want to be the first guys out there having HD undercover gear when people start asking for it. There are certain people starting to ask for it for certain shows now.

So, the robotics stuff: Totally in HD, and the infrared night stuff is totally in high definition. Now we're working on the glasses, the pens, the necklaces—all of our equipment changed to HD.

Fireproof/Microwave and Airplanes

We've done arson investigations where we've mounted cameras in fireproof boxes in vehicles we thought would be torched. The video is then microwaved to an airplane so that, when the arsonist strikes and the wires melt, we'll still have the pictures. If the fire department is standing by and they get to the car as soon as possible, we can retrieve the fireproof box and perhaps save the camera. The airplane was a Florida Highway Patrol plane, a Cessna with three antennae underneath the wings. They were circling because you can't follow a perp in a chopper; they're going to know it every time. When you have a plane that is 2,800 feet up and two miles out, just constantly circling with the right microwave, you're making great pictures and the person you're following will never know.

Standard Broadcast Cameras

When I've got to do normal end surveillance out of a vehicle, I go with the DSR500 DV cam with a 33× Canon lens with a 2× extender. We get big vehicles because if they shake, the shot is lost. When I work a "ride along" with the cops, all of that is done with small three-chip cameras that I "trick out" with a matte box and a little, invisible infrared light.

Constant Creativity

Name the item and place "cam" after it and Wagenberg's company can make it. This could be a "book cam." I'm writing with a "pen cam" (which actually exists). Sound like fun? It is. Wagenberg's imagination and creativity have solved countless production problems and placed cameras in positions where they would never be expected. Creating a new invention, watching it work, ridding the world of yet another criminal, network execs ooh and ahh over your work. Who wouldn't love that job?

Camera Operatives

Wagenberg is not alone in his company. His father and brother work there, too. He also hires outside operators as the jobs dictate. Doing undercover work is not for everyone. A lot of what you do is based on deceit but, hopefully, for the better good. There's no other way to get around that statement.

I have freelancers, a few guys and a few gals. If I'm going into a factory in Chinatown to buy garments or look for a job, I can't be a thirty-year-old Chinese woman, so there are certain freelancers out there who fit the mold. They walk the walk and talk the talk and freelance on a regular basis. Most of the workers, they don't rig themselves up; we've got somebody to do that. We make it so that it's really simple. Years ago things were really big and tough to do.

These days, tiny hard drives are difficult to detect. When you go into a strip club, you get patted down; you get wanded *[scanned with a metal detector]*. We've got ways around all that. We put little recorders right down in a jock strap down your pants. Wear a belt, and the belt motivates the wand to go off so security doesn't detect the recorder.

You still can't get through metal detectors, although there are times we did. We got through security by sheer force of numbers. You send four or five guys in when it's busy, overwhelm security, and get in. Invariably, guys will get stopped, and they'll go, "What's that?" "Well, nothing." And they say, "Take it out of your pocket," and you just walk away. But, eventually, one the guys slips through. For years, we did a lot of raves. Law enforcement or the media went out and were looking to show parents what kids were doing at raves. They were on all sorts of high-end Ecstasy, multiple drugs, and we would see people passed out on the floor. Parents just don't know what this rave thing is all about.

I had a crew of women who were all in their twenties, but they could make themselves look like they were sixteen or seventeen. They went in all tricked-out with hidden cameras that were extremely light sensitive, with tiny little infrared emitters on them to make their own light.

We'd expose a lot of what goes on in Puerto Vallarta and Cancun during spring break where it's all you can drink. High schoolers are just passed out with alcohol poisoning all over the place. These are all the things we do. It's more than "news you can use"; it's alerting parents when their kid says, "I'm going with my friend down to Cancun for spring break." They don't really know what goes on down there.

For *60 Minutes*, I had to get a picture of a guy who stole fifty million dollars from a firm, and no one knew what the guy looked like. I couldn't park a van on the street outside his Greenwich, Connecticut, mansion because the cops would be there in a second. So you've got to think, What do you do? Well, I've got three joggers and three people on bicycles going around this house. It has only one driveway in and out. We can't trespass on the property, we're not going in there as a florist or something else, so it took us four, five, maybe six days to get the shot. We were starting at eight o'clock in the morning and going until eight at night. Finally, we timed it right and the guy backed out of the driveway; somebody on a bicycle—it was my brother who works in the business with me—stopped in front of the car and just asked directions. He was wired and, boom, we had our shot of the guy. So you've got to get a little clever sometimes.

You have to learn about whatever the subject matter of the story is; otherwise, you look like an idiot. So we're constantly doing research into the topics we cover. You can go in there just as a buddy if somebody else is doing the talking. Often times, I say the biggest thing you always do in situations that allow it is to always have a woman with you. If you have a woman undercover with you, a lot of times it brings the tension level down on the whole situation. We like to send women operatives in to do a lot of the stuff that we do if it's cool with the scenario. The women I have are all great shooters, and they fit the part. They're good looking, although you don't want them drop-dead gorgeous. You want them to just be there and do it and get out. You need to pick the right crew, the right tools for the job. That's what it comes down to in the end.

To Catch a Predator

Back in the States and thousands of miles from the pedophiles of Svay Pak, Wagenberg and crew have spent a great deal of time on the Dateline *series "To Catch a Predator." Here in the U.S., they're able to bring considerably more undercover assets to bear. The results are clear to the communities they're working in and the network they're working for.* It's the best ratings the show ever had. This new series has really kind of invigorated them, and, as a public service, they're getting these bad guys off the street and informing parents. With *Dateline*, you've got eight million people watching per show, and it gives good exposure to the problem; it's changing legislation.

We set up sting houses, twenty-four cameras, static, robotics, and body wear. We work with law enforcement, but we don't cross the line. *Dateline* is in the house as the journalist, and law enforcement is in the house next door, or attached apartments or a mobile vehicle. The predators chat online with who they think are twelve- and thirteen-year-old kids, but really they're a group of about seventy volunteer adults, called Perverted Justice, posing as children.

The predators think they're going to a house to meet a child while the parents are away. All the Internet conversations and Web-cam interactions are printed out, the transcript is printed out, the Web stuff is printed out. They broke the law just by going online with who they think is a thirteen-year-old. Even if it's not, if they think it's a thirteen-year-old they've broken the law. So, before they get to the house they broke the law; when they come into the house, it's pure intent. The volunteers tell the predators, "Don't forget to bring me some chocolate." So, we know they have something that they said they were going to bring to prove why they're there.

A nineteen-year-old who looks like a twelve-year-old, meets the predator at the door. She or he says, "Come on in," and they walk into what's usually a kitchen. They come up with an excuse to leave for a moment and then, boom, out comes the correspondent, Chris Hansen, who asks, "What are you doing here?"

We'll get thirty to fifty guys in a three-day shoot, which is why we have to have a big task force of cops. There's a lot of processing to be done and it's a big operation.

On the TV end, too. I've got between sixteen and twenty-four hidden cameras going, and the cops are also wearing body wear *[hidden cameras]*.

A typical NBC "Predator" series control room: There are 22 covert cameras—12 robotic, 6 static, and 4 undercover body wear. All images and audio are recorded to digital and simultaneously fed via microwave to secure locations for law enforcement "takedowns." Images are a mix of high-resolution color and infrared and thermal imaging.

Interrogation rooms have cameras; the cars that they bring them down to the jail in have cameras. So, it's a lot of hidden cameras, the whole gamut, from the robotics to the car cams. It's an eight- to ten-man operation to keep everything going.

On one occasion, a predator walks in stark naked. He walks around the house like that, and then Chris Hansen walks out and hands him a towel. The next day, we caught him online again. He goes to McDonald's to meet another twelve-year-old boy. We get set up at McDonald's, this predator shows up again, and Chris walks out and he says to the suspect, "In twenty-four years of broadcasting, I am for the first time speechless. After yesterday, I'm just speechless."

Hidden Camera Legalities and Ethics

There are a number of legal issues surrounding the use of hidden cameras. Privacy laws, trespass laws, and entrapment laws change from country to country, state to state, and town to town. At the network level, there are lawyers retained to advise on the legal implications of each undercover story.

There are a number of states that are one-party states *[where only one party needs to know that they are being recorded]* and some that are two-party states *[where both parties need to know that they are being recorded]*. Some states are tougher than others, some states we have to stay away from. In the states that have a single-party rule, you can shoot anybody you want, anywhere, except where there is a presumed right of privacy.

You can't record a two-way conversation on the phone anywhere in the country without a court order; that's a federal law. California is a two-party state, but if a third party is involved or near the conversation, it could be legal to record that. Florida is a two-party state, but we shot in our private house. All we had to do, legally, was put up a little sign that said, "This house is under video and audio surveillance," like something that would be on your ADT sign. It wasn't hidden. When you walked to the front door, you would see it, but it was a sign that looked like something you would see anywhere. That, legally, allowed the network to go in and do what they had to do in that jurisdiction.

Each state and municipality in that state has different laws, but the lawyers are on top of that. I go to a lot of meetings involving lawyers because, once we get involved, they advise what we can do and what we can't do, where we're allowed to go, where we're not allowed to go. Lawyers live and die on what we can and can't do, and they want you to be very careful. We always back ourselves up that way. Lawsuits have really put a damper on the whole network news business. All the networks have their big faux pas. They all mess up and make mistakes, but in the end hidden cameras are around and are always going to be around.

The first two times we did the *Dateline* "Predator" series, tons of e-mails came into NBC saying, "Where were the cops? You guys let these guys go into the streets among the people again?" Then we started to get involved with law enforcement. We're getting involved in law enforcement, and a lot of the other networks had problems with that because what is Wagenberg? Is he a cop, or is he a journalist? Well, I do ride that line, no doubt about it, but I try to keep it separate and distinct because you can't be a journalist and a cop; you can only be one or the other. With this particular series, we're getting a lot of grief from other journalists—holier than thou people—saying, this isn't real news reporting; this is the cops doing stings.

In the end, it's going to get harder for the predators. Those guys aren't going to come out; they'll be afraid they're going to get busted. If they stop coming out, the series will end. So, it's going to solve the problem at the expense of the program and, in the end, that's fine with me.

Now Congress is going to pass laws against soliciting minors on the Net. That's what investigative reporting is all about: changing society for the better.

Going undercover and using hidden cameras without legal advice and the backup of a large news organization can get you in a lot of trouble. Because there are guys out there who are going to sue you when they can, and you won't have the backup money. I'm not going to go to India undercover, or Afghanistan, the poppy fields, or anywhere unless it's for a legitimate news organization. I know that if I get into a jam with ABC, CBS, or NBC, my ass is covered. I know if I'm in a hot spot, there's going to be a lawyer somewhere in that country that will come to my aid. Sometimes, you can't say the same thing depending on what intelligence agency you're working for. The police agencies and most law enforcement agencies you can. They're going to cover you if you're working with them on something. In the end, the people I do trust are those I'm working for.

Undercover Safety and Schedules
Dangerous Work

Undercover, hidden camera work is not without its moments of adrenaline-filled danger. One of Wagenberg's main concerns is safety. Safety comes from planning and experience and a sixth sense about your next move when seconds count. It doesn't get dangerous too often, but it gets close sometimes, it gets tight. You get confronted. You've got to be ready for it. You've got to have eyes in the back of your head, especially in a place like Cambodia or any foreign country where you don't speak the language. I've got a tough time with my Spanish; my English is sometimes an issue. You've always got to have a fixer with you, that's the bottom line. When you have a good fixer *[someone who really knows the lay of the land]* with you, you're golden.

For safety and the success of his undercover work, Wagenberg also takes great precautions to keep his identity private. You never see pictures of me. I make no bones about it; there are never pictures of me in anything we do. I don't go to any award shows. I'm a behind-the-scenes guy and whatever happens, happens, but no pictures are allowed. In one-on-one undercover encounters and long-term investigations that will lead to indictments or to investigations, you just don't want to be the guy that was recognizable.

Undercover Takes Time

Working undercover can be very time consuming and painfully boring. Once everything is set, you just wait. Watch any cop show where they stake out a house all night, and the shot of the cops peering through a van window lasts ten seconds. In reality, that same "shot" lasts ten hours or much, much more. You've got to persevere in this work; you can't expect to come back with a story in three days overseas. It doesn't work like that. Sometimes it does and sometimes it doesn't. For *60 Minutes*, our assignment was to catch Edwin Edwards, the governor of Louisiana, gambling with state money down in Lake Tahoe with his girlfriend.

Well, for a forty-second shot of him gambling at the poker tables, we went in there—we used small tricks that aren't illegal. I put a little scanner in my pocket and a little wireless in my ear, and I'm listening to the casino security frequency and, actually, I heard them talking about me and my brother when we were sitting at the same table as the governor. We know they're looking out for us, so we left them there and my brother got in the elevator with the governor and his girlfriend going up twenty-six flights. We got some great shots gambling, but for that thirty- or forty-second shot, we were in Lake Tahoe for ten days.

Repercussions

The work that Mitchell Wagenberg and his company do rarely ends with a simple tagline, with the story all neatly wrapped up. Often, it's just the first salvo in an ongoing battle to expose an injustice that was previously invisible to the public. Dateline NBC's *"Children for Sale" investigation did not end in Svay Pak with the rescued children. In Cambodia, six suspects were found guilty and sentenced to up to fifteen years. The madam in Phnom Penh selling the virgin, "three days, 600 dollars," received a twenty-year sentence.* The laws actually changed, and there is now training for Cambodians on how to confront this thing the right way. After this investigation, for the first time in Australia two guys were extradited from Canberra and sent back to Phnom Penh. It was the first time ever that Westerners were actually brought back for prosecution. You might as well slit your wrists right now if you're going to prison in Cambodia for twenty years.

A few weeks later in Saipan, Dateline *found the American doctor they had met in Cambodia offering personal details of his experiences with child prostitution.*

What I love most is when I'm undercover in a bar in Cambodia, and there's this American doctor—he's a little suspicious of me. I'm getting pictures of him with his buddy using a wrist cam. Then, I went and shot him as a regular Beta cameraman, with a camera on my shoulder coming right up to him when Chris Hansen, the correspondent, confronts him. The doctor was working as a radiologist in Saipan, and I know when he turned and looked at me, he did a double take, saying, "That's the guy, that's the guy I saw in Phnom Penh." He saw me before; he knew I was the one. That's when my glory comes in. "Yeah, I am the one, that's me, take a good look. You're not going to be going anywhere for a while."

If *Dateline* had not been there, the doctor would not have been caught. Even if he did get arrested, his lawyer might come in and get him out on bail. But when ten million people are watching on TV, "Your shit is over, man."

Through ingenious camera designs and surveillance techniques, Mitchell Wagenberg has refined the art of catching and exposing pedophile/predators. He has dedicated his life to making the world a better place by saving one child at a time.

I, I, I usually take -- don't take girls that are very, very young. I mean 15,16 and older.

Reporter Chris Hansen confronts an American doctor with an undercover tape.

The watchdog has teeth. Most of the time it's kept behind the fence sniffing the air for a scent of trouble, then making just enough racket to let the world know when something's wrong. Other times it has to protect the junkyard.

The tiny remote in Mitchell Wagenberg's pocket vibrates once.

CHAPTER 12

Heidi McGuire

The One-Woman Band

Heidi McGuire
Backpack Journalist

WFMY-TV News 2, Greensboro, North Carolina
Society of Professional Journalists, First Place for Spot News

*I*t's springtime in Greensboro, North Carolina. The grass needs mowing, there are leaves on the trees, and Simpson's clouds float in a cheerful blue sky. Morning sun warms the dashboard of a white Dodge minivan peacefully motoring down the road along with all the other minivans carpooling to work and school. Shaken loose from under the seats—papers, plates, old fast-food wrappers, and drink cups bounce around on the floor. A tennis shoe moves off the gas pedal to kick a brightly colored cardboard sandwich box back out of sight. Behind the wheel, Heidi McGuire is thinking about spring cleaning, blooming flowers, and a fresh coat of paint to brighten the day. She's not thinking about cleaning the minivan or painting the house; she's planning how to shoot today's story.

Heidi McGuire is a BPJ. "Backpack journalist" is one of a growing number of names given to one-man bands or, in McGuire's case, a one-woman band. She does it all: finds the story, sets it up, shoots it—interviews, stand-ups, and B-roll—writes and edits it, and, from time to time, goes live during the newscast to introduce it. Day after day.

The trash on the floor settles down as McGuire pulls to a stop at her location. A quick look in the mirror is more habit than anything else. There's no time for lipstick and a brush, and this is not the story for a "glamour arrival." Not that you'd ever step out of a minivan with WFMY News 2 printed on the sides and pull that off.

Heidi McGuire pulls her camera equipment from the back of a specially modified minivan. Smoked windows hide the set-up from prying eyes and offer a bit of privacy. Sometimes privacy is essential on long stories. The back seats have been replaced by a desk—a desk is just as efficient as bench seats when it comes to hiding sporks and Tupperware. McGuire puts a fresh battery on the camera, still warm from the charger running off the minivan's DC-AC inverter.

EQUIPMENT

Sony PD-170 camera

Tripod

Light kit: 2 tough spun lights, gels

Lectro CR-187 wireless microphone and transmitter

Panasonic Tough Book (laptop) with Avid Newscutter

Caravan Minivan with desk, AC power, and lights for editing

Headphones and desktop speakers

Steady bag

Handheld microphone

A. Flowers are used as the opening shot for the story. Spring introduces bright colors.

B, C. A team of DOT workers repaints the road lines every year after winter weather dulls the color; they are out to brighten things up.

Camera in hand, she walks toward large yellow highway trucks, blonde hair blowing in the spring air—it's a beautiful day . . . for a story about big, heavy, greasy road-painting vehicles. But for Heidi McGuire, the story is more about blooming flowers on the side of the road and a fresh coat of paint to spruce up the lanes. It's about springtime.

Framing brightly colored flowers and freshly painted asphalt, McGuire shoots her story. The caravan of Department of Transportation (DOT) vehicles lumbers down the road at a break-neck speed of five miles per hour. Diesel and paint fumes fill the air. McGuire is a skilled photographer, and her visual sense of storytelling comes naturally. Everything is falling into place for McGuire: The wide shots are interesting and establish location, the close-ups come alive with detail and motion.

Now it's time for the tricky stuff—continue photographer job; add reporter layer. McGuire doesn't let the photographic part of her work slide as she moves into reporting—the "look" needs to be seamless. Photojournalists and reporters are both responsible for story content, but when the two jobs are held by one person, that person needs to be in front of the camera from time to time, conducting interviews and doing stand-ups.

Framing and headroom are a challenge for every shot Heidi McGuire appears in. Finding unique ways to mount the camera, frame the shot, and shoot themselves while carrying out interviews and doing stand-ups requires a special resourcefulness—a MacGyver ability to make a shot work with the tools at hand. McGuire sets the interview shot: A DOT worker will be kneeling down by the line in the road—a very relevant place for an interview. She kneels across the line from him and makes sure the interview will be comfortable. "Stay here; I'm gonna set my shot."

At the camera she adjusts the headroom in the frame for him—he's a little taller—and allows room for her on the other side. McGuire pushes the record button; this is not for the actual interview, it's a test.

She quickly takes her place in the frame and makes some small talk. "Excuse me," McGuire is back at the camera checking the shot in play-back. It's good. "You ready?" she calls from the camera as she starts recording. A second later, she's in the shot and the interview is going—perfectly framed.

McGuire's pleasant demeanor puts her subjects at ease and often gets her access to story elements that might be off limits. You can catch more flies with honey than with vinegar. It's time for the stand-up. The best place for a stand-up in this story is in the driver's seat of the DOT paint truck as it's driving down the road.

As a BPJ, she's always looking for ways to do stand-ups from interesting angles, and that often means finding new methods and unusual places to secure the camera. For this shot, the tripod moved too much, so McGuire uses a steady bag (a nylon bean bag that conforms to the base of the camera) to hold down the camera. Again, guess the headroom, set the shot, record a little, play back, readjust if necessary, roll. It's easy to see that the methods Heidi McGuire and other BPJs use take more time and patience than a standard two- or three-man crew. But the results are unique to the individual BPJs themselves. It is complete authorship. The whole story—start to finish—is theirs.

The DOT crew surprises McGuire by changing the warning board that signals traffic work. The story opened on a flower and closed on a light-hearted moment as the trucks drive away. The sign on top flashes, "Reporter Painting." The package ends. It's been a Heidi McGuire story from the first frame to the last.

Stand-up: "Look at me, I'm painting and talking at the same time!"

"Get off the road!" This is McGuire's favorite closing shot.

The Evolution of the One-Person Band

The concept of BPJs, one-person band, solo journalist, is not new. These positions have existed in small markets around the United States for decades. Largely as a matter of finances, small stations need to keep things simple, inexpensive. Small markets also serve as a training ground for journalists eager to hone their craft and climb the ladder to larger cities and international assignments. Many top broadcast *journalists today started out as one-person bands in small markets. But once they move on to a larger market, they tend to specialize in either reporting or photojournalism and work as part of a crew, sharing responsibilities.*

Enter the new millennium. Dwindling advertising revenues in large markets, followed by the shrinking size of broadcast-quality cameras and the availability of inexpensive laptop editing solutions, made the appearance of one-person bands in large-market television an attractive alternative to the status quo. Add to that the new breed of journalists, BPJs, who have developed reporting styles that fit into the large-market story rotation, while using the smaller "prosumer" equipment and executing lightning-fast laptop deadlines. All of these developments have created openings for enterprising one-person bands to work in top news organizations around the world.

The backpack journalist is a specialist, although he or she covers a wide variety of subjects. It takes a special person to gather news and compete with the newsgathering/storytelling firepower of a seasoned crew of photojournalist and reporter. Often BPJs gravitate more toward feature stories where their complete authorship shines as a singular point of view. In organizations where there are both standard crews and BPJs, the standard crews may get assigned more of the heavy lifting—although not always. Most BPJs are expected to enterprise and turn around the same number of stories with the same deadlines as the rest of the staff. "It's nice that you're a BPJ—Now feed the beast."

The odds of creating a successful staff made solely of BPJs covering a large market are low, although nothing is impossible. Success in news is based on ratings, which the station converts to advertising revenues, which helps pay for newsroom assets—both people and equipment. If a station's full news-gathering personnel are all BPJs and they're number one in their market, the station has achieved the Holy Grail of news production: top ratings with half the labor costs. However, if ratings are slipping, the staff reduced to cut costs, the remaining forced into BPJ positions or lose their jobs, all in the hopes of regaining profit margin before quality—it doesn't take an MBA to figure that one out. The whirlpool sucks down.

A great BPJ is rare, and the ones that are great know it. They've found their journalistic voice through a combination of a unique personality, limitations of equipment and resources, and the adaptations required to survive alone. They excel at every aspect of the news-gathering process and have developed individual styles that accentuate their strong points and make their handicaps invisible.

Being a BPJ is not for everyone. It takes a strong individual with a lone wolf mentality and a dedication to one's own vision. A day in the life of a BPJ can be exhausting, and part of the skill is being able to deal with the demands of the newsroom while telling the uniquely crafted stories you are expected to crank out. McGuire knows how to balance news deadlines with her personal style of story-telling. One-man bands are often asked to perform the same duties under the same deadlines as everyone else. So it is crucial for a one-man band to understand and practice good time management throughout the day.

Like the other reporters in our shop, I'm asked to bring two leadable story ideas to the table every day at our nine o'clock editorial meeting. From there, I'm expected to turn a story for the 5:00 P.M. or 6:00 P.M. newscast and, in some cases, both. At the end of my day, like the other reporters, I'm also expected to do a cut-down version of my story for the morning and post my story to our Web site. When I started, I would work twelve-hour days just trying to get everything done. But, I've gotten faster, and now I work nine to ten hours a day.

"The shots here are from a fun story about a local camp that had a one-of-kind, sixty-foot alpine climbing tower. I used my tripod to shoot this stand-up in segments. 'As you can see this camp really has it all . . .' *Cut to shot looking down at me climbing.* (I stopped and moved the camera.) '. . . even a sixty-foot alpine climbing tower.' *Cut to medium shot of me at the top.* 'And once you get to the top, there is only one way down . . .' *Cut to shot of me on the swing.* '. . . a giant swing.' In all, it was a four-part stand-up that took a half hour to shoot. I was able to pull it off by setting up my shot, saying my lines, and rewinding to check it."

The Methods of a Backpack Journalist

In the field, BPJs look and work differently from standard news crews. Their equipment is smaller and lighter, but it still may take a few trips to the truck to assemble all the gear needed for a particular story. Their methods for gathering news are different, too. Heidi McGuire rarely uses a reporter's notepad; instead, she uses her camera to take notes, playing back the audio like a memo recorder. "Note to self . . . check teeth next time."

Just Shoot Me

The biggest hurdle BPJs face is shooting themselves while still making great images. Stand-ups are always creative challenges.

First, my philosophy on stand-ups is that they only be used to advance the story or show the viewer something he/she wouldn't otherwise see with video alone. For me, when it comes to stand-ups, I like breaking the conventional thought that the reporter, especially as one-man band, is just standing in front of the camera. I always incorporate movement in my stand-ups by using cutaways and overlapping action. The trick to getting it right is rewinding your tape and watching what you have. Remember, what matters to the viewer is the information and what you're showing them, not that you shot it yourself, so you have to get it right. Putting a multipart stand-up together happens in the editing room. To make sure the shots and cutaways match, it's important to have overlapping action.

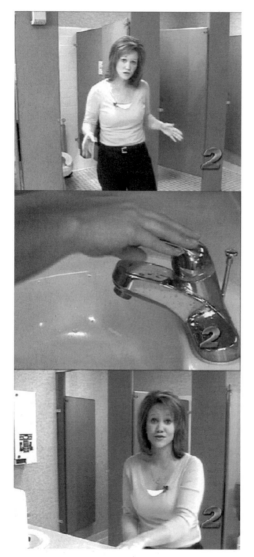

"This was a simple stand-up I shot in our bathroom at work while doing a story on strep throat. 'And it starts right here in the bathroom . . .' *Cut to tight shot . . . hands turning water on . . . Cut to shot in mirror.* 'Doctors say the best way to make sure you don't end up at their office is to simply wash your hands.'"

I never give someone my camera to help me shoot a stand-up. I always want to be in control of my equipment unless it's another photographer helping me.

When shooting a stand-up inside, I take the time to set up lights. It's worth it every time. Also, a good trick is using the back light as a marker. I raise the light on the stand to my height and place it where I'll be standing. I set my framing, focus, and headroom on the back light, then move the stand back out of camera view into its intended position for lighting separation. The more I do this, the easier it gets to guess the back light position of the stand and light head so the light highlights me properly.

Always make sure light is not hitting the front element of the lens. This will wash out your image and draw attention to any dirt you have on the lens—which of course won't be there because you take photography seriously and a dirty lens is amateurish and the result of laziness.

With practice and proper time management, you can execute fun, multipart stand-ups that add interest and a higher level of production value to your story. Much better than standing there, poorly lit, with a stick mic saying something that would be better left illustrated by the story or said by the anchor as a lead-in. Bring value to your stand-ups.

Talk to Me, I'm All Alone

Conducting an interview by yourself without a crew has some big advantages in terms of the content and comments you'll record. In most interview situations, one-man bands can be at great advantage, especially when you are one on one with a person. I find that when it's just me, people are more comfortable, plus my equipment is smaller and slightly less intimidating. When setting up for my interviews, I use this time as a chance to get to know the person I'm getting ready to interview. It's also a great opportunity for them to get to know you before the camera is rolling.

A. "From a story called 'MySpace.com Mom' about the dangers of online communities such as MySpace. This was not a day turn, so I took my time and set up four lights. I used a key light and a back light on the interviewee and two more lights to accent the wall and bedroom in the background."

B. "Never Too Much." "An employee at a local restaurant says minimum wage is too low. I used just one key light for this shot and let him come to me in between his time waiting on customers. This is a good example of adapting to your surroundings, not the other way around."

C. "Textile workers at a local uniform shop are getting ready to break the mold. The uniforms were on a belt, so I thought it would be neat to place the camera farther back to capture both the interview and what was going on around us. It also made the interviewee more comfortable not to have the camera in her face."

Angela Hayes
Royal Park Employee

Sit-down interviews are the easiest. When a person is sitting, you can pretty much set the camera on the tripod, press record, and chat away. Unless the person is in a chair that moves, rocks, or rolls, you can assume that they will stay in that same spot. But you'll still need to glance over from time to time. I tend to also reach over and pull out or zoom in during my interviews to change the shot for variation.

I'd say the hardest thing for any one-man band is to interview from the right side of the camera, especially when the person you are interviewing is standing. On the right side, you can't see into your viewfinder. You have to shoot from both sides to provide visual balance; there's no way around it.

When I do have to shoot an interview from the right side, I politely let the person know that I've got my camera set, and I ask them not to step from side to side. But guess what? It always happens. I've gotten interviews back where I could only see half of the person's face. To keep that from happening, it's good to pause now and then to walk to the other side of the camera and check your shot. That's perfectly fine. In fact, sometimes it gives your interviewee time to take a deep breath and relax. Also, just a general rule: shoot wider when you're on the right side. That way, if the interviewee moves, it won't be as detrimental to the shot like it would if you were tight.

Breaking or spot news can be a lot harder on BPJs. Lugging equipment, shooting as soon as you arrive on location, trying to anticipate changes as the story unfolds while taking notes and finding the right person to interview, stretches the capacity of even the most skilled BPJ. Whether it's the fire chief or the lady whose dog is stuck in the burning house, you've got to know when to drop your sticks and move, "run and gun." If you don't move quickly, you could lose the opportunity for great sound. In this case, it's okay to shoot off the shoulder and use your shotgun mic for sound.

The same goes for gathering "Man-on-the-Street" (MOS) interviews. The term MOS has two meanings in television production depending on the context in which it is used. In traditional "film" terms, MOS means "Mit Out Sound," which comes from early European film directors calling for a scene to be shot without sound. The MOS scene would generally end up on the B-roll. In this case, MOS means "man on the street."

These are actually my least favorite, but not hard to shoot. This is where you find an average Joe or Jane on the street to talk about a particular topic. In some cases, people will avoid you like the plague because they don't want to be on TV. And then you'll always get the clown who just wants to be on TV but has nothing to say. I say these are my least favorite because you're trying to keep up with equipment while tracking people down.

My advice on approaching all interviews: Bring a good attitude!

It's Just Me and My Camera

Just shooting the story requires cunning and determination if you're going to get those great shots and create sequences that cut together. Working solo means no one is there to help you lug the tripod up the hill or half a mile into the forest. You'll be driving yourself while shooting out the window (and obeying all traffic laws). With the mundane tasks of navigating, driving, and hiking requiring as much focus as framing a shot, it would be easy to let the quality of your images slide. Again, the best BPJs have the ability to do it all and make the end result look effortless.

Being a reporter and a photographer is a challenge, and I love challenges. Whether I'm the only person on a story or bumping elbows with crews from other stations, I want my story to be the best. And it doesn't just happen; you have to make it happen. I want to get the shot no one else has, stretch my imagination to find a different angle, or just try something new. You won't hit home runs every day, but if you try, it's more likely to happen every once in a while than if you don't.

I always like to knock out my key interviews before I shoot my B-roll. It gives me a

"When gas prices hit the roof, I followed this guy to see how some people are avoiding the pump. I played around with this shot to get it just right. I wanted the bike in the foreground and ended up using my jacket and shoe to get the camera angle exactly where I needed it."

A. "This shot was made while I was sitting in the driver's seat at a stop light. I got ahead of my subject and waited for him to come into the shot. Thank goodness the light was red."

B. "Again in the driver's seat, this time I was tailing the rider. We were almost at our destination and out of the hectic traffic, so I could slow down and shoot and drive. In most situations, it's not a good idea, but a smaller camera helped me pull it off."

C. "This shot illustrated part of the ride into work through the countryside. During this shoot, I was in and out of the van to get all the shots of the biker coming and going."

better idea of what the story is about. From there, I look around and determine what objects, people, and actions can help me tell the story. It's also perfectly okay to ask the person you're interviewing what they may have in mind to help you tell their story. And remember, before you press record, ask yourself, "Why do I need this shot?" If you don't know, chances are you don't need it, so move on.

From Your Left Side—No, Your Other Left

Heidi McGuire's frequent use of mirrors, multipart stand-ups, matching action, and moving shots requires a firm grasp of "screen direction" and the "180-degree rule." The use of these tools and shooting methods creates compelling storytelling with high production values. Values not normally associated with a BPJ. It's important to understand the rules in order to consistently apply them and, in the right circumstances, break them.

Screen Direction

Screen direction is an aspect of the visual language that occurs as part of the relationship between shots and the apparent "direction" of the action and attention. An understanding of screen direction is necessary to keep all the action flowing in the proper direction. To ensure the correct screen direction, an imaginary line is drawn through the scene. The "line" is also called the "line of action" or "axis of action," and the concept is referred to as the 180-degree rule. Breaking the rule is called "crossing the line," "breaking the line of action," or "breaking the 180-degree line."

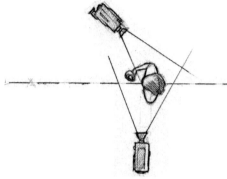

The figure on the left shows the line going though the center of the woman's head, running the same angle as her point of view. When there are two people, the line goes through both of their heads. With more than two, the line may divide the scene in any number of ways. What is important is to establish the line and not cross the camera over it.

Reverse screen direction happens when the camera crosses the line. The woman faces left as she's watching the bird. If the camera crosses the line, she's looking right, apparently not looking at the bird at all, even though in reality she is. Cut together, the two shots appear to show the woman watching herself.

In the "Alaskan Bald Eagle" story introduced in Chapter 8, the line ran through the reporter and ranger and the camera stayed on the right side of the reporter (see A on facing page).

In figure B on page 205, you can see which angles work and which ones don't. If we established the interview on the right side of the reporter from camera position 2, camera position 1 works as the reverse. It appears that they are talking to one another. If the interview starts on the left side of the reporter from camera position 4, camera position 3 works as the reverse from this angle; it also appears that they are talking to one another.

But cross the line between the ranger and the reporter, and they're both looking in the same direction, not looking at one another at all, even though in reality they are. Shots 1 and 4 and shots 2 and 3 cannot be cut together. Screen direction is particularly important when portraying reality. Mistakes in screen direction confuse the viewer and destroy the flow of your story.

For most news stories, you'll want to establish the line and stick with it throughout your shooting. Editing is much easier with clear screen direction. You can change the theoretical position of the line as you shoot only if you know how the story will be edited. The line can be changed as long as the shot before and after is within the 180-degree radius established by the preceding shot. You can "jump" the 180-degree line by going to a neutral shot that doesn't "lead" the screen direction—a shot that is "dead on." From that point, you can redefine the 180-degree line. Figures A, B, and C on page 206 illustrate inserting a neutral shot to cross the line.

You can also use a continuous move to cross the line. A dolly move can take you "across the line" or you can follow your subjects as they cross and redefine the line's angle.

Jumping the 180 degrees can get very complicated if you do it more than once and is not advisable without discussing the edit with the editor.

Screen direction only matters in the relationship between two shots.

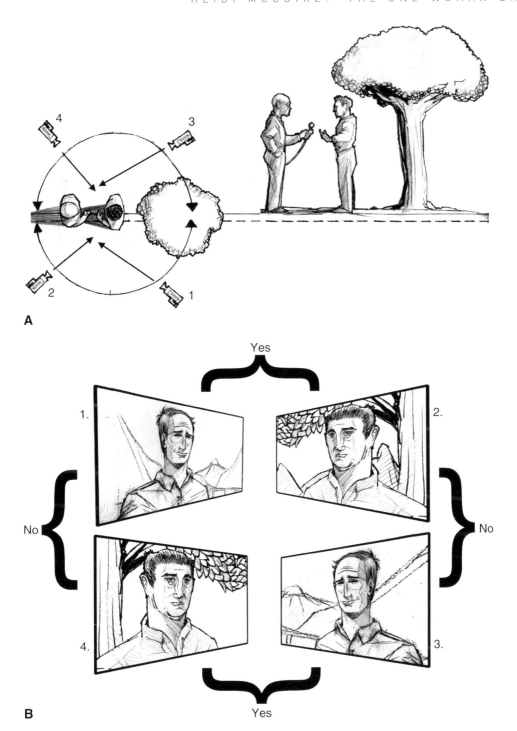

A. If a majority of the story is shot from the right side of the subject, a cut to the left side will seem out of place.

B. Shoot a neutral shot to allow the editor to cross the line.

C. Any neutral shot in the sequence will allow the editor to cross the line.

Dolly Around

D. One continuous move can allow you to cross the line.

Doing It All in the Field

Much of Heidi McGuire's work life is about streamlining—leaving the unnecessary behind and focusing on the essentials. She finds new ways to skin the old cat. Unlike most, if not all, reporters, I do not carry a reporter's notebook. At best, I'll have a folded-up piece of paper in my pocket and a pen. Since I already have a lot to carry—camera, mic, tripod, lights—I can't ever seem to keep up with a notepad. It's always the first thing I leave behind. Instead, I use my camera as my pen and pad.

With that being said, I try not to ask any questions related to my story until the camera is rolling. Prior to pressing record, I'll ask the interviewee other questions as a way to break the ice before the interview. And it never fails—people always want to know what you are going to ask them. I have no problem discussing that, but I'll ask them to save their answers for the interview, or I'll just ask them again when the camera is rolling.

As a BPJ, I am mobile in my position. All of my equipment can go with me, so on any given day I can work at the station or I can work out of my customized van. If I'm out in the field, I can work from the desk in my van. I write my script on a legal pad, not a computer. Once I'm finished writing, I call my script in to the station for approval.

I edit on an Avid laptop computer. Laptop editing is wonderful; it saves so much time. If my story is twenty miles away from the station and I don't get done shooting everything until one or two o'clock, and then waste another twenty minutes riding back to the station and twenty minutes back out to my live shot—that's forty minutes of my time. Forty minutes that I could have been writing or editing or working on my story.

With laptop editing, I can go in the back of my Caravan with my custom desk, take the video from my camera, put it into my laptop, and cut away. The only problem right now is that the technology is not there yet to send the video fast enough without a microwave truck. If I'm going live and feeding my story from the field, they'll send a microwave truck and a photographer. The photographer will set up my live shots while we microwave the story back to the station. Luckily, I don't have to shoot my own live shots. That's the only thing that I don't do by myself.

One of the biggest problems reporters and photographers say they have is communication. You know, I don't have that problem—my reporter and photographer are pretty much on the same page. *In the field, both thought processes of a reporter and a photographer must be working, complementing each other—on task—in order to complete the assignment. The mix of duties can be confusing at first.* I'd say the most difficult part of one-man banding in the beginning is thinking like a reporter and a photographer. I remember when I first started, I'd set up the camera for the interview, sit down, ask the first question, and think, "Did I remember to white-balance?" Or I'd be thinking about the technical side of things and completely forget the question I was going to ask. Like any job, you get better with practice. But you can guarantee, even once you think you have it all down, it's still a balancing act. But it does get easier.

The Key to Survival

Proper time management can save your sanity, allow for better work, and keep you safe. Being distracted and harried is no way to go through work or life; important emotional and even life-saving details get missed. Don't be scattered. Time management is a tough one—it's so crucial to what you do—and oftentimes that means you don't get lunch, you don't get time to make calls on stories for the next day, or you work late to get the cut-down and Web story done. That can be very frustrating when reporters and/or photographers seem to have plenty of time.

So Why Be a Backpack Journalist?

I do it because the feeling I get when it's 5:15 P.M. and my story just aired and I can look at what I accomplished and say, "That's all my hard work, 100 percent of it." But know this: Just as you (the one-man band) get to take all the credit if it's great, you also take all the blame if it stinks.

I feel, in order to be successful at one-man banding, you have to want to do it all! You have to want to be good at shooting, writing, and editing. Each aspect is as important as the other. Probably more so with shooting and editing because you can tell a story without writing by editing together pictures and sound bites.

One of the best parts about being a one-man band is the amount of freedom you get. Freedom to make the right calls, freedom to express yourself with your camera, your writing, and editing. But just like everyone else, you are held accountable for everything you write, shoot, say, and edit.

You may have noticed that Heidi McGuire refers to herself more often as a one-man band than as a backpack journalist. Clarity in her communication wins out—everyone understands the term "one-man band" while "backpack journalist," or "BPJ," is more of a branding name for the company. She really does not have a backpack that is essential to her journalistic endeavors. Camping is rarely required.

But, TV news is a business, and proper marketing is essential to sustain a healthy newsroom budget. While backpack journalist *shows up on her business card and carries no gender labeling, one-man band is her description of choice. And what of that one-"man" band moniker? It's not completely accurate when referring to Heidi. McGuire's point of view—being a woman—adds a different perspective to the job; the job title does not. Clarity, basic.*

A Woman's Point of View

Women can see things a little bit differently—a different perspective, a feminine angle. Women tend to be more emotional. Certain stories strike a different chord with them than it would a male. Naturally it does, but I don't think that makes a woman's story better. We all have different perspectives and that's great.

I think it really says something when WFMY hired their BPJs, they hired two women. So, I think what that says is that we're just as capable of doing this job as any guy out there. I think what really helps is the equipment is smaller and more manageable. If you told me tomorrow that I had to switch over and go back to carrying a DVC Pro camera, I don't know that I could continue to shoot for very long. So, the equipment has definitely made it much more manageable. Just by having women out there, doing this job, period, says that we can do it. It doesn't matter, gender, anymore. You can get the job done.

All BPJs are expected to be presentable on air. It may be unfair that a man can have rugged good looks but rugged messy hair on a woman isn't considered good television. Not that men aren't vain; many wear makeup for on-air field work, too. But there's an extra expectation to look presentable if you're a woman, and that can be difficult even if you are gifted with good bone structure and manageable hair. Sometimes, it's just a matter of priorities. I learned really fast that this is not a pretty job and it's not a glamorous job at all. What's important to me is not how great I look on TV but how well I told the story. Even if I don't get my fifteen seconds in front of the camera that night, that's okay.

Sure, you want to look great when it's time for that big, live shot, but when it comes down to putting on lipstick and getting my story ready for air, I'll skip the lipstick if I need to. There have been times when I didn't even have a chance to look in the mirror before a live shot, and while I really didn't like that, I got over it. When it comes to being a one-man band, sometimes you have to put yourself last. You have to prioritize. For me, there has never been a day when lipstick and hairspray were more important than the story I was telling.

When it comes to maintaining my look throughout the day, well, let's just say I put my makeup on in the morning and, if I have enough time, I'll refresh it before I go on air. I'm not one to put on fresh lipstick several times a day, even if I had the time. I believe in always looking presentable, but you also have to be reasonable when it comes to your time. So far, I haven't gotten any complaints and I've never missed slot because I was primping.

I feel the same about my appearance in stand-ups as I do with live shots. You want to look your best, but let's say you're in the woods and you have to walk a half a mile to retrieve a hairbrush and lipstick, all the while carrying your gear because you don't want to leave it behind. That's right, you do what I did. Go without it. So what if I'm wearing a knit cap and I don't have any lipstick? I'm in the woods! I think that's story-appropriate.

A female backpack journalist can encounter different risks than a male in the same position, and the risks are harder to defend than they would be for a standard news crew. I always say that the only issue that you run into being a female in this business is the fact that you're out by yourself. There have been times when I've been out by myself in places I shouldn't have been. I get a false sense of security a lot of times when I'm carrying that camera around, wearing the WFMY news crew jacket. You still have to be aware that you're by yourself. Safety's definitely an issue; it needs to be part of the discussion before you walk out the door. Is the situation going to be safe? And if it's not, how can we make it safer? Maybe we need to send a photographer with you.

One of my coworkers—the other BPJ—went out on a story about a broken water main. This guy calls up. He said, "Hey, there's water everywhere." So she goes out there and she spends the day with him and he's showing her where water is flooding everywhere and he takes her down underneath this bridge where it's particularly bad. Well, after this story runs, someone calls up and says, "That guy's not even supposed to be out of his house. He's on house arrest." Apparently, he's even in the sex offender registry. He's a convicted sex offender and she was out underneath this bridge with this guy by herself. For those situations, it's after the fact where you think, "Shit. That was not a good deal."

Learn as much safety as you can from any source you can and keep aware of your surroundings at all times. By yourself, you are vulnerable; with a camera taking up half your peripheral vision, you are twice as vulnerable—a woman without defense training even more so.

Risk is reduced by planning! Keep your eyes open, always look for a safe exit, and don't needlessly put yourself in risky situations. You'll want to be around for that great story you'll shoot tomorrow.

A Hard Row to Hoe

Starting out in broadcast journalism, many newcomers will be searching smaller markets for positions as backpack journalists or one-man bands or some other name that means "Okay, do it all yourself and make it great." The challenge will be answered by countless wide-eyed optimists clamoring for their big break. The biggest adjustments to a young BPJ's outlook happens in the first years—take it from someone who's been there. For anybody starting out, it's hard. It's hard to even get your foot in the door. It took me three months to get my first job, and I had to move all the way to South Dakota to do it. I had no idea when I took my first job how much work it was going to be.

I was a one-man band out of a bureau in Aberdeen, two hundred miles away from the main station. This is the way a lot of one-man bands start out. I was covering fifteen counties in northeast South Dakota. They'd say, "Heidi, get as much as you can." So there were days I did up to two packages and two or three VO/SOTs—regardless of quality. It was about quantity.

Time management obviously was crucial, and I've learned that very fast. Also how important it was to have a good attitude. There were a lot of days that just really sucked, being a one-man band out in the middle of nowhere. But I realized that there were things about the job that I couldn't change and I could either accept it and go on and have the best attitude that I could, or I could get upset about it and be miserable. I knew that this was something that I wanted to do, so being miserable was not going to get me anywhere. At my first TV station, I learned plenty about the job, but I learned even more about myself and what I was capable of.

When I went to WFMY, the focus shifted to quality. "You've only got to do one package a day, but we want it to be really great." So, there was all this pressure on me all of a sudden not to get a lot done but to do a great job. When you move to a bigger market, the bar needs to rise. Just because I'm a one-man band doesn't mean that I'm going to be underneath that bar. I hope to be setting it.

You know, I got into this business partially because I like to learn. Every day, we're forced to become experts on whatever story it is that we're telling. I'm also finding that I get to learn every day on the job about my job. And for me that's really fun because I see that that there's so much room for growth in photography, reporting, and editing.

The one-person band can be considered both an entry-level position and a veteran post as seasoned journalists exercised their singular voice. The work is challenging and certainly not for everyone. But for those who choose this road, all realize close to complete control over their craft. Experiment, succeed or fail, readjust, try again—it's a very personal experience. For better or for worse.

And if you're ever on Sixteenth Avenue in Greensboro, North Carolina, there's a new left turn lane you'll probably want to watch for.

CHAPTER 13

Greg Stickney

Live—What TV News
Does Best

Greg Stickney
Chief Photographer

KNSD-TV, San Diego
Emmy Award for *Making a Marine*, documentary, 1996
Golden Mic Award for "Chased by Fire," spot news, 1988

*I*t's late October under a dark red twilight. Streetlights glow as motorists search for shelter in downtown hotels. A few masked citizens point up at the low, bleeding sky, squinting through ash that falls like snow. Coughing through surgical masks, they weigh their chances. "Will there be a home to return to?" It's twelve noon, but it looks and feels like nighttime in hell.

Just a day before, strong Santa Ana winds blew in hot, dry air from the desert, clearing the southern California sky to a vibrant blue. Saturday in San Diego: America's Finest City goes to sleep as a lost hunter's signal fire rages out of control in the Cleveland National Forest. By morning, the fire has killed thirteen people as it races toward the coast. Now called the Cedar Fire, it charges over rural hilltops to the footsteps of suburbia and beyond.

Hot westerly winds fan the flames that push thick, acrid smoke over San Diego and miles out into the Pacific. Many people start their day to forced evacuations. A few mementos and important documents are packed into cars as families scour the city for available rooms.

EQUIPMENT

Helicopter:
  Bell 206 Jet Ranger III
  Sony camera for exterior
  Sony lipstick camera for interior
  Wescam Gyrostabilized lens housing
  Troll Smartlink camera and microwave control
  Troll Skypod microwave system

Live Truck:
  Frontline-manufactured Ford E350 Hightop
  MRC Code Runner microwave transmitter
  DVCPro laptop videotape editor
  IFB Plus wireless integrated cell phone/radio
  Copperhead fiber-optic cable system
  DVCPro 810 camera
  Lectrosonic wireless mic
  Miller System 20 tripod
  Lowel lighting kit, softbox/Scrim Jim

Satellite Truck:
  Frontline-manufactured Chevrolet C5500
  Triple-path satellite/single-path microwave
  3 Tandberg Voyager digital encoders and
     receivers
  Miteq Upconverter
  Steller ezv transmitter
  Vertex satellite locator/antenna controller
  MRC Code Runner microwave transmitter
  DVCPro laptop videotape editor
  3 IFB Plus wireless integrated cell phone/radio
  3 Copperhead fiber-optic cable systems
  DVCPro 810 camera
  Lectrosonic wireless mic
  Miller System 20 tripod
  Lowel lighting kit, softbox/Scrim Jim

A. The Cedar Fire rolls over the hills as police force evacuations.

B. A whirlwind of flame leads the devastating Cedar Fire into suburban San Diego.

C. The tornado of fire passes behind a live truck mast.

Every bar and hotel lobby has the television on. The fire's close; there's so much smoke in the air you can smell the live shots that flicker on the screen, flames in every shot.

Ten miles away and closing fast, a Bell Jet Ranger chops through the turbulent air. The helicopter is sending one of those live signals. In the cockpit, the pilot navigates through the dangerous smoke clouds. Next to him, KNSD-TV chief photographer Greg Stickney focuses on a small, high-contrast monitor. Neither can believe the image that's unfolding a few hundred feet below them.

A fire tornado.

Leading the charge of flame that's spilling across the valley is a vortex of fire spinning up into the darkened sky. More frightening, it's moving as fast as the helicopter, incinerating everything in its path. Stickney works the knobs, dials, and levers built into the control box balanced on his knees. Something like playing a video game, he steers the gyrostabilized camera mounted on the nose of the chopper. Focus, zoom, pan, tilt, exposure—all controlled in unison to chase the fire. Stickney and the pilot bounce in their seats as the hot air from the fire and wind from the Santa Ana buffet their craft. The camera lens stays rock steady, cradled in a black ball where gyros eliminate the erratic movement. The camera signal: sharp, steady, a terrifying nightmare beamed back to the station downtown, then on air—instantly. Live.

From the ground, a microwave truck plans for a quick retreat as the fire tornado races across the horizon. As the photographer shoots, he is recording as well. There's no telling what will happen and whether he'll be on air live when it does.

These signals and many others are gathered at the station. Located in the heart of the city and a few blocks from the bay, KNSD is about as far west as you can get before getting wet. The signals collected above the office tower come from remote cameras permanently mounted around the city, microwave trucks, a satellite truck, and Greg Stickney's camera following the fire as it moves closer to downtown.

We just ducked under the smoke, flying very low along the freeway heading west. On the other side was where my house was. The fire made a beeline at my house. I'm just watching in shock and fear. "That's the end of my house." Then it jumped Interstate 15, which is twelve lanes of solid concrete, like it was nothing. Usually that's where a fire stops, that's what they count on. But once it jumped over, it's now in a high-density urban area. The wind swept it along, just missing my house. For a moment I was relieved, but the fire wasn't over, my home wasn't really safe, and many more homes would vanish before the day was over.

The homes in this area are ten feet apart and they range from very large ones to smaller, older homes. The ones that really got hit hard were up on the edges of the canyons. The wind carries embers and hot air in front of the fire, and that preheats the brush ahead, so when the fire hit's it, the brush just explodes. Giant 2,000- and 3,000-square-foot homes just got obliterated. The fire came up out of the canyon and took out sixty homes.

Qualcomm Stadium becomes an evacuation site for the displaced. Located directly on the other side of Interstate 15, it's just eight miles from downtown. Its safety falls into question as the fire jumps the twelve lanes of the interstate on its journey west.

Back in the bar, stunned residents watch for hours, hoping to make out some small detail of their neighborhoods. This is where live television really pays off. This is the situation where we can tell people, to the best of our knowledge, the fire's going this way, it's going that way; if you're here, you need to leave. The police department will call us and tell us we need to get the word out. This is why we do live. This is where it pays off for the community.

There were neighborhoods that people wouldn't think a brush fire could happen in and, suddenly, it rolls over the hill and it wipes out forty or fifty homes. If we can warn them ten minutes ahead of time, maybe that ten can let them grab a few more possessions and get out before it becomes a serious situation.

We can let people know to avoid certain areas. If they really want to see what's happening, we'll bring them the best pictures we can, closer and safer than they could see on their own. That also keeps people off the road and allows the fire guys do their job or the police guys do theirs.

Live, that's what we do. We can bring you the information right now. We can break into programming at anytime; we are on the air twenty-four hours a day. The fire started in the middle of the night on Saturday. We started doing live cut-ins at five Sunday morning and went nonstop for the next two, three days.

All the stations are just doing full, constant live programming. We called in everybody we could call in; we sent every live truck out. On a fire like this, no matter where you set up a truck, you are going to see something.

We have photographers being reporters because the photographers are generally easier to

The fire leaps onto the roadways, blocking traffic.

contact. They get in the truck; they go, set up the shot, set up the camera, set the mic on the top of the camera, and just start talking while the camera signal goes live. So, we put photographers on the air. We put everybody on the air—I was on the air.

The red and black news helicopter flies along a few feet under a smoke ceiling, particulate and ash wreaking havoc on the jet engine. Low visibility, high thermals—this is dangerous work. Acutely aware of the risks, Corporate Helicopter's pilot Brad Kygar nimbly maneuvers the craft and camera to optimum shooting positions. Greg Stickney's images are immediately broadcast on air, part of the mix of components gathered to keep a community informed.

At the station, the complete news-gathering assets come together. Live images, graphic maps, emergency announcements all updated by the minute; a moment's notice could save lives.

Live coverage is about presenting news content instantly. The benefits for the audience are immediate and as varied as any form of communication. Live can warn a community of impending danger, announce a political event, and, by its instantaneous nature, add excitement to the news program. When the program goes live to a location, it ups the apparent news value of the story.

Why Go Live?

News You Need to Know Now

There are some reasons you go live. The first is you take the viewer to something as it is happening right now, immediately. This is what separates us from newspapers. They come out at a set time, once a day; we can take you there anytime. If it's an emergency situation where you may really need to know because you may be evacuated, that's where we provide the information in a very timely fashion, and that's what live brings to the viewer. We can take you right there. We can talk to the people that are involved with the issues. We can get the information out much quicker. It's a little bit akin to radio, only you can see what's happening as opposed to just having it described to you.

Your local television nightly news program is live already. The show isn't taped earlier for later broadcast. Note that some late-night news is a rerun of the 10:00 or 11:00 P.M. show. Sometimes, the live signal from the field just broadens the news "set" and expands the production value of the news program.

Live—Because We Can

Another reason to go live is really a little bit more along the entertainment angle of what we do. Some of our live shots actually are just to break the show up, involve viewers, bring them into our program, get them excited by our program.

Going live from the field connects any story to the present moment. It also connects the reporter to a pretaped package. Last-minute updates and reporter/anchor question-and-answer discussions can personalize the story while "teasing" further developments.

It's a way to get the reporter who did the story involved in the 5:00 P.M. newscast. If a new road opening or ribbon cutting happens at 10:00 A.M., and it's important enough to the community, we'll send the reporter back out to go live for the newscast. As the viewer watches, when they see "Live," they think, it's a little more important—maybe I should pay a little more attention to it.

It's also a way that stations can promote more people than just their anchors. I mean, everybody generally knows the anchors. The reporters sometimes are not as well known. Sometimes you go live to profile your reporter. It might be the reporter that covers the city or the military beat, and you want him live so that your viewers understand, "He's our guy at city hall," or "He's our guy with the military." So putting him out live makes him almost as high profile as your anchor team. It's a way to profile reporters and capture viewers with immediacy and excitement as we throw a lot of flashy graphics onto the screen. *"We're Live."*

Going "live" is a way for a station to rally their assets around a moment, event, or idea. Floods, a county fair, or coverage devoted to AIDS Awareness Week all find enhanced newsworthiness by going live.

Community Involvement

Live shots also involve the community in the show, in both the content of the story and the physical presence of the live crew operating in the neighborhood. A live crew is hard to miss. There are stories that have a reason to be live for the importance of the story to the community. The ribbon cutting was hours ago, but now you have the first people visiting the building. They cut the ribbon at ten, we open to the public at five, and our reporter is standing outside talking to people at five minutes after five as they go in or come out of the new building. There you bring the story full circle. Where if you were not live, all you would have was the ribbon cutting and say, "Tomorrow we'll tell you what people thought of it."

Going live is also a way you can involve a community in your show. When we go live, we say, "We are live from Lincoln Park," or some other area of town, and those people get excited about that, especially if it's a good-news story as opposed to a bad-news story. That shows that you care about their community. You are willing to send your people in there and spend the time and the resources in their community.

They see the truck there. They see you there. Being "live" obviously is a much bigger commitment just by your presence. Your truck is bigger, you put a mast up in the air that people can see, you drag cable out. A lot of times, you have a couple more people there. People see that and they respond to that, and that will translate into people sampling your station where, maybe, they never watched you before. Because we were live in their neighborhood and they want to see what's going on. "I saw the live truck; now I want to see what's going on." It's another aspect that going live brings to a station—it helps draw people in.

"Live" is our way of bringing the immediacy of a story to the viewer. Even if it's not happening right now, we let the viewer know that we think this is important; we pay more attention to it.

Stations pay more attention to a story by marshalling their live news-gathering assets and attacking the story. The original live platform is the microwave truck. The basic technology has been in place for decades, while technical advancements have made "going live" easier and safer.

"Live" Transmissions

The Microwave Live Truck

The microwave truck is the workhorse of this "industry." In most cases, it's a Ford or Dodge van loaded with microwave transmitting equipment. Some will have editing capabilities, a portable

A microwave truck with its mast down.

light kit, and tons of cable. What makes a live truck noticeable to your average citizen—other than brightly painted station logos—is the mast that can go up to fifty-two feet in the air. Microwave transmission requires a line of sight to the receiver. The mast gets the transmitter above local impedances, like buildings and other relatively low obstacles. We use them as daily news gatherers. Our trucks are always on the road, so they are always out somewhere, ready whenever we need them.

Microwave trucks are used both for live shots and for feeding footage from remote places. When setting up for a "live shot" with a microwave truck, there are several steps that need to happen in order for the process to be successful and safe.

Step 1: Choose a Place to Set Up

First of all, pick a safe place to put the truck. There's no reason to get hurt by getting hit by another car or anything else that could cause a hazard to the crew or truck. One of the primary hazards is overhead power lines. *(More on power line safety later in the chapter.)* When positioning and parking the truck, try to figure out where the sun is going to be. You don't want to park on the wrong side of the scene and have the sun go down right behind your reporter, making good exposure impossible. You also don't want the sun to cast a shadow from the microwave mast, where it's going right across the reporter.

Step 2: Choose the Camera Position

The next thing is to start looking for what will be in the background. Is it an audience? Is there something the reporter can interact with? Is it a giant sinkhole? Is it a burned-out building? What is it that I can put behind the reporter that will tell the people why we're live? It's important to have something the reporter can reference.

It's a team effort. You ask what the reporter wants to do. Do they have any ideas? Do they want to walk and talk? Do they want to start over here at the blue car and walk over to the red car? Do they just want to stand there? Some reporters have a lot of input on what they want to do and, at that point, it becomes the photographer's responsibility to say, "We can do that," or "We can do some of that," or "We can't do any of that." You have to decide if you are able to light the distance between the blue car and the red car. Do you have enough light? Do you have enough cable so you can get there? The old, big copper cables work for about 300 feet; the new fiber optics can go thousands of feet. Other systems don't require a cable at all and send wireless signals from the camera to the live truck.

Step 3: Establish the Signal

Establish the microwave signal, which means turn the truck on, start the generator, bring all equipment up inside the truck, turn it all on, and make sure everything is functioning. Check for overhead power lines and put your mast up. It'll take three to four minutes to put your mast up in the air. Orient your dish toward your receiver, which is usually located at some high elevation in the city.

A microwave signal is kind of like a one-way walkie-talkie. The truck is the transmitter; it has to have line of sight to the receiver. We have them on top of our buildings. In some places where the land is very flat, they use their transmitter towers as well. San Diego has some hilly terrain, so we put them on mountaintops as well as in the downtown area on the tops of buildings.

The old analog system, which most people are on right now, is "line-of-sight" signal. Newer systems are digital and don't require a perfect line of sight.

The receiving sight is owned by the station and assigned a particular frequency. There isn't any chance that you are going to screw anybody up if your truck is working properly and if you are on your assigned channel. As you adjust the position of the mast, you just guess the general position of the receiver. Once you've done it for a while, you know where your receivers are and in which general direction they are.

You are in contact with a person receiving the signals. They will call out an AGC reading, which is a signal strength reading. The higher the number, the stronger the signal. You pan your antenna back and forth until you hone in on the center of your signal.

Step 4: Drag and Dress the Cable

Drag the cable out of the truck to where your camera position is. The cable carries the audio and video signal from the camera to the truck. In California, we have certain rules you have to follow when you lay cable. You want to make it safe. You don't want to trip anybody. So you dress the cable, which means you tape it down where it crosses the sidewalk or you try and stash it in the gutter or throw it in the bushes as much as you can.

Step 5: Set the Shot

Once you have that set up, you take all your gear out there, you plug your camera in, and you plug your microphone in. Generally, we set up a small television so the reporter can watch the on-air signal, so that they can see when they are on. It also gives them cues if they are voicing over other video. If it's a car accident they want to talk about, when they see the red car, they can talk about the red car; when they see the blue car, they can talk about the blue car.

If the event is happening right now and they say, "We want you in two minutes," you get your signal in, you get the cable out there, you plug in your camera; you plug the microphone in, hand it to the reporter, and you are on the air. It's like that. You can set up a shot in less than ten minutes. The only thing that is really important is the fact that you and the truck are in a safe location and it's not near any power lines.

Set up the camera and finalize your decisions on movement and camera angles.

Step 6: Light the Live Shot

In conjunction with these steps, you should be making lighting decisions. It's winter, and your live shot is for the 6:00 P.M. show. You set up the microwave signal, camera, and microphone; everything checks out. But by the time the live shot happens, it will be dark—time to run power cables and lights.

Most live trucks have a generator and can power a few lights. If the truck doesn't have a generator, or the live shot location makes setting up lights impractical, go with a battery-powered light.

In any case, expose for the background first. Theoretically, that's why you're there—something's in the background. Then bring the light level on the talent's key light up or down to match the background. Control the light source with scrims, diffusion, or simply panning the light away.

This is the time to really finesse the lighting. The anchor will cut directly to the field reporter, and the difference in quality will be noticeable. So put extra effort into lighting live shots.

Step 7: Rehearse, Rehearse, Rehearse

If the reporter is moving in any way, rehearse the move as many times as it takes to get it right. Take the time to tweak the lights. If the reporter or camera movement changes your focus, preset focus points. Put marks on the ground so the reporter knows where to stop. This can be colored tape or a small sandbag.

"You're Live in Five Minutes"

The producer is in contact with you (the photographer) by radio or cell phone. A wave of the hand in front of the lens or a tilt of the camera lets the producer know you've heard the five-minute warning. You tell the reporter you're five minutes out. He moves into position.

"One Minute." The producer again alerts you to the remaining time before you're live. You let the reporter know.

The reporter is monitoring the on-air signal on a small field monitor or simply listening to the show's audio as the anchor introduces the reporter and story.

Remember not to lock your knees; relax. Passing out in the middle of a "live shot" would be bad. The reporter knows the lead-in lines, so he knows his cues.

Andy Anchorman: "More on that from Reporter Ron in Lincoln Park."

And we're live.

Reporter Ron (in field): "This neighborhood has seen a lot of change . . ."

If the reporter is tossing to a package or pretaped story, the program's director will know the reporter's voice cue and roll the video.

Ron Reporter (in field): ". . . there's more to this neighborhood than meets the eye."

Cut to pretaped package.

Ron (on pretaped package): "New shops are bringing more customers to this part of town."

When the package ends, the director will call for a cut back to the reporter "live in the field" for a wrapup.

Ron Reporter (on pretaped package): ". . . residents expect these changes will improve their community."

Cut to live truck.

Ron Reporter (in field): "And there's more construction expected in the next six months. Back to you, Andy Anchorman."

At this point, there could be some back-and-forth discussion between the reporter and anchor, so be prepared to stay "live."

Andy Anchorman: "So, Ron, you live in that community. Will this change the traffic patterns?"

Ron Reporter: "Residents have been told to expect delays through the end of the year."

Andy Anchorman: "Thanks, Ron. When we come back, Windy Carlson will have the weather."

"You're clear," The producer tells you. Your live shot is over.

Safety First with Live Trucks

A young camera crew races to the sight of a breaking story. The assignment desk is allocating assets to cover the event; producers are restructuring their shows; writers are writing new intros. The crew arrives a few minutes before air—just enough time to get set up.

The adrenaline is pumping. The reporter is in the live truck finishing a cell call as the photographer raises the mast (antenna). The mast's hydraulics moan as it's raised. All of a sudden, everything stops and there is a small spark. A nanosecond later: Enough electricity to power a neighborhood races down the mast and energizes the truck; the photographer's hand on the up switch is the contact for the electricity to find a ground.

All that energy passes from finger to foot and grounds out. In that instant, the wire above explodes as the heat vaporizes the insulation. Sparks fly as the photographer's heart stops, his arm and both legs are missing. There is little chance for survival. The reporter, safe in the truck, knows something is wrong—she hears screams and steps out of the truck. As soon as her foot hits the ground, she, too, carries the voltage. The electricity permanently disfigures her leg.

Look Up and Live!

"Look up and live" is a phrase anyone working in news and working around microwave trucks needs to know. Remember that phrase. Say it to yourself, say it often, and tell other people.

Our example of a microwave truck mast/power line electrocution sounds tragic, and it's not uncommon. Had the photographer looked up, he would not have raised the mast anywhere near the power lines. There are no safe power lines. Once the mast made contact, there was only one outcome for the photographer, but the reporter still had a chance. Just by staying in the live truck, she could have survived. If the live truck was burning and she needed to get out immediately, a large jump far away from the truck might have saved her, landing on two feet and shuffling away from the van. Even a few feet away from the vehicle, the ground can still be energized, and if one foot is far enough from the other, you could get electrocuted.

The important message here is "Never complete the circuit." If one part of you is charged and you ground another part, you will get electrocuted. If there is no ground, you should be fine. Think of the birds that land on the wires; they are fine. They wouldn't be if some part made contact with a connection to the ground.

Many people get injured or killed working around microwave trucks. Engsafety.com lists more than seventy live truck incidents. As a photographer, it's the only piece of equipment we use that will kill you. The camera can't kill you; your editing deck can't kill you unless you hold it above your head and drop it on yourself.

The microwave truck can kill you if you are not paying attention when putting your mast (antenna) up and you hit a power line. Power arcs from the power line to the mast and travels down the mast into the truck. If you are outside the truck, touching the truck and the ground, you are the quickest path to ground for the electricity to travel. The minimum voltage is probably 25,000 to 55,000 volts that runs down the city neighborhood, all the way up to a 300,000-volt line. The lines only have to be fifty feet above the ground, and your mast probably would reach them or would come close enough that the electricity would jump from the power line to your mast.

There are systems that will periodically stop the mast when it either encounters an electro-magnetic field (which is around the power line) or senses an object in the way. But I don't want to trust my life to any system. I am always going to look up, and if I am not sure I am not going to do it.

Accidents can happen any time of day or night and in any weather. Imagine running around the microwave truck late at night in a pouring rain. You can't really look up into the rain, and it's so dark you can't tell what's fifty feet up. STOP!

If you are not 100 percent sure there's not a power line over your head, you don't do the live shot. I don't care how important it is, you just don't do it. You call the station and tell them you've got to move the truck. You go to a place where you know there is no power line. Your boss might be mad at you, but putting your mast into power lines is the last thing you'll do or you will be disfigured for life.

Unfortunately, it happens a lot, and cameras were rolling. I've probably seen ten or fifteen different accidents that were caught on tape and, for every one that's caught on tape, there are probably two or three that nobody caught on tape. It's a horrific thing to see because all the electrical energy enters your body at your hand or whatever is touching the truck. The electricity burns a hole in your hand and travels through your body and burns a hole on its way out one or both of your feet. It destroys most of the tissue in the first eighteen inches of your arm and the last eighteen inches of your leg. The best you can hope for is that your limbs will be disfigured and disabled for the rest of your life. In the worst case, you'll be dead or you may want to be dead because it's a burn so terrible that its recovery is almost impossible. *Scared yet? You should be. That's the point.*

There are two ways to get injured or killed. If your truck becomes energized and you touch the truck and the ground, it's called "touch potential." Your body has just become the electricity's shortest path to ground. Second is what they call "step potential." In "step potential," think of it as dropping a rock into a pool and the waves come out; each wave gets smaller as it moves further from the center.

In "step potential," each one of those waves has a different voltage. So, if you take big steps away, you may have one foot in one voltage and your other foot is in a different voltage. The higher voltage will jump to the lower voltage through your body. So if you are near a truck that's been energized, you have to shuffle away, keep your feet together, and just kind a shuffle along the ground so that your feet never separate. That way, you never cross over different voltages.

222

If you are inside the truck, your best bet is to stay in the truck until emergency crews respond and tell you you're safe to leave. The only reason to get out of the truck is if for some reason the truck caught fire. And of all the ones I've seen, I have never seen a truck catch fire. I have seen a lot of arcing and sparking, a lot of smoking, a lot of tires blowing, in a very uncomfortable situation, but I've never seen one burst into flames. If it did burst into flames, then you would need to jump from the truck, land with your feet together, not fall forward or backward, and not touch the truck. Then shuffle away.

I always establish my signal first, before I pull out cable. This is a safety measure. If you drag your cable before putting up the mast and the mast touches a power line, suddenly, instead of the danger being right around the truck, the electricity now runs down your cable. If you have 300 feet of cable out, you have just sent that electricity 300 feet down the street, endangering a lot more people.

KNSD has a closed-circuit television system in the station. A safety video runs on it all the time for anyone to watch. We require our photographers to watch it and take a test once a year. Safety is something NBC really takes seriously.

Most of the accidents, not all of them, are people who are new to the industry. They are excited about doing this, they're trying to get it on the air as quickly as they can, and it's the one thing they forget to do—and it's the one thing that will kill you. When you start out, you are assigned to a live truck; you work your way toward getting your own car and gear that's assigned to you. Generally it's the newer, younger guys who are in the live trucks, and those are the guys that are running harder, running faster. What takes ten minutes they try to do in five, and that's when they start cutting corners. And it's the corner you cut that kills you.

Again, look up and live!

The Satellite Truck—To Outer Space and Back

The next evolution in land-based, live transmission is the satellite truck. A satellite truck can send a signal from anywhere. The audio and video are sent up to a satellite; the signal is then resent from the satellite to any receiver on earth with the right equipment set to the right frequencies.

The biggest difference between a microwave truck and a satellite truck is that you can go live from more locations with the satellite. The stuff you see coming out of Baghdad that airs on the *Today Show* or the nightly news is a satellite shot from Baghdad to the United States. Depending on how far away or how far around the world you are from the U.S., it may be two shots or two bounces, as we call it. Up once, down to another ground station, and back up, as you're going round the ball (earth). Satellite companies will have stations around the world that will retransmit the signal. They receive it, turn it around, and send it right back up to a different satellite.

The truck has a little computer built into it that finds the satellite for you. The truck has a GPS receiver so it knows where it is on the earth and it knows where the satellite is in relationship to where it is. You pick from a list which satellite you want to send to. You hit enter and the dish moves position and points at the satellite you've selected. Then you fine-tune it on a scope as you look for what are called "haystacks." It's a little hump along this squiggly green line that looks like a haystack; and you fine-tune it to get the highest or largest haystack you can. Each satellite has different transponders—these are the little parts of the satellite that receive the signal—and each has a different frequency. You program your satellite truck to send its signal up on a specific frequency to hit a specific transponder.

Satellites are owned by satellite companies. The ones I use for NBC are owned by a company called Americom. AMC1–AMC9 are their satellites. You pay for satellite time in "windows" or "blocks" of time. You can buy any length of window, the smallest being a five-minute window. I've been on a satellite for as long as four or five hours at a time. They range in price, but seventy dollars for a five-minute window is probably about average.

If you buy a whole hour, you get a little bit of a discount. You call them in advance and reserve a window or spot. Many companies vie for transponder windows on satellites. The farther ahead you get, the more choices you have. It's not like trying to get a table at a really good restaurant; there are a lot of transponders on the satellite.

If I punch the wrong number and don't double-check it and bring it up, I could override another signal. The worst I can do with my truck if I enter the wrong frequency, is knock NBC programming off the air. Usually the operator you are talking to will see where you are coming up and tell you to stop. But I have been knocked off the air by somebody else.

You send the signal up and then, to confirm it for yourself, you downlink the signal and receive it back in your truck. So, now you can see, there it is going up and here is how it looks coming down. I know my signal is good.

Aside from the satellite technology, the ground operations are the same as with a microwave truck. No matter how fast you become at setting up a live shot from a truck, there will always be a way that's faster and arguably much more fun.

The live helicopter is the fastest method of getting pictures of a breaking news event on the air. Helicopters are great things; we can't live without them.

Helicopters, Choppers, Whirlybirds—Live All the Time

When you talk about live television, the conversation usually starts with the helicopter. It's what most news departments really rely on for immediacy, and it is immediate. Before we even lift off, we establish a signal to the mountain top, and from there until we land, that signal is on; no matter where we are, we are live. It's much faster than a microwave truck. Even if you can set it up in ten minutes, that's still ten minutes that the helicopter is already orbiting with the picture coming back. It gets even faster if you are talking about traffic—the truck can take an extra half hour to get across town to where the story is. Anytime we do anything, the helicopter is the first piece of equipment that is up and live and has a picture.

As soon as the helicopter lifts off, the microwave transmitter under the helicopter starts transmitting. It sends the video and audio signal and also "talks" to the ground station. At KNSD, this is located on top of a mountain. Through GPS, the helicopter

A news helicopter in flight: The lens is pointing backward to protect the glass from bugs.

A. The gyrostabilized lens mounts on the nose of the helicopter.

B. The laptop console controls all camera functions.

knows where the ground station is; it also "tells" the ground station where it is so that the ground station knows where to look for the helicopter's signal. Both systems point at each other. The transmitter for the helicopter and the receiver for the ground station follow and track with the motion of the helicopter. This ensures a constant live signal, no matter where the helicopter is.

Camera Systems for Helicopter News Coverage

In our helicopter, there are two cameras. I've seen as many as four or five on some helicopters. Inside, we have a lipstick camera, which looks like a tube of lipstick. It's a very small camera that's maybe four inches long and less than the diameter of a quarter. It sits in a little shock-mounted bracket that's attached to an upright column in the helicopter, and it points to where the talent will be. It's the reporter's camera. You just turn it on, white-balance it (there's a locking ring so the focus won't change), and it's done.

Mounted outside the helicopter is a remote-control ball that rotates on all axes. Helicopters vibrate, and they have a bunch of spinning and moving parts. So, there's a lot of inherent shaking in a helicopter. The lens is isolated by the gyros, and it stays—as one of the manufacturers of the ball states—"Rock solid worldwide." It looks like the camera is sitting on a tripod.

From the lens, mounted by itself in the ball, a cable that looks like a garden hose runs to the luggage compartment of the helicopter. There the cable hooks to an adapter plate on an ENG camera where the lens used to be. From the gyrostabilized ball and camera, all control cables run into the cockpit. The lens controls and the camera controls—on/off, gain, bars, all of those things—are remoted to a console on your lap.

From the console, you zoom, focus, and pan the camera ball right and left, tilt up and down, iris, turn the bars on, or throw the doubler (a 2x extender on the lens) in. You can do everything from the console.

Seat belt fastened, ready for take off. It's a whole new world up there for photographers. There's a new set of skills to be mastered.

Shooting Aerials

Working the outside camera is kind of like playing a video game. While the pilot flies the helicopter, you fly the camera. The camera will turn 360 degrees in a circle and will point nearly straight down. There's a toggle switch that lets us switch between sending images from the inside and outside cameras. It's the ultimate fun ride in TV news.

Because all of the controls are remote, it's hard to get a feel for how all the systems react. Instead of touching the lens to control the iris, you're touching a little knob. There's a bit of a delay, and if you don't anticipate it, you overcompensate. Start learning by turning the controls slowly and seeing how long it takes each system to respond and how much turn or back pressure you need to exert on the console controls.

The trick is setting the reaction speeds for the servos to react in a manner that feels comfortable to you. You use both hands, controlling all functions all the time. You wish you had an extra hand when things get busy.

Sometimes we put the camera in auto-iris if the lighting is changing a lot and there's a lot of camera motion. This, of course, is not ideal. On the ground, you'd never go auto-iris, but up in a helicopter, sometimes it's necessary. Then just as you make that decision to switch to auto, a white cop car or ambulance will race through your shot, catch a glint from the sun, and your image will go dark. No matter what happens, you need to react fast, but at the same time don't overreact with the controls. Focus, obviously, in a helicopter is not as crucial; you are so far away, you are almost nearly in infinity all the time. It's really a feel thing. You get to know the system; you get to know the limitations and its abilities.

To get great images, the pilot and photographer must work in unison. Clear, concise dialog is essential in an ever-changing shooting environment.

Helicopter Communication

You talk to the pilot; he tells you what he can and can't do. The pilot should have an understanding of flying a camera-equipped helicopter because there are certain ways you fly. You make your turns flatter, you need not bank the helicopter, you just make an orbit as flat as you can, keeping the helicopter as level as you can. If you bank the helicopter, your microwave signal now is shooting up in the sky or straight into the ground instead of out to the horizon, to your mountain top.

You work with the station to find out where they want you to go. Then you work with the pilot to see how you can get there. We have the Thomas Brothers "map" just like every other ground crew in town has. The interesting part is that I can't just find a 100 block easily by looking at a house from the air. So you find some landmarks on the page—a park, a shopping center—and go from there. If it's a big enough news event, you'll see the flashing lights or smoke; whatever it is you are going for will be easier to find.

The cameraperson talks to the station and relays to the pilot. I always have a relationship with the pilots on a first-name basis. Most of them really want to get you into position, so they will bring it around quickly to get to the shot and then go slow while you shoot; then you go around quickly and go slow. They don't take pride in the picture that goes on the TV; they take pride in the fact that they were able to put you in the place to get the picture that's very still.

Drawbacks and Benefits of Helicopter News Coverage
The biggest drawback for me is you are not in contact with the story, so to speak. You are very separated from the story. You're not meeting people; you're not experiencing the story. That's a little bit of a drawback, but you usually are the first guy there, and you see a lot more than some of the ground guys.

Some of the nice things: at the brush fire I don't have to walk up the hill; the helicopter takes me there. I don't have to argue with the cop to let me in the closed street; we just fly over.

Issues from the Air
One of the issues that can get TV stations in trouble is where that fine line of private property and privacy comes into effect. With your camera always being hot, you need to be real careful about what you show. At five hundred feet, you can read a license plate. There are certain things you have to be really careful about.

We have seen a lot of it, especially in Los Angeles, with car chases. We start carrying chases live and suddenly, by accident, show the public something that they may not want to see. Somebody being shot by a police officer, somebody being run over by a car being chased. Something we would probably never put on the air if it was on tape, but because we are carrying it live it gets on the air. Here, we make a conscious effort to be very careful about that. When a chase comes to an end we generally pull out, even though it's kind of against what you want to do.

For Some, Flying Is for the Birds
Not everyone is cut out for hours in a helicopter, circling a point on the ground. If you're prone to motion sickness, I would stay away from aerial photography because it will get you real fast. You have to stay concentrated on your screen, which is like looking in your viewfinder, while the helicopter is turning to the left and your camera follows to the right. It's disorienting; it can kind of mess with your body, and you can get ill; that will end your day quickly.

Helicopter Safety
Just like in an airliner, the flight crew is responsible for giving you a safety briefing. Learn all the safety aspects of your helicopter in particular. You'll want to know where the door handles are, how the seat belt latch releases, where the life vests are—even if you're not planning on flying over the ocean. In an emergency, the pilot may choose to put it down in a lake as opposed to a crowded street. It would be a shame to survive the crash only to drown in a small lake.

There will be crash procedures that the pilot will run through with you. They may change from helicopter to helicopter, so pay attention.

Always approach a helicopter from the front. The top blades are usually out of harm's way, although everyone ducks on the way to the cabin. The back blades are deadly; they are usually about head height, and not paying attention can get you killed. Avoid the rear of the helicopter.

Accidents do happen, from mechanical failure to pilot error. Hitting power lines is an all-too-frequent cause of helicopter accidents. When you're not shooting or in an unfamiliar area, all eyes count, including yours. Look for power lines. A few seconds' notice could save your life.

Helicopters Provide a Degree of Safety . . .

. . . from situations that are unsafe on the ground. The helicopter also provides safety for our crews. In the Cedar Fire situation, the live trucks can't move out of the way as fast as a helicopter. When you set up a truck, you can't drive it away when you got a forty-foot mast in the air and 200-foot cable hanging out from that door. If you've got to run, it takes a little while for that mast to come down, takes a little while to get that cable back onto the truck. In a helicopter, you can fly just about anywhere and be fairly safe.

It's a perfect tool for covering spot news. A guy could shoot at the helicopter, but he's more likely to shoot at a news van sitting on the side of the road than shoot up in the air at a helicopter. We have long enough lenses that we can sit a couple thousand feet up in the air and still bring all the pictures you need and be well out of the range of any immediate danger. It really is the one piece of equipment the newsroom relies on the most for the immediacy of live coverage.

Helicopters, camera systems, pilots, fuel, maintenance, and insurance make news helicopter coverage an expensive proposition. Every flight minute is expensive. Calling a local helicopter company for an hour's flight may cost you five hundred dollars. Now, the station's paying you your salary to go fly. That means you can't be looking out the window going, "This is wonderful!" You are really up there concentrating on your job and staying focused on what you are doing.

Up, Up, and Away

Skim over snow-covered ridge tops, pan across clouds at sunset, track with a train as it cuts through the countryside; now you're flying.

There's no beating a steady helicopter image for putting perspective in a story—it's the ultimate at portraying "where we are." It's fast, it's instant, it's cool. With a little practice on the controls, you'll go from just following your subject to using the helicopter as a shooting platform or tool. Pans, tracking shots, and point-of-view shots can all be used to communicate and add production value to the story.

Back on the Ground

Whether it's a helicopter, microwave truck, satellite, or some other form of "live" video acquisition, all of these high-tech tools are allocated daily by the assignment desk to gather news and enhance the newscast. The funds and manpower required to operate them are weighed against the newsworthiness of the story and a perceived production value for the newscast. Generally, your lead story or your second story will be a live shot. The stories that are farther down in your show, in your "B" or your "C" blocks, probably will not be live.

"Live" provides a service to the community and, at the same time, keeps viewers locked into the moment as it unfolds in front of them. Going "live" is also good business. We are profit businesses, and we need to have a news show that people watch so that we can sell advertiseing and make money to pay our bills and our people. A lot of times as photographers, we may think, "Why am I live?" But

sometimes it's a bigger picture than just what the photographers think. Sometimes the reason is that it helps pay our salaries.

The Cedar Fire burned out of control for three days, but smoldered in wood debris and in the minds of residents for months afterward. Accusations, lawsuits, and a criminal trial gave little comfort to those who lost loved ones and homes in Southern California's worst wildfire. By the time the Cedar Fire burned out, it had consumed 721,791 acres and destroyed 3,640 homes. One hundred and four firefighters were injured trying to contain the blaze. The fire claimed the lives of thirteen civilians and one firefighter.

On his drive home, Greg Stickney can still see evidence of the fire: blackened mats of earth, dead and gnarled trees—too many to remove. He pulls his news car up the driveway to a home that survived by luck, fate, or a simple shift in the wind.

His destiny decided in an instant—an instant captured live.

CHAPTER 14

Sam Allen

Get into the Game—
Athletic Photography

Sam Allen
Director of Photography

Sam Allen Productions, NFL Films
Former Chief Photographer KBTV, now KUSA (9News), Denver
NPPA Ernie Crisp Television News Photographer of the Year, 1977
National Iris Award, *Rocky Hockey Picture Show*
National Sports Emmy (Cinematography, HBO's *Inside the NFL*)

*N*ew England snow fills the air for a second day in a row. Not light flurries, but wet, frozen puffs that stick to everything, carpeting the landscape like an Arctic tundra. The view out the hotel window is only seen in varying shades of white. The brightness makes the room seem dark. This is a snow day and anyone who doesn't have to be out is not. Except for those determined fans braving the elements to see the Raiders play the Patriots. Football wins over traffic advisories every time.

The roads are treacherous; there's as much slipping and sliding as actual driving. Fender-benders and roadside cursing highlight the trip to Foxboro Stadium. For some, it's a miserable day. For Sam Allen, smiling in the back of a fifteen-passenger crew van as it pulls into the parking lot, it's a perfect day for a game. There's something special in the air—snow! All the other NFL Films cameramen who are shooting in domes or on the West Coast are laughing at us. It's going to be sloppy work. But we knew we had the best game in the world right now. Why? "Snow games" are better because a lot of things happen in snow games. If it's a beautiful day, it's not going to be as exciting.

EQUIPMENT

For NFL Films:
- Arriflex Super 16-HS SR2 or SR3 film camera
- Canon 7.8-164 mm lens—converted standard video lens modified to a film camera
- Canon 35× or a fixed 400 mm lens when shooting long lens
- Sony F-900 CineAlta HD camera
- Fujinon or Canon 15× lens/22× lens

For Extreme Shows:
- Arriflex Super 16 camera
- Sony F-900 CineAlta HD camera
- Panasonic VariCam
- Sony Zu-1 HD-DVCAM

Lighting Kit:
- Mole Baby-Baby 1K Light head with Chimera
- Mole 650 light head
- 2 Lowel 250 light heads
- Lowel 500 Chimera LC-55 light head
- 1 or 2 Diva 200s and 1 or 2 Diva 400s
- 5- or 10-ton grip truck rented for larger productions

Not only is it a snow game, but this will be the last game ever played in Foxboro Stadium. So it's a snow game and the last time any cameramen will record a football game in this old stadium.

Today, there are nine cameras shooting 16mm film for NFL Films. It's an elite group; only the very best sports cameramen work for NFL Films and, of that group, the ground-level guys are the top in their field. To cover this game, there are two handheld, ground-level cameras shooting 48 fps (frames per second), one up high in the end zone (he will shoot 32 fps or 48 fps), one shooting high center (he will shoot 32 fps or 48 fps), a couple of sync sound cameras shooting 24 fps, and one shooting high-speed 90 fps to 120 fps (he will be on a high hat or handheld). Sam Allen is one of the handheld 48 fps ground-level guys—with an old 12 to 240 Angenieux zoom lens (not used any more).

The NFL Films Company started 300 miles away in Philadelphia. In 1962, Ed Sabol was selling top-coats for his father-in-law's clothing company. Ed and his wife received a Bell and Howell film camera as a wedding gift. Now, with their son Steve playing high school football, Ed would break out the old wedding gift and film the games. Part-time hobby turned to passion as Sabol founded a small film company named after his daughter—Blair Motion Pictures. Then, in a bold move, Sabol contacted NFL Commissioner Pete Rozelle and bid $3,000 for the rights to shoot the 1962 NFL Championship Game between the New York Giants and Green Bay Packers. He won the bid, and Pete Rozelle called his footage "The best football film" he had ever seen.

Within two years, Ed's company employed six filmmakers. He convinced Rozelle that the NFL needed their own film company and in 1964, under NFL ownership, NFL Films was born. Ed's son, Steve, began working as a cameraman on the sidelines and is today president of NFL Films, overseeing 275 employees and more than 1,000 miles of 16mm film shot each season.

Film as a recording medium has long been removed from all of the news-gathering organizations outlined in this book, immediacy and the expense of film origination being the overriding cause. However, few would debate film's ability to capture beauty in a way that exceeds today's video technology. NFL Films does what the name says; they film. They use film and believe in film as a medium. From the NFL Films Web site:

Film goes to the core of what NFL Films is all about. We are filmmakers, romanticists, and storytellers. Film has a sense of history about it, while video is too immediate. Film is like wood—it has a texture. Video is like Formica—it is shallow and one-dimensional.

One of the top NFL Films filmmakers is Sam Allen. Wearing long underwear, boots, and fingerless gloves, Allen hikes his equipment from the parking lot into the stadium. Sled dogs would have come in handy to help move all the cases of film equipment. The snow is six to eight inches deep, and we finally get to the field. We are now about one hour behind schedule because of the traffic and the weather. The field is wet and muddy with more and more snow falling. We have to build tents in this weather to try and keep everything dry. You have to try to keep your lens dry and your magazines dry because if you put a wet mag on the camera, the film can stick to the gate, causing a film break or mag jam that causes a chain reaction to other problems. Film can get really brittle in cold weather and can snap at any moment. There are all these things you have to think about, and the game hasn't even started yet.

Now we have to shoot pregame. Every cameraman will do his job to tell the story about what is about to take place. The snow is falling, stadium crews are cleaning it off the stands and the field with snowblowers or shovels. Wide shots of the stadium inside and out, players warming up, and coaches talking to each other about what a beautiful warm evening we are having for this match-up.

Allen's assistant cameraperson prepares for the game, preloading film magazines so he can quickly reload without missing a shot. All his equipment is accounted for and positioned for instant access so that when it's needed, there's no fumbling around trying to find the right gear. The crowds are in their seats, players on the field. Allen shoulders his Arri SR2 under a protective camera cover. The lens is still dry—for now. He thumbs the "on" button and the Arri screams to life, high-speed 16mm film racing across the gate at 72 feet a minute, 48 fps. That's a 100 percent faster-than-normal action; the faster shutter speed ensures razor-sharp images, each one a frozen snapshot of time.

When displayed at normal speed, a three-second shot will take six seconds to watch, crushing scrimmages, floating footballs, and diving receivers become a ballet of intense competition. At normal speed, 24 fps, the image framed on the viewfinder's ground glass flickers. At this speed, it's hardly noticeable. Add intense concentration and focus, and it's like you're right there—two feet away from . . .

. . . Kick-off

The game starts and it's snowing straight down. It's everything you ever wanted in a game because they're slipping and sliding they're catching the ball, they're not catching the ball, they're falling—everything you'd every want in a game.

Of course, football is an athletic sport requiring strength, physical stamina, and a keen understanding of every element of the game. Shooting the game for NFL Films is an athletic sport requiring strength, physical stamina and a keen understanding of every element in the game. Allen runs up and down the sidelines carrying twenty to twenty-five pounds of equipment, diving onto knee pads to set his shot for the best angle of each play.

We shoot from our knees because you're shooting up and we get the crowd in the background, which is the prettier shot. *He then runs to the next position; the game's not going to wait for him. These are sports Allen loves passionately, both the game of football and his aggressive camerawork. Asked to draw a diagram of his coverage over a printed football field, Allen scribbles wildly for 15 seconds and then says, "That's it." It was an honest depiction, an Etch-A-Sketch in the hands of a man possessed by football and filmmaking—a "cine-athlete."*

I can run end zone to end zone in fourteen to fifteen seconds if it's not raining or snowing. There is a lot of running up and down the sidelines involved in football games just to try and keep up with the game. If you miss a play, that could be the play that really tells the story of the game because it could be the only touchdown or field goal scored. So, we have to try and shoot every single play in the game. We will also take chances with extreme angles, so we will miss a few plays during the course of a game, but we have a cameraperson perched high up in the stadium. That person never misses a play—we hope.

On the field, Allen is keeping ahead of the game, keeping a good average anticipating the plays, logging many of those great long-lens shots through falling snow. From the quarterback, to spinning pig skin spiraling toward the camera, to big hands plucking it from the sky and carrying it into the end zone, Allen exposes the drama in one smooth shot. At NFL Films, the rule of thumb is: Try to get the whole play from the snap to the reaction. Play after play, defense, offense, running up and down the sidelines covering more ground than many of the players while pulling focus, adjusting the zoom, and following the action. Allen calls for a fresh magazine.

The mag runner takes the exposed magazine and spent batteries back to the assistant cameraperson (who can't even see the game because they are under cover from the snow and too busy to take a break), while Allen snaps the new magazine on his camera. The assistant cameraperson will carefully download the mag and label the film, treating it like the Crown Jewels. These moments on film can never be recovered.

All of a sudden, I see an unbelievable, backlit shot of the crowd with the Patriot's flag floating through the air and the snow now falling at a rapid pace, with this rake of light coming from behind the crowd—and it's beautiful. It's cold, steam is rising above the dark faces, and it looks so surreal. As I am looking at this scene, I am rolling footage because the scene may not be the same five minutes later. To this day, I still see that shot when they associate that night with the Patriots. It's one of my favorite shots.

The game continues. Allen is in heaven; he knows what he's shot is spectacular, battery after battery, mag after mag, and images from vantage points only he has raced to position himself. All of the cameramen will produce images completely different from each other. Unique to each, unique to Sam Allen, all prized by NFL Films. The very last shot of the game is a field goal, and I start head to toe then zoom in on his face and try to stay as tight as I can on the field goal kicker, so, when it's over I can see his face and see him being lifted up and carried away by team members. This field goal ends up being the greatest part of the whole night, but it was the snow that made this story. Maybe it was cold, but I wasn't cold because it was a beautiful winter game.

Behind the Highlights

Sam Allen has been shooting for NFL Films for twenty-five years. With that kind of sideline, long lens experience, his insight and techniques are invaluable to anyone attempting national-level sports photography. With sketchpad left behind, Allen takes us through some of his favorite shots as he narrates his "highlight reel."

A 48 fps low-angle shot of the Denver Bronco cheerleaders at Invesco Field at Mile High Stadium.

News and Sports Mix into a Prize Assignment

Allen's love of sports and athletic talents led to great news opportunities and a chance to rub elbows with the President of the United States. I was the only one who actually could ski without poles and carry a camera—or at least I thought I could ski. I had a CP-16 film camera. I was the only one allowed to ski with President Ford because I could shoot and not have to look through the lens and ski at the same time and, also, keep up with the group surrounding the President. I got all the tracking shots needed for the story, so now it's time to do something stupid. We were skiing down a pretty flat run about a third of the way down the mountain. This was before we arrived at the first group of cameramen, who were set up about halfway down the mountain, all on tripods, waiting for a shot of the President to ski up to them.

It was time to get my lower-angle shots, so I sat down with my butt on the backs of my skis and the camera in my lap. The President decides to make a right turn, and I'm already two or three feet from him. I know I'm too close for comfort, but I can't get up in time. The backs of his skis catch the top part of my skis, and it almost knocked him over. I almost crashed but was able to stand up, and he was able to get out of it without falling down and breaking a leg or arm.

Almost immediately, I had a secret service agent out of nowhere grab me, stop me, look me in the eye, and say, "If you ever do that again, I'm going to break your ass." "Yes sir." He could have said something like dismembering parts of my body, but that quick conversation is a blur. I didn't get that close to him from then on. The footage was pretty good, and you could see the shot where this stupid cameraman got too close and almost knocked him over. I was young, dumb, and aggressive. What did I know?

In 1977, Sam Allen wins NPPA Ernie Crisp Television News Photographer of the Year and takes over the reins from his mentor, Tom Baer, to become chief photographer. It's the same year the station wins its first NPPA Television News Station of the Year, recognizing all the photographers on the staff. Baer has achieved his goal; a tradition has begun.

Our creative services guy, Harvey Mars, was a bit of an inspiration because he pounded it into our heads that he wanted good stuff and, if we were doing a special, we would work with him. He gave me more inspiration than anybody because he would applaud me for the silliest little thing that I did. Then he decided he was going to make a commercial about me and put it on the air. It was a shock to me. That's when photographers were recognized on Channel 9.

Today, there are commercials on the air about the photographers and editors winning the National Press Photographers Association, Station of the Year, Photographer of the Year, and Regional Emmys. It was something we started back in the late 1970s, and today camera-people from all over the country venture to this station to prove they are the best in the business.

In the photographic department, Allen specialized in feature stories and sports, shooting all the Denver Bronco games ground level on film, with Don Brookins shooting topside camera for the weekly highlight show. The ground-level film reel he put together from his Bronco footage attracted NFL Films, and he's been running the sidelines for them ever since.

How do you go from news to NFL Films? Well, news and sports are the same thing. You don't get a second chance. When the fire is burning, it's burning—same with sports. You can't ask John Elway to pull that ball back and do it again because you are resetting your camera, cleaning the gate, or checking your lens. You have to be ready for whatever action is going on. If you are shooting an event, you only get one shot at it.

I specialized in sports because I started to get tired of news. In sports, it's not about life, death, and tragedy. This is only sports. So you lost a football game, big deal, you don't have to feel bad. Plus, whether it's an event or a snowboarding feature or a heli-skiing feature or a basketball feature, you have a little more time to tell the story than you do in news.

I got a promotion that took me out of the news department and into the promotional department, and that led me into commercials. I was also able to shoot football games on weekends. This became my love and passion. I didn't want to shoot news anymore. I think I found my niche.

If You Love Sports . . .

. . . you probably love extreme sports, too. What's the difference in covering the traditional versus the extreme? It jumps into extreme when it's not a controlled situation—mountain boarding, mountain biking, skateboarding, helicopter skiing. You don't have teams with players, but you are competing against the elements—dirt, mud, cliffs, rock, snow, and ice—now that's extreme. The risk factor is a lot higher. Body parts break; property damage, brain damage, and damage to cameras are a bigger possibility.

Heli-skiing is a natural extreme sport for Allen's talents. You have to be physically fit, capture great moments, and love the sport. Allen's first heli-ski shoot started before sunup in rain and fog. You get up in the morning and pack all your stuff in backpacks and take it out to the helicopter. Everything fits in this big basket on the side of the helicopter. It's the week following the last week of the heli-ski season, and it's raining and foggy in the valley where the chalet and helicopters are located, so we think there's not any great snow left.

When the rain stops, they fly us up to the top of a mountain and, much to our surprise, there is plenty of snow in the Monishes and the Caribou ranges. You have to wait for the weather to be somewhat clear because you don't want to get caught in the sucker holes. That's when you fly into a second or third location about six- to eight-thousand feet, land, and then the helicopter leaves to get more fuel in the valley. The clouds start to close in, and it's like a fog. Now you are stuck on the mountain, dig a snow cave, and spend a nice evening wondering what the hot dinner is in the chalet.

The pilot lands, drops us off, and we have our skis, backpacks, film cameras, and survival packs. Now the helicopter leaves. It's very quiet: beautiful mountain range as far as you can see, a few clouds—picture perfect everywhere you look. Now, all of a sudden, there is this gut-wrenching feeling deep down inside because you have to get down the mountain on your own with equipment and you've never been out of bounds where none of the ski runs are groomed. On this trip, we did have a professional ski guide and an avalanche dog (Tomba), but that definitely was the scariest moment to me. I almost got sick because the helicopter just left and I knew that was going to happen, but you don't realize it 'til it really happens.

All the mistakes that you can make are usually in the beginning of any production, so learn from your mistakes. For anyone to shoot helicopter-skiing/snowboarding, you must have radios that work in the mountains. Think about all your shots in the helicopter and at the top of the mountain. Have a plan, even if it's not a great plan, and then you work your way down the run. You had better be in shape because you will have to ski down in all the cruddy parts because you want all the nice snow in the middle of the run looking perfect for the skier and for your shot.

We have two cameramen and four snowboarders on this shoot. All have radios so we can talk to each other from anywhere on the run. We do what we call leapfrog, where one cameraman shoots from near the top and the second cameraman is at least a hundred yards down the run. You send the boarders one by one or all at the same time, depending on what you need for this sequence. As they ride down the virgin run, they pass the first cameraman real close and keep going toward the second cameraman, so you can get more footage without having to stop so many times. You then leapfrog. The cameraman at the end of this scene is now the first and skies down to be the second position on the next scene. We continue swapping positions as the snowboarders pass us.

You can set up for a crisscross shot or set up on the same side of the run for more of a continuity shot. If you shoot where there are cliffs, you have to set up a camera at the edge of a cliff and send the other cameraman to find a way to the bottom of the cliff. You probably don't want to jump off the cliff with your gear. It can really hurt, and the equipment is hard to replace where you are located. You're skiing on snow that is probably fifteen to twenty feet deep, so you always have to listen to your guide for your safety and the success of the production.

Try to set up where you can get a twenty- to twenty-five-second shot because somewhere in that twenty-five seconds is the four-second shot your editor is going want. You should try to shoot your scenes back-lit, and please expose for the snow. Never expose for the shadows. Snow will really screw up your shot if you're not careful, and, especially in video, you never want to overexpose high-definition or standard-definition video.

Rock music accompanies the action sequences as skiers sail through virgin snow at the Powder 8 Championships—hosted by Mike Wiegele Helicopter Skiing Company—in Blue River, British Columbia. Allen fills in the photographic details.

Shot A on the previous page, taken with long lens on a trusty Sony Beta-Cam, was set up with two skiers coming down a slope with great powder as the helicopter flies over them. You can see the skiers and the helicopter in the same shot to give you the excitement of heli-skiing. Using radios, a guide on top of the mountain coordinates the skiers, cueing them and the helicopter pilot to come around at a precise time so that no one gets hurt or killed.

This is a one-take shot because you want snow with no tracks, except those laid down by the skiers. To get the shot with pristine snow, we had to ski down with backpacks, camera equipment, and tripod way to the right or left of the area we were going to shoot. It was a little difficult, but the shot turned out beautiful, lasting all of twenty-five seconds.

Shot B on the previous page is also at Powder 8 Championships for the feature about two contestants. I had to chase expert skiers down a powder run with a Sony Beta-Cam, obviously without poles. We were trying to get tracking shots alongside and behind them at maybe half speed—that's when you fly head over heels, or skis, as it were. You better be in shape to hold the camera up while not getting your body beat up or the camera buried in snow. Electronic cameras hate to get wet and it's difficult to find a replacement Beta-Cam in Blue River, BC. We got several shots to compliment the feature, and no one except me was injured or tortured and no animals were harmed.

For the top shot on this page, we set up in Canada under a jump because it was snowing and we needed the trees in the background to show the skiers in flight. A Beta-Cam was handheld because the snow was so deep we could not use a tripod. Again, we skied into position and used radios and guides to get us into and out of the tree runs. To get the different shots, we were dropped off on the mountaintop by helicopter, then all skied into place.

To get a series of shots of skiers in trees and very deep powder, you ski into place, take off your backpack, pull out a camera and shoot, then put it back in and ski to the next spot and do it all over again. If I had a dollar for every time I've pulled a camera out of a backpack, put it back in, and skied to the next spot, I would have enough money to take a trip to an Hawaiian beach and shoot footage from a tripod. I will keep dreaming.

The bottom image on the previous page is a great tracking shot, if you can get it. Try skiing next to expert skiers, keep your eyes on them while looking to the front and side, trying to not loose them in frame. The best way is to cradle the camera in your hands, not on your shoulder; this way you can steady the shot with your arms and use your legs and hands to absorb the vibration you get at higher speeds. Try talking to them and keeping them at your side or a little behind you. They never listen and take off ahead, so you can get that tracking-from-behind shot. To keep you on your skies and close to the action, not on your face, it's best to do leg lifts for about a month before heading out on your great adventure. As you can see, the experts go fast and furious; you are just a cameraperson trying to take beautiful shots.

Shots taken for the first Burton Snowboard "cult" film; it was a setup using a 16 mm Arri SR with a wide-angle 5.7 mm film lens at 48 and 64 fps.

There Are Levels of Extreme

The action moves up a notch with snowboarding. Heli-skiing with snowboarders is similar to heli-skiing with skiers, except they're crazier. A beautiful blue sky is torn in half by a snowboarder looking straight down at Allen in the series of shots on this page.

We tried to let the riders get as much air as they could over the jump. The camera was handheld in order to put it as close to the snowboard as I could without smashing the lens or destroying the camera or cameraman (that would be me). We hiked up and under the cliff so we could get a shot of the riders flying off with a nice mountain backdrop. It was shot at 64 fps with a handheld 16 mm Arri SR and a 12–120 zoom lens to get as much as possible on film during the five-second jump.

Later, we had hiked to the dead center of the cliff to get the riders in the air with only sky as background. We used the old yelling technique instead of radios to get all four on film. "He's coming, he's airborne, over you." I cranked the camera to about 75 fps to keep them in the air as long as possible during the three-second airtime. Back then snowboarders were dudes who were renegade types (probably why I could relate to them); most ski areas would not allow them on the slopes. So, we were learning about the sport way before it was accepted. Now it's an Olympic sport that draws more spectators than downhill racing. We found out how much fun it was—the speed, the recklessness—and how they could do all kinds of tricks to make it worth watching.

Extreme Documentary, with Extreme Forces

Pushing the limits in ski filming has played a large part in Allen's career, from the President Ford fumble to heli-skiing to a documentary on the Army Special Forces. Those who hire Allen know his skills well. In an extreme environment where anything can happen, his success rate of capturing stunning images is one of the highest in the industry. It's not that he's just willing to race down a mountain. He knows what to do with his camera every step of the way. He knows how to tell a story, especially one where the subject, the people, the photographer, and the environment are all extreme.

I was contacted by a Colorado producer to shoot handheld Sony CineAlta HD 24p footage of the Army Special Forces for Digital Ranch, a California company. They needed someone who could shoot handheld on skies for a documentary and commercial for the Web and broadcast. We found the Winter Park/Mary Jane Mountain ski area that had a beautiful snow-covered moun-

tain backdrop and somewhat steep terrain with chair lifts so that we could shoot many runs without the use of snowmobiles. This was a set-up shot at the 12,060-foot top of Parsenn Bowl on the Mary Jane side of the mountain—getting gloves on, snapping boots in, and checking goggles. It was a cold morning with blue skies and lots of snow. I tried some low-angle shots to give viewers the larger-

"This is a handheld, tracking shot of a Special Forces' guy to show speed on a downhill run. I am trying to get as close as possible to show a low-angle POV shot without hitting him and causing a crash. The runs were through trees, so we had a reference of speed to show that they're 'bad asses' so don't mess with them."

"Here, I'm skiing in a reverse snowplow so the guy can bring the gun right up to my lens, with the sun in the background to give it some drama. I had to keep telling him to ski closer and shove the gun in my face, not to be afraid of knocking me over. It took 40 to 50 seconds to get the 5-second shot. Trees were on each side to show speed."

than-life look. The Sony F-900 was set up for 24p, so we could get the film look they needed for the production.

Chasing Great Images or Great Danger

Capturing all the thrill-packed moments only a handful of people get to live can be dangerous, no matter what the sport is. The closer you get to the action, the more involved you are, but also the more danger you're in. Another reason to know the sport you're filming—get a realistic idea of the risks. Again, hiking the camera around and losing half your vision to the camera body puts you at a disadvantage. The people you're filming are probably pros, and they're only thinking about their sport. You, on the other hand, are trying to think what they're thinking, anticipate their moves, get great shots, and think about your safety, all while being in the middle of the action just like your subjects. Anticipate your risks.

There's another hazard waiting to injure anyone with a lens. Many photographers have been injured or killed watching the screen in the viewfinder. What I mean is that the viewfinder's image becomes a movie that they're watching, not completely aware of their actual surroundings. They become thrilled and mesmerized by the images coming through the viewfinder. There have been stories of photographers following the last para-trooper out of a plane without a parachute of their own. Jumping was not their plan. The photographer wanted to keep the frame and was mentally drawn out of the plane before he knew to stop. Whether this story is true or not, anyone who has experienced this effect knows how it could happen. Be aware!

Keep Healthy by Working Out—It's Sports Afterall

If you want to be an extreme cameraperson, you will have to work out. You should lift weights, run, jog, and use as many machines as possible: treadmill, bike, and elliptical stepper. Do as much working out as possible because, when you're out in the middle of the mountains and you run out of strength, you might miss that great closing shot just over the next rise. So work out, be strong, and go for it. I work out two and a half hours per day—four days this week—and I still should work out more.

It's Not Dedication—If It's Love

At fifty-nine, Sam Allen can outrun most people half his age. There's no secret. He loves what he does and makes sure he can put himself and his lens exactly where it needs to be to capture the shot he wants, the instant he wants it. He lives the sports he shoots and knows the minute details that make memorable moments of competition and photography. What makes a great Sam Allen shot? Why is he constantly sought out for traditional and extreme assignments?

It's love. Thanks, Sam, for all those great moments. I'm a fan.

CHAPTER 15

Brian Weister

Editing—A Cut
Above

Brian Weister
News Editor

KMGH-TV, Denver
High Noon Entertainment
NPPA Cutting Edge Editor of the Year, 2002 and 2005
NPPA National Editor of the Year, 2003 and 2004

*I*t's 4:35 P.M. A fresh cassette from the field is ushered into the newsroom with the same focused intensity as a critical patient being rushed to an ER.

On a dark monitor, the first frame of video pops to life. The remains of a collapsed building stand frozen against falling snow and rescue efforts. Emergency lights flash on the screen, illuminating Brian Weister in a transparent cage. He's an editor, the final voice that "tells" the story. A quiet craftsman in a dimly lit room, huddled over a colored keyboard and script. Like an "editor encounter" in some futuristic zoo, a row of glass doors allow a view into this final stage of storytelling, Room after room hums with the business of assembling stories.

This has been Weister's roost for the past six years. While in captivity (employment) at KMGH-TV, Denver, he has risen to the top of his field, winning numerous national awards for editing and creativity. There's an element other than editing the story that competes for Weister's attention: The deadline.

Only twenty minutes to air an A-2 package—the second story on the 5:00 P.M. newscast. No one knows time like an editor, where seconds are thought of as frames. Weister can sense time going by in one-thirtieth-of-a-second increments. The reporter's script and narration arrive, roughed out in the field and recorded in a small booth down the hall. Weister makes a few quick notes as the sound is ingested (digitized). Years of expertise tell him this deadline will be close.

The temperature behind the sliding glass door has gone up a few degrees in the last couple of minutes; the icy images seem out of place in the sweltering heat. Beads of sweat begin to appear on Weister's forehead as he cuts the story.

Cuts *refer to the process of editing. The term "cut" means an instant transition between images from the last frame of one shot and the first frame of the next. While the human eye observes all that's in visual range, the mind "cuts," instantaneously directing attention from one element to the next,*

EQUIPMENT

Avid News Cutter XP

assembling a coherent flow of thought. An editor then creates a coherent flow of thought from the sights and sounds captured by the photojournalist. Just as the mind pops seamlessly from one element to the next, a skilled editor can make these transitions invisible to average viewers as they ride along the narrative journey.

Weister's eyes dart back and forth among three screens and the clock as his fingers attack the command keys. One screen shows the video clips he chooses from; the other is playback; the third is the Avid menu. Wide shots, mediums, close-ups all fly by. The clock on the wall represents death as much as the sickle-wielding reaper from Igmar Bergman's Seventh Seal.

Tick-tock, Brian Weister, the end is coming.

Sixteen Minutes to Air

The video is assembled on a nonlinear editing system, or NLE, a computer that allows Weister to place any shot at any point in the story's timeline and trim that shot's beginning and ending frames. Timeline refers to all of the points in time from the first to last frame in a story. An older "linear" editing system requires the editor to assemble the story in the exact order it will be presented. Alterations in the middle of the story's timeline are very difficult with this type of editing.

Weister knows where different scenes are called out in the script. He cuts in a shot of a third rescue truck arriving on top of the reporter stating, ". . . more crews are brought in." He then places a shot of an ambulance racing away from the building as a closing shot. There are many holes in the timeline, spaces where the video has yet to be inserted.

A news video editor is more of a "selector/director" than a computer operator, punching buttons to assemble digital files. Editors select what the viewer will finally see, for how long, and in what order. The pace set by the editor can raise anxiety, quicken pulses, or relax and open the viewer's experience to absorb every element in a single shot. The shots are selected and assembled to direct the viewer's attention to the important aspects of the story. The craft of editing exerts an extremely "subjective" influence.

A survivor screams in agony as he's brought out of the building. Weister opens the timeline to allow for this shot and its natural sound to play on its own, punctuating the story, breaking the pace, and bringing the viewer back to the danger of the situation. The story automatically gains three seconds in length. The additional length is worth the storytelling power this "full-stop" visual punctuation creates in the story.

Through editing, sequences are assembled. They are the sentences in the story, connecting images to make one complete thought. Thoughts or sequences are connected and presented in a way that engages the viewer to follow the story to its conclusion. The editor unwraps the mystery.

The wall clock plays mind games with Weister, taunting him as the second hand clicks forward in a maddening rhythm. His decisions are coming too slow, his fingers not moving fast enough. Random paranoia sets in, "It's Alzheimer's, arthritis, and a heart attack all at the same time." My heart is just racing like you wouldn't believe and just pounding in my chest uncontrollably to the point that my fingers start shaking as I'm trying to punch the keys to make my next edit. I know that I've only got twelve minutes left before the story has got to hit air, and I still have thirty seconds of the story to cover.

Masters of Time and Space

Editors control time and space in their unique video reality, condensing the actual reality of days, hours, and minutes to a few precious seconds, or expanding a brief glimpse into a complete photographic study. It seems unfair that those manipulations can't be brought to bear in the real world. A few more seconds might save the day and help Weister make his A-2 time slot.

There's little time for finesse; the timeline shows a few holes left. Dropping shot after shot into the timeline, Weister checks for jump cuts (two shots that are so similar that the transition between them is jarring). He knows there's one waiting for him in the interview between two sound bites from the same subject. A reverse of the reporter will fix the cut if he can get there in time.

The glass door slides open, diverting Weister's attention to the hallway and away from the edit. "Are you going to make it?" Jeramy, another editor, asks, aware that this intrusion might release an animal fury with dire consequences. Anxiety and deadlines go hand in hand even for the best editors. I keep making more mistakes because I'm so nervous about missing slot. I have to keep going back and redoing things again and again and again. I've got hair on my arms standing up just from the fright of not knowing whether this is going to be the time that I miss my deadline.

The End Is Near—Eight Minutes to Air

Weister trims the beginning and the end of a few shots that have been bugging him, which leaves only the best for the viewer to see. The phone in the edit cage rings and rings and rings. Weister swears at the receiver, not picking it up. It's the show producer behind the unanswered phone. "Shut up. I know, I'm getting it done as fast as I can. Just leave me alone. You're not speeding things up by calling back here." *The phone stops ringing for a moment, as if the producer heard Weister's tirade, then starts up again. A bad joke with a tired punch line.*

A reverse shot of the reporter gets placed over the jump cut and visually smoothes out the interview. Weister pushes the red record button on the tape machine and starts to dub the story. It's one minute and thirty-five seconds in length after the countdown leader.

Four Minutes to Air

Weister watches the story dub. Not bad. The story's structure is clearly evident. The reporter's sound track is compelling and sets a nice pace for Weister's editing to dance around. The photographer's images are steady and graphically strong, perfect for getting the viewer to sit up and take notice. The arrangement of elements composed by Weister makes a strong story.

The survivor's scream happens at just the right moment, clearing the viewer's palate and connecting two segments of the story by saying, "Stop! Look at this!" The sound from the reporter's stand-up starts under a montage (a series of shots related by a common theme to create a sequence) and ends with the last shot of the montage being the continuation of the reporter's stand-up. Nice cut. The last sound plays out as the final shot lingers a few seconds longer than the audio track.

Black. It's done! Hit "Stop." Shuttle back to the head. Hit "Eject."

The blue "Eject" light glows as the recorder's machinery unhands the tape. The gears move as if they're stuck in molasses. Weister's heartbeat is in his ears, pounding louder than the noise from all the editing bays combined as he slides the door open, waiting for the machine to give up the tape.

Two Minutes to Air

The tape is finally free from the grips of the machine. Weister grabs the cassette and runs down the hall. The phone rings from his edit bay as he turns the corner. The producer must be going mad. The newscast's opening music plays throughout the newsroom. The first bell tolls for Weister; the reaper is on his heels. I've got this tape under my arm like a football player, like a little Heisman Trophy candidate. I am bobbing and weaving and dodging people as I'm running. It seems like two city blocks back to the other side of the building to the tape room in engineering. Eternity is when you've got a minute to run down the hall and you know it's going to take you forty-five seconds to get there.

Panting and out of breath, Weister skids to a cartoon stop in front of a tape operator, who looks at him like a scolding parent recapturing a lost child at the mall. "Where – have – you – been?" his eyes say in question and accusation.

"A-2 is here." The tape operator drones dryly into the microphone connected to the show's directing booth. The hand-off of the tape is a connection between two worlds. Weister's face is flushed with anxiety; the tape operator's, dispassionately removed, with a fluorescent pallor. The tape machine sucks the cassette into its maw, digests for a second, then sits contently in pause. It's cued. Brian Weister made his slot.

The Last Word

A video editor is the last person in the chain of newspeople responsible for the content and mood of a story. From the producers, who have edited out all the bad ideas and selected the stories that will run tonight, to the assignment desk, where decisions are made about who will cover what and if a breaking news story warrants coverage, to the reporters and photographers, who bring their selective impressions from the field—all are editors of the story. The last editor is the video editor, who takes the efforts of the entire team and assembles them into a coherent and engaging final presentation.

Being an editor, being a reporter, being a storyteller, the most important thing is being able to relate to your viewers. If you're using some angles that no one can comprehend and you're writing stories that have words that people don't understand and you're editing so fast that nobody can even see what they're supposed to be seeing, then you missed the whole point. A photojournalist should be able to relate to the people who are watching the news.

The whole shebang with news is we're trying to get people to watch so there will be better ratings, so that we'll make lots of money, so that we'll all keep our jobs. So how do you keep your viewers? Well, I think a great way to keep viewers is to try to make them a part of the story by communicating in a way they can relate to. Not just with visuals but with sounds and editing techniques that keep viewers involved and following the story.

The Tools of an Editor

Packed inside a computer and ready at the touch of a keyboard are all the creative tools used by an editor. The ability to cut, dissolve, trim, and place media all happen here. A story's visual language is brought to life by manipulating the software to the editor's discretion. To be an editor you need to know how to edit in a nonlinear environment. All the software's kind of the same. I prefer Avid because that was what I learned nonlinear on. The workflow varies greatly depending on which system you're using and how your station ingests (digitizes) video.

The Software

All NLE software is basically the same. There are certain brands of software that many news stations use (Avid, Final Cut Pro, and so on), so there are better NLEs to master than others. If you understand the basic concept of editing in a nonlinear environment, you can switch software from one brand to another without too much difficulty.

Basics of NLE Software

- All NLEs utilize a timeline. The timeline is where you assemble all the pieces of your story. It's like a video piggybank. It starts out empty, with nothing to see or hear. Slowly you add to it until you've met your goal (finishing the story).

- All NLEs utilize digitized video clips. Typically this involves shooting video and audio on a video camera, then hooking the camera or a stand-alone video deck to a computer. Using your NLE, you digitize, or ingest, the video into your computer.

- All NLEs utilize "In" and "Out" points. These points tell the NLE where to start and where to stop when you edit a video clip. Typically you open a video clip in your NLE that you have recently ingested. You mark an In point on this clip where you want it to begin and an Out point where you want it to stop.

- All NLEs utilize an "insert video" key. After you have marked your In/Out points on your video clip, you need to get this shot into your timeline. You do this with the "insert video" key. With each new clip you choose to add to the timeline, you "insert" it with this key. Most NLEs use an "insert" key and an "overwrite" key. Inserting the new clip will move your entire existing clip in the timeline down in the story. If you place the timeline bar in the middle of a clip in the timeline and then "insert" another clip, it will be split in two by your new clip. If you use the "overwrite" key, it will simply write over whatever clip is in front of it.

What is really important in mastering nonlinear editing is the concept. If you can understand that you're simply selecting a portion of a clip using In/Out points and then moving these clips into a workspace called a timeline, you've got it. Avid, FCP (Final Cut Pro), Premiere—they all work basically the same. They just have different interfaces.

Editing on a Basic NLE System

For Weister, organization comes before creativity. Organization allows more time for creativity by condensing the time and effort it takes to complete basic tasks like searching for a video clip or audio file.

I assemble all the sound, or A-roll, for the package first. This gives me the backbone of the story, at which point I can cover the rest of the piece with whatever time I have remaining. A-roll includes all reporter track and sound bites. Because of this, I digitize in the reporter track (recorded in a sound booth down the hall) and the sound bites (interviews and stand-ups) first. I take note on the script where all the sound bites are and which tapes are being used. Starting at the beginning of the first tape, I "dig" *[digitize]* in all sound bites from tape one, and then move to tape two and three, and so on.

I name each clip by its time code. This way, when I'm assembling the story and I see the time code in the script, I know exactly which clip to move into the timeline. I open each track and bite in the source window of my edit system, marking an In point at the exact first frame of speech, and an Out point a second or so after the end of speech. Why a second after instead of precisely when the bite or track ends? Because I'm using key frames at the end of this sound to ramp the audio down for a clean audio transition.

Typically, I've got four to ten frames in between my key frames for a clean audio dissolve. You can achieve similar results by simply adding a four- to ten-frame centered dissolve at the end of your clip, but by using key frames you have absolute precise control of where your audio ends. This technique is also referred to as "rubberbanding" because of the effect of key frames lowering and raising your audio within the timeline.

Using key frames on your audio in this way also makes pacing your story easier. I find it's faster to simply lop off the end of a clip for timing purposes than to go into your NLE's trim mode and extend frames on the clip. Making the clip longer to begin with and simply lopping off the end of the clip that you don't need takes fewer steps and will make you a quicker editor.

Now to the simple, clear, and basic part. On a deadline story, I create two folders (or "bins," as Avid calls them) within my NLE to dig clips into. One for "Sound," the other for "Cover." All the reporter tracks and story bites go in the Sound bin. Everything else (B-roll, natural sound, graphics) goes in the Cover bin. I create my A-roll in the timeline, pulling only from the sound bin—this makes it easier because I know all the clips are right next to each other. I then dig in from the raw tapes all of the cover video I'll need.

If I'm under a strict deadline, I'll scan the tape quickly and just find the shots I need (after consulting the script). If more time allows, I'll dig in more shots to give me more options while editing. When the story is covered, I'll watch it back for accuracy one time (time permitting) and record the timeline back to tape. I would never digitize in an entire tape when I have to do the ingesting because it's a waste of time. If I only need three sound bites, why would I dig in an entire twenty-minute interview?

Editing on a Server-based System

On a server-based system, all tapes are ingested at a central location in the newsroom. This is not typically done by an editor but by a "media manager" or the like. With this option, you have no choice but to work with very large clips (up to forty minutes long!), which can be quite difficult. Using this method, I will still build my A-roll first, pulling from the large clips for sound (assuming the reporter's track makes its way to the server as well).

To quickly break down the large clips into something more usable, I will subclip the large clips into smaller, more workable segments of like material. If the photographer shot two minutes of building exteriors before an interview, I'll subclip just the exteriors into my Cover bin and label them accordingly. This will help me keep track of video so, when the clip calls for something specific, I should be able to pull it from one of my subclips. On this system, when the story is finished, it simply runs off the server. No dubbing to tape is necessary.

Basics of the Desktop Setup and Editing Process

- Create two folders (bins) in your NLE, one for sound, the other for "Video Cover" (B-roll).
- Digitize the reporter track and sound bites for your story into the "Sound" folder.
- Digitize your select B-roll shots (not everything, just what you think you'll need) into the Video Cover folder.
- Edit all of your sound, or A-roll, into the timeline first.
- Using shots from your B-roll folder, cover the story with shots that match the script.

In reality, editing doesn't get to be clear or basic until you've mastered it. Beginning editors need to know about things like subclipping and key frames and a dozen more techniques I haven't described to truly understand what they are capable of in a nonlinear editing environment.

After the story is finished, and time permitting, I go back to the raw video and look for good nat *[natural]* sound. If it's available, I insert it into the piece where appropriate for transitioning, dramatic effect, and so on. This is the beauty of working fast. The faster you get the "meat" of the story done, the more time you'll have to spend on the creative end, making the story "sing" for your audience.

Fast, Accurate, Creative

This is the phrase I live by in the editing world: Fast, Accurate, Creative. It's kind of my editing mantra. The words apply to any—and all—editing situations. Follow this code, work very hard, and you'll be successful.

Fast

This is at the front of the list because it's always the most important factor in edit decision making. Edit fast, and you're in the clear. Make all your deadlines, and people learn to trust and rely on you. Edit fast, and you are dependable to others. Even when you have all the time in the world, still edit fast. Your eyes and hands won't easily forget their movements. This will give you a huge advantage the next time you've only got twenty minutes to edit a one-minute, thirty-second package. Miss slot, lose your job.

Accurate

A close second on the list, accuracy is key in storytelling—from showing the correct individual when reporting a story to making seamless, crisp edits. If you're sloppy, you'll find yourself in big trouble. If you run video of the wrong man during a crime-related story, you could find your employer in a lawsuit. You can also find yourself in the unemployment line. Also, a few frames can make all the difference in the world. If you're not editing accurately and precisely, people will notice. Viewers will notice your sloppy work. Your story will suffer, and that's a disservice to the folks at home watching. A little effort goes a long way.

Creative

Although last on the list, it's not any less important. Without creativity, you're nothing but a button pusher. Your job is not to re-create the script that was handed to you in audio/video form. It's an editor's job to bring a story to life—to make viewers at home feel something—and feel like they are part of the story. If you can't do this, the story will suffer and you have failed. Constructing creative sequences, inserting natural sound to transition from one part of a story to the next, and simply avoiding jump cuts and pop cuts can get the job done. No one is asking you to be Picasso, but you have a duty to the viewers at home to engage them with the story that "you" edited—that "you" created.

Creativity is what will differentiate you from everybody else who does your job. Anybody can edit fast; anybody can get the facts right. But not everybody can be creative. Most of the time, it's by choice. Most of the time, people just don't have the motivation to take their work to the next level. Your creativity can send your story from being a "watchable story" to a "watercooler story" that people are talking about the next day.

Keep P.A.C.E.

P.A.C.E. is an acronym created by Brian Weister that represents editing concepts that raise the bar for quality and speed.

P Is for Pacing

This is the life of your story; it sets the mood. A great story can be ruined by bad pacing. An okay story can be brought to life with the correct pacing. That said, there are no hard-and-fast rules for how a story should be paced. The key is the story itself. Does it make you feel something when you watch it? Does it feel right? Do you notice the edits, or are they smooth and seamless? Are you engaged by the storytelling, or is it jarring? If a story just doesn't look right (ask your coworkers; ask your family at home), the pacing is probably off. One pop cut can be so distracting it throws off the rest of a story. If a story with serious, heavy information or emotion just zips by with lightning-quick edits, the pacing is probably off.

In general, the content and the available video will determine the pacing of a story. Emotional stories are often slower and breathe more (there's more time between the end of one line and the beginning of another—maybe only ten frames, but it can mean the world). Long, slow dissolves are often found in these stories, which can be useful when used correctly. If it doesn't look right, it isn't!

Stories with lots of action will often be faster paced with quick cuts. Highway construction, sports, and other active stories will usually be edited this way. Remember, if an edit is so short a viewer at home can't make out what he just saw, you edited too fast. There is a technique to using extremely fast edits (one frame to ten or so frames) in a sequence to create visual and/or sound transitions. This makes the viewer "feel" something without actually having to understand exactly what it is he's seeing. The "you can't break the rules until you know what they are" rule applies here. Figure out how to do things right; then you can break all the rules you want and stretch your creative legs.

A Is for Audio

Audio should be seamless. It should ramp and flow up and down to create an aural experience for your viewers. When your audio drops off (or falls off a cliff, as I like to say) instead of smoothly dissolving out or ramping down, you just created an audio jump cut—just as bad as a video jump. Utilize several layers of your timeline to mix and weave reporter track, sound bites, natural sound, and music.

C Is for Communication

Relationships are vital in any job, not just TV news. You need to get along with everyone, and everyone should get along with you. That is the fantasy world, of course, as there will always be someone who just has to bump heads with you. I've found that I'm successful when it comes to building relationships because people feel they can trust their work in my hands. If you haven't developed that trust with a reporter or producer or assignment desk manager, it's time to start. Better stories come to those who simply say, "Hi," and are friendly toward the assignment desk. Better stories result from a reporter and photographer talking about the best way to tell the daily story or the best way to use the material they have gathered. And it all comes together in the edit bay.

The more information that is communicated to the editor, the better the end result. A simple "I got great sound of sprinklers running at the end of tape two" is plenty. When I'm under deadline, I may not have a chance to look for something like this. Tell me about it, and I promise it'll make the story. End result—a better story for the viewers at home because of better communication in the newsroom.

E Is for Efficiency

Learn how you work the fastest and develop a routine. Know immediately how many Avid bins you need to create, what you're going to call them, and when you can start digitizing video. An inefficient workspace can intrude into your story. If you don't have shots/sound bites/reporter track/nat sound grouped together, how will you find what you need quickly? Take the extra few minutes to keep your computer desktop organized, and you'll easily make that time up in increased efficiency during the edit process.

Shoot for the Editor

In editing, and in your mind while shooting, are the concepts and terms that describe the action the shot will have on the sequence. So not only is a shot a close-up, low-angle shot; it may also be "used" as a

A, B. Jump cuts.

C, D. A change in image size and angle makes a better transition.

cutaway or cut-in. Knowing how your shots and sequences may be used in editing can inspire the techniques you employ in the field.

A cutaway *is any shot that is used to cut "away" from the action. It's important to keep cutaways relevant to their moment in the story. A cut-in must match the action and appear connected to an adjacent shot. It implies a closer look.*

A jump cut *is any cut that is similar in framing and action but doesn't match exactly. The jolting effect seems like we've jumped ahead in time. Instantly, body positions pop or "jump" to the new shot. If the angle is too similar or the action mismatched, a jump cut can still occur even if the framing is changed.*

Jump cuts can be avoided by altering the size and angle of the subject from one frame to the next. For this reason, don't shoot wide, medium, and tight from only one camera position. Move the camera to make better shots as you get closer. Avoid jump cuts unless you're going for a jarring effect.

A *pop cut* is not unlike a jump cut, except in a pop cut there's nothing in the frame that has magically moved or changed places. A pop cut occurs when two or more shots are taken from the same spot and at the same angle, using different focal lengths. I prefer the idiot's explanation, which is "You shot wide, medium, and tight of a building from the same spot, without moving the camera, just by zooming from wide to tight. Then in your story, you edited two of these shots back to back. Because they are taken from the exact same angle, they look bad."

It's visually jarring to see two shots from the exact same perspective shown one right after another. This is the easiest mistake to fix. Continue shooting wide, medium, and tight of the building, but pick up your tripod and move ten feet away. Now change the height of your sticks. Now shoot wide, medium, and tight again. When editing, edit one shot from one angle, the next shot from the other. Although we're seeing the same building, it's not jarring anymore. It's not as if we're jumping through space and time from one shot to the next from the same perspective. We've changed angles and perspective, and now the shots cut fine.

Photographers should always remember to "shoot and move." Get wide, medium, and tight from several angles, and, when editing, cut from one angle to another. Visually, it's very watchable and seamless.

A *match cut* is vital for proper sequencing. When someone is performing an action repetitively (mowing a lawn, writing on paper, operating a machine), you have an excellent opportunity to create a sequence of matched action. You have wide, medium, and tight shots from several different angles of a single action occurring. By cutting from one angle to another on the performed action, you create a very vivid action sequence. It's as if we're seeing an action occur from several different points if view.

If a match cut is technically right, but somehow looks wrong, it's wrong. Match cuts should be done technically first and then by feel to finesse the transition. Some match cuts work better going from a close-up to a wide shot because there's more information for the viewer to accept in the wide shot and the minute details get lost in the transition.

"Cutting on action" is a great way to disguise what may otherwise be a jump cut. By cutting on action (that is, someone cutting paper snowflakes with scissors), the scene you're creating remains fluid and seamless. *If you cut to a still shot and the action happens a second or two later, the cut appears late and draws attention to the abrupt transition.*

A *dissolve* denotes a passage of time and can be done by the use of a video dissolve. *One image fades out while another image simultaneously fades in. The center of a dissolve is a double exposure where both images are mixed.* It's a simple way to transfer from day to night or from one location to another. My preferred method of transitioning (without a dissolve) is a close-up shot with natural sound. We get from the office interview to the campus parking lot with a close-up of a quarter going into a parking meter (with the accompanying natural sound). Tight shots make for great transitions. If you can get natural sound on a tight shot, you can transition time and location and add a little breathing room before your next track or bite begins.

A *transition shot* allows time passage and location change without the use of video effects (dissolves, and so on). The best transition shots are close-ups. They are descriptive without being too telling. Natural sound makes for better transition shots. From the "swish" of an office door opening to the rumble of tires on the road to a high school locker door slamming shut, viewers can associate sound with their personal experiences. Not only does natural sound help the transition and help with the pacing of your story; it also helps your viewers to "feel" like they're on location, to "feel" like part of the story.

"Natural sound" is one of the biggest things that can be added to your story that will differentiate it from your competitors. It advances the sense of place so much more than just visuals alone. Nat sound is great for transitioning between tracks and sound bites. It's great for bringing your viewers to the scene—that's its best attribute. When you've got this great natural sound woven throughout your story, accentuating points and transitioning between others, then I think people are more apt to stick around and watch the entire story. That's what it's all about. It's getting viewers involved in the story. They're not just watching the news; they're a part of it. A big way of doing that is by making sure that sound makes it into the story. You've got to spice it up a little bit. *(For more about sound, refer to Appendix D.)*

Screen direction, *as discussed in Chapter 12, is the direction of the action and attention. Proper screen direction is necessary to keep all the action flowing from one shot to the next in the proper direction.*

Montage *is an editing term that refers to the arrangement of shots with a unifying theme, often assembled without the restrictions of traditional screen direction or editing techniques. A montage could be made up from shots of a bald eagle flying ("Bald Eagle Flying Montage"). It could also be created by intercutting bald eagle flying shots with people watching ("Bird Watching Montage"). Eagle shots could be mixed with shots of factory pollution ("America's Skies Are Polluted Montage"). Each montage has a message it is trying to impart. Each shot in a montage must be different enough to avoid an unwanted jump cut. Changing angles and frame sizes often can help avoid this.*

Shot duration *is the length in seconds and frames an image is usable. Make sure you record enough of each scene with adequate static time on both sides of a camera move. Roll at least eight to ten seconds on every shot, even if it won't be onscreen for more than three seconds or less.* This is something that I've always struggled with. I want to change shots often enough to keep viewers interested, but leave shots up long enough so viewers can understand what they're seeing. It's a constant dilemma. In a more quickly paced story, I try to make sure there are enough shots that stay up long enough for viewers to understand the story.

I also may have some quick sequences of rapid-fire edits to act as an exclamation point on a sound bite or to transition from one topic to another. Viewers will probably not understand what they're seeing in this quickly passed montage, but they will "feel" the sense of urgency that I want them to feel. It's a fine line between editing fast for the sake of it and editing fast to evoke a viewer's emotions. I always strive for the latter.

Shoot clean entrances *and* clean exits *when shooting action. In the cooking scene (here and on the facing page), the first shot easily cuts with the second before the hand comes in to turn up the flame. Matching action isn't necessary.*

A clean entrance.

A clean exit.

If we start with the hand turning up the flame, all we have to do is allow the hand to exit the frame to allow for a good cut from the close-up to the wide shot. In practice, while shooting this scene, you would anticipate the hand on the controls and set up to capture the moment. You would get both the clean entrance and the clean exit to allow more options for the editor.

A clean exit.

A clean entrance and a clean exit in shot 2.

While following a jeep from the city to the country, a clean exit from the city allows you to cut directly to the jeep already in the frame somewhere in the country. If you have a clean entrance in the country, you can cut from a shot of the jeep in the city without waiting for it to leave frame.

You should always "shoot" clean entrances and clean exits. You "edit" a clean exit to anything and from anything to a clean entrance. You rarely edit "clean" to "clean," as the pauses are unnecessary and ruin the pace.

From Field to Screen

Most good photojournalists will come back to their editor with a wide variety of shots. They're going to have everything from an extreme wide shot that gives you a great location and lets you know exactly where you are in the story, all the way to extreme close-ups. We're talking the entire gamut here. Shooting with editing techniques in mind allows for a greater range of possibilities when assembling the final story.

The "Alaskan Bald Eagle" Story from an Editor's Perspective

Remember the shots and sequences that we captured in the field? The shooting happened in order of importance and control. What could change was shot first, the interview second; finally, when our time was our own, we shot the reporter stand-up. An editor looks at all of these shots and decides how best to arrange them to convey the content, pace, and mood of the story.

Shots 1 through 5 in the diagram below are B-roll and tell the story. There could be many more variations on this. These shots could also be used as cutaways for the interview. As the ranger discusses the plight of the bald eagle in his interview, you can cut away to a flying eagle. One of the shots will open your story,

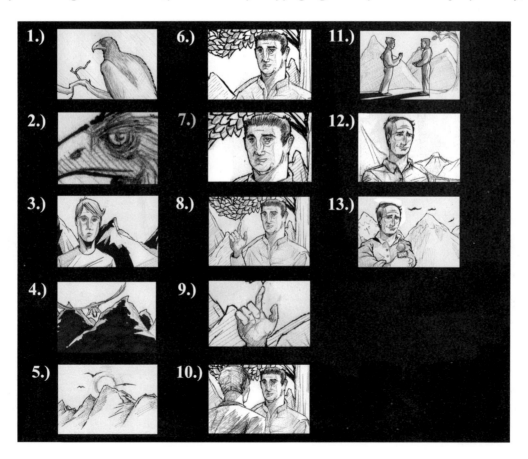

but not necessarily establish the location. A close-up of the eagle might be the most powerful opening, while the shot of the mountains and a flying eagle could become your "establishing shot."

Shots 6 through 8 are the interview. You may roll for five, ten, or more minutes as the reporter asks questions. Shot 9 would be used as a cut-in, and the action will have to match any adjacent shot meant to be in the same timeline.

From the moment you start your interview, you'll be thinking about coverage. Coverage *refers to all the shots necessary to create a smooth sequence in both interview footage and B-roll. The next few shot examples show why it is important to have all of these shots ready to use in your story.*

Once you finish the interview, make sure to roll on over-the-shoulder and interview-establishing shots long enough to be able to match action. Shots 10 and 11 have to have both the interviewee talking and listening to the reporter's questions as well as the reporter asking questions and listening. In editing, you may try to match action with these shots, but they are too wide to be considered cut-ins.

The reporter "reverse" in shot 12 can be a cutaway. It's also a reaction shot, and, if he asks a question, it can be used as a line of dialog.

The interview runs on and on; there might be three different clips that, when tied together clearly, tell the story. No one would sit through a five-minute rambling interview only to hear fifteen to twenty seconds of important information. So we need to be able to cut together the different sound clips. As we cut the video and audio together, it's easy to see jump cuts at the edit points of the sound clips.

That's where the reverse shot comes in handy. It smoothly connects the two sound clips by showing the reporter listening while the interviewee keeps talking. The edit for shot 12 can go anywhere on top of the edit point for the two sound clips, thus masking the jump cut. Now we can condense and connect separate sound clips while keeping the interview section of our story flowing.

The interview rambles on. If we want to use two different sections back to back, the interviewee's hand will pop onto the screen at the edit point, making a jump cut.

By inserting the reporter reverse shot, it's as if he's listening at the moment the edit happens, which masks the jump cut.

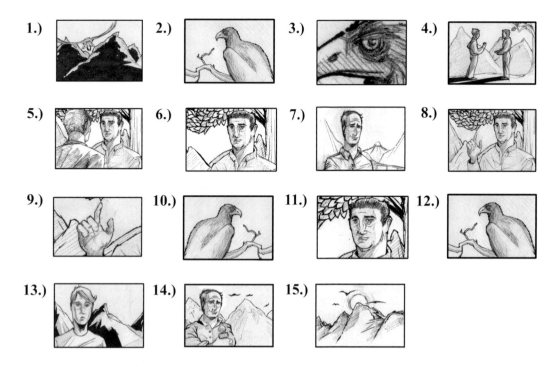

Assembling the "Alaskan Bald Eagle" Story

The diagram here takes the shots from the field and assembles them into a story. In this "storyboard," the numbers now correspond to the shot order in the finished story.

A strong opening shot grabs the audience and, in this case, establishes the location. Perhaps a bit of natural sound opens the story. As the narration starts, various shots of the eagles illustrate the story. There's an authority, the ranger, who must be introduced; frame 4 does that, with the narration, and establishes the setting. Frame 5 brings us closer; we see more of the ranger as the interview sets up.

Variations on this interview sequence are endless. Some interviews can be introduced on the same shot as the "interview" (frame 6) with the reporter's introduction fading out just as the interviewee starts talking. If the interviewee is concise and to the point, there may be no need for a reverse, but interview coverage is always shot just in case.

During the interview, the ranger has a habit of pointing to the eagles. The close-up shot of his hand is cut in, matching action from the interview as he points. The pointing hand then cuts to what he's talking about—the eagle perched in the tree. The reporter's narration talks about how much this preservation means to the next generation just as the eagle flies away. The boy in frame 13 reacts with a look of awe. In frame 14, the reporter says a few lines of factual support in a stand-up. The eagles then fly into the sunset as the reporter sums up the story in frame 15.

Motivation and Art

Flash for the sake of flash is just flash; it doesn't advance the story, or concept, and rarely is aesthetic enough to be considered art. Every edit should be motivated. This is a very important concept for beginning editors to understand. You don't just throw in dissolves and other effects because you can. You can't just throw in a random shot because you think it looks cool. Everything you do needs to advance the story you're trying to tell. If there's no reason to make an edit, don't.

You should be able to justify each and every edit (both audio and video) in any story without question. If there's no motivation for a certain shot or a certain pacing, you've done more harm to the story than good. Editing is much like painting. You can't just throw paint on a canvas, let it dry, and call it art. Telling a great story is an art form in itself. Each edit should be precisely timed and placed within the story to be both visually pleasing and emotionally reactive.

Join the Story of the Month Club

If you can come up with one story every month that you're really proud of, you've succeeded. The strength of that story is going to keep you motivated to get you through the next one. I never even made it that far. I was lucky to get six or eight good stories in a year. But this goal improved my work dramatically.

The Future of Editing

Basic storytelling will remain no matter what equipment comes along to make the process more streamlined. Server systems will allow access to field media from multiple work stations. High definition requires much more computing power than standard definition, and systems will be developed to handle the unique load of a news operation. Laptop editing is already making field editing by one-man bands commonplace.

The machines are coming. More and more jobs in the newsroom are being automated, and scores of people are losing their jobs. Instead of a control room full of people making sure the cogs in a newscast run to a smooth perfection, one or two individuals run the show with a few clicks of a mouse. Automation in newsrooms is already here, and editors could be the next to fall. Editors are not button pushers; we are skilled craftsmen in the art of video. A machine will never be able to bring the emotion to a story that an editor can.

Editing is not astrophysics. There's no higher math, no unsolvable equations, and really nothing mind numbing about the concept of piecing together video and sound. When it's done right, however, editing can be a sweet science. The weaving together of layer on layer of sound, the perfect amount of silence following an emotional sound bite, the masterful sequencing of video timed to the frame—editing is easy to do but very hard to do well. As an editor, you are a gatekeeper of information. Thousands, even millions, of people will hear and see only what you choose to show them. It's a big responsibility and not something to be taken lightly.

It's 5:05 P.M. as Weister quickly enters the newsroom moments after handing his A-2 package to the tape operator. Monitors hang from the ceiling playing the night's newscast for the small crowds that gather near each one. Brian looks up just as the anchor's lead-in shows a graphic of the collapsed building story hovering over his shoulder. It's going to run. The first frame comes up; the package runs flawlessly.

Brian Weister's day is over, having delivered a story with seconds to spare, or frames, depending on how you count time.

CHAPTER 16

Mike Elwell

Embedded—War Coverage

Mike Elwell
Freelance Cameraman

National Emmy, *Brothers in Arms*, ABC News, 2003
National Emmy nomination, *Martha Stewart Living*, 1997
Peabody Award, *Politics of Poison*, 1978

*C*old wind blows dust into the open window as Mike Elwell watches endless sand roll by.

He grinds desert grit in his teeth and wonders how far they'll get today. Blinking often to clear his eyes, he lets out a long reflective sigh. "What have I gotten myself into?" A moment later, like the flip of a switch, the scene changes as the drums of war spring to life. Thump, thump, thump—an explosive tympani roars a few feet above his head as the fifty-caliber machine gun mounted on the roof rocks the cab. Flames jump out of the muzzle and point the way to the target.

Spent shells rain down on Elwell as the Humvee that carries him and four others races towards Baghdad. The first burst leaves a deafening echo that reverberates throughout the cab. The gunner stands on the Humvee's hump that separates the left and right seats. Elwell's on the left side, staring up into the hatch on the roof as a wide-eyed marine squeezes death from his automatic cannon. We took off like cowboys when we got word it was time to go. Now all hell had broken loose and it seemed like there was shooting from everywhere. I kept trying to make myself as small as possible.

Thump, thump, thump. His heartbeat is almost as loud as the bullets exploding above. Elwell's partner is correspondent Mike Cerre, who's riding shotgun with a

EQUIPMENT

Sony PD150 DVcam
4 Sony PC110 single-chip Mini DV cameras
Small two-channel mixer
2 Lectrosonic wireless mics
Sennheiser shotgun mic
2 RBGAN satellite dishes
Talking Head videophone
Compaq laptop with store-and-forward editing
    software
Thuraya satellite phone
Electrovoice hand mic
Inexpensive tripod
Reasonably priced monopod
4 power inverters
Solar battery charger
Night vision scope from an outdoor supply store
Shortwave radio
Lots of resealable bags, canned air, lens brushes,
    and baby wipes

view out the dust-covered windshield. With enough adrenaline to revive a corpse, Elwell's mouth is bone dry as he yells up to Cerre, "Where's it coming from?" Cerre's response is overpowered by more thundering from the fifty-caliber machine gun.

A few shells bounce off the camera that he's poking though the roof. Elwell focuses on the fold-out monitor that's hovering above him on a monopod and pointing in the same direction as the machine gun fire. Tiny points of daylight appear in the doors as gun smoke defines the stream of light. White dots sprout up on the other side. Bullets had gone all the way through the Humvee. They promised me the Humvees were armored— ha! I had the windows down and just hoped there where no bullets that had my name on them. I was just trying to find a heavy door post where I could scrunch up and be small and hold my camera.

A rocket-propelled grenade (RPG) whistles by and explodes in front of them, sending more smoke, sand, and shrapnel into the air. The driver swerves around the pothole and punches the gas.

It's hard to know where the action is coming from. At home, my skills are honed to follow the action and be on top of it as much as I can. But in war the chaos is so intense it's hard to do that. I would ride side by side in the Humvee with this very experienced marine who was in Vietnam, and I trusted his judgment the most. He would warn us and point out snipers and say something's at twelve o'clock, and we knew there was something bad over in that direction. *Thump, thump, thump. Shell casings eject from the machine gun and bounce off the roof; a few, still smoking, find their way into the cab and onto the seat.*

Our strategy was to drive like hell from one end of town to the other, then slow down when it got relatively safe and assess the damage before racing on to the next town. I can't really remember being terrified. I think cameramen have a feeling that they're impervious to danger as long as they're shooting. At the end of the day, our Humvee had ten to fifteen bullet holes and no one was injured.

Later that night, we were the first ones to announce that the war had started. We called into ABC's War Room on the satellite phone and said, "We're at war." They put us on hold while they

checked it out. The following morning, we filed our first report over a Talking Head (a satellite–video camera combination with a slow frame rate and low resolution). The jerky image was of Mike Cerre announcing that the war had begun.

Elwell is an "embed" with the Marines of Fox 2/5 F Company, 2nd Battalion, 25th Marines, 4th Division. He's

A Humvee in convoy toting a fifty-caliber machine gun; the Marines call it "the ultimate in drive-by shooting."

Training at Camp Pendleton prior to deployment to Kuwait.

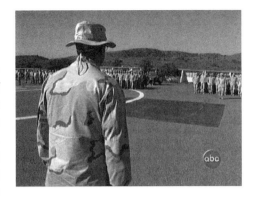

working for Cerre's company and providing coverage for ABC and Nightline. *For Elwell, the embed process started months before with a project inspired by a magazine article written during the Korean War, where one company was followed from boot camp through combat.*

Before the war began, we started going down to Camp Pendleton in Southern California once a week and photographing the Marines. Major General James Mattis, the commanding officer of the Marine Expeditionary Force, remembered the story and approached Mike Cerre about the idea. He said we could jump into their personalities in the beginning and as they go through training, and he might be able to get us into Iraq if they go.

Elwell and Cerre shot the preparations for war: weddings, babies being born, and the daily lives of the Marines of Fox 2/5. From combat drills to tearful good-byes as they left for Iraq, Elwell was getting to know the Marines, and, equally important, they were getting to know him. Cerre got a call one night that said the company was leaving the very next day. So he called me and said, "We are leaving tomorrow, can you do it?" I had a lot of other things scheduled, and I couldn't go that day, but I could meet them in a week or so. Mike went on the plane with the Marines to Iraq and spent a week or two there by himself, shooting their first "boots on the ground" in Kuwait.

Elwell spent the next few days collecting equipment and preparing to fly to Kuwait. Mike would call me every other day and say, "Bring a tent, bring handy wipes, bring me a bottle of Scotch," which was confiscated when I went through Kuwait. When we finally reunited in Kuwait, we lived with the Marines for three or four days in the preliminary camps and filed stories about their training and conditions. We were really the first ones to do any kind of coverage of regular grunts in camp waiting for the war to start. We would go back to the bureau in Kuwait City and file reports and stories for a couple of days and then go back to the Marines. We were kind of grizzled veterans by the time the rest of the embeds showed up a month and a half later.

Embedded

An embed is a journalist who is part of the company or battalion. They feed you and protect you and transport you, but you can't really leave their pres-

"Countless WMD alerts and exercises in camp prior to deployment to Iraq—you had to be able to get your gas mask on at any time in less than nine seconds."

ence. That's your sphere of influence: about 100 yards one way or the other. The unilaterals were the news guys who got their own car and took off across the desert and probably got better coverage and more coverage of Iraqis. A lot of unilaterals were killed as a result of not having the same protection that the embeds had from the Marines. There were many more accredited unilaterals in Iraq, about 2,100, and only 600 embeds.

The military held the press responsible for the failure in Vietnam because they felt the press showed too much. Back then, they weren't really embedded but more bounced around. The military thought the press sabotaged the war, and that made for a deep distrust of the press. Every war since, the press has been tightly controlled and been narrowed to briefing rooms and news conferences, which drove the press nuts in Gulf War I and in Afghanistan. They wanted to control the media and control the information going out. In Afghanistan, they didn't really need the press and they didn't need a sympathetic public by way of the press.

I think, in Iraq, they needed to keep it public and create a sympathetic public. So the embeds were introduced into the second Iraq war. The Pentagon said, "If we bring the press into the war, so they feel like they're a part of the whole thing and shoulder to shoulder with some eighteen-year-old, bright-eyed patriot, then this is how we will win public support." I think the Pentagon still mistrusts the media, but realizes it has to sell the war. What better way to do it than to throw back the curtains and see what the press has to say about the guys who ate with them, slept with them, and protected them from the "bad guys"?

The official government version is very close to Elwell's description. Following is an excerpt from a pamphlet with the title, "Public Affairs Guidance (PAG) on Embedding Media During Possible Future Operations/Deployments in the U.S. Central Commands (CENTCOM) Area of Responsibility (AOR)."

2A. The Department of Defense (DOD) policy on media coverage of future military operations is that media will have long-term, minimally restrictive access to U.S. air, ground, and naval forces through embedding media coverage of any future operation will, to a large extent, shape public perception of the national security environment now and in the years ahead.

Our ultimate strategic success in bringing peace and security to this region will come in our long-term commitment to supporting our democratic ideals. To tell the factual story—good or bad—before others seed the media with disinformation and distortions, as they most certainly will continue to do. Our people in the field need to tell our story—only commanders can ensure the media get to the story alongside the troops.

To accomplish this, we will embed media with our units. These embedded media will live, work, and travel as part of the units with which they are embedded to facilitate maximum, in-depth coverage of U.S. forces in combat and related operations.

Commanders and public affairs officers must work together to balance the need for media access with the need for operational security.

Elwell became an embed through his relationship and ongoing project with the Marines of Fox 2/5. There was also a prescribed method of becoming embedded that most journalists had to go through.

Before embeds were official, I had heard rumors that the Pentagon was going to do this. But the first thing I actually saw was in the newspaper comics. It was the "Doonesbury" strip focusing on the so-called media boot camps run by the Army. Fortunately, neither Mike nor I had to go through these training camps. It probably was a good idea to have the camps to weed out the really out-of-shape reporters or the ones who really couldn't handle the steady diet of MREs. The training camp was in Arlington, Virginia, and was two weeks long. They didn't turn anyone away who went all the way through it.

Each major network was allowed six embed crews, but because Mike and I had already established a relationship with this Marine company, they sort of slipped our names onto the "official" list. This was a pretty sweet deal all around, as ABC would get an extra embed and we could operate more independently than the other crews but still have the relative security of being attached to an actual unit. Our prime goal was to get to Baghdad, and neither Mike nor I was ready to test the "unilateral" method of renting a car and heading off through a war zone. Besides, we were committed to following our one company through to the end.

Elwell's Equipment

Packing equipment for an extended stay in a hostile environment takes a lot of forethought. What will the conditions be like? What equipment will work the best for the job? How will I protect my gear?

We decided early on to shoot MiniDV and DVcam. I took one main camera, a Sony P150, and four cheap, throw-away, one-chip cameras. We used those because they were super portable and great on battery power. I brought a small, two-channel mixer that could power my 416 shotgun mic and a couple of wirelesses. I was a one-man band, so I was camera and sound.

We took a night vision scope that I had gotten from a hunting supply place for 400 dollars, and I had a mount for a microscope that I was able to cut slots in so it would slide in and mount on the camera.

I had an old, funky Electrovoice 635 microphone, the kind you used to see in ads where they would pound nails with them. That's the one we used for interviews, and it worked great.

A Sony Handycam with a custom night scope.

Cerre broadcasts live at the beginning of the Iraq War on a "night vision scope," reporting on crossing the berm between Kuwait and Iraq, April 17, 2003.

A. Dust from the desert environment was a never-ending concern. Not only was this true for the camera equipment, the military hardware was also vulnerable.

B. The talcum-powdery dust got into everything, and keeping gear clean became a critical obsession.

We also used a laptop with store-and-forward software to cut our selects and put them on the bird with RBGAN satellite dishes. The only problem was that it took so long to feed via the Internet on the link—one hour per one minute of video—we never got to use it. We would either run out of battery power or loose the satellite link or the Marines would be on the move. We did get pretty good at feeding raw footage that they were able to cut into a story back in New York.

They told us we could only bring what we could carry. I was limited to anything I could fit in a camping pack—not only the equipment I had to carry but my sleeping bag and clothes and food and anything else I would need. A box of Cubans bought us a two-foot cube in one of the Humvees to store all the extra stuff.

Protecting Gear from Sand and Dust

What we really needed were things to protect the cameras and mics from the harsh environment we were taking them into. We had to assume that once the war started there would be no shopping for supplies along the way to Baghdad. I ended up buying all kinds of food storage containers to hold batteries and tape, resealable plastic bags to cover the little one-chip MiniDV cameras we brought as backup, photo blower brushes to clean lenses, and all kinds of goggles and scarves to protect us from the dust. Dust is the biggest headache when shooting in the desert, especially shooting MiniDV. Any dust on the tape will clog the heads or, at best, cause dropouts. I tried to be extra careful keeping things clean.

I had tried out various ready-made camera covers for the Sony PD150 before we left California and was unhappy with their inability to completely seal out dust and moisture. So I decided to make my own cover out of a kayaker's dry bag. I cut some hand holes in the side, made a lens port out of some wet suit material, and glued it all together with a hot glue gun. That skill no doubt came from my *Martha Stewart Living* days. Once I stuck the camera in the bag, it stayed there 'til we got to Baghdad.

I had this fear that I would start out with four cameras and then get to Baghdad for the story of my life and all the cameras would be broken. By the time we finished, three of the four Sony PC110s would break down.

The capacity of the solar charger was enough to charge only the small batteries. The equipment charged off the Humvees. We ended up burning up all sorts of inverters and alternators, and the Marines really didn't like that. It was a big problem. I had to spend a lot of time finding a way to charge batteries, and we never found a good way to go with that. When we ran out of cigars to swap, I resorted to giving the Marines liberal use of my satellite phone to call home. I also let them use my RBGAN Internet link to send flowers to their girlfriends via *1800flowers. com*. It was the best money ABC ever spent.

Solar charger.

On a Desert Highway

After the first days of the war, the fighting stops. Elwell and crew think the war might be over as they keep up their steady pace heading toward Baghdad.

Forty miles from Baghdad, Elwell and Cerre are crammed into an armored assault vehicle with twenty other Marines who've been without showers for weeks. They are safer here than in their old Humvee, when they were sitting on top of 1,500 pounds of high explosives in what now looks more like Swiss cheese than the world's most expensive SUV. The motor of the assault vehicle rumbles along as complete boredom numbs Elwell's thoughts.

The Whistle Comes First

On April 4, as soon as we crossed the Tigris River on our way to Baghdad, all hell broke loose. RPGs were flying everywhere. *Through a hatch in the roof Marines are firing away just a few feet above Elwell. The armored vehicle doesn't have windows like the Humvee. There's no way to see out, only a view of sand-colored fatigues jockeying for fighting positions. There are lots of explosions, yelling, and small arms fire as the caravan moves down the road. Elwell finds just enough room to push his camera up through the opening when—Whamm!—an ammo dump explodes in a huge fire ball. The vehicle immediately in front of them takes the worst*

A. The convoy headed north to Baghdad with air support.

B. An ammo dump explodes as the convoy passes, and shrapnel from the explosion hits Sergeant Smith.

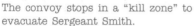

The convoy stops in a "kill zone" to evacuate Sergeant Smith.

Marines carry Smith to a medivac helicopter.

of the explosion as shrapnel peppers the troops shooting from the hatch. First Sergeant Smith, a twenty-year veteran, suffers a head wound from the explosion.

The Marines call for Sergeant Smith to be evacuated as they continue the firefight. Rain starts to fall as the day turns darker; the weather mirrors Elwell's emotions.

A medivac helicopter spins whirlwinds of dirt, mud, and rain while Sergeant Smith is carefully placed inside. The Marines watch through mist and debris as he takes off, unsure of his condition, hoping for the best.

The firefight rages for five hours before they're clear to move on. The caravan continues toward Baghdad, a little slower, more cautious, each man reflecting on the battle.

The marines went from boys to men that day because Sergeant Smith was like the strength of all of them. He had already signed his retirement papers when he was asked to be in Iraq for this one mission, and he said yes. He was the first one in our group to be injured. A few days before, all the commanding officers attended a meeting and were discussing how to motivate all the troops because it had been almost a week and no one had fired a shot, and the grunts were all depressed that the war was over. Sergeant Smith said, "Tell your men to be careful what they wish for, because it could come in a way that they don't want." This was not the end to our grief that day.

The Market at Night

Elwell, Cerre, and company set up camp in a small market. The Marines set up a road block to stop traffic and protect the camp. Elwell plugs in his night scope. An eerie green hue lights up on the viewfinder, making images in almost no light. Two glowing shapes crouch by the road, aiming into darkness.

Bang! One shot. Bang! Bang! A few more followed by a stream of automatic gunfire, then silence and muffled discussion. When a vehicle would come down the road, they would shoot warning shots over the top of it. This one car just kept coming, so they opened fire. They killed two men in the front seat and injured some kids and a woman in the back seat.

We were shooting footage of the Marines treating their injuries when Marine snipers started firing warning shots at other vehicles coming down the road. These vehicles also didn't heed the warning and continued through the checkpoint. The first truck looked like a military vehicle. This truck flipped over, killing the driver. Behind the truck was a minibus full of civilians. In the confu-

A. Marine sentries at the checkpoint seen through a nightscope.

B. Injured Iraqi civilians after being fired on when their vehicle tried to run the Marine checkpoint, seen through a nightscope.

C. Marines inspecting dead civilians in a bus that attempted to run the checkpoint.

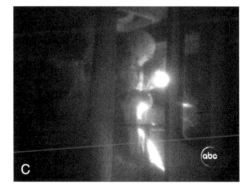

sion, the Marines fired on the minibus, killing three children and two women. I've never seen anything so horrific. I've never seen gunshot wounds so close, and these were children. By the end of the night, our unit was involved in shootings that left eight civilians dead. This was probably the worst nightmare for the Defense Department concerning the embed process, because we were right there when this civilian tragedy happened.

After all we'd been through that day, the only time I was really scared was when we camped in the market. Late at night, they started firing RPGs at the camp. The Humvees were put in a circle, and they started blowing up all around. I thought I was better off not in a vehicle at this point, so I went and laid in one of the vegetable stalls. I covered my face and listened to RPGs whistle by, then explode a moment later. The smell of rotted vegetables and urine was everywhere. I prayed I wouldn't die as I huddled in garbage.

The entire night was a horrible scene, and I think it upset the Marines as much as it did Mike Cerre and me. The incident at the checkpoint really put the embed process to the test. The question always was, "Would the embedded journalists be able to report stories that put the military in a bad light, either through censorship or reluctance to criticize our friends and protectors?" This was never a question as we set up and did a videophone report for ABC News the next morning . . . pulling no punches. While Cerre was doing the live report, the executive officer and two platoon sergeants stood behind me at the camera. After the report, they all said it was fair even though Mike was harshly critical of the incident.

A few days later, we all learned that Sergeant Smith had died from his injuries. His death knocked the wind out of the Marines. It was hard on me, too. I had shared a tent with him at the Kuwait base camp and had gotten to know him pretty well in the two months or so I had been with the company. We shared a special need for coffee in the morning, and although it was sometimes difficult to secure some once we were on the move, he always seemed to supply me with a cup. Maybe that is one of the down sides of getting close to the troops during an embed. You never know when you might lose a friend.

Elwell and Cerre make it to Baghdad for the toppling of Saddam Hussein's statue. For them, the assignment is over. Their project, **Brothers in Arms,** *an ABC Primetime special, will go into postproduction and air four months later. They make it back to Kuwait, but not without detours, bandits, endless waiting, and a bird ripping a hole in the wing of their plane as it flies out of Baghdad.* The pilots kept us airborne and got us safely to Kuwait City. I went to the cockpit to watch, and it reminded me of Doctor Strangelove. We were flying fifty feet above the ground to avoid artillery radar. The first thing we did when we landed was go to a Dairy Queen and have the best ice cream cone I think I've ever had in my life.

Reflections from the Front

Elwell is quick to point out he is not a combat cameraman, although this experience puts him in that league. He says this was his one and only time and he went there as much for the story of the California Marines from Fox 2/5 as for the experience of covering a war. As someone new to the embedding process, and combat in general, his insight and experience will be valuable to anyone following in his footsteps to the front lines.

It's not going to take courage because everybody is scared. You have to have a certain amount of fortitude just to deal with the inconvenience of it. It really is a miserable way to live. The Marines are constantly on the move, and they are always moving at night. It was impossible to sleep. Your hygiene was totally out the window. I went a month with taking a shower. You couldn't go to the bathroom behind the tree because there were probably mines behind it. So everything takes place in front of 150 other guys. You have to give up some of your modesty and things you've lived with for most of your life. There is a fair amount of enterprise that takes place with stories. There are always different stories within each tent, so you don't have to dig very deep to come up with a story.

You want to be honest in the way you're shooting. Respect the people you are photographing and be able to step back and assess your situation.

In a war zone, you get tunnel vision; you focus on what's in front of you and not what's all around you. You are more prone to hurt yourself. I always try to shoot with two eyes. It was harder to actually see what was going on without shooting than when I was shooting. It hit me harder.

One time in the market, I was searching for a place to charge the batteries. There were all these abandoned cars, and I went around and opened the doors to find a cigarette lighter to use for the chargers. Each time I opened a car door, there were at least two dead bodies in the car. The only way I could deal with this was to tell myself I was on a mission to charge these batteries. I think that actually the physical act of having a job to do really helps in those types of situations.

You definitely need to think small and keep your politics to yourself. Be in as good shape as you can. There is a lot of hiking and carrying stuff and hanging on for dear life hours on end.

I try to stay safe. I didn't have anything to prove. It's TV; it's not worth getting shot over. I didn't want to be a worry for the Marines because I didn't want to have them bring their attention to us and not see someone shooting at them. Try and figure out what your escape plan might be and where the action may flow in the next two minutes. Anyone who wants to do this has to know it isn't a constant adrenaline rush. There are weeks of absolute boredom and then there are weeks of absolute terror.

The Toll

There's a price to pay for covering the bleeding edge of history, as wars are waged and governments fall. The Committee to Protect Journalists keeps a tally of those who have died while on duty, reporting from the front lines. The complete list can be found on www.cpj.org.

As of this writing, February 2007, 93 journalists have been killed in Iraq since hostilities began in March 2003—37 more if you consider media support workers. The year 2006 was the worst so far, with 26 casualties. The vast majority of media killed are Iraqi nationals. The war has claimed 25 photojournalists (including still photographers and camera operators); 55 directors, reporters, and editors; 7 producers; and 6 technicians. Of those, 6 were embedded journalists and the rest were "unilateral."

For comparison, fewer journalists have died in other wars. The Freedom Forum (www.freedomforum. org) lists 62 journalists killed in Vietnam from 1965 to 1975, 17 in the Korean War, and 69 in World War II; in World War I, only 2 journalists died covering the battlefield.

In Arlington, Virginia's Freedom Park, the Freedom Forum Journalists Memorial is etched with the names of 1,665 journalists who have died while trying to report the news. The memorial is rededicated each year as the list grows longer.

When I was over there, I told my wife, "I'll be back in two weeks," because I thought there wouldn't be a war. But, it was almost three months later when I came home. In the back of my head, it was one of those things I wanted to be able to say I did. I had a buddy who was an old ABC cameraman during Vietnam, and he would tell me stories. I think that every cameraman wants to have that experience and see how they would hold up in those situations. It's history. I think that's why camerapeople want to experience these things. It would be great not to have war, but we do. So maybe we should experience it.

I was there; I know what it looks like, what the sun feels like, the cold wind off the desert.

Hopefully, the pictures I take will help those who see them understand the horrible reality of war.

CHAPTER 17

Bart Noonan

World Coverage—From
the Top Down

Bart Noonan
Chief Cameraman

Reuters, London
Course Instructor, "TV News Production," Reuters Foundation

*I*t's the week before Christmas as Finnair flight 427 from Helsinki to Rovaniemi, Finland, flies over the Arctic Circle, 2,260 kilometers from London, where little Lily Lou Noonan is tucked snug in her bed with dreams of her daddy and the holiday ahead. It's been a while since Reuters's cameraman Bart Noonan has been home to see his daughter. He recounts the days as he stares out the jet's window; his traveling companion, a Panasonic 615 camera, is stashed safely in the overhead compartment.

Noonan smiles as he pictures his daughter leaving cookies and milk for someone special on Christmas Eve. He remembers his own childhood Christmases in Rhode Island. One of the stations in Providence used to do these big productions on Christmas Eve. I still remember this from the days of black and white. The weatherman had one of those old magnetic weather maps, and he had Santa's sleigh on the map with billowy clouds and snowflakes. They would run a story from the airport in Rhode Island, where the reporter would point to a blip on the radar screen and say, "There's Santa now, somewhere over Hartford." And then the airport guy would say, "We've cleared a special flight path for Santa tonight, and of course the reindeer will help him through the snowfall we've been having. . . ."

This is the top of the world. Outside, the 3:00 P.M. afternoon light fades to a gloomy dusk. At this time of year, there are only four hours of light. Endless forests of snow-covered pine trees give way to fields of ice, reflecting blue hues from the early Purkinje Shift. This is home to the native Sami (Laplander) reindeer herders. They and their herds of tens of

EQUIPMENT

Panasonic 615 DVCPRO 25 4:3 camera with
   FireWire output
Fujinon 8-121 mm lens
Canon wide-angle adapter
Kata neoprene camera cover with rain jacket
Padded Portabrace shoulder strap
Beyer Dynamic MCE 86 shotgun mic with Rycote
   windjammer
X3 PAG 5 Ah Ni-Cad batteries
PAG camera light
Sachtler Hotpod with video 18 MK3 head and
   carrying strap
Chamois cloth for cleaning the lens
6- to 4-pin FireWire cable for playback into laptop
IFB earphone on mini jack

thousands of reindeer roam nomadically for three seasons a year across a vast pristine land, north of the Arctic Circle, from the Norwegian Atlantic coast into Northwest Russia. With temperatures from −15 to −37 degrees Celsius, it's almost uninhabitable except for the Sami, who say, "There is no such thing as bad weather, only bad clothing." It's also home to the real Santa Claus!

With some research, we found the real Santa Claus. Not these phonies who go to some convention every year and drink booze and smoke cigars in public, or the tawdry bunch skulking around shopping malls—pretenders to the throne. I mean we found the real thing. And if any readers are laughing about this, you are very close to getting coal and old onions in your stocking.

That's why Noonan, aka "Santa's Cameraman" (a title he received from a local newspaper that made him a celebrity), is coming. It's a trip he's made every year for the past ten years—to meet perhaps the only other person who's been to as many countries and logged as many flight hours as he has—although the "sleigh" doesn't have business class.

You know you are headed to Lapland when the snack trolley comes around on the flight—no pretzels, no potato chips. One thing on the menu: cold, sliced reindeer sandwiches. No word of a lie. Think about what I've heard from the kids in the ten years of flying up to Santa's Village. "Mummy, this isn't Rudolph we're eating, is it? Whaaaa! *The aircraft's lights turn on and illuminate frozen snowflakes racing by Noonan's window. The airport rotates into view, and the ground lights glow like candles in the snow.*

The plane, with livery that proudly states, "The Official Airline of Santa Claus," pulls to a stop on the frozen tarmac. If you start in with "Why does he need an official airline when he's got the reindeer and sleigh?" then you're really asking for a single lump of coal this year. And you'll be lucky if he leaves you that, so just don't even start! *It's a short walk to the terminal, but it's one you won't forget.*

When you step out of the aircraft onto the staircase to the runway, the cold rushes straight to the depth of your lungs in an instant. You can feel it circulate around your body as your heart works faster to keep up with the unexpected freeze. By the time I crunched through the packed snow on the Arctic runway to visit Santa, I'd been on the move across two continents, three flights, three countries, eleven time zones, and in the cold for forty-eight hours. I was ready to hit the hay when I arrived in Rovaniemi. There was a relaxing, steamy sauna at the hotel that would be followed by a piping hot plate of reindeer stew and a crisp, chilled vodka. Then a long Arctic night's sleep.

But that never happens to Noonan when he's in Rovaniemi—Santa's village—right before Christmas. The elves aren't the only ones who are busy that time of year. Noonan's cab pulls to a snow-crunching stop outside Santa's office. I pulled a few basics from my single flight case and shared a hot coffee with The Big Man before starting to film. He had children to meet and letters to answer from his post office. We filmed inside for a few hours.

After filming with Santa, Noonan bundles up in thermals, flannel-lined jeans and shirt, and an old, comfortable down jacket. Tonight he'll wait in minus-below-nothing temperature with his camera frosting up, just hoping to get some shots of the northern lights. Even the elves tire out before he does.

The next day starts out early. The temperature has gone up to some other negative number. By this time, Noonan can feel the difference—it's downright balmy. There is not a lot of daylight in the Arctic in December. So you have to make good use of every chance to film with Santa. It's peak season

282

for him. Each year I visit, I try to add something a little different to the Santa story. One year, he got e-mail. His computer sang out, "Good morning, Santa, you have 20,000 new e-mails!" Another year, it was climate change. We'll do more of that in the future. I've also done stories on ecotourism in the Arctic and traveled on snowmobile safaris. And some years, World Rally car teams are in the area to practice for the Rally of Lapland. This year, it's a charity for terminally ill children who are coming up for Christmas. Santa puts a lot of his spare time into helping this charity and its children.

After ten years, Bart and Santa have become friends. They both look forward to the visit, when Santa and his cameraman try to bring something special into the world, a picture of hope and joy and goodwill. After filming Santa with his reindeer and sleigh in the daytime, we headed out in his sleigh for a night's work with the kids. That's what this shoot is all about every year, kids. And trying to put something on TV they might enjoy and let them feel like kids in whatever country or situation they live in. Because some folks in Providence did that for me back in the 1960s, in the days of black and white. And I remember.

Bart Noonan will be home soon, with plenty of time scheduled for family and friends. However, "scheduled" is a loose term, subject to any number of global stories that could send him to some far-flung piece of real estate many time zones away. This holiday, the world takes a break.

Traveling the world is a large part of Noonan's work. He's chief cameraman for Reuters, working out of their London headquarters. He is also a course instructor for the Reuters Foundation.

The Reuters Organization

Reuters News Agency

Reuters is the world's largest multimedia international news agency. Reuters Television has nearly 100 bureaus and more than 500 international clients around the world. Some bureaus, like Berlin, are big offices with five crews and a dedicated uplink. Other offices may be one guy with his own minicam who looks after a whole country for us and shoots weddings on weekends. We started off a long time ago as British Commonwealth Overseas Film and Television. More recently, it was called Visnews and was owned by NBC, the BBC, and Reuters. Reuters TV works like your local newspaper: You pay one price; then you get the paper every day. Now, if you are a small station, you pay a small price and you probably just get one news feed each day. If you are a big broadcaster like the BBC, you pay a bigger price, but then you are getting something like the *Sunday Times* every day. Twenty-four hours of news feeds and live stories.

The Reuters Foundation

The Reuters Foundation is a charity. The main mission of the foundation is to teach journalism in developing markets and countries. The foundation strives to teach good fundamentals and balanced reporting. I developed and teach the TV news class and really enjoy it. I've had the chance to teach around 1,500 working TV professionals in thirty-some countries for the past eleven years. It's been a great experience to meet all these people and see what TV news is like in so many different countries. It's also allowed me to have the chance to give something back for all the fabulous colleagues, drivers, fixers, and translators I've worked with.

The Road to Reuters's Top Slot

Noonan started shooting in the early 1980s, but his desire to travel the world was born some years later. I remember vividly, watching the Berlin Wall come down on TV. I was freelancing in Washington, D.C., and thinking to myself, I wish I was there. What I wouldn't give to be a cameraman at all these historical events—really being there and seeing it all happen instead of being here in D.C., listening to what the government has to say about it. Especially when the Wall came down. The world changed overnight.

In 1989, I had been freelancing for Visnews in D.C. on a very regular basis. Then the one staff guy was going to get married and the other freelancer was going to be a best man at an upcoming wedding. It was around the time of the Bush/Gorbachev summit in Malta, and so the Washington office asked me to go. Wow, that was wild! Getting asked out of the blue to go to this little place in the middle of a faraway ocean. So I went and worked real hard with a great bunch of people from London and Paris and Rome. Two months later, they gave me a job opening their new office in Berlin. Next thing I knew, I arrived there in Berlin with a bag of clothes and a full-time job! What a twist of fate!

In 1990, Visnews was a little group of maybe 200 people worldwide with a big office in London. The company was very different back then. There was a pub in the Visnews HQ in London immediately above the newsroom! Visnews was a newsreel company that first began back in the fifties, and it retained that character for its entire life. It's a small group of dedicated and talented people who hang together.

Reuters was at one time called the Family News Agency, and Visnews became its TV division. To this day, the best thing about working for the company is the sense of family. I've got an extended family of brothers and sisters around the world. We get along and respect each other by virtue of doing the same demanding job of TV news coverage. Wherever we are from, there is friendship, respect, and camaraderie among the people who work in the field. Some of us know more about lighting, others know more about covering a war, and others know how to "work" a very difficult local system under the eyes of the government, militias, or populations that simply do not like to be filmed. But we love making good picture stories and delivering them against deadlines, getting the news out for the world to know what is happening in our "patch"—to use the British expression for turf.

From Berlin to Brussels to London with a Promotion

After three years of wars and riots in Eastern Europe, the Middle East, and the Soviet Union, Noonan moved to Brussels. He was called to support a new Visnews project called GMTV—the United Kingdom's most popular breakfast-time program. Over two years he worked on feature stories throughout Western Europe, a welcome change of pace. Visnews was absorbed into the Reuters brand, and Noonan was promoted to the London office and became senior cameraman for Reuters.

I may be the chief cameraman at Reuters HQ, but that certainly doesn't mean I am the "best" or even the most experienced cameraman or camerawoman in the company. Far from it. My great privilege is that, through assignments and my teaching, I have had a chance to meet almost everyone who works for us worldwide. I've tried to share everyone's knowledge and experience across the company. For example, the guys in D.C. know loads about lighting because they do it every day. So I can give some of their ideas to, maybe, the crews in Jo'burg. They don't have much call for fancy lighting there, but know how to operate in civil conflict.

Some of our folks have worked for us relentlessly for decades, called on maybe once a year to get the big, breaking story of the month out; they deliver unfailingly due to their devotion to their vocation. Everyone does things their own way, and a little differently. But there are fabulous professionals working for us around the globe, and I have a great deal of respect for all of them.

Today's Newsreel Camerapeople

Basically, a news cameraman in our company today is a lot like a cameraman in the old newsreel days. It's one person that can go out with a TV camera and tell a story with pictures. You need to be able to handle the camera alone. You edit your material, understand the story, get the quotes and the spelling of the names right. You need to be able to write at least a basic dope sheet if not a full script to go with it. You need to find your way to the feed point in a strange country where you don't speak the language, or find a traveler at the airport who might be willing to take your tape on the flight with them and deliver it to a waiting colleague in another country. If somebody calls you now and says, "I need footage out of Romania tonight," you should be able to go get a few thousand bucks, hop a plane, do it, and get the footage back on time, before you check into a hotel. That's what we do for a living—go anywhere at any time, do the story, get the material back, know what you're going to do the next day before you go to sleep.

Reuters employs camerapersons around the world. We have great local people working for us all over the world. They come from very different backgrounds, but all share a passion for what we do in the field. Some people may have started as translators or couriers. Others have received years of classical training. As Eastern Europe opened up, we took on a number of people who had spent years studying filmmaking at the Moscow Film Academy.

The Reuters Style

Operating much like the newsreel camera operators from the last century, the Reuters camerapeople shoot so that their footage can be used in countless ways once it's fed to clients. You can build a story one way in Germany, another way in Vietnam. Some languages take longer to speak, so they use the full length of the shot; others speak quickly and select the middle of the scene or recut quick sequences from the same material. Reuters provides the entire story and the ability for clients to customize stories to their needs.

Shooting to produce stories that can be customized around the world creates a kind of style for Reuters. Each one of their clients knows what it can expect. However, inside that style lies the varied talents and shooting styles of the camerapeople based in far corners of the world, who bring their own special vision and cultural influences to the work they produce.

When Noonan talks of work, he takes inspiration from still photographers Walker Evans, Robert Frank, and Henri Cartier-Bresson. A solid foundation from the past that rings true today.

I tell people, if you set a camera on a tripod, you've got to think like Walker Evans (the famous photographer known for his work for the Farm Security Administration documenting the Great Depression). You're looking for the graphic aspect of things. You're looking for how light and shadow come together to give you a geometrical frame. You're concentrating on the pictorial element of things—strong lines and shapes built with light and shadow.

If you've got the camera on your shoulder, you think like Robert Frank, another famous photographer who shot the 1958 book *The Americans*. Robert Frank's style is just kind of catching things as they happen without many people knowing that he's around. He's just catching that interest in the moment, that combination of the lens and real life on camera.

If it's quick and candid, you think like Henri Cartier-Bresson, considered a father of modern photojournalism. That's how you shoot. How do you teach people to do that? You've got to make people interested in what a camera can do and what they can do with the camera.

Noonan also draws inspiration from the early cinéma vérité documentaries by Richie Leacock and D. A. Pennebaker and Frederick Wiseman. Those movies still stand up today—no narration, reporters, or what we now consider traditional interviews—just real life on camera.

Not an Office Job

Being chief photographer at Reuters does not mean Noonan gets a break from the field. In addition to his yearly flight to Santa, he's seen many of the world's top stories in the past fifteen years. He recounts some of his most notable assignments—highlights from around the world.

East Berlin

There was a giant, six-story-tall marble statue of Lenin on *Leninalle* (Lenin Avenue) in East Berlin. Sometime after unification, the German authorities decided to remove it. They built a large scaffold around the statue and brought in diamond-edged power saws to cut it apart, piece by piece. Every day of the dismantling, there were violent demonstrations by radical leftists. A lot of East Germans were sorry to see aspects of the old system go. They had guaranteed jobs, health coverage, and a social system based on the need of sharing items not easily purchased in state-run stores.

Radical leftists called *Autonomen* or the "Black Block" had barricaded themselves in heavily fortified apartments on *Mainzstrasse* (Mainz Street) in

East Berlin. There were hundreds of them armed with petrol bombs, slingshots, and paving stones. They defied the police to root them out of the buildings, and a seriously violent fight lasted six hours. You can see the Berlin riot police being attacked with petrol bombs from the balconies above (see bottom image on previous page). In the end, the Munich antiterrorist squad was brought in to get the leftists out. It was late 1991.

Georgia

This material was recorded outside Zugdidi, Georgia, during the second phase of the civil war in that country (see A and B above). There was a blockade imposed on the country by the Russians. It was hard to get fuel or food. The producers and I often relied on the great generosity of the Georgians we met. It was cold, and they had an unusually heavy snowfall. Some days we had to walk for miles to get to the fighting. These images show the National Guard returning fire against rebels hidden in a forest. I'd been caught in crossfire twice earlier in the day.

Bosnia

This is the Serbian army assault on the historic town of Visegrad, Bosnia. I was working alone with a translator. There was a small TV station nearby, and they had three-quarter-inch gear.

So I took a BVU110 from our Belgrade office and hooked it to my Betacam with a BNC cable. I taught the translator how to operate the Record/Pause button. We went into combat and managed to record camera edits on the BVU and feed from the local station two or three times a day. The competition had to drive four hours back to Belgrade each evening.

Iraq

It was the summer of 1992 when U.S.–Iraqi tensions were high. I was based in Baghdad for a month and a half. The Iraqi government flew some members of the foreign press to Basra and the surrounding areas. It was strange to fly in a U.S.-built Huey with an Iraqi pilot who spoke English with a Texan accent! He'd learned to fly in Texas, where they made Hueys, and learned his English there as well. We went to see the "Marsh Arabs." These people were anti-Saddam Shiites living as they had for ages in the swamps in the south of the country.

They had a nearly primitive lifestyle. Their homes were small huts made of straw and mud, and their slender, fabric-hulled wooden canoes were handmade and covered with a kind of dung and tar mixture to waterproof them. The faithful of the Ba'ath party were herded out before the cameras to demonstrate people's loyalty to Saddam.

The Iraqi town of Safwan was cut off and trapped between U.S. forces to the north and the Kuwaiti border to the south after coalition forces established themselves in southern Iraq. Hunger soon set in. The U.S. military brought in food, medical care, and other humanitarian aid. But on the first day of the operation, a Saudi Army truck pulled up near the Americans. The Saudis started throwing food out of the back of the truck. Chaos and a riot ensued. Adults were beating children to take away their food. I climbed into the Saudi truck to film the desperation on the faces of the civilians. This happened before the Kurdish crisis began up in the North.

London

We cover London fashion week twice a year. Julien Macdonald often provides a glamorous show. Last year, Paris Hilton was first down the catwalk. Fashion is a challenge to shoot. The camera platforms can be crowded with as many as thirty TV cameras and sixty photographers. Then you need to get in close to see the cut of the material and the texture of the

A. Iraqis carrying a portrait of Saddem.

B. The starving Iraqis of Safwau.

fabrics on a model moving toward your camera. So you need to ride the focus and keep a decent frame on the long end of the lens in sometimes very low light, and try to finish the tilt on the model's face as she pauses for a moment on the close end of the runway. You need to know what you are doing and concentrate to produce good results.

Ireland

The last Sunday of every July, around 25,000 pilgrims climb the 900-meter-high St. Patrick's Mountain in the west of Ireland. It is where legend has it that St. Patrick fasted for forty days and forty nights and heard the voice of God. Many of the pilgrims climb the rocky slopes barefoot, enduring the climb as a kind of penance, and many of the faithful are Irish speakers from the surrounding area. There is a chapel on the summit, where church services are held in Irish and English throughout the day. The priest in the picture is leaning on a staff that he will use to descend the steep path down the mountain. It is a difficult shoot to do as a one-man band.

One year, I took a broadcast camera and tripod up with the help of my cousin, Enda, a photographer who lives in the west. We were exhausted by the time we got down! On this occasion, I went up with a PD170. It was much easier. The three people in the background *(see top right figure)* remind me of the image of three crosses on the hill at the crucifixion. The mountain is by the sea, and the weather can be hot and sunny one minute and windy, rainy, and cold the next. A real pint of Irish Guinness at the end of the day is always a pleasure!

Having shot in so many places around the world, Noonan has developed guidelines that make international travel for other crews a little easier. Other Reuters colleagues have also added their two cents.

Bart's Rules of the Road

I have been to more than eighty countries—some of them don't even exist any more, and some have changed beyond recognition. My journeys have taken me into incredibly dangerous, disastrous, humorous, wondrous, and wild situations. I haven't had a single disastrous failure along the way (knock on wood). For more than sixteen years, I've been traveling, shooting, interviewing, producing, editing, writing, and teaching around this amazing world and, for the most part, things have gone well. Of course, I've had the chance to work with many very talented coworkers and wouldn't have gone far without them. Working abroad certainly demands good teamwork in many instances. If you are not working with people from your own organization, then you are working with people involved in the story you are covering.

Sure, there have been threats, attacks, broken equipment, frozen equipment, corrupt officials, and everyone and their sister who wants to be paid for being in a wide shot of Main Street. But I've managed to make it happen, get the pictures delivered on time, and put my feet up for a well-deserved beer at the end of a long, productive day.

Working abroad regularly is all about planning, organization, and the ability to think on your feet. You should be prepared and able to fly abroad at short notice, drive to a story, shoot and cut a piece, and feed the material before checking in to your hotel.

Your Papers Please—Passports, Carnets, and Equipment Lists

Passports (Yes, Plural)

If you are going to travel abroad regularly, it may be useful to obtain a second passport. There is a good reason for this; some countries will not let you enter if your passport contains a stamp from certain other countries. For example, Israel will allow you to enter if you have been to Arab nations, but most Arab nations will not let you enter if you have an Israeli stamp. If you go to Israel, you can ask for an "Insert Visa." Your entry and exit visas will be stapled into your passport and so easily removed later.

But if you are traveling a lot, you may need to send your passport to the embassy of the country you are going to visit to obtain a visa before you travel. This can be a time-consuming business. If you need to travel in the meantime, you will need a second passport. If you get two, use one for visas from countries whose stamps are easily accepted elsewhere, and the second passport to visit countries whose stamps are not welcome in other places.

Equipment Documentation

Sometimes TV gear needs its own passport, just like people. The documentation is used to allow people to bring expensive items like TV gear into and out of a country without paying import duties. There are essentially three different kinds of documents used for transporting equipment internationally.

The ATA Carnet This is an *Admission Temporaire*—temporary admission—pronounced *car-nay*. A carnet is an official, multipage document. It lists equipment along with serial numbers, makes and model numbers, countries of manufacture, and values. The document states that import duties on the gear are paid in the country where the kit is based. There are different pages in the document for instances when the gear leaves base, enters and exits a different country, and returns to base. The list of gear is printed in the carnet. They only need to be signed and dated on presentation at customs. They can also be amended. There are lines to fill in what items are not there. Carnets are recognized by many countries; *http://www.export.gov/logistics/exp_000969.asp* is a Web site that gives a very thorough rundown on carnets.

It may take a little time to organize and pay the fees on a carnet, but even the most demanding customs official will allow you through if your papers (including the carnet) are in order!

Duplicate Lists These are not official documents; they are gear lists printed on company letterhead. They list the gear models, manufacturers, serial numbers for big items (camera, lens, edit gear), countries where the kit was made, and the value of each item. The value should be declared at around half or a third of the actual value. The reason for this is difficult customs officers. If an officer doesn't like the way you look or doesn't like the press or foreigners, etcetera, they may ask you to post a bond. A *bond* is a deposit on the value of the equipment. You may be asked to leave cash or at least a credit card swipe for the value of the gear until you leave the country and customs is convinced all the gear is going out with you.

If you are using a duplicate list to transport equipment, take at least six with you. Two are presented to customs on departure from home. One is kept by customs in your country. The other is stamped. Keep it in a safe place! It guarantees your gear can get back into your base country. Another two are presented to customs when you arrive on assignment. They keep one and you retain one, which is stamped with your date of entry. That must be presented back to customs and presented with the gear when you leave the country. If you leave the country separately from the gear, the duplicate list must be handed over to your replacement so they can get the gear out. The other duplicate lists are carried in anticipation of being moved on to another country with your gear. We only write the serial numbers for the big items for purposes of flexibility.

For example, if there is a broken Sachtler tripod in the country of your destination, you can leave the good one you brought in and take the other one out for repair. If the serial numbers are not on your list, there is no way for customs to know exactly which Sachtler tripod you have. If you think your camera gear will return home with you but the editing equipment may stay behind on location for the next crew that comes in to replace you, be sure to make a separate list for the edit gear. But make sure the stamped list is kept with the editing gear at all times.

The third kind of document that can list equipment you're transporting is your own *personal passport*. It is not unusual, especially in the Middle East, for customs officers to scrawl in passports their own description of what you're carrying. Do not depend on this system for transporting gear. Bring a carnet or at least a duplicate list. If it is the custom of a particular country to write in passports, officials will most likely transcribe some information from any documents you bring.

Before You Leave Town

It is essential that your team communicates closely. Each member must be aware of his or her role in planning and preparation before the journey begins. The team must know what everyone is going to do to optimize time spent on the ground.

Travel light. Don't work with more than you can carry—maybe with the exception of a light kit. (Put the "porter" back into reporter.) Now, if some of my colleagues are reading this, they are going to have a laugh because I used to carry a load of things with me when I traveled. You'd think an Everest expedition was on if you had seen me at the airport years ago. No more. A flight case smaller than a normal suitcase. A tripod tube. A light kit. Camera. Trust me, you tend to be on the hop when you travel. Leave the trolley at home; it's just more stuff to deal with. If you have four batteries at home, take three (if they are in good shape).

First, make time to understand the story before traveling anywhere. Identify the main players, key locations, and critical events that will be central to your story. Begin to plan how different elements of the story can be covered and delivered. All the soft lights, radio microphones, wide-angle lenses, and bean bags in the world won't help you if you don't know about the story and people you are going to cover. Any journalist who works with a switched-on cameraman is going to be much more responsive to giving you the little extra time you need to make an exceptional shot. Make sure that you are as prepared as your gear.

Have this stuff good to go for trips away from home:

- A cheap watch with alarm and two time zones to keep track of time at home.
- A small flashlight; keep it by your bed at night so you can find your way around dark, unfamiliar hotel rooms.
- A multipurpose tool.
- A shortwave radio. The Voice of America (VOA) and the British Broadcasting Corporation (BBC) offer twenty-four hours of news on shortwave, on the hour, every day in just about every corner of the world. Check their Web sites to get frequencies for your destination.
- Maps of where you're traveling.
- At least a simple first-aid kit.
- At least one spare pair of glasses if you wear them, and doctors' prescriptions for medications.
- A half dozen or so ID photos of yourself. They are useful for getting accredited quickly. Count on giving two photos for every accreditation or visa you require.

You should have all the contacts, communications, locations, directions, and editorial background information to accomplish the assignment quickly and efficiently. Know how you will feed your material before you get to your location whenever possible. Sometimes you are just sent to the airport; other times you have the chance to prepare.

Airport Routine

You don't need things going wrong before you leave your base. Plenty can go wrong at the airport, but keeping to a routine and observing a few small details can ensure things go smoothly. Here is a checklist for airport procedure that can be modified according to local conditions:

- Check that you have tickets, passports, money, and gear documentation before you leave home.
- Count the number of bags and flight cases you are taking. In fact, count your gear boxes every time they are moved—from office to cab, cab to curbside.
- If you have a large number of boxes, two people should count them. This is done to make sure nothing is accidentally left behind. We used to travel into places like Baghdad

or Moscow with eighty flight cases, including an uplink, editing equipment, a few camera rigs, and accessories.

At the Airport

Keep cameras and personal bags with you at all times, and do not let them out of your sight! Different airports and countries have different customs routines. Here is one example of how to check in with items to be presented to customs officers. Go to the check-in desk first. If you have to present gear documentation to leave your base, be ready for everything on this list:

1. Tell the airline you have items to show to customs.
2. They will call a porter to escort you to customs after check-in is completed.
3. Recount the number of bags you are checking in.
4. Baggage is weighed.
5. Make sure the check-in person tags your bags for the correct destination!
6. Count your baggage tags and ensure you have the right number of tags for the number of bags you have checked in.
7. If needed, pay excess baggage charges at the ticket desk of that airline or a dedicated excess baggage cashier.
8. Go to customs and present gear documentation.
9. Customs is usually interested in seeing the main items on an equipment list—for example, a camera and lens. But all listed equipment must be ready for inspection by customs officials.
10. Documents are stamped.
11. Keep stamped documents in a safe place! The gear may travel back to base or onward in the field without you. The documents will have to be passed to the next person who takes charge of the kit.
12. When traveling to airports, do not let gear go in a car by itself. Ensure that there is a team member traveling with equipment at all times.

When You Land

Count all your bags and make sure they have all arrived with you. Then one person in the team can deal with customs while another takes care of the rental car. That person will need driver's licenses. Always use two people to pass through customs in case there are difficulties. Never let one person deal with all the kit. If you don't already have local currency, get some at the airport. Don't worry if you do not get a great exchange rate. Concentrate on getting the story.

Shooting out of Town and out of Country

Now that you've landed in a different country, it's time to start working. Working outside of your comfort zone might make it difficult to produce the same quality of work you were shooting back home. Common sense and an open mind will take you far. There are a few ideas common to all the trips I've taken, journeys I've enjoyed, and stories I've covered over the years. Some ideas have come from my own experience, and many are pieces of advice given to me by fabulous friends and colleagues.

Local journalists, crews, and photographers in locations abroad know the story better than you ever will and will stay and live with the situation after you leave. You may be a hotshot, first-call, award-winning cameraperson at home, but when you are away, you are on someone else's turf. They know the story, the people, the locations, the short cuts, the cops, the other journalists, and all the rest. Just like you do on your patch.

Learn to respect the local journalists and crews everywhere you go. No one is going to think you are special just because you traveled a long way to cover the story. They may not have gear as fancy as yours, or may work in what seems like an outmoded or strange way, but that's their livelihood. Demonstrating a little respect goes a long way everywhere. Nobody likes a loud-mouth, self-important superstar.

Take a moment to get to know people, and you can save yourself lots of time and headaches. And be ready to give something back to people for their time—give yours. Learn to listen. Or just take a moment to say hi and introduce yourself. TV news crews tend to be one big family around the world, and meeting someone from somewhere else can be fun. You have a chance to exchange ideas and working practices and find a good place to eat. You can also get useful information about a story and maybe even some footage from that station. You will be surprised to discover how often people are willing to share video material. If a big international story is breaking in a small place, the local TV station is a good place to meet people, make friends, and stay across (know) what's going on.

Take 110-Percent Responsibility for Everything

The shooting schedule, finances and receipts, local helpers (called fixers), and a spare tire for the rental car are all in your hands—so is everything else.

Unless you are traveling with a big network team on a major story, there is a good chance you will be working with one or maybe two other people. It's not the time to regard yourself as a "button presser" (that's a translation from the French term *presse button*, or someone who waits to be told what to do at all times). If you are one, you probably won't be asked to travel anyhow.

When you are traveling, it's not enough to deliver great pictures and well-crafted edits. There are always multiple aspects of planning, logistics, and the story itself. (If the story weren't a big deal then you wouldn't be sent, would you?)

You need to be prepared to work as a field producer and second journalist when you are working abroad. "When you're on the road, share the load." (Catchy as flypaper, that.)

Preparation, Planning, Backups, Alternatives

Be mentally prepared for each shoot—visualize the story. Keep your eyes, ears, and mind open on location. Your gear and working methods should be second nature—build in backups and alternatives to everything you need to do.

New techniques and technologies make working globally much easier. GPS navigation can help you find your way anywhere in the world. Satellite phones can put you in touch from locations that don't have cell service. New video delivery systems make your stories much easier to file.

It can be intimidating to work in a country and culture where you don't speak the language, where you are unfamiliar with the routines and protocols used to gain access to a local feed point or TV station, and where just doing what you can do at home without thinking twice about it suddenly becomes an effort.

Store-and-forward technology can make life a lot easier. You can keep matters in your own hands instead of making endless phone calls and faxes to arrange a feed, which you drive like mad to get to at the last minute and which, at the end of the day, leaves you in someone else's hands.

So learn how to cut, compress, and transmit with a laptop. FTP (File Transfer Protocol) is the method used to deliver what is essentially a big mother of a file over the Net. There are loads of programs out there to edit with and just as many to deliver with.

But I can't emphasize enough the tranquility you gain by being able to transmit in your own time from your hotel room or an Internet café or even a nice pub, with a creamy pint on the bar. It beats driving like a pizza delivery guy through red lights, then standing nervously in the guard house at some foreign TV station waiting for someone you don't know to arrive and escort you through miles of hallways you'll never find your way out of to an MCR (master control room) reeking of ancient cigarette smoke where there is a playout machine that might have been in use during the Boer War.

Preparation and Risk

Many of the assignments for Reuters involve risk. Stories come from war zones and politically unstable countries. Reuters insists on proper training for everyone who goes into a conflict zone. There are a number of organizations in the U.K. and the U.S. that provide training and security services for journalists and other people who might have to travel inside war zones. What they do for journalism organizations is provide weeklong courses on how people should behave in dangerous situations, mostly war zones. So they'll tell you how armies think, how armies act. They'll teach you a lot of battlefield first aid. They'll tell you how you have to prepare yourself, how to act in such a way that won't draw attention or act in a threatening manner. How do deal with situations like roadblocks and people pointing guns at your head, which isn't a lot of fun.

Reuters Foundation Workshops—Worldwide

Noonan shares his time between his duties as chief photographer and course instructor with the Reuters Foundation. Again, more travel. The object here is to travel to developing nations and share production and journalistic techniques with working professionals in countries where there is often no high school or university training in broadcast journalism.

Privatization has changed international TV. Before the Wall came down, most countries had one or two state-run channels. But that has all changed. First, Eastern Europe exploded with many new television stations, and the same is now happening in the Arab world. There are thousands more TV stations now than there were fifteen years ago. And the young people working in developing markets are always hungry and thankful for knowledge. They all want to improve themselves.

Noonan presents a toolbox of methods and techniques—concepts that can be adapted to different situations, countries, and cultures. With the vast number of countries that have their own way of doing TV, what works in one place doesn't work in another place. What we try to do is to present the students with tools. We try to help them select the right tool for the right job. When we go to countries, we don't say this is the Reuters way and you must do it this way, because everybody has got their own way of doing things.

The biggest problem most TV stations have is the relationships between reporters and camera crews. There is a great hierarchy in a lot of stations and in a lot of cultures, too. We try to spend a lot of time helping people learn how to communicate on the job in such a way that they can get along better, have more fun, work more efficiently as a unit, so they can work as a creative team rather than separate employees.

The Reuters Foundation decides which countries they'll offer classes in and invites local stations to nominate one or two working professionals to take part in the class. The Web address is www.foundation. reuters.com.

Noonan's five-day workshop is designed to establish the fundamentals and give students a new jumping-off point to explore their creativity.

The Workshop

There are exercises throughout the week. We send the journalists out with digital cameras and ask them to shoot photo essays. We get the camera folks to write and conduct interviews. Everyone works on structure and focus exercises.

Day 1: Structure, research, critical viewing, visualization. The Reuters Trust Principles, which focus on accuracy and balance.

Day 2: Visual grammar and the camera. It's not about buttons and switches but about when to stay on the action, when to try a sequence, the use of sound. Photojournalism and impressionism.

Day 3: Writing to pictures, interview technique, stand-ups.

Day 4: Editing and pace, rhythm, the dynamics of the frame, the essence of the shot.

Day 5: Wrap-up and final exercises.

During the class, and specifically on the second day, we cover a lot the visual basics about framing, about how you need to use close-ups, light and shadow, foreground, background, and clearly seen subjects. You see so much stuff on TV where the subject is really not clear. It's either too small or too obscured, or it's half hidden or there's a bad camera angle. It's got to be a clearly seen subject.

When we do these classes, we tell the reporters and the photographers we want them both to be bilingual. We want the reporters to understand the language of images, and we want the visual journalists to understand how to write to pictures and how to make a connection to an image through writing.

We conduct most exercises two times, once to get people used to the idea and another time to give them the opportunity to improve on what they did the first time.

Photographers have to understand how a narrative needs to work and how you have to have certain elements that allow a reporter to connect an idea to a picture. You've got to give me something to write about. Perhaps if I'm going to talk about elections, you can go to horse racing; because horse racing is a big thing here in Britain and Ireland. Connecting the idea of horse racing to people jockeying for position in their candidacy could be one way to go. We make the photographers write. They learn to write stories to try to connect a certain kind of idea in a certain way through pictures and understand how that works. At Reuters, everyone strives to understand the story.

Noonan has seen many of his students go on to produce incredible stories and advance their careers. It's something he's extremely proud of. His workshops often help provide a new outlook for a career and a life for those who may have had little hope of a career just a few years ago. There are just so many people who live in not such great circumstances. For example, in Colombia, every person in my class, all fourteen students, had at least one person from their station that had been kidnapped or killed by the rebels or by the government.

For all the kidnappings of journalists that take place in certain countries, they still just walk out and do it because they love it. That's something to be admired. Great lighting, yeah, that's one thing; a great eye is another. But just going out and doing the job under difficult circumstances and in dangerous countries, just so you can feed your kids and put them through school—that's a whole different ballgame. That's something to be admired.

Teaching journalism in emerging markets often means that those markets have been through significant upheaval. Some of the workshops have taken place in cities where Noonan's been before, and they're not always nice to visit.

I recently ran a five-day class in Bucharest, Romania. It was very interesting to be back there for the first time in sixteen years. When I was last in town, it had been taken over by former secret police, common criminals, and brutal coal miners from the Carpathians, an "army of around 10,000." They all claimed they were there to "protect the constitution," an old communist subterfuge. They were, in fact, trying to topple the new government through a popular uprising of violence. People were abducted and disappeared. Students and anyone who got in their way were beaten in broad daylight. All the TV crews were working under serious duress. Some crews were badly beaten in the streets. Others had left the country completely. Many cameras were smashed. Some of the coal miners saw me filming from the fifth-floor balcony of my hotel room and rushed the door of the hotel—a group of a half dozen with pick axes and staves.

I was terrified. I didn't know what to do and was sure I would be caught if I tried to escape on the stairs or in the lift. I looked around the sparse room at the basic set of gear I had with me. Just the essentials: camera, tripod, and three batteries. I stuffed my flight case and tripod tube under the bed. Then I threw the accessories into my fabric suitcase and dumped my laundry on top. Finally I whipped the lens and camera light off the camera. I stuffed everything under a stack of pillows on the bed. Then I grabbed a paperback and sat up in bed with the pillows propped up behind me, the camera digging into the small of my back.

Moments later the door crashed open and the miners stormed in. They were shouting, "Camera! camera!" while clenching their axes in the air. I was certainly startled when they broke the door open. But when they looked around the room and only saw a guy reading a book, they settled down. I think they were looking to catch somebody with a camera or find an empty room. But as I was just sitting there with a book in my lap, they were a little confounded; nothing they found fit their expectations. They left after a few seconds and broke into the room next door. Then they left the hotel. I can tell you, now, how good it was to head out for a beer with our local photographer that night.

Of course, back then there was just one national TV station in the country; it had been a propaganda machine for the old dictator, Ceaucescu. But the people who ran the international MCR and got our material out for the world to see were brilliant.

The journalists and cameramen in my class in Bucharest were stunned to see the footage I had shot sixteen years ago. Many of them were kids or teenagers. Because the national broadcaster at the time had little to show, my class saw some events for the first time. My story about the reopening of the opposition newspaper even featured the boss of one of the stations that had sent three journalists to the class! The footage of sixteen years ago laid the foundation for one of the best classes I have had. Some stories come full circle.

The Reuters Foundation Workshops offer Noonan a different perspective than he would have in the same location as a cameraman. It helps him connect with the culture on a more personal level. Teaching and exchanging ideas through different customs and languages is a learning experience for both student and teacher. I'm always lucky because, when I go to these countries, I'm there with our local cameraman. I get a chance at an insider's view of the life in that country. I feel very privileged to be in with these people.

Whether it's teaching or shooting, Noonan's life on the road has been the fulfillment of a dream. He easily shares stories that educate and enlighten, whether he's behind the lens or in front of a class. Traveling and being a witness to all that the world has to offer keeps Noonan on the road.

Working Internationally

I've been working internationally for more than sixteen years and have visited more than eighty countries. Technology, globalization, open frontiers, and a host of other facts and factors have caused an evolution of what it means to be an international TV news cameraman. Long gone are the days when a cameraman was a member of a crew of at least half a dozen dedicated professionals.

There are many aspects of location shoots abroad that have nothing to do with good camera-work: Teamwork, planning, organization, flexibility, calmness, and an open mind. Don't expect things to work or happen like they do at home. Learn patience because things take longer to happen in some places. Trust your gut instinct about people's human qualities, but always think twice. Don't walk around with loads of gear trying to make everything look perfect, but employ some backups and alternatives. Find a good fixer in a place you don't know. That person needs to speak your language and be energetic and curious and positive. Know how to cut on a computer and deliver over the Net.

Don't do anything without telling home base, and stay in regular touch with them when abroad. Let them know what you are up to, and stay in regular contact, even if it is just a text message or e-mail every three hours to say, "Things moving along." Don't ever forget how important local journalists are on a story. Meet them, be polite, even humble, and you will learn loads and maybe make friends. They always know the story well.

Don't waste time on looking for pretty shots. Buy ten postcards and get your fixer or a taxi to take you to the places where the postcard shots were done. Saves time. If you have to feed or do a live shot with a dish, remember that satellite time is calculated in GMT (Greenwich Mean Time), not EST, Central, or anything else. There is someone who speaks English in most pharmacies.

Keep money in a hotel safety deposit box. Only take what you need daily. Don't be conspicuous by behavior, actions, or possessions. If you are unsure about food, eat something that is local and grilled. Pizza may not be good, but is safe in most places. Bottled drinks only. Carry aspirin and tummy medicine. The main reason people will ask you to travel abroad is because they expect you to come up with the goods. Consistently. And whatever you do, enjoy it as much as you can and with a smile on your face. It beats a nine to five.

British Airways flight 0799 bounces down through the last 1,000 feet of airspace. The lights of London reflect off the snow in a Charles Dickens picture of Christmas. Bart Noonan is strapped in as the bells start to chime—"Tray tables and seat backs to their full, upright position." They bank gently over neighborhood chimneys on the last leg to Heathrow.

Not far behind will be another world traveler, if you believe like little Lily Lou Noonan, her face pressed to the window watching for Santa and Dad.

CHAPTER 18

David Hands

Freelancing in
TV News

David Hands

Freelance Cameraman and Editor

Principal, Crewhouse Media Ltd. (*tvcameramen.com*), Nicosia, Cyprus

*W*hite clouds build early against a cobalt sky, fueled by the rising temperature across Eastern Africa. Staying low, peering over tall grass, freelancer David Hands works his way closer to the herd. With him are an East African correspondent, an AP photographer, and six armed rangers from the Kenyan Wildlife Society Antipoaching Unit. They've hiked two hours into the bush following a group of elephants for a story on ivory poaching.

The story is as much about the Antipoaching Unit working the refuge as it is about the elephants and their precious ivory tusks. When there's a good shot of an elephant, Hands steadies himself and rolls a few seconds. The elephants that were getting nervous being followed by a group of men started growling and shrieking, warning us to back off. We stayed well out of their way, but continued filming. We still needed more images.

Moving through the grass, Hands captures images of rangers in camouflage scanning the horizon for poachers and danger. Framed just over their shoulders lies the herd. The record light glows in the viewfinder as he captures both elements of the story in one shot. I was behind three rangers crouched in the tall grass looking in the direction of where the herd was. Suddenly I heard a loud trumpetlike sound and an angry elephant appeared from behind a tree.

Twelve-thousand pounds of angry elephant charge at twenty-five miles per hour, closing the "safe" distance in a matter of seconds. As it got closer, I

EQUIPMENT

Sony DNW90WSP SX camera with Canon J17 × 7.7 lens

Sony DSR570 camera with Canon J14a × 8.5 lens

Sony HVR-Z1E camera

Sachtler Vision tripods

PAG NMH100 batteries with chargers

Wireless and cabled microphones

Red Eye wide-angle adaptor

Reflectors and camera lights

Dedo and Arri lighting kits

SX edit packs with microphone and speaker

Mac PowerBook with Final Cut Pro

A. Tracking a herd of elephants in Kenya.

B. Hands shooting members of the Antipoaching Unit.

C. Rangers get close to an elephant.

D. A charging elephant.

E. With his camera rolling, Hands runs to escape the charging elephant.

could feel the earth beneath my feet vibrate as the rangers started running away and firing their weapons in the air and over my head! *Flying bullets, charging elephants, rangers on the run—the situation deteriorates to pandemonium. Hands runs too, not behind the rangers shooting in his direction, not toward the charging elephant determined to crush him, but sideways, camera still rolling.*

As soon as he hits his stride, "Whoa!" The world spins in painful somersaults. Hands stares up through dancing blades of grass into blue heavens and billowing clouds, out of breath and disoriented, his broken camera digging into his back. Not bullets or elephants but a hidden tree limb stops Hands's escape. I lay there for few seconds while I could hear the elephant growling nearby. The moment I thought it was safe for me to move, I picked up the camera and ran to where the rest of the group was.

By running sideways, I turned faster than the large elephant could maneuver, so I'm not surprised the elephant did not get me. I'm more surprised I hadn't been shot by accident. The truth of the matter was that this armed unit had no experience with elephants; their job was to hunt poachers, so we could not blame them for panicking and trying to shoot us.

The viewfinder on my BVW-400 was smashed to pieces, so we were unable to continue, but did get enough pictures for the story. I filmed the whole thing, including the fall and my electrocution (live cables were hanging out) as I tried to pick the camera up.

For his adventure in Kenya, Hands is paid between $750 and $900 per day for his services and his gear. The fees are deposited directly into his company's account. He is paid on actual instead of per diem, which means he is required to provide a receipt. The stay at the Kenyan Wildlife Services Base Camp, the air fare to Nairobi and to the base camp in the National Park in a single-engine Cessna, and all other expenses are covered by the client.

My client eventually paid for the replacement camera, even though they tried to get away with it, claiming that, since I was a freelancer, it was my problem. My camera was out of action for more three weeks, in which time I received no compensation.

This is the world of a freelance television news photojournalist.

An Independent Spirit

David Hands has been freelancing out of Nicosia, Cyprus, covering famine, disease, natural disasters, and the wars in Bosnia, Somalia, Zaire, Rwanda, Burundi, South Sudan, Israel, Lebanon, Kosovo, and Iraq. His global client base is made up of ABC, CBS, and CNN; BBC, ITN, and Channel 4, Sky in the United Kingdom; and in Germany ZDF and ARD. I cover anything, anywhere, mostly Middle East, Africa, and Eastern Europe.

Hands chose Nicosia as his base for several reasons. It's safe for his family, with a good standard of living, and Cyprus is situated in the middle of three continents; he can get to the story fast. It's also his home country, being born to Anglo-Cypriot parents and having moved from London to Cyprus when he was very young.

The roads to freelancing are as varied as the dirt paths and blacktops that crisscross the globe. Each person finds the path when ready for the journey.

Hands's independent spirit came early in his life. I was an amateur photographer since I was fifteen. I had no interest in other school lessons. I was kicked out of school one year before graduation and then attended a paid school just to get the high school diploma.

Hands went through college studying "Graphic Arts and Advertising Design." It was the closest to photography that was available at the time in Cyprus. After college, I could not get a job as a graphic designer mainly because I could not draw even if my life depended on it. I went to the U.K. to look for a job and, after four months of mostly rejections, unemployment, and construction work, I came back to Cyprus and got a job in a racing car shop (every kid's dream—got to drive some cool cars).

A good friend of Hands who thought playing with racing cars was a waste of time introduced him to a relative who owned a photo studio. When they saw Hands's still photographs, he was offered a job as an assistant. I took the job (huge pay cut) and worked there for two years. I became the studio photographer for advertising and portraits and did lots of weddings. I was also responsible for all black-and-white developing and printing.

The photo studio had a sister company that shot film and video. When they needed extra help, Hands volunteered and got his first taste of filmmaking. The company shot on 35 mm motion picture film, and Hands was brought on as first assistant camera.

From there, Hands went to work for another video production house, which was considered the best in Cyprus. Even though his experience in video was limited, within three weeks he was promoted to chief cameraman. I got the job based on my still photography, but I spent all my first few weeks learning everything I could about video. During the holidays, the studio was closed, so I spent every day and every night learning how to edit. It took me nine hours to make my first dissolve as the "edit enable" switch on the vision mixer was not enabled. Even though I was happy working as a director of photography for a production house, I started growing more and more apprehensive about my future.

Again, Hands's independent spirit called as he and his girlfriend opened their own photographic studio, shooting advertising and fashion. Their biggest fear was the loss of a steady income. "Will I have any work?" I wondered. I was young, and those fears were less scary than if I had to do it all over again now at thirty-seven years old. My confidence was riding high, and some people I worked with believed that I could do it alone. Some offered support, and some of the clients that I worked with also offered jobs. I was moving from being a DP at a film production studio to being a photographer. There was no competition between my new venture and my old job.

Focus on Shooting and Editing

The studio was short-lived, ended by a phone call from Vanguard TV, a company that provided crews for international news assignments. The equipment was owned by Vanguard TV, and the crews were all freelance. Hands took an assignment in Lebanon as a soundman/assistant to "learn the ropes." I knew nothing about how to make news. I loved it. By the second day, I knew this was what I wanted to do from now on. Next they sent me to Bosnia for six months as a soundman with ABC. In those six months, I learned how news is made and I learned how to edit fast. This proved to be a good move, as I was watching and learning from others and did not have the pressure that a cameraman has. I realized that competition for camera work was fierce, and I wanted to be sure when I did it that I would be good enough to get more.

One day I just announced that I was now a cameraman/editor. I turned down any job as a soundman until they finally gave me my first shoot, again for ABC News in Bosnia. The rest is history, as they say.

Vanguard TV wanted to open an office in Nairobi and offered Hands the job of setting it up and being their cameraman/editor. They provided equipment and a guarantee of eight-days-a-month work. In Nairobi, Hands continued to learn how to work on his own and how to deal with clients. That knowledge made Hands even more independent. In 1998, I left and took a long break by going to Thailand for a month and then to Australia for seven months.

While on break, a Nairobi client recommended Hands for a contract in Jerusalem with RTL4 Holland and RTL Germany. Luckily, Hands accepted the contract. While working in Israel, he fell in love with his producer, Petra, and got married. I had enough from the story and the living in Israel. With Petra and her daughter, Maya, we decided to live in a peaceful place, so we moved to Cyprus. We had nothing arranged—I had no work and neither did Petra. The only sure thing was that Maya was going to a good school. Slowly, I picked up work and Petra was offered a job as head of broadcast in Hellas Sat, a Greek Satellite company.

Turning Freelance

In Cyprus, Hands established his base as a freelancer. It was do or die for the young family as they carved out their lives and charted a course filled with uncertainty. Freelancing is not for everyone. Some people need security in their life. As a freelancer, you have a lot of time on your hands that is up to you to fill in before boredom takes over. Sometimes it can take months before your next job, and in those months you need to keep yourself from going insane. Freelancing is a loner's job. You need to be a person happy to be on your own.

Often people have said to me that they would love having my life. I remember once my brother, also in TV but behind a desk, married with two kids, was giving me a lift to the airport so I could catch a flight to yet another adventure. He said he wished he was coming with me, and I replied that I wished I could stay home with my family. The grass is always greener on the other side.

When You're a Freelancer, You're Running a Small Company

Being a good cameraperson is not enough; you need to market yourself and handle the business aspects of your company. The company of "you" will have all the complications of any small company, with some additional ramifications because of the nature of the industry. Hands's experience with his personal companies sheds light on concerns anyone contemplating going freelance should consider. It takes much more than hanging a shingle.

Open for Business

You need to think about setting up and remaining within the law. That means either setting up a company or working as self-employed (each one has advantages/disadvantages, depending on where you live). Either way, you need to pay social security, income tax, VAT (value added tax in Europe), and you need to have liability insurance. You need an accountant to keep the books for you. Of course, all this costs money, which comes from your own pocket.

Marketing

There is no point in being freelance if no one knows you are there. This is something that I know I lack, and many others do also. You need to be self-promoting, to be able to talk and convince a client that you are as good as you say you are. This is not as easy as it sounds. You need a certain degree of arrogance for this.

Public Relations

You need to keep up with your clients. Most of my clients have also become friends, so it is easy to keep up and learn their news.

Training

You need to stay ahead of technology and techniques, so you need to spend time and money learning all the time. I am the type of person who likes to be self-taught. I would spend weeks learning something new.

Hands recently heard from a colleague about a high-paying, two-month editing contract in Baghdad. There was a shortage of experienced Final Cut Pro editors wanting to work in a war zone. Even though the job for the colleague and Hands was uncertain, he said he'd be ready to go in a month. For three weeks,

Hands trained on the system. Unfortunately, he did not get the job so he did not need me. But I learned a new program and kept busy for a while.

Insurance

When it comes to health and travel insurance, equipment insurance, social security, income tax—everything, you are on your own. Many of the big networks will insure you when you are on a job, especially a dangerous one, but that only covers you when you are working for them. In between, you have nothing. I remember once, in Australia, I met a freelance cameraman with his own gear who broke his leg very badly. He was not insured, and he was going to be out of action for more than four months. He had a mortgage to pay off his camera gear. He was left stranded with no help and no income.

Also, sometimes you get sick after the assignment is over. I got malaria by being in Burundi once, but I did not get sick until two days after I was back in Nairobi. Malaria was not expensive to treat, but I was out of action for two to three weeks when I couldn't earn any money. It is almost impossible to claim this from any company. The same happened when I got amoebic dysentery in Egypt. So it is important to have good insurance, but that can prove expensive and sometimes hard to get. Most insurance companies will not insure you for high-risk zones and, if you do get coverage because of the high risk, it's expensive.

Now I have full coverage for all equipment in the field. This insurance will cover damage and loss, but has some restrictions, such as not covered if stolen from inside a vehicle that was left unattended and no coverage for war-related incidents (bullet holes and such). The cost is about 3.5 percent of the total value of the equipment.

Expenses

All the expenses you have as a freelancer are your responsibility unless these expenses occur while on assignment. As a freelancer, you are expected to cover all the expenses needed to get you there. It is rare that a client will give you money in advance for expenses. Of course, if I think that the client is not reliable, I will ask for money up front, but that is rare. So all expenses, flights, taxis, and anything else has to be paid by me first and then I get it reimbursed on my final invoice.

All expenses while on location are dealt with by the client. Different companies use either of two methods:

- All expenses are paid by the client. This includes all job expenses, laundry, and all meals and drinks. Personal expenses such us alcohol, cigarettes, entertainment are not covered.
- The client pays a per diem, a fixed amount that you receive every day that you are on the job. Companies usually have a table on the amount depending on the country you are in. An average amount is $65 per day. This amount is to cover food and drinks. All other work-related expenses are covered by the client (hotels, laundry, taxis, and so on).

Making and Keeping Money

I have my standard daily rate, but my rate will drop slightly when (1) it's a long shoot, more than 10 days or (2) it's a regular client. The longer the shoot is, the lower I may go on my rate—a bit like a package deal. But that also depends on the client. Some clients demand a lot more from you than others. A small station means that I would be doing one story a day. I would shoot during the day, edit early evening, feed, and the have the rest of the evening off. And some days we would not produce stories, especially on weekends. But the international, twenty-four-hour news stations are a lot more demanding, with stories throughout the day and night. Usually the big, twenty-four-hour ones have more than one crew but, work is more and harder. I like working for both for their own reasons. When the shoot is worth it, I am also willing to work without my gear. Once the day rate is established, we then talk about costs of disposables such as tapes.

I ask for one-third payment in advance if they are new clients or not well known in the industry. In some extreme cases, I insist on payment of invoice before tapes are delivered. Normally, I invoice at the end of shoot, payable within thirty days. That rarely ever happens, but I expect to receive payment within sixty days.

I use basic bookkeeping methods by using Microsoft's Money. The important thing with recordkeeping is to keep all receipts and remember to include them on relevant invoices, which should be clear and honest. Any faulty accounting can lead to delayed payments and unnecessary time wasted trying to sort it out. Also, you have to make sure that the invoice goes to the right person.

Currency is a problem when working internationally. I used to charge all non-European clients in U.S. dollars, but because the dollar dropped so low, I now only charge in Euros; that has a constant rate with the Cyprus Pound. At the end of the day, the money I make needs to be converted to the currency in the country I live in, so I keep an eye on exchange rates.

Honesty is very important for a freelancer. After all, your client, who may not know you that well, is entrusting you with confidentiality and money. When on a shoot, all expenses are paid by the client. That means that you need to keep receipts, which are not always possible. For example, in Africa bribing is common and of course you get no receipt for it. You need to build such a trust with your clients that, when you tell them you have to pay $100 to get through the border, they believe you. Cheating them with expenses is easy but stupid. You may make a hundred dollars, but you stand to lose a client who in the long run will give you thousands.

Word gets around, and company accountants are known to compare notes. I once heard a story that someone was caught cheating with expenses simply because two accountants from different companies were having lunch together. One said to the other that the Bosnian war was costing them a lot of money, and the other was surprised. Once they compared notes, they figured out that there was no consistency between the two crews on the ground. After an investigation, a few people were distressfully fired.

A Freelancer's Camera and Equipment

As a freelancer, you have two choices. One is to have your own gear. The format depends on what the majority of clients need. During the 1990s, it was easy because it was only Betacam SP. But by the late 1990s and early 2000s, Betacam SX, DVCPRO, DVCam, and Digibeta all came into the picture, making the choice of format harder. The other option is to rent the gear, which is a good way to go if you have different clients using different formats. This is not the best financial way, but it is safer as you do not have the initial investment and the cost of maintenance and insurance.

Most of the time, the clients choose which format they want. If not, then the format is chosen by me according to the budget and the story. When shooting high-end productions, I add a matte box with filters: graduate ND, graduate sunset, white soft, black soft, polarizer. For black mist, I sometimes use a nylon stocking stretched over the lens.

To Buy or Rent

Hands asks the following questions when deciding to make an equipment purchase or simply rent and return.

- What is the cost of the equipment, complete, to buy?
- What is the cost of equipment to rent?
- What is the life span of the equipment? Is it something that will be out of date soon?
- Will I use it regularly, or is it a specialist kit that I may not ever use again?
- Does it have high maintenance costs?
- How much money will it return from the confirmed booking?
- What is the availability of renting the equipment on short notice?
- Will I have new opportunities for work if I own this piece of equipment?

The following is an example in dollars that will help direct anyone to make a purchase/or-not decision. Here are the factors:

- A kit costing $10,000 to buy might rent for $100 per day.
- The kit has a long life span and requires little or no maintenance.
- The confirmed booking is for ten days.
- I think I will use it again for another forty days maximum.

With this equation, I would rather rent as I only have $1,000 guaranteed and I estimate that I will only make $5,000 back in total. So that is a loss of $5,000.

But if I think I can use it for more than a hundred days, then it is worth buying. Plus, I always have the option of selling it if, as time goes by, I do not think it will reach the target of return. Also, I do take into consideration the fact that if we own a piece of equipment it will always be available whenever we need it.

How Do You Start Freelancing?

You've established the company. You've got the gear. What's next? You need to have already established yourself in the industry and have made some contacts. You are on a high when there is work and clients keep calling; you are at a low when there is a breaking news story and nobody called you. If that happens, you need to get everybody informed that you exist.

Hands's clients come from all over the world. From national networks to small production companies, they find him through his reputation. All a freelancer has is a reputation, so treat yours and the people you work with as if it were gold.

Don't just sit by the phone and wait for a call. Freelancers need to market themselves and let the world know where they are. If there is a breaking news story, Hands will often call clients and let them know he's available for work. In some cases, Hands gets hired when clients don't want to send their own staff into a danger zone. Hands keeps an up-to-date demo reel ready to go should a client request one. Some clients find him through his online listings.

Advice to beginners: Take all jobs that come along to gain experience and contacts. Eat humble pie to begin with. You have to be prepared to prove yourself over and over again. Respect the ones that have been there and done it; in return, they will help out.

International Freelancers

You need to be able to adapt, country to country. You need to know the culture and respect it; then they respect you back. I found out that if you show respect to the people, they usually help you out more than they should. I also try and learn a few words of their own language, as it helps with breaking the ice. In most cultures, people find foreigners speaking a few broken words so funny that you instantly make friends as they try and teach you more. I also try and learn the right way of greeting people; for example, in Muslim countries you greet them by placing your right arm on your chest as you say, "salaam alaikum" *(peace with you)*. When entering a mosque or an Arab house, you need to take your shoes off.

Note: Always wear socks with no holes in them; otherwise, it is embarrassing. On Shabbat, religious Jews do not like to be filmed. Once, in Rwanda, I got caught filming something that I was told by the military specifically not to film. They were so pissed off that a guy stuck his AK47 assault rifle in my face and cocked it, ready to shoot. The soldier spoke no English and no French. A fellow journalist said to him in broken Swahili something on the lines of "Take it easy. We are all friends." Suddenly, he burst out laughing at the sound of the broken Swahili, and that released the tension. It saved my life.

You also need to be aware of the sensitivities of a place. For example, if you are talking to a Palestinian, you should not call the West Bank by its Jewish name, Judea. That will not go down very well. At a Croatian checkpoint, a friend accidentally showed his Serbian press card. The sight of Serb official cards pissed off the Croats so much that they almost shot him on the spot. It was only by talking to them that he was let go at the end.

As a freelancer, you are often on your own; there's no big corporation that will come to your aid and rescue you at the last minute. In his constant quest to be completely self-reliant, Hands has been through AKE Group's Hostile Environment Training. Being prepared reflects well on you and your clients and may also save your life.

The Fraternity of Freelancers

Freelance cameramen in the early 1990s were a bit like a boys' club. We all knew each other, and we were all glad to be in a war. Jokes and pranks were many, and I think, looking back at it, that was what kept us sane. In every big news story, there is always a hotel that most journalists stay in. In Kigali, it was the Mille Colline hotel (watch the movie *Hotel Rwanda*). Staying in the main journalist hotel is always my preference, as I get to see so many of my friends. It's like a school reunion. People that you have not seen for a while are all gathered together, and you get to hear their news and tell yours. You have friends to go out for a drink with and talk to about anything, but mostly you talk about the story. You also talk about story ideas and safety issues. You find the people who are interested in the same story you are doing (but are not competition), so you travel together just to feel safer.

As a freelancer, you can always turn down assignments that you do not want or do not feel are safe. I think it's becoming more dangerous to cover stories because more and more people have access to television and do not like what they see and take it out on the messenger. A lot more camerapeople are running around in war zones, so that has two effects: More there, more killed. Also, I believe the novelty status that a cameraman has in a war zone has been diminished a bit. What I mean is that, in places where there are only few of us, the locals treat us nicer. When there are too many of us, we lose the individuality and we are all accountable for any cameraman's mistake.

I once read "Too far, and you do not get the picture; too close, and you do not live to see it." Safety first, but not to the point that you cannot work; after all, you are in a war zone. I always want to know where I'm going, what the dangers are there, where the dangerous spots are, a get-away route, safe spots, and so on. I get this information by asking anyone who may have information. Never, ever try and be a hero. No image is worth dying for. Also, the people you are with have to be of the same mindset that you are. If there is one stupid "hero," then things can get rough as they try and force you into doing something that you would usually not do. Stand your ground if you believe you are right. It is better to have one idiot thinking you are a coward than to be dead.

It's Not Always about a Day Rate

For me as a freelancer, Tingi-Tingi was an eye opener. *Hands was staying at a small hotel in Goma, Zaire, while working for the Swiss. They were covering the large refugee camp in Goma when a rumor that Tingi-Tingi, a small camp in the middle of the rain forest, was in a bad state. The only way in was on a UN flight, with the possibility of not making it back the same day. A day in Tingi-Tingi would be hell; a night, unimaginable. Hands teamed up with a BBC journalist and hopped the C130 cargo plane that was taking in medical supplies and bringing out the wounded.*

On the Ground in Tingi-Tingi
The rebel army forced the evacuation of Tingi-Tingi. All that remained were those who were dead or too weak to leave, scattered on the ground with the waste and refuse of an abandoned camp. In the distance, Hands saw a small child in a black blanket lying on the ground.

As I approached the small child, I noticed that the blanket covering her was moving in an unusual fashion. As I got even closer, the blanket seemed to rise to the air and I realized the small child was covered by millions of flies. I was no threat to them, and they slowly settled down again.

I walked around the child, my eyes scanning the skinny body, and as I came to the face my sight just locked on it. Now, I did not know if I should shoot film or not. She once must have been beautiful, and I could imagine her playing in the same spot where she was now lying. Her eyes were shut, her skin was withdrawn back into the bone, her cheeks were no longer visible, and her head seemed out of proportion with the rest of her skinny body. Her wrinkled, aged skin barely covered her bones; it was holding on as a last attempt to protect her. This was an image that will haunt me for the rest of my life.

I got my senses back momentarily, and I realized that this was going to be a fantastic shot. I had the dead child's body in my foreground and the deserted refugee camp in the background. I set up my tripod, ready to film this amazing shot, when this breathless child, this dead child, opened her eyes and stared straight into mine. She desperately tried to focus her swollen eyes, probably only seeing a bare shadow standing above her. She seemed frightened; maybe she thought I was one of the soldiers who caused her this suffering returning to finish her off. But as her eyes slowly adjusted to the light, she did not see a soldier but a white man standing above her motionless. With all the strength she could muster, she forced all her remaining energy into raising her hand toward me. Her palms were slightly open and her lips were moving, but I could not hear what she was saying. I began to feel helpless.

Like a man possessed, I called out for help. Charlie, the UNICEF officer, came running up the hill and, when he saw what I was seeing, he froze, just like I did a few moments before. Once the initial shock was over, Charlie bent down and gave her some water. That is when I started filming my first shot. I knew I had missed the best shots earlier, and for once this did not seem to matter. We organized a stretcher and took her to the field hospital, and once she was in the hands of experts, I turned and walked away. I do not even know her name, but she has been with me ever since.

When I got back, we went to the BBC makeshift edit room and I handed my tape to the editor. As he started playing the tape, everyone fell silent. The pictures were the strongest pictures to that point that anyone had seen. This was not because of me but because of the situation. Nevertheless, everybody in the room congratulated me for an excellent job. As a freelancer, this was great as I not only pleased the Swiss, who were paying me, but also proved myself to another client, the BBC. I do believe that after this job I was moved up in their lineup. I think this story played a major factor a year later when I was offered a staff job with them. Ironically, one of the reasons I turned down the BBC offer was because of this story. I had had enough in Africa and I wanted out.

At night, back in the hotel, while I was trying to force myself to eat something, my pictures appeared on French Satellite TV. The room was full of journalists, photographers, cameramen, and locals. Everyone again fell silent as they were watching pictures from a place so near but yet so isolated. Another great strike for a freelancer, this was an exclusive and everyone knew they were my pictures. But instead of this making me glow and feel on top of the world, I felt I was in a dark pit with no light around. I remember very strongly how alone I felt and how low I felt as a human being.

Tingi-Tingi questioned my humanity and the work of a freelancer. My high income and my well-

Aid workers comfort the young girl in Tingi-Tingi.

being depended so much on other people's misery. Without wars and suffering, I would not have had so much work. Sometimes we even joked, saying that a freelance cameraman would never be unemployed as there will always be wars. I felt like a pimp making money from the hardship of the prostitute. I figured out that my rate of $900 per day was enough to feed this child for years in a place where the average income was $30 per month.

Putting things in this perspective does eventually drive you mad.

I now know that things are not that simple, but it had a major effect on my life as a person and as a freelancer. After this story, I became more willing to drop my rate and go on an assignment that I felt was worth telling. Tingi-Tingi made me realize that the greatest gain from being a news cameraman was not the high income but the impact your pictures could have in making things better. This, of course, is an indirect and uncontrollable effect that you may have and it does sometimes make things worse. But I can live with that as long as I know that I went for the right reasons and that my intentions were honest.

One of the things that is only now becoming apparent is the physiological effect that experiences such as this have on people. Companies now see this and provide psychological assistance to their personnel who have been exposed to "some serious shit." But as a freelancer, you are on your own as the psychological strain may not just come from one assignment alone. And if it does, no company will cover a freelancer. After all, how can you prove that what happened to your mind happened at a specific assignment?

Freelancing Is Not for Everyone

You need to have the personality that goes with it. Freelancing is not a job, but it is a lifestyle. You need to be comfortable to drop everything at a moment's notice and hit the road running. But you also need to be comfortable sitting at home for weeks on end. Boredom is a great factor in a freelancer's life. This is where one can distinguish if they are cut out for freelancing. I know fellow cameramen who spend their free time making furniture or are simply being happy playing computer games. I used to kill my time with photography, and, in 1999, I made *tvcameramen. com*, which has kept me busy when not shooting.

You also need understanding family and friends. I have missed many Christmases and many birthdays; I even missed my mother's last moments. But when I heard that my mother was ill, I flew straight back to Cyprus and told her that I was thinking of moving back just to be with her. She gave me the bollocks. She did not want me to stop my career for her, she understood why I was away, and she did go on to add that I need to do what I do. This kind of support, I must admit, I had throughout my life from many dear to me, and they are the ones who made me who I am. Not the job, but my family and friends. The same with my wife. She understands why I need to do this.

You need to be able to survive without the feeling of "security" that so many people seek in life. When I uprooted my family and moved to Cyprus, neither my wife nor I had any income. We were both in our mid-thirties with a teenage child. The only certainty was that we were going to spend a lot of money with this move. We would have to rent a place, buy a car, and put the kid in a private school, and all this without an income. But we both felt confident that we could handle it and, indeed, we did. But I realize that many people think of me as foolish to make these

Crewhouse Media Ltd. specializes in production and providing crews for international clients and is now home to a network of freelance television photojournalists.

risky moves. The truth is that nothing is done foolishly. If you believe in yourself and have faith that things are going to work out, they usually do.

I also have my insecurities about "security," especially as I get older, but the thing I always try and remember is that there is no point being "secure" and unhappy. And after all, we only live once so we might as well make the best of it.

In 2005, Hands joined two other freelance cameramen and formed Crewhouse Media Ltd., a company that specializes in production and providing crews for international clients. This move was important for me, as I joined like-minded people and I no longer stand alone; we are all there to offer support to each other if and when needed. For someone who spent his life as a freelancer, this is the obvious next step.

Now Crewhouse is home to a network of freelance television photojournalists working worldwide, with an emphasis on the Middle East, Africa, and Europe. In addition to shooting and running a company, Hands owns and manages tvcameramen.com, *an online magazine with industry articles, equipment reviews, classified ads, and insider tips.*

Through all his endeavors, David Hands uses his freelance experience to support and educate the community of television photojournalists. His work behind the lens and in the industry has made a difference.

CHAPTER 19

Rustin Thompson

From News to
Independent Documentaries

Rustin Thompson
Director of Photography

Independent Documentary Filmmaker
White Noise Productions, Seattle
Best Documentary, Chicago Underground Film Festival and Portland Festival
of World Cinema
Gold Jury Prize, Chicago Underground Film Festival
National Emmy, Best Breaking News

*L*ate in the afternoon, the air is wet and the sky is dark gray. All the color has been drained from the streets as throngs of demonstrators stand opposite a line of police.

Like a press clipping from the 1960s, they wave banners and chant slogans of peace and protest. The scene is complete with a young man handing flowers to policemen, while acoustic guitars strum on the street corner. Rustin Thompson has entered a time machine, and the images from decades past now play in his viewfinder. It's like living in Haskell Wexler's 1969 film Medium Cool. Almost on cue, peaceful protest turns to confrontation.

In dark riot gear with faces obscured by gas masks and visors, they march toward the crowd. Yesterday's friendly neighborhood cop, today's storm trooper, part of a faceless wall of authority summoned to control the crowd. It's a time machine for them, too. Each side plays the role it has been assigned; all can see what's coming.

Welcome to the 1999 World Trade Organization Convention in Seattle, Washington, which is host to 350 delegates from 173 countries gathered to discuss global trade policies. Outside, 50,000 demonstrators pack the downtown

EQUIPMENT

Sony HVR-V1U HDV Pro camcorder
Sony TRV-9 and PD-150 cameras
Tram lavalier
Sony ECM lavalier
Azden SGM1X shotgun mic
Sennheiser wireless
Sony wireless
Sachtler fluid head
Canon wide-angle adaptor
Canon 2x extender
Canon macro adaptor
Hoodman cover for flip-out viewfinder
Lowel Tota-lights
Chimera soft boxes
Riffa light

A. At the Seattle WTO meeting, 50,000 demonstrators protest.

B. King County police in a stand-off with protestors in downtown Seattle.

C. A bottleneck develops as protestors stop delegates from attending the WTO meeting.

D. Police-fired tear gas scatters people.

E. Demonstrators light a dumpster on fire.

area in an attempt to keep delegates away and disrupt the meetings. The primary debate is free trade versus environmental and labor interests, but in the street many other causes attach themselves to the protest.

Chants turn to yells, yells to screams, as rubber bullets and tear gas canisters bounce off buildings in a crowded intersection. Thompson's decision to go on his own is now being realized. Limping from a rubber bullet, with a bandana over his nose and mouth to keep the tear gas at bay, Thompson clearly looks more like a guerilla filmmaker than the traditional network news photographer he was just days before. Today, his transition into documentary filmmaker has been cemented. I'd been capturing images of increasing agitation, threat, and confrontation. Suddenly we were inundated with tear gas canisters. People were overturning dumpsters and garbage cans, trying to hide behind them as the cops were shooting rubber bullets.

This is getting ugly. Someone sets one of the dumpsters on fire. I begin to wonder if I should be concerned for my safety. The demonstrators are sticking it out, so I decide I'm going to stick it out, too.

The crowd demands the release of demonstrators held at the King County jail.

A cloud of gas rolls down the urban boulevard, strolling with the gentle breeze. Thompson easily moves with the crowd, capturing images on a mini digital video camera not much larger than a beer can. It was very liberating just being down on the streets shooting it all. I still felt I had the cachet of a legitimate news photojournalist because I had the press credentials, so I was able to go back behind police lines. I thought, "Huh, this is interesting. I've got the credibility of a legitimate newsperson, but I've got the sensibility of a guerrilla filmmaker." I liked the feel of that. "Maybe this could lead somewhere."

Thompson is now an independent. No longer backed by the networks, he's on his own. Without a clear vision of how his footage will be used, he simply follows his intuition as years of news experience pay dividends for his lens.

He hears the rhythmic sound first; it's different from all the others. Thompson hits record as he turns toward the street. A squadron of police in riot gear bang their legs with batons as they march in unison, the drumming sounds echoing off downtown buildings. The moment unfolds in front of Thompson's camera with the sound playing a powerful role supporting the story and, at some point in the future, placing the viewer at the scene. I decided to shoot using only the microphone on the camera, which is usually something you wouldn't do, especially with smaller digital video cameras. But from my news background I knew what would work. I had a plan.

By getting close to the action, not only would I get better shots, but I also would get better sound. I also realized that a lot of the sound was coming from speakers, people singing, and people talking into megaphones. I would just point my camera directly at the source and the sound would be good. Once I figured out the sound thing, that really freed me up and I thought, "This is really going to work." I just loved the fact that I was often surrounded by cameramen from ABC, CBS, NBC, all of the foreign networks, and they all had the big cameras that I used to have. With my little camera, I found myself way ahead of these guys, always getting to a place before they could. I didn't need to check with a producer or reporter. It was really liberating for me as a cameraman to decide where to go and get there fast.

Thompson continues shooting the events surrounding the five-day WTO Convention, wondering where his footage might find an audience, questioning his decision to go it alone, and relying on his instincts and training from television news to guide him and his lens through the protest.

Police make a show of force to discourage more protesting.

Breaking Free from the Past

Thompson's journey in the time machine and to an independent lens began a few days before the WTO Convention with a call from CBS News, his main freelance client. They wanted me to go to the eastern part of the state and shoot a story on trade involving apples, because the WTO is all about trade. I didn't really want to leave Seattle and shoot something on trade. I asked, "Don't you think the real story is going to be here in Seattle with all the demonstrations?" The person at the news desk in Los Angeles said they didn't really care about people waving signs and standing on street corners chanting—that's not really going to be a big story. The real story is trade; that is the issue.

I remember I had this moment where I thought, "If I turn down this gig with CBS, I'm walking away from something like five- to seven-thousand dollars." I thought, "Okay, I can either hook up with these guys and make a lot of money and be stuck possibly doing live interviews all day long on a street corner or I can go my own route." At that moment, I turned down the job, and I think that was the key breaking point for me.

Thompson picked up press credentials for the WTO Convention, hoping to get work with one of the nongovernmental agencies that were coming to Seattle. We started to hear rumbles that there were going to be protest demonstrations in the streets, and this was going to be a big deal as they would try to shut the WTO Convention down. I had recently bought a small mini digital camera just to play around with. It was still new technology, and I was thinking I'd go down on the street and shoot some stuff. I went with my little camera and started shooting on the first day of the WTO. Sure enough, as the week progressed all hell did break loose and there were protests, riots, vandalism, and arrests. This is crazy.

Postproduction: A Documentary Voice Emerges

Two months after the tear gas had cleared, the crowds and delegates returned home, and city life returned to normal, it is time again for the annual Seattle International Film Festival. The tiny video cassettes will play again. I hadn't touched the footage in quite a while when I heard the film festival was coming up. I thought, "Hey, why don't I make a documentary? I'll just start putting it together." I wasn't making a lot of money at the time, and this was before you could purchase a home-editing system like Final Cut Pro or Avid Express. I rented an Avid suite that I had installed in my house. It cost me $2,000 for the one week, and I started to just put a film together in a week.

With the clock ticking, Thompson assembles his first pass at a documentary. The conventional approach tries to cover all the trade issues with an objective point of view. A script is written, and a scratch narration is matched with Thompson's footage for a short test run. It was a third-person, omniscient, objective, very PBS-style narration, and it sucked. It was horrible;

Police breathe their own tear gas after protestors throw the canisters back at them.

I sounded like I had no authority, and it was boring. I showed it to three or four people, and they said, "Well, Russ, I don't know, this doesn't sound like you. What are you doing with this?"

I realized at that point that the only way I could make it work was to do it as a first-person point of view of a journalist in the streets, having my consciousness raised not only by the issues surrounding world trade but also by the common citizens of this country, still being able to rise up and have their voices heard outside normal bureaucratic channels. That way, too, it freed me up from having to cover trade issues. It freed me up from having to use other footage, which I really didn't want to do. I can tell the truth in this documentary, the truth the way I see it. I was able to shoot myself looking at the footage in the editing room while commenting on what I saw. That was a valid viewpoint, and to this day many of the positive comments about the film are about that aspect.

The Cameraman Is Often Silent

I think it's interesting to finally hear from a cameraman on what he was thinking, what he was looking at, and what he was listening for while shooting. It's a valuable perspective because cameramen are the first ones to experience what we see on the screen. Doing a documentary the way I did it, for the first time I was able to talk about that. Everything from the conflicts and tear gas to more random thoughts like, "When will these people get tired and go home?" and "Where were they all going to the bathroom? There's no place around here."

It was important to me to try and make the film without anybody else's footage. I don't know if I would have made the film if I hadn't gotten the footage that I did. I was lucky to be in a few places where there was really dramatic stuff going on. I wanted that through line of all of this footage to be mine because then I could comment on it.

By taking this first-person approach and being very honest about what I was feeling, it set my documentary apart from the three or four documentaries that were made about the same subject. It was only while I was actually editing the film that I thought, "Oh my God, I'm making my first independent feature documentary."

Along with editing his first documentary, Thompson was also writing an article for MovieMaker Magazine *about filmmaker Jean Luc Godard. From his research into Godard came the inspiration for the title of the documentary,* 30 Frames a Second: The WTO in Seattle. The title, *30 Frames a Second*, comes from a Godard quote in *Le Petite Soldat*: "Film is truth at 24 frames a second." What that means is film is only a subjective truth; it can only be what I choose to contain in the viewfinder. I thought this was appropriate for my film, too, so I changed it to *30 Frames a Second* because that's the rate of video. The film is about "my truth."

White Noise Opens in Seattle

After completing the seventy-two-minute documentary, Thompson entered it in a few film festivals, where it began winning awards. It won best documentary at three or four of the festivals, and I realized that I could really make a living, make a go of this as a filmmaker.

Around the same time my wife was getting tired of her job in public relations, so we decided to start a documentary production company, White Noise Productions. We took a look at the new digital technology and saw you could buy an entire system—camera, editing, the whole thing—for about 15,000 bucks, and that's what we did. We got a loan, we set up our own home studio, and we started contacting the local nonprofit agencies in our area because that's what we wanted our niche to be. We didn't want to work for corporations, and we didn't want to work for news organizations. We wanted to do our own thing.

We started marketing ourselves as documentary-style filmmakers for nonprofit organizations. Our approach was to apply documentary techniques and storytelling to give the nonprofit issue or agenda an emotional resonance for the viewer. We started making money, and at the same time I was able to do a couple of other independent documentaries on the side. Once I realized that I could now have complete creative control—I could shoot, edit, write, and do music; my wife could write and produce, and we could do our own interviews—I never looked back. I never took another network freelance job.

The Transition from Television News to Independent Documentaries

Thompson started his career as a television news photographer in the early 1980s, working his way from local news to freelance network assignments around the world. His background proved to be the perfect experience for the transition into documentaries. In news, every single day you're going out and making a little film; you're getting this wealth of skills, which is a tremendous value, and, as your skills become assimilated, they become second nature. Experience is the key to learning how to be a good storyteller with your camera.

I realized while I was shooting the documentary that I didn't have to worry about a lot of stuff that the other guys out there, with those little digital video cameras, were worrying about. My news background paid off in that I didn't have to think about composition or back lighting or sound in the ways that they had to worry about. All the decisions that you make when you're a news cameraman working in very competitive situations—those were just second nature to me.

Thompson adds the skills he learned shooting the Seattle Seahawks and Seattle Sonics to those that are essential to him and his documentary. I tell people that shooting sports is great training for knowing how to move the camera either on a tripod or on your shoulder. You need to follow the ball, and you need to do it by keeping things in focus. You need to anticipate, know the arc of the ball, and have a sense of the length of a playing field. That came to bear in the documentary when a big melee broke out and cops were lobbing tear gas canisters. Even though they were really difficult to see, I knew enough to see something being thrown from a cop's hand and I was able to focus on that object and follow its trajectory. It landed and exploded, and that was just like shooting sports.

Improvisation is an essential skill in television photojournalism and documentary production. Adapting to the environment and making the tools at hand work to your advantage allow you to focus more on the story and less on technical distractions. I didn't have a tripod when I was out shooting, and I'm really glad I didn't, but I still had to make sure the image was absolutely steady. When you're out in that kind of situation, you go with what you can get. If you really need a shot that's steady, you set it on a trashcan, you put it on a curb, you use your hand underneath it to be a little wedge brace to make a steady shot. I was doing all those things that had taken me years and years to get comfortable with knowing how to do.

The ability you gain with experience is not only the technical aspects of composition, focus, exposure, sound, and camera movement, but also the ability to move your body when you're out in a crowd. You need to know where to hold the camera to protect it. You've got to know how to use your body to protect yourself when you're in a crowd, and you've got to be able to move and then set up quickly.

Shooting both documentary footage and news footage is about telling the stories you've seen and heard. You should be listening to as well as capturing the world in front of your lens. Listen to people and don't just think about what it is you, alone, want to get out of them; let them tell their story. You never know what's going to come up through the interview.

Everything that I use is a stripped-down version of what I used to shoot with. The skills I learned when I was shooting TV news still come to bear, but everything is just less expensive and much easier to work with as a one-man band.

People say, "Oh, I bought Final Cut Pro and I have the latest Canon camera. How do I get into the business? How do I start shooting? I don't know what to do." You just have to make a lot of product. You just have to shoot a lot of stuff, especially people who want to do documentaries. Going through a small TV news station and working every single day, getting practice and the training—that's the best way you're going to do it. I would not be where I am now if I had not put in all those years doing television news. It's invaluable.

Making Documentaries

Making documentaries is a journey of exploration and discovery. Every step is in new and uncharted territory; only your experience and cinematic aesthetics can navigate the venture. You don't quite know where the beginning, the middle, and the end are until you sit down and start looking at all the footage. Then the arc of the story becomes clear. Even if you're doing a story on a child from age six to twelve, the beginning of your story isn't necessarily going to be when he's six. It could be when he goes to middle school. It could be on his ninth birthday. You never know when the turning point in those six years will be, and that makes your story what it is; it makes your story come alive.

In any documentary, you're exploring; you just start shooting, and eventually the story reveals itself. You have to have faith that there's going to be a story. You also have to be very much aware of when there is no story. We've started a few projects where we think it could be a documentary. We go out and shoot several hours of tape, and when we come back it's obvious the story's not going to play out.

A documentary filmmaker mixes cinematic talent with the ability to both emotionally connect with real subject matter and craft that information into a compelling, feature-length story. While a news story is shot and on the air the same day, a documentary requires patience to follow the story over the course of a few months to sometimes many years. You have to have the ability to keep coming back into that emotional space of your subject matter again and again. You might shoot something for a few days and then leave that project for a month and go do something else, and then come back to it.

I think you have to approach it more artfully, too. You have to think in terms of what metaphorical images you can get. If you're coming from a news camera background, you have to start thinking beyond strictly visual images. You have to think about transitions from one part of the story to the next because you're going to be moving over a long period of time through a lot of different characters. They talk a lot in TV news about finding your character. I think that's great training, but it really comes true in documentaries. You're going to have to find your characters and know who they are. You're going to have to spend time with them and develop them, and that not only requires that you get emotionally more involved in your subject matter; it also requires patience and a willingness to be bored a little bit.

In order for a documentary to really work over an hour or an hour and a half, you've got to have a lot more going on than just sensationalizing surface issues. You've got to have real characters that you spend time with and really learn about.

Making the Leap

"Make the Leap and the Net Will Appear" is a code I've always lived by. Just decide: I'm going to do this and commit to it. Know you've got the experience and skills that are going to carry you through and that work is going to be there, the subject's going to be there, the documentary is going to come out of nowhere and fall into your lap, and you're going to be off and running. If you have confidence in your abilities and your ability with people, the leap can be made. The most important thing in making the jump is knowing your goals. Who do you want to make films for? You have to know why you're doing it.

It's a Good Time to Make Documentaries

More people are able to make independent documentaries because of the whole explosion of small, affordable equipment that allows for new filmmakers and projects. That has led to people turning in more personal, idiosyncratic stories—fewer issue-oriented, PBS-style stories. Documentaries have just become more interesting to watch. You have a greater part of the audience who finally, after all these years, have come around to consider documentary pieces as entertaining. You used to have ten documentaries a year, and five of them would be good; now you've got two hundred documentaries a year and maybe thirty of them are good.

With more documentaries in the marketplace, more are finding mainstream acceptance; with that acceptance comes ticket sales, money, and what Thompson refers to as the Hollywood formula. The formula is this: The underdog has to overcome some obstacle, usually in a competition in order to achieve an epiphany at the end, where there is some kind of prize. Whether the prize is a trophy or greater self-knowledge, it still fits the formula. The competition documentary will usually feature cute kids.

Another category in the genre is the first-person, muckracking documentaries like Michael Moore's *Fahrenheit 9/11* or Morgan Spurlock's *Supersize Me.* For those to work, you need to put yourself on camera. You need to be a real character, an extrovert who's willing to get into people's faces and challenge them.

A longtime mainstay in the documentary world is the wildlife piece, with National Geographic and Mutual of Omaha playing a large role. Found only in the backcountry of obscure television timeslots and high school AV departments until Imax came along, now wildlife documentaries are moving from the big round screen to bigger audiences. Films like *March of the Penguins* are taking wildlife documentaries beyond Imax theaters and into mainstream cinema.

Thompson has a few favorites when discussing the work of other documentarians who bring their vision to the screen. I really like the idiosyncratic profile pieces by Werner Herzog with *Grizzly Man* and Errol Morris with *The Fog of War.* I happen to like those kinds of documentaries because they're extremely well done. They're competently made, and you can really sense the director's point of view. You can really sense the auteur theory coming through on those kinds of films.

The Business of Independent Documentary Filmmaking

Independent documentaries are just that—independent. Filmmakers often need to raise funds for their projects. The goal is to be able to have the resources to complete the documentary and have it find a paying audience. Often, completion takes a mixture of available (unpaid) time, access to cameras and editing equipment, and financial aid from an outside source. If you have your own equipment and don't need to rent, there's still the cost of narration talent, music, and other finishing and distribution expenses. Your project is a commercial success if it generates more income than it cost to produce. Any margin is a good one, and larger margins allow for more freedom on your next documentary.

Thompson and White Noise Productions have raised money for their upcoming projects. In their case, they attack the project on two fronts. Because they own their own equipment, they generally start shooting to assess the viability of a documentary as soon as the decision is made to move ahead, and at the same time they begin their fundraising efforts. Their independent documentary production takes place in between the shorter documentary-style projects they do for paying clients.

Thompson outlines the potential money trail of today's independent documentary from sources for fundraising to distribution.

Grants

The International Documentary Association lists seventy grant sources on their Web site at *http://www.documentary.org/resources/grants.php.* You can apply for grants, but you're then often at the mercy of granting cycles, which are sometimes six months to a year. The Sundance Documentary Fund doesn't have grant cycles, but it's very competitive and gets a lot of applications.

Pass the Hat

Another way that we've done it is, once we've completed a film and now want to raise a little bit of money to pay for our time spent, we'll hold screenings and pass the hat and ask people to write checks. You show them clips or a rough cut from your film, and you get a bunch of little donations.

Profit from Nonprofits

When we do a documentary project, we ally ourselves with a local nonprofit cooperative—that is, a 501c3—501c3 is their tax status. It means that they're a nonprofit and if a person donates money to that nonprofit for a particular project they're representing (which would be the film we're making), that person can get a tax break. They can deduct the donation from their taxes, so if they're donating a huge amount, say $10,000, that's a good tax break. Often, the 501c3 is going to take a percentage and then disburse the funds to the filmmakers. This is one way to raise money where you don't have any tax issues.

The Independent Feature Project is a 501c3 based in New York. We work with Women Make Movies. They're a production and distribution company. There's a Seattle-based 501c3 called 911 Media Arts. A lot of cities have media arts nonprofits, places where people can come and take classes and rent equipment. Those are all 501c3s.

The 501c3s don't do any of the fundraising; we still have to do that. We still have to drum up the money. If we go to a philanthropist who does this kind of thing a lot, they say, "Yes, I'll write you a $10,000 check." We'll say, "Okay. Make it out to our 501c3 and write the name of our project on the memo line of the check." Then those funds will be deposited into an account for our film after the 501c3 takes their cut—anywhere from 5 percent to 8 percent and sometimes 10 percent.

Presell

You can also try to presell a project. If you get hooked up with HBO or Showtime, they will sometimes agree to buy the film from you ahead of time so you can go ahead, make the film, and know you're selling it.

If you're doing a documentary with a particular subject matter that appeals to certain organizations, they can sometimes decide to contribute to your film as well.

Web Presence

Having a Web site is a big help because you can have a link saying, "If you want to donate to this project, send a check here."

Festivals—The Red Carpet

Once you've finished the documentary, you should start sending it out to film festivals; in the documentary world, there are a lot. There's the Full Frame Documentary Film Festival. There's the Silver Docs Film Festival in Washington, D.C. In Europe, there's the Thessaloniki Festival, which is in Greece. There's a festival called Hot Docs in Toronto and the Hot Springs Documentary Festival in Arkansas. You should try to get it into the bigger festivals like Sundance, Toronto, Cannes, and Tribeca. You hope that a company is going to see your documentary at the festivals and want to buy it, and that what they'll pay for it is enough money to cover the cost of the documentary.

Distribution

There have never been more avenues available to distribute your film; there has never been more competition; there has never been less money.

The first tier of distribution would be theatrical—very few documentaries make that cut. Lion's Gate, Think Film, Focus Features, and Miramax buy documentaries. They'll buy your film anywhere from maybe $500,000 to $1,500,000. The second tier is television, which is usually HBO, although a lot of times an HBO film will also play theatrically. HBO might pay $100,000 to

$150,000. Then you've got the third tier, right below HBO, which is PBS venues like Independent Lens or POV or Wide Angle. POV might pay $35,000 for a seventy-five-minute documentary; Independent Lens, $15,000 to $20,000—something like that. Those are the three main things that a documentary filmmaker hopes to get: theatrical, HBO, or somewhere on one of the PBS venues. After that, it gets a lot tougher.

You can sometimes get a small theatrical run, which means you're going to play in maybe New York, Los Angeles, Seattle, San Francisco, Chicago, and that's it. Your film will probably play at a small art house venue that doesn't advertise very much, and it'll probably play one week and never be heard from again at a theater.

Then you've got the whole video and educational market, where you can get your film hooked up with an educational distributor like Bullfrog Films, Women Make Movies, New Day Films, and Filmmakers Library. They will not pay you upfront for your film, but you'll give them your film and then they'll market it to colleges, libraries, organizations, and churches, and you get a percentage of every unit that they sell.

The pay off for something like that is that the distributor usually takes about 70 percent, you get 30 percent. So you have to sell a lot of units before you make any money doing it that way. But at least your film is being seen and it's actually having a good effect. It's being used for educational purposes, so you're reaching a lot of people with your film.

You can also try to sell it over your Web site or get a distributor like IndieDocs, IndieFlix, or Film Movement. You can try to sell it to a local PBS station in your area. They have practically no money to spend on independent documentaries. We sold a couple to them for $1,000 and $1,500. That's it. You don't make much money with just a documentary. That's the truth of it.

If you want to have a popular, money-making documentary, then you have to appeal to the widest audience possible and it's got to be a positive story. You have to make it about a subject that helps people in some personal way without it being uncomfortable or disturbing. That's if you want to make a popular documentary. If you want to make a successful documentary, meaning that it's successful on an artistic level or on a personal level, I think you need to be true to your vision. You need to make the film you want to make rather than the film you think people want to see.

From Rubber Bullets and Tear Gas: The Dream of a Lifetime

The mass demonstration at the World Trade Organization Convention in Seattle launches Thompson's documentary career. Now, with a few more documentaries under his belt, he can reflect on the choices he made in late November 1999. It has been a great move. I've been

Police arrive in riot gear in an attempt to quell the protests.

waiting for this for a long time. When I went to college, I wanted to be a filmmaker and I got into the TV news biz. That was pretty satisfying for a long time. It taught me a lot.

When I got to what I considered the pinnacle of my news profession, which was being based in Seattle, shooting for the networks, going to exotic places around the world, I won a national Emmy for some shooting I did in North Korea. The very height of what I was doing as a news cameraman is when I got the most disgruntled and disillusioned with the work. I called myself an overpaid electronic stenographer. Then, luckily, this explosion in digital technology happened—editing systems became affordable, and you could put them in your home. I thought, "Oh my God, this is what I've wanted all my life."

Democracy and the Documentary

A plastic earth balloon bounces overhead as bongos keep the beat for hula-hoops. Thompson's documentary is experiential, woven with personal insight from a television photojournalist's perspective and filled with the natural sounds of protest.

"This is what democracy looks like," goes the chant from a young woman broadcasting on a megaphone. The crowd marches through Seattle, making their voices heard, shutting down the World Trade Organization Convention, and effecting change. Thompson calls it "an unruly outbreak of democracy." During a week in November, on posters, over megaphones, and in improvised folk songs, 50,000 citizens find a forum for their voices.

It's easy to see the passion and celebration free speech brings to life in the flash point the convention provides. A few days later, life in the city is back to normal, the streets are cleared, and face paint has been exchanged for office makeup. Where are the voices now? Have the issues gone away? Like the proverbial tree falling in the woods, can a voice find freedom if it's never heard?

Now, for seventy-two minutes, democracy looks like Rustin Thompson's film. At thirty frames a second, Thompson can see the democratizing effect new technology has had on the mediums of film and television. Small, easy-to-use, inexpensive video cameras and editing systems have given a visual forum to everyone, including Thompson.

He's now free to use the medium for his own voice, the voice of a TV photojournalist.

CHAPTER 20

Kevin Sites

The Future of
Journalism

Kevin Sites
Journalist

Yahoo!
Edward R. Murrow Award, War in Kosovo, 1999
***Wired Magazine* Rave Award, Mosque Shooting, Kevin Sites Blog, 2005**
Payne Ethics Award, Mosque Shooting, Kevin Sites Blog, 2005
Daniel Pearl Award for Courage and Integrity in Journalism, 2006

Arrows of neon and flashing marquees out on main street

Chicago, New York, Detroit it's all on the same street

Your typical city involved in a typical daydream

Hang it up and see what tomorrow brings

Sometimes the light's all shining on me

Other times I can barely see

Lately it occurs to me

What a long strange trip it's been

> *From "Truckin'" written by Jerry Garcia, Bob Weir,*
> *Phil Lesh, and lyricist Robert Hunter*

*H*awaiian Sumo wrestlers Akebono and Konishiki had taken the top two rankings in a sport that had never seen a non-Japanese champion. Akebono was the first to reach Yokozuna, *the highest rank. Konishiki, nicknamed "The Dump Truck," is* Ozeki, *the second-highest rank. Both men wrestled their titles from the status quo. While the hierarchy of Sumo wrestling may not have broad influence in a global sense, the namesakes of these two champions would change the world.*

1994

In a trailer on the campus of Stanford University, Jerry Yang's workstation, named "Akebono," hums quietly with a list of personal-interest Web sites that is titled "Jerry's Guide to the World Wide Web." It's a distraction that keeps Jerry and fellow Ph.D. candidate and "deadhead"

EQUIPMENT

Sony HDR-HC1 high-definition digital camcorder
Samsung SC-X105L camcorder with "headcam"
Apple 12-inch PowerBook computer
Thrane Explorer 500 satellite modem
Thuraya/Hughes 7101 satellite phone
Palm Treo 650 GSM mobile "smart" phone

Akebono becomes Yokozuna

Jerry Yang & David Filo Start Yahoo

| 1993 | 1994 | 1995 | 2004 | 2005 | The Future |

David Filo from completing their doctoral dissertations. When the lists become too big, they break them down into categories, then subcategories—a core concept of a new business is born.

Filo's computer, "Konishiki," runs the software that drives what will become known as Yahoo! "Yet Another Hierarchical Officious Oracle" is a nice phrase to establish the acronym, but Yang and Filo insist that the name is inspired by the definition set by Jonathan Swift in Gulliver's Travels—*rude, unsophisticated, uncouth." The world is waiting for Yahoo!—a single place to find useful Web sites. By the fall of 1994, Yahoo! celebrates its first million-hit day.*

The Next Year

Honored as an "American icon" and named the thirteenth-greatest guitar player of all time by Rolling Stone, *vocalist and lead guitarist for The Grateful Dead, Jerry Garcia, dies of a heart attack. Thousands attend memorial services at Golden Gate Park, San Francisco. David Filo mourns as well and scours the Internet for news of the tragedy. Knowing Yahoo! users will want to know more too, he puts together a page that links information about The Grateful Dead and Jerry Garcia and articles about the legend's life and death. The death of Jerry Garcia marks the first time Yahoo! places news on their front page. From there, this new idea of bringing together different news sources from around the Internet begins as Yahoo! forges relationships with news content providers such as Reuters and the Associated Press.*

Akebono becomes Yokozuna   **Jerry Garcia Dies**

Jerry Yang & David Filo Start Yahoo

| 1993 | 1994 | 1995 | 2004 | 2005 | The Future |

Nine Years Later

"He's f–king faking he's dead—he's faking he's f–king dead." *(Bang)*

"Well, he's dead now."

The smell of gunpowder fills a mosque in South Fallujah, Iraq, as the report echoes off bullet-ridden walls. Kevin Sites captures a scene that will change his life.

Freelancing for NBC and embedded with the U.S. Marines in Operation Iraqi Freedom, Sites's camera is rolling when a Marine fires point-blank into a wounded insurgent. The recorded video and audio make the story seem clear. Sites's mind reels with the implications. I'm so shocked at what's just happened. I had to process it. When I heard him say, "He's faking he's f–king dead," I thought he was going to cover him. Maybe he'd hold his weapon there while someone else was going to search him if they thought he was booby-trapped or something like that. But then he pulled the trigger and

Akebono becomes Yokozuna   **Jerry Garcia Dies**

Jerry Yang & David Filo Start Yahoo   **Sites in Fallujah**

| 1993 | 1994 | 1995 | 2004 | 2005 | The Future |

330

blew his brains up against the wall. He just shot this guy, spun on his heels, and walked out.

At that point I wasn't a journalist anymore. I stopped cold. I wasn't exactly sure what I needed to do. I was certain this was going to become propaganda for the insurgents. So there are all kinds of conflicting thoughts going through my mind.

Through a pool arrangement with NBC, many networks, including the BBC and Al Jazeera, gain access to Sites's footage. The footage became very controversial on a number of different levels. Obviously, just because of the very dramatic nature of what had happened there but also because of the debate that it engendered in terms of what this meant as a piece of journalism. What did this mean in a time of war? Where is the loyalty of a journalist? Is it to the troops or Marines he's embedded with or is it to a country or is it to the truth itself and what happened there?

When the footage was released, it just got huge worldwide circulation and it was shown everywhere to some degree. People would use different snippets of it. In the U.S., I don't believe the actual shooting itself was ever shown except on a Web site when I released it later. Al Jazeera certainly showed it, and other people did, too, and there became this debate on whether this is propaganda. Is it going to serve the purpose of the insurgents? One of the most important aspects of that debate was that we decided to self-censor ourselves at NBC and not show the entire piece. We would show up to the point when the marine raised his weapon but not the entire video.

Looking back at that, I think that was a mistake on our part because we created a lot of confusion. We didn't provide the whole context, and people in some ways didn't understand what had happened in there. Some people felt like the Marine had been justified and that we basically were being opportunistic with this sensational piece of video and decided to use it for our own purposes. I think most people didn't really understand what took place in there, what led up to it, and what was involved before that shooting and after that shooting. Because we didn't show the full piece of videotape, there was a lot of criticism and a lot confusion.

So I had to use an independent "blog" that I kept, not something that was making any money but just something to record my own impressions of the coverage that I was doing out there. I wrote an open letter to the Devil Dogs of the 3.1, on Sunday, November 21, 2004, to help clear up the confusion about my coverage.

The explosion of the Internet has allowed millions to place content on the Web. Some content is updated often and written in journal style, like online diaries. Web logs help establish online communities about news and special interests. The term blog *is a contraction of "Web log" and is also used as a verb meaning "to maintain or add text, photographs, audio, or video" to a blog.*

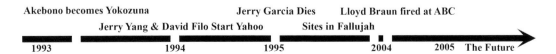

Akebono becomes Yokozuna   Jerry Garcia Dies   Lloyd Braun fired at ABC
    Jerry Yang & David Filo Start Yahoo   Sites in Fallujah

1993	1994	1995	2004	2005	The Future

After being fired from his position as chairman of ABC Entertainment Group for greenlighting the most expensive TV pilot in history, Lloyd Braun joins Yahoo! to run the Yahoo Media Group. The $12,000,000 pilot launches Lost *and becomes a huge success for ABC. Braun sees Sites's reports on NBC and reads his blog.*

I released the letter on my blog, and it got picked up worldwide. At that point, I really began to understand the power of the Internet. Television didn't fully convey what was going on here for a number of reasons, partly because of self-censorship and partly because of the limitations of the medium. This particular blog ended up mitigating a lot of the anger that was directed toward me and more fully explained what happened in that story.

Opportunity Knocks

Upon his return from Iraq, Sites meets with his lawyer and family friend Joel Behr, who has an idea he's been cooking up. He asked me, "Are you interested in doing anything besides network news?" I said, "Yeah." At that point, I really was kind of burned out after what had happened in Fallujah, and when he mentioned it might be an opportunity with the Internet *(Joel Behr knows Lloyd Braun, now firmly perched in his new roost at Yahoo Media Group)*, I thought so much the better. He said, "What do you think of the idea—*Kevin Sites in the Hot Zone*? You would cover different things that interest you. You would control the agenda, you would be Yahoo!'s only reporter and you would report on a multimedia level, doing video, text dispatches, and still photography." *Joel Behr pitches the idea to Lloyd Braun who immediately likes the idea. Braun meets Sites and agrees to launch* Kevin Sites in the Hot Zone *for Yahoo! News.*

Timeline

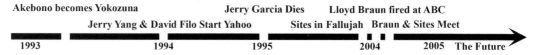

Akebono becomes Yokozuna		Jerry Garcia Dies		Lloyd Braun fired at ABC	
	Jerry Yang & David Filo Start Yahoo		Sites in Fallujah	Braun & Sites Meet	
1993	1994	1995		2004	2005	The Future

To me, that was a dream come true. I could do multimedia disciplines, all provided on one platform. TV reporting, print reporting, and still photography all delivered through the Internet. It sounded like an incredible idea and that's really where it started—that was the impetus.

From Sumo wrestlers to Stanford grad students to the death of Jerry Garcia, blogs, and a television network executive to a freelance correspondent—one path to the future of photojournalism has been set.

Yahoo! and Sites Build *The Hot Zone*

Kevin Sites is joined at Yahoo! by Yahoo! News general manager Neil Budde, senior producer Robert Padavick, researcher Lisa Liu, and associate producer Erin Green. Other than Sites, the team will remain in California to coordinate and assemble the reports sent back from the field.

Their goals: *to cover every armed conflict in the world within one year and to provide a clear idea of the combatants, victims, causes, and costs of each of these struggles and their global impact. Sites will pursue the stories that aren't getting mainstream coverage and look for the human element behind the conflict.*

There's a lot riding on this Yahoo! initiative. Longtime users and the traditional media will be watching.

The idea is to complement existing news content from providers already in partnership with Yahoo! while attracting new users with something original. Although Sites has a history creating journalistic content, Yahoo! does not. They must raise the bar and prove that they can provide stories and adhere to the same standards as traditional media. To highlight that intent, they post their ethical statement on the Web site. From the Hot Zone Mission Statement:

We are professional journalists and will apply to our work the ethical code of conduct as outlined by the Society of Professional Journalists:

1. To seek and report the truth.
2. To minimize harm.
3. To act independently.
4. To be accountable.

We strongly believe, as stated in the preamble of this code, that public enlightenment is the forerunner of justice and the foundation of democracy. We also will add four more criteria to our work that will take us above the journalistic code. We also pledge in our reporting and storytelling:

Transparency: an honest and authentic accounting of both our failures and successes, to pull back the curtain on our editorial and technological process. We refuse to propagate the myths of the omniscient, infallible correspondent.

Vulnerability: we will strive to live, breathe, and experience the lives of the people we are covering—including the daily dangers they're exposed to from combat, disease, and hardship.

Empathy: we may not always agree with our sources, but we will make every effort to understand their positions and report them with clarity, so that our audience may have context and perspective.

Solutions: our site will contain links to organizations and groups that are working to aid victims of these conflicts and assist in their peaceful resolutions.

As the team ramps up to start a year of conflict coverage, the designers at Yahoo! go to work making the Web site for The Hot Zone, *now the company's only original news content.*

Launch of *The Hot Zone* Web Site

Kevin Sites in the Hot Zone *is posted on the Web at* http://hotzone.yahoo.com. *The September 26, 2005, front page leads with a feature story with links to text dispatches, photo essays, and video stories. The page's design and navigation make accessing the content easy.*

Timeline

Akebono becomes Yokozuna
Jerry Yang & David Filo Start Yahoo
Jerry Garcia Dies
Sites in Fallujah
Lloyd Braun fired at ABC
Braun & Sites Meet
Yahoo! Launches the Hot Zone

1993   1994   1995   2004   2005   The Future

The front page of a 2006 *Kevin Sites in the Hot Zone.*

The featured report.

The video interface for playing video reports.

A link to the photo essay.

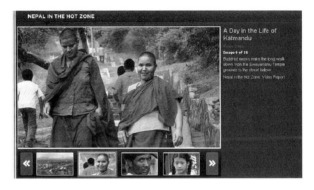

The photo essay interface.

Additional coverage.

Different Media All Rolled up into One

The Internet offers some unique abilities that combine elements from more traditional media. On the Internet, you can take your time and read, get more in depth, like a magazine article; you can listen to audio like radio; and you can watch video like television. Bandwidth and modem speeds limit the quality for now. For Sites, the Internet also has some other benefits. He's free to tell his story in any medium he sees fit.

If it's better as a photo essay, that's what it is. If it requires more in-depth analysis, he writes it; if video tells the story better, he shoots it. He gets to pair the medium with the message. And to top it off, there are no real deadlines on the Internet; it's done when it's done. When Sites says it's done. There's no 5:00 P.M. timeslot that needs to be filled, and, unlike television, when the story is over it stays up, ready to be played for the next user who chooses to watch.

Kevin and a Camera

Much of the content that is displayed on The Hot Zone *is visual in nature, with the text dispatches adding expanded detail and impressions. As a one-man band, or solo journalist, his camerawork is as important as his reporting. While Sites has always been a journalist, he had to learn video skills later in his career. He took a two-year sabbatical following his assignment in Kosovo for NBC to teach at California Polytechnic Institute (Cal Poly).*

I was traveling pretty consistently. I was married at the time, and my marriage wasn't going well; I needed to get off the road. So I promised my ex-wife I would take some time and teach for two years. I'd been a producer, so I hadn't been shooting a lot of video. I was directing camera crews but not shooting myself. Basically, I learned to shoot and edit while teaching my students to do the same. I got divorced, and when my two years was up I went back to work for NBC just as the war in Afghanistan was getting ready to start.

NBC sent me to Afghanistan, and I was working with a correspondent as a producer. I ended up on the front line with the camera and the means to transmit those pictures by myself without the correspondent. So they asked me to report, and at that point I just kept on shooting and reporting.

A Background in Photojournalism

Sites's first inspiration in photojournalism came from the black-and-white war photography of Eugene Smith. I was a still photographer very early in my career, and when I say very early I mean my first job. I was fifteen years old and worked for a local newspaper with a circulation of 6,000. I got a camera one Christmas, and I put together a portfolio. I said I was a photographer, and they hired me to take Cub Scout pictures and pictures of study groups and service organizations and sports events—things like that.

I never considered myself professional with video until I started to do it in the field. I still don't consider that my greatest skill. I think that I am fairly aggressive with a camera and try to get things as honest as I can, but I am not much of a technical master. I understand exposure, and I understand the basis of composition, but there are people who can run circles around me who do only the photographic work, and I have to combine that with my other skills. I think I am able to do it effectively.

The up side of this is that I'm able to travel alone. I can get into a situation where I don't necessarily change the dynamic like some reporters do. If you are coming in with a full crew, a $50,000 Ikegami camera, and a soundman with a boom mic, and maybe even a producer, you've got four people standing there trying to interview a normal person in the field. That person is going to do one of two things. They become a public relations professional—you know, put on their best voice and give you a show; or they become a deer in the headlights. Neither of those things is an accurate portrayal of what was happening in that circumstance.

So, it's my desire to interrupt the least amount that I can. When I shoot an interview, I use a very small camera and I hold it to my chest and maintain eye contact. Sometimes the camera is shaky. I try to keep it as steady as possible. If I am doing a long interview, I put it on tripod. But for the most part, the idea is to capture the moment. The goal is to go out there and put a human element to an issue, to connect them together. We can do that very well through the visual.

The default tagline for our whole project has been "Putting a Human Face on Global Conflict," and it's just ended up being that way. The stories that we wanted to tell were the small stories in front of and behind the conflicts—not the large, macro geopolitical stories, but the small, intimate stories. Along with that intimacy came the proximity to the camera, picking up this still or video camera and looking into that person's eyes. Hopefully getting an honest response as we capture that image. That's what I try to do.

A One-man Band

Quite honestly, in television news the one-man band isn't a new concept. I would like to pretend that I created it, but it's not the truth. People have been doing this in local news because of pure economic reasons. I mean it's fairly common in small markets around America.

It started to become a little bit more prevalent in war scenarios and combat scenarios because it lent itself to that. Production values suffer a little bit when you have fewer people. If you can control the environment and provide a boom mic and a great photographer and a producer, you can make something look very polished. But, in a war environment, you are not afraid to show the gritty nature of things, and that's probably why it is more successful in those environments. People aren't necessarily expecting things to look beautiful; they are expecting them to look real and gritty.

I don't think we are going to become the standard overnight, and it may not necessarily be the best case to become the standard. It's probably more appropriate to have a mix of things, especially when you are talking about high-production television magazine work, where you really need to control the environment to some extent. But as the equipment becomes lighter and smaller, and we can move a little bit easier, it does present a good opportunity to make the reporting more real by not disturbing the environment to such a great degree that people are aware of the technology.

If you have a lot of people out there doing this, yes, you will save the network money, but the problem is that you don't have people with multiskill levels to do all these things. Someone might be an incredible writer but never wants to edit or never wants to shoot a picture, and vice versa on the other skills. So, it takes an individual who's fairly well motivated, not necessarily smarter than your average bear but someone willing to do the donkey work that it takes to do all this stuff.

I don't consider myself a very technically skilled person, but I am motivated enough and, I think, selfish

Sites with video and still cameras.

enough in some ways that I want to tell my story; I want to tell the story I am going after. I like collaboration in postproduction and preproduction. I don't necessarily like collaboration when I'm in the field that much.

When I was out in the field, I was reporting from eight in the morning to seven or eight at night. By the time you get back, you are very tired from just reporting. And then you have to write your story. You're doing about a thousand-word dispatch every night. You've got to input your pictures into the computer and the video. I would actually do a rough cut of the video I had. So, I'm working in three different mediums, and I have to transmit this all through the satellite modem.

The first month that I was in Africa I thought, "This is crazy." We started to develop a rhythm. We started to see that, maybe, we should focus on the print story first, make sure that we have the notes and that the story is well told. Then we'll add the photographs and then we're going to add the video. Once we figured out that rhythm, I think things became a bit smoother.

You give up a lot of in terms of relationships. There are definitely a lot of lonely moments that are part of it. It's a mixed bag. I think that what we gain is worth the price of what it costs us personally, but I wouldn't want to do this forever. This has certainly been one of the most trying times physically and professionally for me. When you have to drop yourself into Somalia and the Congo and Uganda and Iraq and all these places one week after another, it does take its toll.

It's a killer.

Equipment for *The Hot Zone*

It's certain that we can look forward to increased image quality and resolution as cameras become lighter and more ergonomic. Although cameras are available now that are very small, photographers generally prefer some substance to their cameras.

Kevin Sites has been outfitted with the latest technology, which allows him to cover the world's conflict zones with little more than what fits into a backpack. Sites's main camera is a Sony HDR-HC1 (see A at

left) high-definition digital camcorder with an 0.7 wide-angle converter lens. He tends to work very close to his subjects, and the wide adapter allows for better composition and more options for framing.

Sites records 1080i image resolution in a 16:9 ratio. Kevin prefers this model to the slightly larger Sony HDR-FX1 because the HC1 is less obtrusive in the field. It's easy to shoot from hip level while maintaining eye contact with interviewees and it doesn't belie its presence with an obvious microphone or a large, rectangular lens shade.

Sites connects the camera to an Apple PowerBook through a FireWire/IEEE 1394 interface and edits in Final Cut Pro. The camera weighs about 0.7 kilograms (1.5 pounds). Sites's second camera is a Samsung SC-X105L digital camcorder with headcam (see B at left).

This camera is used in situations where Sites needs two free hands, or as a backup. The Samsung records in MPEG4 format and carries enough memory to store anywhere from twenty-two minutes to more than two hours of video, depending on the resolution. The remote headcam accessory is a camera and lens that connects to the SC-X105L

A

B

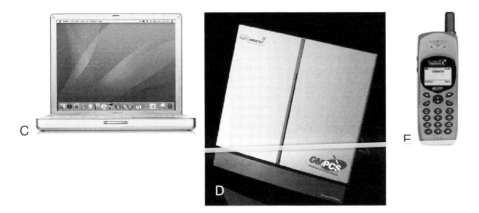

body through a cable. The headcam is mounted in an elastic headband that Sites wears for POV shots or when he needs both hands free. It weighs 150 grams (0.33 pounds).

Sites's twelve-inch Apple PowerBook (C) has a 100 GB hard drive and 1 GB of RAM and weighs 2.1 kilograms (4.6 pounds). The laptop serves as his workbench, typewriter, and editing studio. For video editing, Sites uses Final Cut Pro and iMovie HD; for still images, he uses Adobe Photoshop; and for writing, Microsoft Office. For live reports and interactive chat sessions, Sites carries an Apple iSight Web camera, which mounts to the top of the PowerBook screen and connects to the laptop's FireWire port.

Sites uses a Thrane Explorer 500 satellite modem (D) to send images and computer data back to Yahoo! News. It's his main data link to the outside world. The satellite modem is about the same size and weight as a laptop computer. It operates throughout Europe, Africa, the Middle East, and Asia and weighs 1.3 kilograms (2.9 pounds).

The Thuraya/Hughes 7101 portable satellite phone (E) is used where other cell phones can't get a signal. It operates on the same satellite network as the Hughes satellite modem. The phone can determine its position using the GPS network and transmit those coordinates, which helps Sites's U.S. team keep track of him.

Sites's standard cell phone is the Palm® Treo 650™ GSM mobile "smart" phone (bottom figure). It's a standard mobile phone/organizer combo for calling under normal circumstances. He uses the GSM model, which is the standard in most of the world outside the United States. Sites's contacts and schedules are synchronized with his laptop.

Up and Rolling at Full Speed

By the time Sites's tour of conflict zones hits Kabul on March 20, 2006, the show is firing on all cylinders. Gear issues have been worked out, communication is flowing smoothly, and the Web presence has an established following. Sites files a story called "Child Bride" about an orphan who was forced into an arranged marriage at the age of four, where she was tortured and beaten by a family who made her their slave.

She escaped the family and was taken to an orphanage in Kabul. Now, at twelve, the girl is full of life and vitality despite all that she'd been through. The story touches on all the elements Sites is working with to showcase in his reporting: the triumph of the human spirit even in the face of such adversity and conflict. On The Hot Zone Web site, there's an open message board for every story. The "Child Bride" story results in 7,500 comments from users.

There is also an e-mail account set up so that Sites's fixer in Kabul can retrieve messages of support and give them to the girl. That e-mail address has received more than 15,000 messages. The outpouring of support for this girl and the story takes on a life of its own and becomes the story that gets the most e-mails on Yahoo! for three days running.

Yahoo! News has now grown to become the largest news Web site on the Internet, with anywhere from 27,000,000 to 30,000,000 users per month. In addition to Kevin Sites in the Hot Zone, Yahoo! carries news content from established new organizations such as Associated Press, The New York Times, the BBC, and others. Mixing the latest technology with solid journalistic storytelling has paved the way for the future of Yahoo! News and perhaps the industry as a whole.

Where Are the Flying Cars and Robots?

Most predictions about the future fall short. Our imaginations run wild with the "dreams" of today and pass over the "needs" that will fuel advancement. While we wait for flying cars, computers shrink from the size of a room down to cell phone proportions and language changes to discuss new technologies and methodologies. Our constant evolution will take us places we can't imagine and may not be able to appreciate unless we look back. Leaving robots behind, here are some things the future will likely have in store.

The future of journalism is constantly evolving. I think a lot of people thought when we started off with The Hot Zone that we were going to be competition for the networks or competition with newspapers, that it was another kind of death knell of the old media. I don't believe that at all. I think, in a lot of ways, all the media that we have evolves directly after the initiation of new media. The strengths a particular current medium holds continue to grow, but perhaps in a different way. For instance, with the advent of television and radio, general-interest magazines became niche-market magazines; that's how they were able to survive, by catering to specific interests.

Radio, it's the same. It used to be a dramatic medium used for entertainment value with written drama and comedy; now it's moved to a music and talk format. I think the Internet and this particular brand of journalism that we are doing is also going to force those existing mediums to evolve in different ways.

It will force television to do what it does best—provide the visual impact of the story. It used to be that television provided not only visual impact but also immediacy. If something was breaking at that moment, you could see it on television, whereas newspapers had already printed their story and it was old the minute something new happened within a particular news event.

Now the Internet is taking over that position of being the most immediate news medium there is. Everything is updated much faster on the Internet than it is on television, and in some ways people begin to use that media mix to the best advantage. You get the breaking news from the Internet. If something's happening right now, perhaps you'll want to see the visual element a little bit stronger; then you turn to television to see it. One medium amplifies the other.

A lot of people feel that the newspapers don't necessarily provide news any more but a value-added side of things, a narrative that can be held in your hand rather than a longer narrative that's read on the Internet. Some people don't like to read very long stories on the Internet. But the fact is, the Internet can amplify and direct people toward newspapers and magazines, while at the same time magazines can direct people back to the Internet for more information, for links that go beyond that particular story. I think that what you'll find is that the Internet, rather than being an old media killer, is going to be an amplifier. You will see something in one medium and then use another to gather more information, or one medium will spark your interest in another.

Yahoo! doesn't own the market on Internet news, although it does garner the largest audience. Most television stations now operate a Web presence. Some offer basic contact and public relations content, while others treat it as a second transmission for their stories, keeping the content updated right along with the latest broadcast events. There will always be an active race to deliver timely local news in any manner that will connect a news provider with a viewer. The future will undoubtedly bring the Internet and television closer together in terms of sharing content and revenue.

Better Tools for Storytellers

The future holds better equipment and communication tools for storytellers to tell stories. No matter what the medium, the core product journalists and photojournalists provide is stories. Without innovative, engaging stories, all the technological advancements in the world could stay in the lab for the effect they would have on the viewing public. So what do storytellers want? Which windows of communication will be opened for journalists?

A clean, solid connection to their subjects and to their viewers will continue to create the bleeding edge of the industry. Cameras will shrink, image will improve, workflow will become more streamlined, and the ability to store and send large amounts of data will become easier and easier. Technology will lead the way, fueled more and more by global commerce rather than by the niche market of video journalism.

Luckily, fast, effortless communication is required in the business world and intuitive controls are needed to keep the content flowing to support the global economy. Many innovations will continue to come to journalism as happy accidents in technology's race to have every company and every being in the world connected.

The Future of News Stories

On-Demand, Interactive, and Appointment Viewing

The technology is here now; there are a few bugs, but they're being squashed as you read this. What attracts you? What draws your interest? How long will you stay? These variables are being considered by many news organizations around the world. What will you want to view? On the Internet, there's a built-in rating system; the success or interest in a story can be instantly quantified. What will stick and what will fall into the trash?

Good stories will stay! The ability to tell a good story will keep viewers engaged no matter what the medium. Talking-head, live-shot journalism had better deliver the same user-retaining power as a well-told and well-visualized story. To see the future, ask yourself, "Given the choice, would I click the button to see a local reporter doing a stand-up in front of a house fire or police shooting or school board meeting? Or would I click on the button that illustrates the story behind the rise in arsons, rising crime rates in a neighborhood, or new programs that will affect my kids?"

When you get to choose and aren't forced to wait as you're spoonfed news content, you get picky. And that's good. Live shots will always have their place, but on-demand will raise the bar for every type of coverage.

The Internet is going to be a unique tool in terms of the interactive aspects of journalism simply because the same tool that you use to read information you can use to respond to it as well. If you're watching television or reading a newspaper or magazine and you get excited about a story and want to respond to it, either in an intellectual or an emotional way, you have to pick up a phone or you have to go to the computer and write something.

While the Internet is there to provide the information, it also offers the means to respond to it immediately. That provides a very fast turnaround on what's been read. But at the same time, perhaps the drawback is that responses aren't as thoughtful or as well thought out as if someone actually took time to sit down and write it outside of that particular scope of emotion that they are feeling after reading something.

Log on to the Internet at a specified time and contribute to a "Town Hall" discussion on topics that affect your neighborhood. Appointment viewing through the Internet will offer everyone a voice in the discussions of the day. By sending e-mail or instant messaging content, news moderators can poll the audience during the program. Viewer comments become part of the program. Fifteen seconds of fame may be only a Web cam away in the not too distant future.

You're viewing a story about tornadoes in the Midwest, and, as you're watching, an icon appears that will direct you at the end of the story to a site with an emergency preparedness list, something you can save or print out. Later, another link asks if you'd like to get online alerts when a tornado watch is in your area. As the report continues, a survival shop owner talks about the basics for a shelter; a link opens with his contact information and directions to his shop. The reporter is doing a poll on how many people have had their homes damaged and repaired with insurance. You can instantly enter your answer. The results of the poll will be used in an update to this story.

Viral Content

Viral content is content spread on the Internet by users. When a story "goes viral," it means that many people are e-mailing the content, or links to it, and viewership explodes exponentially.

If your servers can handle it, this type of viral is good. Your story has found a wide audience that is passionate enough for viewers to take the time and recommend your story to others. No doubt viral news content will be a well-discussed goal.

The Cost of the Future

*Technology may illuminate the road ahead, but costs might actually drive the future. Business is business. (*Period.*) Television news is a business, and the business needs to survive before the employees do. Diminished market share, an eroding advertising base, and the costs of doing business are all factors that tend to compress the industry. Fewer people have to do more with less.*

Luckily, in industry, just like in your neighborhood, keeping up with the Joneses is a powerful motivator. All industry moves forward or dies. New innovations and business models will bring opportunity to places we haven't even dreamt of yet. One thing is for certain: The need for visual content is growing, not shrinking. And, keeping the Joneses in mind, higher quality always speaks better for anyone in a competitive market.

Who pays for the future? Advertisers, the businesses that pay for your attention. Under the current media model, advertisers wield a mighty hammer that attempts to influence the content of the programs or the networks they're affiliated with. News organizations in most markets have long avoided influence from advertisers. Not that continued funding of their programs or executive raises aren't enticing. But once the manipulation of news content is for sale, the organization can no longer be considered impartial and, therefore, is vulnerable in terms of credibility in the news arena. The public's trust has been violated.

As news expands into new mediums, there will be more attempts by advertisers to influence the content. The new news providers will have to have very deep pockets to withstand the fickleness of advertising if they want to survive and retain the degree of respect traditional media enjoy.

The Hot Zone Continues

The Yahoo! News initiative has been a success. The year of conflict coverage is up. Sites has traveled to twenty-two conflict zones in nineteen countries. Now, in the next phase, Sites and his team will focus on untold stories in America, bringing powerful still and video images to the computer screen. People have responded to what we're doing. I certainly know the power of an image from my experience in Fallujah in a very controversial way. I think people also respond to our images when they don't necessarily have to do with controversial things. Sometimes it's the basic conflict of life and how a particular person is dealing with that conflict. Is it a conflict that has forced them to surrender? Has it in some way defeated them? Or is it something that is able to show a representation of their human spirit and the indomitable nature of that?

One day in November 2004 changed Kevin Sites's life forever and would redirect his future in a way he never saw coming. The controversy surrounding his footage has become part of his career legacy and will be connected to him forever. Sites addresses the controversy on his blog in an open letter to the Devil Dogs of the 3.1. The letter concludes:

> I interviewed your Commanding Officer, Lieutenant Colonel Willy Buhl, before the battle for Fallujah began. He said something very powerful at the time—something that now seems prophetic. It was this:
>
> > We're the good guys. We are Americans. We are fighting a gentleman's war here—because we don't behead people, we don't come down to the same level of the people we're combating. That's a very difficult thing for a young 18-year-old Marine who's been trained to locate,

close with and destroy the enemy with fire and close combat. That's a very difficult thing for a 42-year-old lieutenant colonel with 23 years experience in the service, who was trained to do the same thing once upon a time, and who now has a thousand-plus men to lead, guide, coach, mentor—and ensure we remain the good guys and keep the moral high ground.

I listened carefully when he said those words. I believed them.

So here, ultimately, is how it all plays out: when the Iraqi man in the mosque posed a threat, he was your enemy; when he was subdued, he was your responsibility; when he was killed in front of my eyes and my camera, the story of his death became my responsibility.

The burdens of war, as you so well know, are unforgiving for all of us.

I pray for your soon and safe return. –KS

Fast Forward

No one knows what the future may hold in store. Life springs twists and turns on us that defy prediction. One tragedy leads to opportunity; an opportunity turns tragic. Giggles and tears, soul-clearing belly laughs, and weeping sobs—the ups and downs that define every life—will make the future. That much is certain.

The human condition will lead the way, captured and told by enterprising storytellers on whatever medium is available at the time. The future is coming, frame by frame, second by second. Hang on for dear life and enjoy the dizziness of the ride.

And, no matter where you find yourself in the days that lie ahead, you'll certainly look back and be able to quote Jerry Garcia: "What a long strange trip it's been."

Parting Shots

"F/8 and Be There" is an old adage wielded by Arthur Felig, aka Weegee, in the 1920s and 1930s. The translation might be described as follows: Simplicity in the technical is equal to being present and prepared. No complicated photographic technique here, just a basic setting (f/8) with enough depth of field for most subjects. And then "being there" in the right place, right time, tuned in to your surroundings, ready to shoot the perfect moment when it unfolds in front of your lens.

That is how great photojournalism is done, whether with a Depression-era still camera or the latest, fully loaded high-definition camcorder. Photographic skill is essential, and it must be second nature, coming second place to the subjects you are shooting. Make the camera work without thinking about the technical, be on the edge of history, and capture the world through your eyes. Your work will stand out and enlighten viewers with images and sounds that carry the human element with all its emotional tapestry. The story of our lives will be told by you—because you were there, ready to observe. From this standpoint, it's hard to begrudge Arthur Felig his well-known photo credit stamped on the back of each image: "Credit Photo by Weegee the Famous." Humor without modesty, a characteristic trait of all photojournalists.

Each photojournalist's interview in this book mirrors the preceding comments. They count themselves as storytellers first, photographers second, and technical wizards somewhere down the line from there. Even the inventive Mitchell Wagenberg, with his shop of secret gadgets, serves the story first. They are students of the human condition, observing and making note of all things grand and all things subtle. They know how to anticipate life from the dawning of a simple smile to the explosive violence of armed confrontation. They are at the right place, at the right time—consistently.

In stories big and small, they relish the telling of the story, expertly weaving the details and setting the direction of the narrative path. Viewers are engaged, locked from the first image, held through an experience that's captured on a tiny photosensitive chip, and released at the conclusion to find themselves better informed for the journey.

Just the Facts

There are highly acclaimed men and women who do this job, who haven't had the opportunity to voice their thoughts on the printed page. David Hands and the industry Web site tvcameramen.com conducted a survey for Roll! in an attempt to paint a picture of the working lives of television photojournalists around the world. The 100 respon-dents came from 34 countries and 76 cities. The following table shows the results from our unscientific survey.

Question	Response	Percentage of Respondents
What title do you use to identify yourself?	Cameraman	44
	Lighting cameraman	17
	Photojournalist	10
	Digital photographer	9
	Videographer	9
	Photographer	5
	Cameraperson	3
	Photog	2
	Shooter	1
If you work alone, what title do you use to identify what you do?	One-man band	46
	Video journalist	21
	SoJo	3
	Backpack	2
	Do not work alone	28
Where are you based?	United States	36
	Continental Europe	30
	Oceania	12
	Asia	9
	Canada	6
	Middle East	5
	Africa	1
	South America	1
What area do you cover?	World	45
	Regional	35
	Local	20
How large is your crew?	One person	28
	Two persons	38
	Three persons	20
	Four or more	14
Is this a healthy job?	Very bad	4
	Not great	28
	Okay	39
	Good	0
	Very good	1
	Not answered	28
Are you satisfied with your job?	Very bad	2
	Not great	4
	Okay	22
	Good	37
	Very good	35
Is there room for happiness in your personal life?	Very bad	11
	Not great	11
	Okay	30
	Good	33
	Very good	15

In addition to the questions in the table, we asked how much the respondents made and what other local jobs paid the same. The following are the countries that seem to have the highest pay: Australia, Canada, Denmark, United Kingdom, Ireland, New Zealand, Turkey, and the United States—southern California, District of Columbia, and New York top the list for best pay.

When asked what other jobs paid the same as television photojournalist, the majority stated teachers, principals, and university professors. This group was followed closely by firefighters, paramedics, nurses, and bank tellers. A few pointed out that they made the same as reporters. The United Kingdom logged: fire eaters, acrobats, fishermen, and train drivers. The Republic of the Marshall Islands: file clerk or boat captain.

Not many surprises in the U.S. market. Photojournalists in Michigan ranked themselves as comparatively paid to auto workers; Louisiana: crawfishermen; North Carolina: cable installers and sanitation engineers. Alabama offered mobile home manufacturer; Las Vegas, illusion engineer.

The data seem to paint a picture that camerapeople are happy and have a high level of job satisfaction; however, they may have to work at keeping themselves healthy. This is roughly the same picture presented by everyone in the book. Most said they were healthy, stating that staying healthy is an essential part of their lifestyle.

On the question of relationships, the answers were all over the map. The first response was often "Great!" but upon further discussion, some said it was often difficult to balance home life and work. Considering the travel involved and the hours away from home, extra effort in relationships should be the order of the day—good advice for anyone. The larger-market photojournalists made the most money, with pay going up with foreign assignments. In all, television photojournalists are generally happy, easy going, and enjoy life. It's a good thing; they're paid to capture life.

Where Do We Go from Here?

Organizations and Workshops

Television photojournalism is the ultimate daily learning experience. There's something new in each story, location, and subject. If you love to learn, your life will be constantly enriched by this calling. There are also organizations, Web sites, and workshops designed for the further education and support of television photojournalists.

Most of the U.S.-based photojournalists in this book belong to the National Press Photographers Association (NPPA), and many have won the organization's highest honor, the NPPA Ernie Crisp Television News Photographer of the Year award. The organization's members are print and television photographers, editors, students, and representatives of businesses that serve the photojournalism industry. The membership totals more than 10,000. The organization was founded in 1946 and published the first issue of its magazine, the National Press Photographer. *On the front page: "With this issue is born a voice, one that has been mute much too long." The voice continues to this day with monthly installments.*

Alicia Wagner Calzada, past president of the NPPA, heads the organization's advocacy efforts to fight the "Orphan Works" copyright legislation and support photojournalists' freedom to shoot in public. Education is a large part of the NPPA's mission. They offer several workshops throughout the year.

The weeklong NPPA NewsVideo Workshop *is held every year in Norman, Oklahoma, with Sharon Levy Freed as its director. It heavily emphasizes storytelling and boasts an internationally recognized faculty of*

NPPA award recipients, network correspondents, and photojournalists. For additional information, see https://www.nppa.org/professional_development/workshops_and_seminars/NewsVideo_workshop/.

The Cutting Edge *is a traveling seminar sponsored by the NPPA; the primary focus is on the craft of editing news. The seminars are open to everyone. An award-winning staff of the nation's best editors comes together to help all attendees increase their skills in editing. Everything from the basics of editing to highly produced stories is discussed.*

The NPPF Airborne TV Seminar *lasts one day and travels to different towns with an award-winning faculty. The seminar is presented by The National Press Photographers Foundation, a nonprofit organization founded in 1976. It is open to both photographers and reporters. The organization's Web site is* www. nppa.org, *and membership, workshops, the* National Press Photographer *magazine, and competition information can be found there.*

The Photography, Film, Video & Digital Media Workshops, *located in Rockport, Maine, offer documentary and photojournalism workshops. Founded in 1973 as a summer conservatory for the world's photographers and filmmakers, The Workshops program has grown into a year-round college and learning center. They offer 250 one-week workshops and master classes. Rockport College came into existence in 1996 and now offers an Associate of Arts degree, a Master of Fine Arts degree, and a one-year Professional Certificate program. Contact them at* theworkshops.com *or 877-577-7700.*

The Poynter Institute *in St. Petersburg, Florida, is a school dedicated to teaching and inspiring journalists and media leaders. It stands for a journalism that informs citizens and enlightens public discourse. It carries forward Nelson Poynter's belief in the value of independent journalism in the public interest. Contact them at Poynter Online, Everything You Need to Be a Better Journalist (*www.poynter.org*) or 888-769-6837.*

Continuing on the Web

TVCAMERAMEN.COM, *The Online Magazine (*tvcameramen.com*), is run from Cyprus by David Hands. It is designed exclusively for the working camera operator. The site provides nonbiased information about the industry and includes articles, interviews, links, news, equipment reviews, job opportunities, and classified advertisements.*

b-roll.net *Television Photography (*b-roll.net*), is run by Kevin Johnson out of Washington, D.C. The site is heavily weighted toward TV news photographers. It features message boards, classified ads, job listings, and tips and tricks.*

Photog's Lounge, *The Online TV News Photog Magazine (*photogslounge.net*), is run by Tim Rutherford and offers news, gossip, entertainment, and humorous articles. The site, which refers to itself as "the voice of the television news photographer and cameraman," explores the culture and grind of TV news.*

Assignment Editor, *The Newsroom Home Page (*assignmenteditor.com*), is a clearinghouse site with links to all topics of news and journalism. Great for research.*

AlertNet, *Alerting humanitarians to emergencies (*www.alertnet.org*), is a humanitarian news network sponsored by the Reuters Foundation that aims to keep relief professionals and the wider public up to date on humanitarian crises around the globe. The site attracts sixteen million users a year and has a network of four-hundred contributing humanitarian organizations.*

ZeroRisk, *the News Safety Information Database (*zerorisk-international.com*), is an online worldwide support database for news industry safety, security, and risk management. The site is supported by the News*

Security Risk Management Group, which is made up of senior managers and editors from APTN, BBC, CNN, ITN, and Reuters. The site carries information and intelligence for news crews working in hostile environments.

Listen and Learn

In an attempt to convey their individual personalities and offer a deeper view into what kind of creativity inspires them, I asked each photojournalist interviewed for the book for a favorite song. The list is as varied as the personalities. Put on the headphones and enjoy.

The mix is published in Apple's iTunes Music Store. The link to the Roll! *iMix is* www.filmspot.tv/roll.html.

Favorite Songs

John DeTarsio *"Crazy" by Gnarls Barkley*

Larry Hatteberg *"In the Rain" by Boney James*

Eric Kehe *"Desire" by U2*

Stephen Hooker *"The Third Man Theme" only on America's Greatest Hits, Vol. 1, 1950*

Christian Parkinson *"I Bet You Look Good on the Dance Floor" by the Arctic Monkeys*

Ray Farkas *"If I Only Had a Brain" from* The Wizard of Oz

Corky Scholl *"True Believers" by The Bouncing Souls*

Lisa Berglund *"Crazy" by Seal*

Ian Pearson *"I Hope" by the Dixie Chicks*

Mitchell Wagenberg *"Sean Flynn" by The Clash*

Heidi McGuire *"Temperature" by Sean Paul*

Greg Stickney *"Come Again" by Sting*

Sam Allen *"Money Can't Buy It" by Annie Lennox*

Brian Weister *"Sugar, We're Going Down" by Fall Out Boy*

Mike Elwell *"Moondance" by Van Morrison*

Bart Noonan *"My Favorite Things" by Kenny Burrel*

David Hands *"Comfortably Numb" by Pink Floyd*

Rustin Thompson *"2 Kool 2 Be 4gotten" by Lucinda Williams*

Kevin Sites *"The Revolution Will Not Be Televised" by Molotov (Spanish version)*

For more than a year, it's been my privilege to puzzle together a collage of voices and ideas from the very best television photojournalists. The interviewees left me in awe of their talents and inspired me to create something that might stand as a tribute to them and their craft. I am eternally grateful for their time, both with me on this project and in their endless hours in the field capturing and telling the stories of our lives. They become our eyes on events we cannot attend; we owe them our thanks for their dedication, artistry, and honesty. We know our world through them.

Keep rolling!

Afterword

They entered the cave, eons ago, carrying flame on stick. Light flickering over beasts inscribed with ochre and charcoal—the human experience held on stone. Wonders captured and shared, unifying as only a well-told story can accomplish. What was once fleeting is now indelible.

In our lives, we owe them all, those who have heard the call to diligently impart truth through art. They've been with us from the beginning, pushing back the horizon, chasing daylight at the far end of the journey. The last illumination of truth where darkness rules. "I have seen, and so shall you," the calling goes. A child's first breath, a soldier's last, a spiritual compassion, a hellish atrocity. Grist for the mill, the storyteller sighs. The planet shrinks as the tribe expands.

A grand theme trumpets the nightly unwind as faces glow in unison before a global fireplace. Luminous tales told in scan lines and pixels, embers of the information age, blown hot by magicians with light. Each image, a charged message shared from some far-off land. Momentary tales flash like lightning; the world is unleashed in vivid detail once captured and held by electric historians.

Our secrets are revealed with a wink as they peer through flickering ports, standing heroic where most fear to tread. Unarmed but for a box of metal and glass that counts our lives in digital code. How we see our world was first viewed by them—

and they've told our story with beautiful and brutal honesty.

Appendix A

High-definition Versus Standard-definition Video Formats

Kerr Cook

Standard definition (SD) refers to the "legacy," old video viewing, storage, and transmission systems, represented by NTSC, PAL, and SECAM when color TV was introduced in the 1950s. When digital video (DV) was introduced, these legacy systems were represented by a pixel (*PI*cture(*X*) *EL*ement) grid digitizing the video content. Tied closely with their legacy, they are limited by the refresh and frame rates of NTSC and PAL (29.97 fps and 25 fps, respectively) as well as the low bandwidth (amount of information per unit of time) of 4 to 6 MHz and the limited number of scan lines allocated (525 and 625, respectively).

Due to limitations from the 1950s and 1960s, not all these scan lines actually carry visual information, and a trick called "interlacing" was done to allow more visual detail to be sent in the limited bandwidth. Interlaced video means that, instead of using a whole frame of visual information (and presenting these stills in rapid succession to simulate movement), a frame is actually updated in parts over two slices of time.

The first slice draws the odd-numbered scan lines, and then the next draws the evens. When displayed, we see both the even and odd lines at once and don't realize that one set is slightly delayed (by one slice of time) from the other. Rather than view whole, entire frames at a lower rate of presentation, which would flicker and have jerky motion, we can create the illusion of a smoother and sharper image by interlacing half frames. Even today, with more bandwidth available and higher refresh rates

Note: The information contained in this appendix was originally written for sonyhdinfo.com *and* camcorderinfo.com. *Used with permission of Kerr Cook and the Web sites.*

(to draw information), not all interlacing is bad and can certainly be used to provide benefits in many situations.

Digital video NTSC then is represented by a grid of 720 × 480 pixels at 29.97 fps for NTSC and 720 × 576 at 25 fps for PAL. These are interlaces, so, actually, there are nearly 60 half frames per second for NTSC and 50 for PAL. We commonly denote DV NTSC as 480i or 480/60i to indicate the 480 pixels vertically (480 scan lines which actually carry visual information of NTSC's 525 total lines), interlaced at 60 fields or half frames per second. These digital specifications are used for MiniDV, Digital8, and DVD recording camcorders, as well as for the DVD-video players of today.

All of the preceding discussions concern the 4:3 aspect ratio of "normal" TV (a legacy of the last forty-plus years). The aspect ratio tells us how wide versus how high. A common old TV screen is 4 parts wide to 3 parts high, or 1.33 to 1, but commonly just written 4:3. Widescreen refers to a screen that is wider than normal—usually 16:9 or 2.35:1, although there have been various aspect ratios used.

Widescreen SD DV is the implementation today of 16:9 video in MiniDV, Digital8, and DVD recording camcorders. This is somewhat of a trick, but what is done is to simply use a *wider* pixel in the grid! For NTSC, there *still* are 720 × 480 pixels in a frame, but those 720 pixels across the screen are not "square" (not as high as wide) but very wide. Putting them side by side fills out a wide screen . . . to a 16:9 overall ratio of the width to the height. This is how DVD-videos and DV camcorders of today utilize "widescreen."

High definition is the new, enhanced video standard. There have actually been several formats, but the standard is settling down to two: 1080i and 720p. Both of these are far superior in color and resolution (sharpness and detail) over standard definition. Almost all HD is in the 16:9 "widescreen" aspect ratio, natively.

The interlaced 1080i provides for a grid of up to 1920 × 1080 pixels! Some implementations use 1440 "wide" pixels (1440 × 1080), which still looks far better than SD widescreen.

Because processing of video information is better today (and cheaper with digital electronics), it is not necessary to always interleave or interlace the video. This gives us full frames for each frame, called "progressive" since each scan line is progressively scanned in each frame. 720p refers to the 1260 × 720 pixel grid of HD in progressive mode. The resolution itself is a bit lower than 1080i, but there are benefits to using full frames instead of interlaced half frames in situations recording high-speed motion where you may want to view the recording in slow motion or take still snapshots of frames.

HD refresh rates vary, but for 720p are commonly 24p (which is very film-like), 25p, 30p, 50p, and 60p for progressive (full frame at a time) video. The interlaced HD refresh rates are 25i, 30i, 50i, and 60i for 1080i.

High definition in any form is much better than the legacy systems. The emerging standards for high-definition video (HDV) is to put the higher resolution HD video stored at a 25 Mbps bit rate onto existing MiniDV tapes using MPEG2 compression. Several manufacturers have committed to this HDV standard, and everyone will benefit from home HD recordings over the limited standard definition DV common today.

Appendix B
Setting up a Video Monitor

Peter Hodges

My background is BBC engineering in studios and on location, where I specialized in special effects and process photography. I patented the Vical in-picture system of setup and video measurement for location operations in 1990, a technique that was developed and marketed by Hamlet Video International, Ltd., under license. In 1993, I set up my own training business aimed at camera operators and photographers new to video operations, and published my first book, *The Video Camera Operator's Handbook*. This was followed by *An Introduction to Video Measurement*, now, in its third edition, retitled *An Introduction to Video and Audio Measurement*.

Nothing creates argument more, gives rise to so much dubious and erroneous practice in the whole of video operations, than how to adjust a picture monitor. The intention here is to unravel a little of the mystery.

First, let us define what the procedure of picture setup should achieve. Ideally, it is to provide the camera operator, photographer, director, art director, designers of various crafts, and all other interested parties with a picture that is similar to that seen by the end viewer.

Such an ideal is, of course, unrealizable. While the up-to-date viewer has the latest widescreen cinema display, next door there could be the oldest TV imaginable with a picture tube long past its best. Our pictures may appear in theatres using high-power projectors, on the smallest iPod screen, or on a mobile phone. Each has its own specification, idiosyncrasies, strengths, and shortcomings. Some will be designed to work in daylight; others require near total dark.

How we deal with this is to fully understand what picture setup is about, determine good practice, and stick to it.

Let us begin by looking at some of the basics.

Note: Peter Hodges is the author of An Introduction to Video and Audio Measurement, *which was published by Focal Press in 2004. This excerpt is used with permission.*

What Is a Picture?

The real-life scene to the eye of an observer exists as tones and colours between black and white. These two extremes set the limits of the contrast range of that scene. The video system also has black-and-white levels, so defining the video contrast range. Black and white are also, by definition, colourless. The video system has a defined "no-colour" condition, that of *grey*, where, in terms of the RGB, red, green, and blue are of equal value.

Return to our real-life scene. Take away all light and the scene will be black. Add light and the scene will grow before our eyes. We can show this with a video camera. Cap the lens and the image in the viewfinder will disappear. Uncap the lens and the image returns. This may seem very basic, but it is upon this simple principle that the whole of the video system, and the pictures it re-creates, is built. Our real-life scene does not disappear because day turns to night or the studio lights are turned off, nor does the camera cease to produce a signal. The video signal is there even when the scene goes black. This is *black level*. It is upon black level that the image is built up through the various tones of grey, all the colours, right up to the maximum the camera can produce, which is *peak white*.

The picture display has its own value for black. It is the screen itself. Switch off the power to the display and we see the screen at its blackest. The point here is that the screen can only go as black as its type and design allow. Screens are also subject to ambient light and manufacturers are constantly striving to make screens less reflective and therefore more black.

Because not every picture will contain black, the video signal always has a reference of true video black. This, the picture display seeks out, latches on to, and builds all the tones and colours to create the picture. For this to happen, video black level should coincide with screen black. This is the point at which the screen is just beginning to produce a light output, and is very critical. It is called *brightness*.

The other principle picture parameter is contrast. This sets how bright the picture whites are. However, contrast cannot be set until brightness has been set.

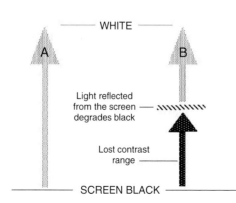

Setting Brightness

So demanding and critical is this adjustment that a number of methods have over years been devised. The requirement, though, hasn't changed: to fix video black to screen black.

The Simplest . . .

Connect a camera to the picture monitor and cap the lens. Adjust the monitor brightness control, first down them up, observe the change in the screen, how the tone changes. A point will be found where the screen will go no darker. Rock the brightness about this point and set the control to just see the screen brighten. The harder you look, the more

critical will be the result, until the smallest change in screen brightness will be observed. It is at this point that the camera black coincides with screen black. This is the point we are seeking. Uncap the camera. The scene should be reasonably represented after adjusting the lens iris for best exposure.

Take the monitor into different lighting conditions and repeat the procedure. A new setting will—or should be—found. Practice and repeat. Get a sense of the monitor's response through your fingers on this all-important brightness control, whether it be rotary knob, up/down buttons, or menu. Observe carefully. Another tip: Open the lens slightly until a semblance of picture appears. See how this affects the result. Open the lens to fully expose the scene and try again; use the darkest part of the picture and re-adjust the brightness control.

Using a monitor with an overscan facility (see the accompanying figure) helps because the slight difference—two or three percent—between the black of a capped camera and true video black makes for more precise observation.

Simplest Is Not Always Best . . .

Setting brightness this way may seem straightforward but each change of scene, ambient light, camera exposure, produces a slightly different result. It also relies on a correctly set-up camera. To prove this, adjust the camera's black level. It may be called black level, lift, or pedestal, and you may have to go into menus. And only do so if you're confident about restoring to the original position. Raise the camera black level high enough to be seen clearly. Now adjust the monitor brightness down. See how adjusting brightness compensates for the camera's maladjustment of black level?

Rule: Do not adjust the monitor to compensate for the camera.

Getting Between Camera and Monitor . . .

To accurately observe and set monitor brightness, we must use a video signal that shows true video black level. A most convenient source of accurate video is colour bars. Freely available on camera, colour bars would seem to offer the ideal solution to picture setup. Beware! The colour bars test signal was devised as the standard test and measurement for recording and transmission and uses the maximum colour values plus video black and peak white. The intensity of the colours makes it difficult, if not impossible, for the eye to observe the fine nuances we are trying to observe at picture black. Not even the black bar, which is true video black, is of much use here because of the presence of these high levels of colour. While alternative forms of this test signal are now available, some of which offer picture setup, one should avoid attempting setup of picture monitor brightness with conventional camera colour bars.

There is now available a range of dedicated picture setup equipment. From small, battery-powered units to full-blown studio facilities, most make use of the eye's acuity in recognizing very small changes in tone or colour. Picture Line Up Generating Equipment (PLUGE), originally developed by the BBC, has mutated into various formats. Another method, Vical, inserts a picture setup signal into the camera monitoring video. Such devices rely on the eye's ability to distinguish small differences of tonal value when seen side by side.

The following is the procedure:

1. Place the monitor in its working situation, preferably in subdued light.
2. Allow one's eyes to get accustomed to the situation.
3. Apply a suitable picture setup signal, such as that based on PLUGE in the previous figure, to the monitor.
4. Observe the dark patterns and adjust brightness such that the darkest patch is barely distinguishable from the background. This setting places true video black slightly high, which most workers prefer. If your system uses higher-than-true video black (e.g., the original NTSC standard uses pedestal, known as "NTSC setup," which is not to be confused with the picture setup procedure described here, or raised black level), the brighter bar should be adjusted to be just distinguishable from background. This would have the effect of pushing down picture brightness to compensate for the pedestal.

Setting Contrast

Setting this correctly really requires that the light output of the screen is measured. Higher-grade monitors may suggest a procedure, either the manufacturer's own or a proprietary method. But, for a single monitor in the field, measurement is much less important than getting the best overall picture for the conditions.

Contrast sets the level of screen white. Adjusted too high and the tonal gradation in the brightest parts of the picture will be lost. Ambient light has a great bearing on screen contrast. The blacker the screen, the better if it is to be used outdoors. However, this is somewhat negated by our eyes adjusting to the ambient light. In bright conditions, we suffer the "can't see in the dark" syndrome and the temptation to adjust the monitor beyond its capabilities is very real. The answer is to shade the screen and let your eyes adjust.

The grey steps of PLUGE are designed to produce specific light outputs. Actual figures will depend on the version used, but the eye will easily see how white and the next step down blend into one as contrast is raised too far. Make sure all the steps are comfortably distinguishable and white is not blooming or "burning out."

On the other hand, setting contrast too low wastes useful tonal range. As with brightness, it's a question of practice, of knowing the display, and that will only come with experience.

Colour

Most picture displays conform to a colour temperature of 6500K, that is typical daylight, or SMPTE D65. Colour setup should be conducted in subdued light of this colour temperature. Proprietary techniques are available to measure colour, but a useful check can be done for colour balance, that is greyscale, by comparing to Kodak Gray Card.

Modern picture displays will normally ship with good greyscale. Unless obviously wrong, don't attempt to alter. The controls are often hidden away. If it's a CRT monitor, this may mean removing covers, which is a safety issue. Here, menu controls are far easier. They are red black, blue black, red white, blue white, although the actual labelling may vary. There may also be green controls but avoid touching these. If you're confident and you're safe, here's the procedure:

1. Ambient light should be as low and close to D65 as possible.
2. Apply a suitable PLUGE or similar signal.
3. Set brightness and contrast as above.
4. Adjust red and blue blacks for neutral or no-colour in the dark bars. This requires a little practice.
5. Adjust red and blue whites to make the white patch true white or no-colour. Compare to Kodak Gray Card.
6. Re-check red and blue blacks, then red and blue whites.

There may be other colour controls such as *chroma phase* or *hue*, and *saturation* or *chroma level*, the latter being set by the *Blue Only* facility. These controls are best left untouched in the field as they also require suitable lighting conditions to observe the procedure properly, not forgetting the time to carry it out. Use colour bars that offer additional features aimed at monitor setup. Saturation, or chroma level, is set by Blue Only. Selecting this reduces the picture display to show the blue component alone. Adjust chroma level until the intensities of the blue bar and the white bar (now also blue) are equal. Where chroma phase is provided, adjust this to make the cyan and magenta bars equal. As can be imagined, this procedure will take practice.

Points to bear in mind:

• Modern monitors are generally reliable as regards maintaining good greyscale and colour.
• Modern cameras maintain good black level and colour.
• It is highly likely your eyes will do neither of these.
• Use PLUGE or other proprietary method to check your monitor periodically and prove all its functions. Likewise, get your camera checked for black level, peak white, and colour balance.

- Then, in the field, when you're moving around from light into shade, the quick check of monitor brightness and contrast as described earlier should be sufficient.
- Iris down or cap the lens.
- Set brightness to see the screen just begin to brighten.
- Open lens and set contrast below highlight distortion.

It's practice and observation, over and over. That is the way to good pictures.

Appendix C
The Power of Lighting

Bill Holshevnikoff

Several years ago, I was working in my office and the telephone rang. It was one of the managers of ARRI's lighting division—he's a film production guy and a real straight-shooter. The conversation went something like this:

"Hi, Bill. If this is a good time, we have a few of us here in New York meeting, and we're all on the speaker phone right now."

"Okay", I say. "What can I do for you guys?"

"Well, we have a question for you. What is a digital light kit?"

Sounding like a setup to a new production joke, I answer, "I don't know. What is a digital light kit?"

"No" he says. "We're asking you. What is a digital light kit?"

The question, and the phone call in general, stumped me for a moment. "Uh, well . . . there really isn't a 'digital light kit' that I'm aware of at the moment—maybe LEDs? Can I ask why you're asking?"

"Sure" he says. "We're getting lots of phone calls lately and people are saying, 'We have our digital camera and our digital edit system. Now, we need a digital light kit.' It's a marketing problem, really. So, we are trying to decide exactly what would be in a digital lighting kit."

After a short laugh, the silence on the other end of the phone led me to realize that they weren't joking. "Um, okay. That's sort of funny."

"Well, it may seem a bit funny, but we need to figure out exactly what's in a digital light kit . . . because, frankly, we need to offer one to our customers. But, I can't bear the thought of calling it "The Digital Kit." I just couldn't sleep with that. Can you put some thought into this, please, and try to come up with some input for us?"

Still thrown by the entire conversation, I reply with "Of course" and we all hang up.

Note: Bill Holshevnikoff's "The Power of Lighting" workshops have been attended by professionals from nearly every major U.S. television network and cable channel.

And that conversation, to my knowledge, was how the ARRI D-Kits were born. In the end, we realized that people were just asking for a smaller, lighter kit. But it was amazing to see that some folks seemed to be almost brainwashed into "digital-think"—that somehow the basics of lighting might be different because they had a *digital* camera. Every ARRI D-Kit includes *The Power of Lighting for Film & Video, Second Edition*, the ARRI Lighting Handbook.*

Open-faced.

Fresnel.

Light with frost.

Light with Softbent.

Hard light.

Soft light.

Bouncing light off a foam core.

Lighting Theories and Techniques
Choosing a Light Source

The two basic types of instruments are the open-faced and the Fresnel-lensed. Both types of light sources provide a focusable, even beam field of light that can be used to create a wide variety of light qualities and moods for productions.

Light quality can be characterized by how "hard" or "soft" the shadow produced by an instrument appears. The quality of light produced by an instrument is determined by the physical size (not the intensity) of the light source used. In general, the larger, more diffused the light source, the softer the light quality. Typically, a diffusion material, such as frost or a silk, might be placed in front of a lighting instrument to increase the working (physical) size of a light source. (When light transmits through a diffusion material, the illuminated diffusion material then becomes the acting light source.)

A sharp, well-defined shadow edge (hard light), like that which is produced by the sun, is most often produced by a small light source. A softer, less-defined shadow edge (soft light), like that of a cloudy day, is most often produced by a larger, more diffused light source, such as a Lightbank.

If you do not have a Lightbank, there are many other ways to create softer light qualities with the instruments contained within this kit. Attaching frost to the barn doors will soften the light quality slightly. Placing a large diffusion panel (silk) in front of the

---

The excerpts that follow are from the ARRI Lighting Handbook. *Images and text © 2000 Bill Holshevnikoff. Reprinted by permission from ARRI and Bill Holshevnikoff.*

source, or bouncing the light off of a white wall, ceiling, or white card, will produce a dramatically softer light quality.

Again, the physical size of the light source is directly related to the quality of light produced. So, ideally, one should consider the appropriate light quality for a shot or scene prior to setting up the lighting. For example, hard light may not be considered a natural light quality for many interior scenes (such as an office with four white walls and overhead fluorescent lighting).

Hard Light Versus Soft Light

There is no hard-and-fast rule as to when to use hard or soft light for a shot or scene. Creating a particular light quality is a judgment call, and there are no wrong or right answers. There are, however, characteristics that are inherent to both hard and soft light, and one must constantly weigh the pros and cons of each prior to lighting a scene.

In general, hard light is easily controlled through the use of the barn doors on the fixture, and it can be used to produce dramatic shadows and attractive lighting effects for film or video. When lighting people for interviews with hard light, one must carefully consider the placement of the light source in order to produce appealing results on camera. An ill-placed Fresnel or open-faced instrument can produce unkind results on even the most photogenic persons.

Fresnel-lensed lights produce an attractive light quality and an extremely even field of light, and are the most popular instrument choice when hard lighting is required for studio and location work.

While Arrilites also produce an even beam field, these instruments generally are not used to light people directly. The Arrilite instrument is most often used to create a fill light source, by bouncing light off of walls, ceilings, or bounce boards (on location), to use with diffusion frost or behind a Lightbank, or to light background areas. When used as a direct source (no diffusion), the glass lens on a Fresnel produces a more pleasing quality of light than an open-faced instrument.

The use of softer light sources can be more forgiving when lighting people, but softer, diffused sources can be much more difficult to control. Diffused light disperses in many directions, and although the light quality may be desirable for a particular shot or scene, the uncontrolled spill light from a diffused source can ruin even the best of shots. Much of lighting has to do with directing the viewer's eye around the screen, and when spill light from your main light sources contaminates the background of your shot, the lighting can appear haphazard and lose visual impact. Once again, careful consideration of your light placement can dramatically improve the results of your lighting.

Light Source Intensity

The intensity of the light source you choose for a shot is an important decision. Brighter is not necessarily better. Depth of field (f/stop = depth of focus) and f/stop selection with your camera should be a conscious decision each time you begin lighting a shot.

Many of the newest video cameras are extremely light sensitive. Lighting a scene with too much light forces you to close down the iris to a deeper f/stop (f/8 to f/11) in order to properly expose the scene. This creates a very deep focus range (depth of field) in your shot. Selective focus is not an option unless you are shooting at the very longest telephoto lens setting on your digital video camera.

Selective focus is a simple method of focusing the attention of the viewer on a particular subject or area in the frame. Using smaller lighting instruments and less light allows you to expose your scene at an iris setting of perhaps f/2.0 or f/2.8. Shooting with an open iris (aperture) creates a shallower depth of field and allows you to utilize selective focus as a creative tool in image making.

Additionally, you can down-lamp your instruments to use smaller wattage bulbs. For example, the ARRI 650 Fresnel also can use a 500W or 300W lamp. This provides you with the wider beam field of the larger Fresnel while still working with lower light output. Many videographers now choose the more compact ARRI D Softbank kits, which use smaller, lower-wattage fixtures. Shooting at lower light levels with the newer cameras allows the use of instruments as small as a 150W ARRI Fresnel. Used in conjunction with proper lighting techniques, shooting with a shallow depth of field can enable you to create more of a film-look when shooting with your video camera.

A Note on Color

The color of the tungsten lighting fixtures is rated at 3,200 degrees on the Kelvin temperature scale. Although the light from these instruments may appear as white light on video or film, it is actually a very warm-colored light relative to the color of daylight. Choosing a tungsten film stock or setting your video camera for tungsten (3,200K) will give you proper color rendering when lighting with these fixtures. Be careful when white balancing your camera that you are balancing your camera for the light in your subject area. Proper white balance will ensure accurate skin tones in your video productions.

Sometimes, you may be shooting in an area with existing ambient light and the color of that ambient light may differ dramatically from the color of light generated by the tungsten-balanced instruments. The color of fluorescent light in office areas, commercial light in retail or industrial settings, and ambient daylight all differ greatly from the color of light created by your tungsten lights. In these cases, it may be necessary to color-correct your lighting instruments to match the color of the ambient light in your scene.

Tungsten lights can be color-corrected through the use of color correction gels. These colored gels can be attached directly to the barn doors of your instruments. Just be aware of the fact that using gels on your lights can greatly reduce the output of light (i.e., full CTB [daylight] correction gel can reduce output by as much as 85 percent). Also, gels can burn when set too close to the lamp or lens on your lights. Careful use of correction gels can help you to manipulate and match the color of the existing light in your scene.

Some Basic Definitions

The Four Primary Light Sources: Key, Fill, Separation, and Background

In this section, the "Lighting Evolution" of images shows the single effect of each of these four sources in a talking head shot.

Key Light

The *key light* is the primary light source for the subject area of the image. The key light is the main source of illumination and often establishes a light quality, whether hard or soft, for the shot or scene. When lighting people for on-camera interviews, the object of the key light is to illuminate the person in an attractive manner and reveal the shape of the person's face through shadow form (modeling). A Fresnel is often the choice for a key light source (due to the ease of use and light control). Lightbanks also are a popular key light source for interviews.

Position of the key light can range from directly above the camera lens to completely behind the subject, depending upon the desired results. Seeing the effects of the key light shadows on the subject's face will help you to determine the best height and location for this light. When lighting for multiple cameras, it is usually best to place the key lights for optimal results on the close-up camera positions for each subject. Regardless of the quality of light you choose, the light from the key source should be confined to the subject area if you hope to achieve a dramatic lighting effect for the image. If a less dramatic effect is desired, the spill light from the key source can be allowed to illuminate the background area as well.

Fill Light

The *fill light* is an additional light source designed to fill in the shadow areas created by the key source. Ideally, the fill light source is a larger, diffused, soft light source that will fill in the shadow area to the desired density (light level) without producing a second, opposing shadow on the subject(s). Think of your fill lighting as ambient light for the shot or scene, and as your visual mood indicator. The less fill light, the more dramatic the lighting. Regardless of whether your key source is hard or soft light, using a hard light source for a fill light can create an unnatural double-shadow effect on the talent/subjects. Use of a large silk, a Lightbank, dense, white diffusion material on the barn doors, or bouncing the light off of a white surface (wall, bounce board, and so on) can produce a natural and effective fill light source. When shooting only a close-up of a single person, often the spill light from your key source can be directed at a large, white bounce card for a soft, shadowless fill light. The position of the fill light can vary greatly, but normally fill light sources are set either near the camera lens or at a position opposite the key light source.

Separation Light (Hair Light)

The *separation light*, or hair light, is designed to help visually separate the subject(s) from the background. A separation light is not always necessary, but without the use of this light, it is possible that the subject could blend with the background. Use of a separation light also helps to bring out

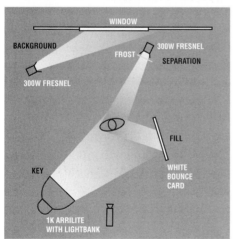

color and texture in the subject's hair. Brightness of the separation light can equal the brightness of the key light source, but for interviews, the separation light is usually less bright than the key.

Position of this source can range from directly behind and above the subject to just outside of the frame line to create a side rim-light. As is true with almost all light placements, the effect of the separation light is dramatically altered by its position. Experiment with different light qualities and placements to find your own favorite look.

Background Light

The *background light* can be the first or final light to be set for a scene or shot, depending on the importance of the background lighting in the scene and your lighting style. If careful consideration has been given to the control of spill light in the subject area, the effect of your background light can be quite dramatic. The addition of a background light also can help to add texture, color, and/or added separation for the subject(s) from the background. Direction of the background light also can help to support key light direction and motivation (i.e., light from a window and so on). Both Fresnels and Arrilites can be used effectively to light background areas.

The accompanying images and diagrams *(see next three pages)* will provide you with basic lighting setups and help you better identify and manipulate the separate components of reflected light.

Basic Lighting Setups	Technical Data
Soft light key, no fill (see A)	1 small Lightbank 1 1000W Arrilite (inside Lightbank) with double-wire scrim 1 300W Arri Fresnel
Key, fill, separation, and background with three lights (see B on next page)	1 small Lightbank 1 1000W Arrilite (inside Lightbank) 2 650W Arri Fresnels (1/2 CTB correction gel on all sources)
Key, fill, and separation with two lights and bounce card (see C on next page)	1 650W Arri Fresnel (bounced off whiteboard) 1 300W Arri Fresnel (GAM 1050 frost on front of barn doors)
One soft light (see D on next page)	1 small Lightbank 1 1000W Arrilite (inside Lightbank) with double-wire scrim
Fresnels (see E on page 367)	2 300W Arri Fresnels
Soft key, two 300W Fresnels (see F on page 367	2 300W Arri Fresnels (GAM 1075 frost on bottom half of barn doors on each key light) 2 C-stands with grip arms 1 small Lightbank 1 1000W Arrilite (inside Lightbank) with double-wire scrim

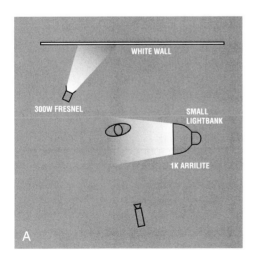

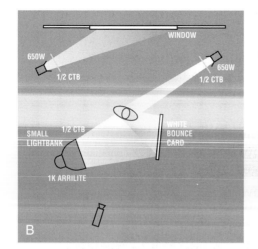

WINDOW

650W
1/2 CTB

650W
1/2 CTB

1/2 CTB

SMALL
LIGHTBANK

WHITE
BOUNCE
CARD

1K ARRILITE

B

B

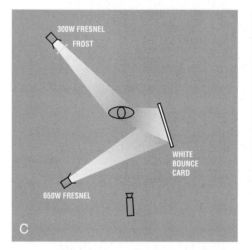

300W FRESNEL
FROST

WHITE
BOUNCE
CARD

650W FRESNEL

C

C

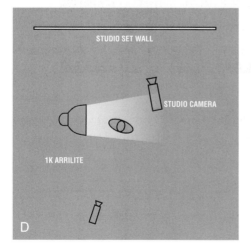

STUDIO SET WALL

STUDIO CAMERA

1K ARRILITE

D

D

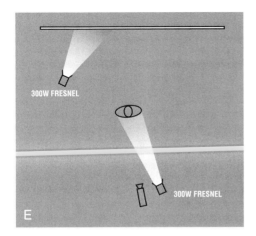

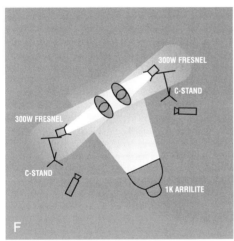

The Inverse-Square Law of Light

Moving the subject or artificial light source twice the distance away will yield only one-quarter the amount of light. In the illustration on the next page, when the distance between the light source and subject is increased from 10 feet to 20 feet, the illumination provided by the light source decreases from 100-foot candles, to 25-foot candles, which is a loss of two f/stops from f/5.6 to f/2.8.

The ratio between the two subjects, one at 10 feet and the other at 20 feet, is 4:1. If you wanted your key-to-fill lighting ratio to be 4:1, you could move your lamp double the distance from your subject or use two double scrims. A double scrim reduces the light by one stop, a single scrim by half a stop.

So, a two-stop difference of key to fill is a 4:1 ratio. A one-stop difference is 2:1.

Appendix D
Sound

Nigel Fox, Location Sound Recordist, or Soundie

*N*igel Fox and his company, Foxprovideo, provide sound services for domestic *and international broadcasters.* As a location soundie, which is Australian slang for a sound recordist, I get the much-maligned and most definitely underrated task of collecting the spoken voice, music, and background noises associated with television productions. But as the old saying states: out of sight out of mind. We're not seen as the "glamour" part of the camera crew. Recently, news departments have been savage in their cutting of two-person camera crews.

Soundies are far more than people who have microphones shrouded in hairy animals on sticks. Not only are we an essential part of the storytelling process, sometimes the audio can overtake the impact of the visual medium quite dramatically. Yet, without sound, television really is nothing more than a collection of moving pictures that make little sense without the spoken word. Try watching it without sound; it can become quite surreal.

When, in a tense interview, the soundie can pick up the rapid drying out of the palate and then signal to the cameraman to do a slow zoom-in—normally the beads of sweat rapidly follow. I can tell you from experience where the palate is drying out, be it the upper front, rear, center, or lower and tongue area. The stress level in a voice changes the pitch of a vocal chord noticeably to us.

In a press pack we can "throw" our boom microphones over the heads of the crowd of still photographers, reporters, and cameramen to capture those all-important words that will be used in a sound bite. From a safety point of view, when the press pack moves, we are there to guide our cameramen backward, walking them around obstacles, making sure they don't get run over or fall down stairs. With crowd situations or civil unrest, we are a second set of eyes, watching out for those who mean harm and controlling crowds as best we can while the journalist does his piece to camera. We do all of this while still capturing the all-important sound for the news report.

Any good soundie will also know where the best coffee shops are and where to get the best food at a good price. They'll navigate the crew car around unfamiliar surroundings and do a hundred other subtle things on a daily basis.

Doing the sound is a much-misunderstood job, as it's not considered a tangible item even though a myriad of studies have shown people are far more susceptible to picking up poor-quality audio than badly shot, poorly exposed pictures.

Bad camerawork can be covered up with a cutaway shot or color-corrected. Sadly, we don't have that much of an option when it comes to working in a fast-paced environment like news and current affairs work. We have to get it right first time, every time.

When you have the luxury of working on a documentary or good-quality production, you can have the time to get "atmos" (background noise, sometimes known as a buzz track, natural sound, or nat sound in the States), effects noise, or specific sounds to be dropped into the audio track during postproduction.

You only have to look at the amount of audio tracks available on most nonlinear systems to see how important sound really is. You may have one or two vision tracks, maybe five effects tracks, and anything up to five hundred tracks for audio! Take a moment to listen through headphones to any animated film that has been released in the last year or two to truly experience the depth of audio and the associated journey it alone will take you on.

The mark of any good television production or film should be the ability to listen to the audio track alone. If the show is any good, it will sound like a play one would hear on the radio, allowing the listener's imagination to put the pictures in place, conjuring up visions splendid within the person's own mind. That is the true mark of an excellent production.

The richness of a well-delivered audio track can add tension to even the most dramatic footage. Even in its earliest guises, sound played an important role in reinforcing a dramatic scene, as witnessed when the *Hindenburg* caught fire and exploded while arriving in Lakehurst, New Jersey, in 1937. The reporter's voice, his emotions caught in the moment, added a raw, emotional edge to what were already spectacular pictures of a terrible event.

Just think how different the footage of Neil Armstrong would be without his commentary as he made that first step from the Lunar Lander to the moon's surface. While you roll off "one small step," the visual will pop into the mind as the sound evokes a far more passionate response than the visual image. The assassination of JFK, Nixon and the Watergate tapes, Walter Cronkite and his reports from Vietnam after the Tet Offensive (which many consider a tipping point in that conflict), phone calls from the Twin Towers and aircraft during 9/11—all major events supported by a recording of the spoken word. Sound really is a far more powerful medium than people think.

Hitchcock understood the musical score perfectly, as the shower scene in *Psycho* so aptly portrays the horror and mental discord of the killer in such striking reality that many people could not bear to watch—while the audio track alone portrayed the horror of the scene to those hiding behind their hands.

While we are on the subject of classic films, how easy is it to remember Bogart in *Casablanca* when people say, "Play it again, Sam," even though that line is not in the film. You might remember the piano playing even if you don't remember the film's main character, Harry.

The deep, ever-increasing notes played in *Jaws* kept a generation away from swimming. The music has surpassed the film in the public subconscious, bringing about an irrational anxiety in many who have never actually seen the film. But you will still hear it used in comedy skits or anyplace where an idea has to be quickly instilled.

Tools of the Trade

We soundies carry quite a diverse mix of equipment during our daily workings. What follows is a breakdown of my equipment in its most common setup. I carry a four-channel mixer in an audio bag with three radio receivers; the fourth channel is reserved for the boom/shotgun microphone.

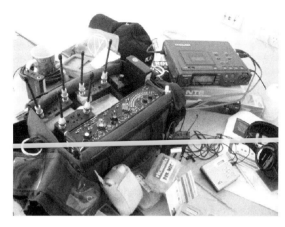

Audio/Mixer Bag

This is a specialized bag made for the sole purpose of keeping all of your equipment "Flex" together. Companies who specialize in such items are Porta-Brace, Kata, Petrol, Rocket, and Versa Flex.

Audio Mixer

I currently use a Sound Devices 442, which is a four-input (channel) audio mixer. With more and more demand for digital audio, I will need to add a Sound Devices 744 T. When the demand for 5.1 surround in the field really takes off, I will buy an Aaton Cantar, which is an eight-track field mixer with a built-in hard-disk drive.

Radio Microphone

This is a two-piece unit consisting of a transmitter, into which you plug a microphone, and a receiver, which feeds the signal to the audio mixer via an audio lead. Generally, they are classed as UHF Diversity or VHF. But remember, if you are using a mix of "digital" and "analog" radio microphones, the analog ones have to have a delay built in to the audio recording device to allow for the digital receivers to process the sound and then spit it out as analog. For example, if feeding into an HDD recorder and then from that directly into the camera, you may end up with lip-sync problems.

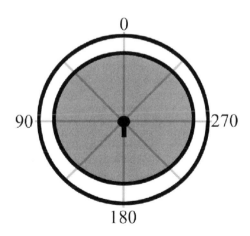

Lavaliere or Lapel Microphone

This is a miniature microphone normally affixed or hidden on a person's clothing, within twenty centimeters or seven inches from a person's mouth. This can take many forms, like the Pin Microphone developed by Ric Creaser of Ricsonix, which has a

Lavaliere microphones have an omni-directional pickup pattern. They pick up sound in all directions around the microphone.

Ricsonix pin microphone.

back plate that pins through the clothing with a microphone head worn externally.

Due to its clever design, the Ricsonix miraculously vanishes before your very eyes. I use these a lot, as they reduce the number of problems one can come across especially with fabric noise, clothing rustle, and so on.

As general-use microphones, they have a good range of sound, plus the MITS-1 is the only microphone on the market that you can actually superglue on buttons or fake jewelery. This is a microphone designed by a fellow sound recordist, hence, why it is so useful in eliminating many of the problems associated with hiding lapel microphones.

Other Mics

Other lapel microphones I use on a day-to-day basis are the Sennheiser MKE-2 and the Sony ECM-77, both chosen for their robust quality as much as for the different sounds both produce. One very important note on using the Sennheiser. The microphone is supplied with two caps: a short cap (Part #MZC2-1, Cat No 76612) and a long cap (Part #MZC2-2, Cat No 74645). The longer cap gives a 3 to 6 db boost to the sound starting at 10,000 Hz and dropping off around 15,000 to 16,000 Hz, which is good if hiding the microphone or using it on musical instruments. If it's mounted around the chest area, it can make the sound of the person talking thinner than the credibility attached to a politician's preelection promises. The difference in length is only around 1 to 2 mm, but the difference in sound quality can be significant.

Which brings me to my tough-as-a-tank Sony ECM-77. It might not be the best lapel microphone on the market, but it is a truly tough piece of equipment. I know of one person who actually put one through a washing machine! It was left to dry plugged in and it still worked—you can't knock that for toughness.

Now the Sony 77 gets used in what can best be described as some wretched working environments, the most common place being on ships at sea. Not only is it at sea, but it is used in places like the engine room while the ship is travelling along at full speed. If you have ever experienced such an environment, it is hot and exceedingly noisy (normally an ear-protection-mandated area), plus it can have an oily presence in the air.

My 77 has survived moving from that environment to deck with driving rain, sea spray, and such on many an occasion and continues its work without a murmur of discontent. If only the same could be said of the talent.

Other more commonly used items are my two "shotties" or should I say shotgun microphones—namely my MKE 416 and ME 66. Out of the two the 416 has a far nicer sound; plus it's a far more directional microphone so, if it's not on target, the off-presence sound can be noticeable. Considering my 416 is some twenty years old (with a visit to the workshop every five years or so), I can truly say it has been a very stable workhorse over many thousands of hours of work.

Over the past two to three years, I have been supplementing the 416 with the ME66, which, due to its fatter pickup pattern, has proved itself quite useful in large press gatherings.

When working in a news environment, a lot of the time, everything we do is a compromise. So, making the available tools work in a most effective manner is very much the situation one normally ends up working in. Again, for this reason, I purchased a Sennheiser ME62, which is a modular k-6 system microphone head with an omnidirectional, pickup pattern.

This microphone is also a good all 'rounder for working in those previously mentioned compromise situations where time is against you but a quick setup is all-important. This microphone is used at press releases or table situations where two or three people are either at a lectern or sitting down in a limited space—where no press splitter box is available. By mounting this microphone in its own, self-contained microphone stand, I can stay out of frame ready with a boom pole should anyone not be picked up and I need to intervene.

The Rode NT-6 is a microphone that I have taken to using for recording multiple, non-professional talent in roundtable discussions for a corporate client. The amazing quality of sound reproduction from this microphone is most certainly up there with many far more expensive units. This microphone is mainly used with a microphone stand mounted above the "talent" just out of camera frame.

At the end of the day, delivering the best-quality sound to the client is what we are here for. Many people over the years have made fun of the sound recordist. We are seen as these static items stuck at the back of a room or studio who complain about everything. But no one ever thinks about the sound until it's not there.

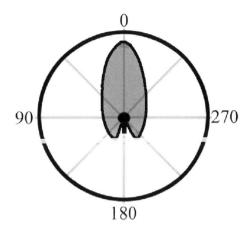

The pickup pattern for a shotgun microphone is very directional.

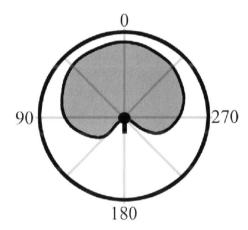

A Cardiod pickup pattern is the standard for reporter's handheld microphones. The pattern is slightly directional and needs to be roughly pointed in the direction of the sound.

Notes and Resources

Notes about the Introduction

I am afraid much of our history is lost, for now. I started doing research for Chapter 1 with ten basic questions in mind. Most were never answered. As my research began, the scope of our history started to expand. Filled with dates and intersecting events that would lead to the present, I had well over 250 pages of notes to pull from. In Chapter 1, Introduction, when dates are left out, the event occurred during the previously mentioned year.

Many dates conflicted depending on different sources. When that happened, I chose the date that appeared most often. Although scholars might take offense at my research methods, sometimes I would use Wikipedia as the deciding factor. In addition to those listed later in the Resources, some of the reference works I used initially follow.

References

Abramson, Albert. (2003) *The History of Television, 1942 to 2000*. Jefferson, NC: McFarland & Co.

Auckland, George, comp. "History of the Magic Lantern." The Magic Lantern Society, 17 June 2006— <http://www.magiclantern.org.uk/history1.htm>

Bianco, Dr. Carl. "Howstuffworks: How Vision Works," 17 June 2006—http://health.howstuffworks.com/ eye2.htm

Dodge, Sam. "Antique 35 mm Movie Cameras." Sam Dodge Antique Motion Picture Studio Cameras, 2 March 2006—<http://www.samdodge.com>

EarlyCinema.Com. "Timeline," 17 June 2006—<http://www.earlycinema.com/timeline/index.html>

"George Eastman House," 17 June 2006—<http://www.eastmanhouse.org>

Fang, Irving E. (1997) *A History of Mass Communication: Six Information Revolutions*. Boston: Focal Press.

Fang, Irving E. "Fang's Media History Timeline, 1996." University of Minnesota, 17 June 2006—<http:// www.mediahistory.umn.edu/time/alltime.html#bc>

Fielding, Raymond. (1972) *The American Newsreel, 1911–1967, 1st ed*. Norman: University of Oklahoma Press.

Freudenrich, Craig. "Howstuffworks: How Light Works," 17 June 2006—<http://science.howstuffworks. com/light.htm>

Genova, Tom. "Television History—the First 75 Years." TV History, 02 March 2006—<http://www. tvhistory.tv>

Hilliard, Robert L., and Michael C. Keith. (2005) *The Broadcast Century and Beyond: A Biography of American Broadcasting, 4th ed*. Boston: Focal Press.

Hitchcock, Don. "Chauvet Cave." Don's Maps, 23 March 2006, 7 June 2006—<http://donsmaps.com/ chauvetcave.html>

Institut-Lumiere.Org. "Institut Lumière," 17 June 2006—<http://www.institut-lumiere.org/english/frames.html>

Kodak.Com. "1878–1929," 17 June 2006—<http://www.kodak.com/global/en/corp/historyOfKodak/1878.jhtml?pq-path=2699>

Leggat, Robert. "A History of Photography"; "Fenton, Roger," 3 January 2006—http://www.rleggat.com/; 17 June 2006—<http://www.rleggat.com/photohistory/history/fenton.htm>

Lester, Dr. Paul M., ed. (1990) *NPPA Special Report: The Ethics of Photojournalism.* National Press Photographers Association. Durham, NC: NPPA.

Mishkind, Barry. "The Broadcast Archive—Radio History on the Web." Oldradio.com, 17 June 2006—<http://www.oldradio.com/>

The Museum of Broadcast Communications. *Encyclopedia of TV, 1st ed,* 3 March 2006—<http://www.museum.tv/>

Museum of the Moving Image. "Television in Quotes," Chum Limited, Steelcase, You TV, Chum City Store, Panasonic, CityTV, 17 June 2006—<http://www.mztv.com/mz.asp>

The National Museum of Photography, Film, and Television. " Resources," 17 June 2006—<http://www.nmpft.org.uk/insight/onexhib_cin.asp>

National Science Foundation, Museum of the Moving Image. "Shutters, Sprockets and Tubes," Verizon Communications, iStreamTV, 17 June 2006—<http://www.movingimage.us>

"Newseum—the Interactive Museum of News," 17 June 2006—<http://www.newseum.org/>

Physical Sciences Information Gateway, Resource Discovery Network. "PSIgate Timeline," 17 June 2006—<http://www.psigate.ac.uk/newsite/chemistry_timeline.html>

The David Sarnoff Library. "Galleries," 3 March 2006—http://www.davidsarnoff.org; "Black and White Television Gallery," 17 June 2006—<http://www.davidsarnoff.org/gallery-tv-bw/gallery-tv-bw-pe.htm>

Schoenherr, Steven. "History of the Newsreel." University of San Diego. 3 October 2005, 17 June 2006—<http://history.sandiego.edu/gen/filmnotes/newsreel.html>

"Sony Global—Sony History," 17 June 2006—<http://www.sony.net/Fun/SH/index.html>

Steeman, Albert. *Internet Encyclopedia of Cinematographers,* 3 March 2006—<http://www.cinematographers.nl>

TFG Transfer. "The Incomparable B&H Filmo 16 mm Camera," 17 June 2006—<http://www.tfgtransfer.com/filmo.htm>

Yesterday's Witness: A Tribute to the American Newsreel. (1977) Documentary series—narrators: Lowell Thomas, Ed Herlihy, and Harry von Zell; written by Raymond Fielding, produced and directed by Christian Blackwood, Blackwood Productions; distributed by Pacific Arts.

Resources

Much of the technical material in the book has been down a well-worn road. The language of film, how lenses work, and many other visual concepts have been written about in countless tomes. Along with the basics, the points of view, techniques, and recommendations offered by the photojournalists in this book bring a new perspective to these tried-and-true methods and focus them specifically on the world of television news. A glossary of terms used in the profession is available on this book's web site at http://books.elsevier.com/9780240808482.

The references that follow have been used to fill out the basics and bring additional content to the educational component of each chapter. A few of the books listed I use in my lectures at San Diego State University. One was the first book I read on the subject and has been out of print for decades. The rest are good reads and should be used to expand the reader's understanding of their respective subjects.

Brandon, B. (2005) *The Complete Digital Video Guide: A Step-by-Step Handbook for Making Great Home Movies Using Your Digital Camcorder*. Pleasantville, NY: Reader's Digest.

Brown, B. (2002) *Cinematography Theory and Practice: Imagemaking for Cinematographers, Directors & Videographers*. Boston: Focal Press.

Cookman, C. (1985) *A Voice Is Born*. Durham: NPPA.

"CPJ Press Freedom Online." (2006) The Committee to Protect Journalists. 3 Mar.—http://www.cpj.org/

Hands, D. (2006) "Tvcameramen.com—Web Site for Professionals," 3 Mar.—<http://www.tvcameramen.com>

Johnson, K. (2006) "B-Roll.Net/Television News Photography," 3 Mar.—<http://b-roll.net>

Leslie, G. P., ed. (2003) *The First Amendment Handbook*. The Reporters Committee for Freedom of the Press. 16 June 2006—<http://www.rcfp.org/handbook/>

Schroeppel, T. (1980) *The Bare Bones Camera Course for Film and Video, 2nd ed*. Coral Gables, FL: Schroeppel.

Sherer, M. D. (1994) *Making the Commitment: Achieving Excellence in Television Photojournalism*. Durham: NPPA.

———. (1996) *Photojournalism and the Law: A Practical Guide to Legal Issues in News Photography*. Durham: NPPA.

Shook, F. (1996) *Television Field Production and Reporting, 2nd ed*. White Plains, NY: Longman.

Stone, V. A., and Hinson B. (1974) *Television Newsfilm Techniques*. New York: Hastings House.

Museums

George Eastman House, 900 East Ave., Rochester, NY 14607, (585) 271-3361—www.eastmanhouse.org

Institut Lumiere, 25 rue du Premier-Film—BP 8051-69352, Lyon Cedex 08, 33 04 78 78 18 95—www.institut-lumiere.org

Museum of the Moving Image, 35th Avenue at 36th Street, Astoria, NY 11106, (718) 784-4520—www.movingimage.us

MZTV Museum of Television, 277 Queen Street West, Toronto, Ontario, Canada, (416) 599-7339—www.mztv.com

National Museum of Photography, Film & Television, Bradford, West Yorkshire BD1 1NQ, UK, 0870 7010200—www.nmpft.org.uk

Pavek Museum of Broadcasting, 3515 Raleigh Avenue, St. Louis Park, MN 55416, (952) 926-8198—www.pavekmuseum.org

David Sarnoff Library, 201 Washington Road, CN 5300, Princeton, NJ 08543, (609) 734-2636—www.davidsarnoff.org

Index